Dreamweaver® CS5

FOR

DUMMIES®

Dreamweaver® CS5

FOR

DUMMIES®

by Janine Warner

WILEY

Wiley Publishing, Inc.

Dreamweaver® CS5 For Dummies®

Published by
Wiley Publishing, Inc.
909 Third Avenue
New York, NY 10022
www.wiley.com

For general information on our other products and services, please contact our Customer Care Department within the U.S. at 877-762-2974, outside the U.S. at 317-572-3993, or fax 317-572-4002.

For technical support, please visit www.wiley.com/techsupport.

Wiley also publishes its books in a variety of electronic formats. Some content that appears in print may not be available in electronic books.

Library of Congress Control Number:

ISBN: 978-0-470-61076-3

Manufactured in the United States of America

10 9 8 7 6 5 4 3 2 1

WILEY

About the Author

Janine Warner is an author, journalist, and partner in the Web design and consulting firm Artesian Media, Inc. Her best-selling books and videos on Web design have won her an international following and earned her speaking and consulting engagements around the world.

Since 1995, she's written and coauthored more than a dozen books about the Internet, including every version of *Dreamweaver For Dummies, Web Sites Do-It-Yourself For Dummies,* and *Teach Yourself Visually Dreamweaver.*

She's also the host of a series of training videos on Dreamweaver and Web design for Kelby Media and Total Training. Her first videos on Dreamweaver have won two multiple industry awards, and excerpts of her videos are featured on both Microsoft.com and Adobe.com.

Janine is a popular speaker at conferences and events throughout the United States and abroad, and she's taught online journalism courses at the University of Southern California and the University of Miami.

An award-winning journalist, her articles and columns have appeared in a variety of publications, including *The Miami Herald, Shape Magazine,* and the Pulitzer Prize-winning *Point Reyes Light* newspaper. She also writes a regular column about Dreamweaver for *Layers* magazine.

Janine has extensive Internet experience working on large and small Web sites. From 1994 to 1998, she ran Visiontec Communications, a Web design business in Northern California, where she worked for a diverse group of clients including Levi Strauss & Co., AirTouch International, and many other small- and medium-size businesses.

In 1998, she joined *The Miami Herald* as their Online Managing Editor. A year later, she was promoted to Director of New Media. She left that position to serve as Director of Latin American Operations for CNET Networks, an international technology media company.

Since 2001, Janine has run her own business as a writer, speaker, and consultant. She lives and works with her husband in Los Angeles. To learn more, visit www.JCWarner.com or www.DigitalFamily.com.

Dedication

To all those who dare to imagine all the ways we can develop sites on the Web: May all your dreams come true.

Author's Acknowledgments

I love teaching Web design because it's so much fun to see what everyone creates on the Internet. Most of all, I want to thank all the people who have read my books or watched my videos over the years and gone on to create Web sites. You are my greatest inspiration, and I sincerely enjoy it when you send me links to your Web sites. Thank you, thank you, thank you.

Thanks to the love my life, David LaFontaine, whose patience and support keep me fed, loved, and (mostly) sane, even when I'm up against impossible deadlines. You are a constant source of inspiration, and I love you more than you will ever know.

For their contributions to this book, special thanks to photographer Jasper Johal (www.jasperphoto.com); to designer Lynn Garrett; and my father, Robin Warner, for his fabulous tree farm.

Thanks to the entire editorial team: Jeff Noble for his superb technical editing and great ideas; Becky Huehls for catching the details, improving the prose, and being a great friend and ally; and Bob Woerner for shepherding this book through the development and publishing process (again and again and again).

Over the years, I've thanked many people in my books — family, friends, teachers, and mentors — but I have been graced by so many wonderful people now that no publisher will give me enough pages to thank them all. So let me conclude by thanking everyone who has ever helped me with a Web site, a book, or any other aspect of writing and research, just so I can go to sleep tonight and know I haven't forgotten anyone.

Publisher's Acknowledgments

We're proud of this book; please send us your comments at http://dummies.custhelp.com. For other comments, please contact our Customer Care Department within the U.S. at 877-762-2974, outside the U.S. at 317-572-3993, or fax 317-572-4002.

Some of the people who helped bring this book to market include the following:

Acquisitions and Editorial

Project Editor: Rebecca Huehls

Executive Editor: Bob Woerner

Senior Copy Editor: Barry Childs-Helton

Technical Editor: Jeff Noble

Editorial Manager: Leah P. Cameron

Editorial Assistant: Amanda Graham

Sr. Editorial Assistant: Cherie Case

Cartoons: Rich Tennant
(www.the5thwave.com)

Composition Services

Associate Project Coordinator: Sheree Montgomery

Layout and Graphics: Ashley Chamberlain, Joyce Haughey

Proofreader: C.M. Jones

Indexer: Rebecca Salerno

Publishing and Editorial for Technology Dummies

Richard Swadley, Vice President and Executive Group Publisher

Andy Cummings, Vice President and Publisher

Mary Bednarek, Executive Acquisitions Director

Mary C. Corder, Editorial Director

Publishing for Consumer Dummies

Diane Graves Steele, Vice President and Publisher

Composition Services

Debbie Stailey, Director of Composition Services

Contents at a Glance

Table of Contents

Introduction

In the 15-plus years that I've been writing about Web design, I've seen
many changes — from the early days (before Dreamweaver even existed)
when you could create only simple pages with HTML 1.0, to the elaborate
designs you can create with Dreamweaver today using XHTML, CSS, AJAX,
multimedia, and more.

If you're not sure what those acronyms mean yet, don't worry. I remember
what it was like to figure out all this stuff, too, so I designed this book to
introduce you to the basic concepts before you get into the more advanced
features. To prepare you for the ever-changing world of Web design, I show
you how to use Dreamweaver to create Web sites that take advantage of the
latest advances in Web technology — such as CSS, AJAX, and Dreamweaver's
newest feature, Business Catalyst.

One of the challenges of Web design today is that Web pages are not only
being displayed on different kinds of computers, but are also being downloaded to computers with monitors as big as widescreen televisions — or as
small as the little screens on cell phones. As a result, creating Web sites that
look good to *all* visitors is a lot more complex than it used to be — and standards have become a lot more important. That's why this book shows you
not only how to use all the great features in Dreamweaver but also how to
determine which of those features best serve your goals and your audience.

About This Book

I designed *Dreamweaver CS5 For Dummies* to help you find the answers you need
when you need them. You don't have to read through this book cover to cover,
and you certainly don't have to memorize it. Consider this a quick study guide
and a reference you can return to. Each section stands alone, giving you easy
answers to specific questions and step-by-step instructions for common tasks.

Want to find out how to change the background color in page properties,
design CSS style rules to align images, or add an interactive photo gallery
with the Swap Image behavior? Jump right to the pages that cover those features. (Hint: The Table of Contents and index can help you find the sections
that interest you most.) Don't worry about getting sand on this book at the
beach or coffee spilled on the pages at breakfast. I promise it won't complain!

You find templates, artwork, and other goodies to use with this book at www.
DigitalFamily.com/dwd.

What's New in Dreamweaver CS5?

Dreamweaver's high-end features make it the preferred choice for professional Web designers, and its easy-to-use graphical interface makes it popular among novices and hobbyists as well. With each new version, Dreamweaver's become more powerful and feature-rich — but this upgrade is arguably the most dramatic, with the following new features:

- **Streamlined site setup features:** Before you work on a new (or existing) Web site in Dreamweaver, it's important to complete the site setup process (covered in Chapter 2). Although setting up a site so Dreamweaver can identify how to set links and images is a basic function — and much the same as it was before — Adobe streamlined the process: Now it's faster and easier to set up a new site, and the more advanced setup options are moved to separate categories. You'll still find all the features that were there before, but you don't have to review them all in detail to set up a site.

- **BrowserLab:** One of the biggest challenges of Web design is making sure your pages look good in the wide variety of Web browsers in use on the Internet. BrowserLab helps by testing your pages in many different browsers — taking a screenshot of each, and then returning the results so you can quickly assess how your pages look in each one. Adobe has been experimenting with BrowserLab for a while, and in Dreamweaver CS5, they've built the online feature into the program by adding an option for BrowserLab to the Preview menu. (Note: You must be online for this feature to work. Okay, you probably knew that; if not, your secret's safe with me.)

- **Business Catalyst:** The most dramatic addition to Dreamweaver is called Business Catalyst. Adobe acquired this suite of tools and integrated them into version CS5 to work in conjunction with InContext Editing. The result is a powerful collection of features that make it easier than ever to add a shopping cart to your site, design and send e-mail newsletters, manage a contact database, and let other people (contributors or clients) update their own Web sites.

- **CSS Enable/Disable:** To make it easier to identify conflicts in style sheet rules, Dreamweaver now features the ability to easily turn any style rule on or off.

- **CSS Inspect:** Following the lead of the popular Firefox toolbar Firebug, CSS Inspect helps you identify and troubleshoot CSS, without having to publish your pages and set up a Firefox extension. This tool is designed to be used with LiveView, which makes it possible to view a Web page as it will look on a server (from a location on your hard drive). To use this feature, click LiveView, and then click the CSS Inspect button, or choose View⇨Inspect.

✔ **CSXS (Creative Suites Extended Services):** This collection of three new features is designed to make collaboration easier. Share My Screen (also included in version CS4) works with Adobe Connect to make it easy to share whatever is on your computer screen with up to three other people over the Internet. Search for Help is the second option in this feature set — a new tool that integrates the best of Adobe's online help directly into Dreamweaver (again, you must have an Internet connection to use this feature). Finally, this tool makes it easier to integrate Dreamweaver with third-party Flash-based services.

✔ **Vertical Split View:** When you choose Split View, Dreamweaver now automatically splits the screen vertically instead of horizontally. That's great if you have a giant monitor — but if you're working on a laptop or other small screen, you can change the split to horizontal by deselecting the vertical settings (choose View⇨Split Vertically to uncheck it the vertical option).

✔ **Dynamically related files:** Building on the features added to Dreamweaver CS4, in CS5, you can now view more dynamically related files simultaneously and you can view files included in other files. This is especially helpful if you're trying to view templates or pages created in a program such as WordPress, Drupal, or Joomla!.

✔ **Optimized linguistic library:** Dreamweaver CS5 is better suited to the increasingly international audience on the Web by including dictionaries and other linguistic support for 37 different languages (CS4 supported only 15 languages). Languages supported in CS5 include Arabic, Bokmal [Norway], Bulgarian, Catalan, Croatian, Czech, Danish, Dutch, English [Canada], English [GB], English [US], Estonian, Finnish, French [Canada], French [France], German [Germany], German [Switzerland], Greek, Hebrew, Hungarian, Italian, Latvian, Lithuanian, Nynorsk [Norway], Polish, Portuguese [Brazil], Portuguese [Portugal], Romanian, Russian, Slovak, Slovenian, Spanish, Swedish, and Turkish.

✔ **PHP code hinting:** Adds many new PHP code hints, as well as the capability to add your own hints.

✔ **Site-specific code hints:** For anyone working on multiple Web sites, this feature makes it easier to create snippets specific to each of your Web sites, keeping them separate to avoid cluttering the interface.

✔ **Workspace enhancements:** You'll also find a few other changes to the interface, including: a new Lock button in the top-left corner that makes it easy to make any page read-only. If you're working on Windows, you'll no longer see the full path of each page in the title bar. This makes it easier to see the final part of the URL, which is all that really matters after you've finished setting up the site.

Using Dreamweaver on a Mac or PC

Dreamweaver works almost identically on Macintosh or Windows computers. To keep screenshots consistent throughout this book, I've used a computer running Windows 7. However, I've tested the program on both platforms, and whenever there is a difference in how a feature works, I indicate that difference in the instructions.

Conventions Used in This Book

Keeping things consistent makes them easier to understand. In this book, those consistent elements are *conventions*. Notice how the word *conventions* is in italics? I frequently put new terms in italics and then define them so you know what they mean. It just makes reading so much *nicer*.

When I type *URLs* (Web addresses) or e-mail addresses within regular paragraph text, they look like this: `www.digitalfamily.com`. Sometimes, however, I set a particular URL on its own line, like this:

```
www.digitalfamily.com
```

That's so you can easily spot the URLs on a page if you want to type them into your browser to visit a site. I also assume that your Web browser doesn't require the introductory `http://` for Web addresses. If you use an older browser, remember to type that quaint prefix before the address (also make sure you include that part of the address when you're creating links in Dreamweaver).

Even though Dreamweaver makes knowing HTML code unnecessary, you may want to wade into HTML waters occasionally. I include HTML code in this book when I think it can help you better understand how things work in design view. Sometimes it's easier to remove or edit a tag in code view than design view. When I do provide examples — such as the following code that links a URL to a Web page — I set off the HTML in the same monospaced type as URLs:

```
<a href="http://www.digitalfamily.com">Janine's Digital
        Family Web Site</a>
```

When I introduce you to a new set of features, such as options in a dialog box, I set those items apart with bullet lists so you can see that they're all related. When I want you to follow instructions, I use numbered step lists to walk you through the process.

What You're Not to Read

If you're like most of the Web designers I know, you don't have time to wade through a thick book before you start working on your Web site. That's why I wrote *Dreamweaver CS5 For Dummies* in a way that makes it easy for you to find the answers you need quickly. You don't have to read this book cover to cover. If you're in a hurry, go right to the information you need most and then get back to work. If you're new to Web design or you want to know the intricacies of Dreamweaver, skim through the chapters to get an overview — and then go back and read what's most relevant to your project in greater detail. Whether you're building a simple site for the first time or working to redesign a complex site for the umpteenth time, you find everything you need in these pages.

Foolish Assumptions

Although Dreamweaver is designed for *professional* developers, I don't assume you're a pro — at least not yet. In keeping with the philosophy behind the *For Dummies* series, this book is an easy-to-use guide designed for readers with a wide range of experience. If you're interested in Web design and want to create a Web site, that's all I expect from you.

If you're an experienced Web designer, *Dreamweaver CS5 For Dummies* is an ideal reference for you because it gets you working quickly with this program — starting with basic Web-page design features and progressing to more advanced options. If you're new to Web design, this book walks you through all you need to know to create a Web site, from creating a new page to publishing your finished project on the Web.

How This Book Is Organized

To ease you through the learning curve associated with any new program, I organized *Dreamweaver CS5 For Dummies* as a complete reference. This section provides a breakdown of the five parts of the book and what you can find in each one. Each chapter walks you through the features of Dreamweaver step by step, providing tips and helping you understand the vocabulary of Web design as you go along.

Part I: Creating Great Web Sites

Part I introduces you to the basic concepts of Web design as well as the main features of Dreamweaver. In Chapter 1, I give you an overview of the many approaches to Web design, so you can best determine how you want to build your Web site before you get into the details of which features in Dreamweaver are best suited to any particular design approach. In Chapter 2, I start you on the road to your first Web site — including creating a new site, importing an existing site, creating new Web pages, applying basic formatting, and setting links. To make this chapter more interesting and help you see how all these features come together, I walk you through creating a real Web page as I show you how the features work.

In Chapter 3, I move onto graphics, with an introduction to creating graphics for the Web, an overview of the differences in formats (GIFs, JPEGs, and PNG files), and detailed instructions for adding and positioning graphics in your pages. In Chapter 4, you discover Dreamweaver's testing and publishing features, so you can make sure that all your links work and your Web site will look good in all the most important Web browsers. After you're sure you're sit is ready to go online, you find everything you need to start uploading pages to the Internet.

Part II: Appreciating Web Design Options

Chapter 5 provides an overview of how Cascading Style Sheets work and how they can save you time. CSS has become *the* way to create page designs and manage formatting on Web pages, and these features have been nicely improved in Dreamweaver CS5. In this chapter, you find descriptions of the style definition options available in Dreamweaver as well as instructions for creating and applying styles. In Chapter 6, I take you further into CSS, introducing you to the power of `<div>` tags, how to create CSS layouts, how to create centered CSS designs and fluid layouts, and how to use Dreamweaver's newest CSS testing features. .

In Chapter 7, I introduce you to some of my favorite Dreamweaver features, including sophisticated template capabilities that enable you to create more consistent designs and make global updates across many pages at once. I also cover Dreamweaver's Library items, which can be used to place and update commonly used elements, such as navigation bars or copyright tags. In Chapter 8, you discover how to use HTML table features (and when they're still recommended on the Web).

Part III: Making It Cool with Advanced Features

In Part III, you discover how cool your site can look when you add interactive image features, audio, video, and Flash. In Chapter 9, you find instructions for creating an interactive photo gallery with the Swap Image behavior, as well as how to use other features in Dreamweaver's Behaviors panel — including the Open New Browser behavior. In Chapter 10, you find out what it takes to add multimedia to your Web pages, including how to insert and create links to a variety of file types — from Flash to video and audio files. In Chapter 11, I cover Dreamweaver's HTML form options, which you can use to add feedback forms, surveys, and much more. In Chapter 12, you discover how great the Spry features are for adding AJAX interactivity to your site. In this chapter, you find instructions for creating and customizing drop-down lists, collapsible panels, and more.

In Part III, Chapter 13, you also learn the basics of how database-driven Web sites work and find an introduction to Dreamweaver's dynamic site-development features. In Chapter 14, you discover Dreamweaver's InContext Editing features, which make it easy to enable other people (your friends, colleagues, cousin Tina) to update a site built in Dreamweaver using nothing more than a Web browser. You also find an introduction to the most dramatic new addition to version CS5, Business Catalyst. This online service is designed to work with InContext Editing and adds a suite of online tools you can use with Dreamweaver, including a shopping cart, traffic tracking and reporting programs, and options for creating and managing bulk e-mail messages for newsletters and other correspondence.

Part IV: The Part of Tens

Part IV features three quick references to help you develop the best Web sites possible. Chapter 15 provides a collection of online resources where you can register domain names and find hosting services, as well as a few services that can help you take care of more advanced challenges (such as setting up an e-commerce system). In Chapter 16, you find ten design tips to help you get the most out of Dreamweaver.

Icons Used in This Book

When I want to point you toward something you can download for your use, I use this icon.

This icon points you toward valuable resources on the Web.

This icon reminds you of an important concept or procedure that you'll want to store away in your own memory banks for future use.

This icon signals technical stuff that you may find informative and interesting, though it isn't essential for using Dreamweaver. Feel free to skip over this information.

This icon indicates a tip or technique that can save you time and money — and a headache — later.

This icon warns you of any potential pitfalls — and gives you the all-important information on how to avoid them.

Where to Go from Here

To familiarize yourself with the latest in Web-design strategies and options, don't skip Chapter 1, which is designed to help guide you through the many ways to create Web sites that you have to choose from today. If you're ready to dive in and build a basic Web site right away, jump ahead to Chapter 2. If you want to find out about a specific trick or technique, consult the Table of Contents or the index; you won't miss a beat as you work to make those impossible Web-design deadlines. Most of all, I wish you great success in all your Web projects!

Part I
Creating Great Web Sites

The 5th Wave   By Rich Tennant

"Games are an important part of my Web site. They cause eye strain."

In this part . . .

1 n Part I, you find an introduction to Web design and an overview of the many ways you can create a Web site in Dreamweaver. Chapter 1 compares different layout techniques and provides an introduction to the toolbars, menus, and panels that make up Dreamweaver's interface.

In Chapter 2, you dive right into setting up a Web site, creating a Web page, and adding text and links. In Chapter 3, you find an introduction to Web graphics and tips for using Photoshop to optimize images in GIF, PNG, and JPEG formats. Chapter 4 covers testing and publishing features, so you can make sure that everything works well on your site and how to publish your site to a Web server.

Chapter 1

The Many Ways to Design a Web Page

*1*n the early days of the Web, designing pages was relatively easy — and vanilla boring. You could combine images and text, but that was about it. No complex layouts, no fancy fonts, and certainly no multimedia or animation.

Over the years, Web design has evolved into an increasingly complex field, and Dreamweaver has evolved with it, adding new features that go way beyond the basics of combining a few words and images.

When I first started learning to create Web sites in the mid-1990s, it was easy to learn — and easy to teach others how to do it. More than a dozen years and a dozen books later, it's a lot more complex. I've come to realize that one of the first things you have to understand about Web design is that there isn't just one way to create a Web site anymore.

Today, you can learn how to design simple Web sites in a matter of hours — or you can spend years developing the advanced programming skills it takes to create complex Web sites like the ones you see at Amazon.com or MSNBC.

For everything in between, Dreamweaver is the clear choice among professional Web designers, as well as among a growing number of people who want to build sites for their hobbies, clubs, families, and small businesses.

In this chapter, you discover the many ways you can create a Web site and the tools Dreamweaver offers to make those designs possible. The more you understand about the various approaches to Web design, the better you can appreciate your options. You also find a quick tour of the Dreamweaver CS5 interface so you understand the basics of moving around the workspace as you begin to design your site.

Understanding How Web Design Works

In a nutshell, building a Web site involves creating individual pages and linking them to other pages. You need to have a *home page,* the first page visitors see when they arrive at your Web address, (also known as your URL), and that page needs to bring them into the rest of the pages of the site, usually with links to each of the main sections of the site. Those pages, in turn, link to subsections that can then lead to deeper subsections.

After you create a Web site, you can test all the links on your own hard drive and then upload the pages to a Web server when everything is ready and working well. You can read more about setting up a site and using Dreamweaver to create pages on your local computer in Chapter 2. In Chapter 4, you discover how to upload your pages to a Web server when you're ready to publish your site on the Internet.

The most important thing to remember is that you need to create a folder on your local computer that will mirror your Web site on your Web server when you publish your site. That's why the site-setup process in Chapter 2 is so important — because it sets up Dreamweaver to help you create these two versions of your site: the version you create and edit on your computer and the perfect copy you need to maintain on the Web server.

Although you have to save all the files in your site in one main folder, you can create subfolders to organize the site. Thus a big part of planning a Web site is determining how to divide the pages of your site into sections and how those sections should link to one another. Dreamweaver makes creating pages and setting links easy, but how you organize the pages is up to you.

If you're new to this, you may think you don't need to worry much about how your Web site will grow and develop. Think again. All good Web sites grow, and the bigger they get, the harder they are to manage. Planning the path of growth for your Web site before you begin can make a tremendous difference later. Neglecting to think about growth is probably one of the most common mistakes among new designers. This becomes even more serious when more than one person is working on the same site. Without a clearly established site organization and some common conventions for tasks such as naming files, confusion reigns.

Managing your site's structure

Managing the structure of a Web site has two sides: the side that users see, which depends on how you set up links, and the side that's behind-the-scenes, which depends on how you organize files and folders.

What the user sees

The side that the user sees is all about navigation. When users arrive at your home page, where do you direct them? How do they move from one page to another in your site? A good Web site is designed so that users navigate easily and intuitively and can make a beeline to the information most relevant to them. As you plan, make sure that users can

✔ Access key information easily from more than one place in the site

✔ Move back and forth easily between pages and sections

✔ Return to main pages and subsections in one step

Setting links is easy in Dreamweaver; the challenge is to make sure that those links are easy for visitors to follow. One of the best ways to ensure that visitors can easily move around your site is to create a navigation or menu bar to include links to the main pages of your site on every page of your site. You find instructions in Chapter 6 for creating a menu bar with CSS. In Chapter 12, you find out how to use Dreamweaver's Spry features to create a drop-down list using AJAX. And in Chapter 7, you find instructions for using Dreamweaver's template and library features, which make menus easier to include on your pages — as well as faster and easier to update.

What's behind the scenes

The second side to managing your Web site structure happens behind the scenes (where your users can't see the information, but you want some kind of organizational system to remember what's what). You'll have files for all the images, HTML pages, animations, sound files, and anything else you put in your Web site. Before you begin building your site with Dreamweaver, think about how to keep track of all these files. At minimum, consider the following:

✔ **A file-naming system:** For example, naming image files consistently can make them easier to find if you need to edit them later. Similarly, giving the main section pages in your site names that match the text of the links on your pages can make setting the links easier. For example, if you add a Contact link on your site's home page, you can easily figure out what page that link should point to if your contact page is named `contact.html`.

✔ **A folder structure:** When your Web site grows past a handful of pages, organizing them in separate folders or directories can help you keep track. Fortunately, Dreamweaver makes this easy by providing a Files panel where you can see all the files of your site — and even move and rename files and folders.

HTM-what? Exploring HTML and XHTML

Contrary to popular belief, HTML isn't a programming language. Rather, it's a *markup* language: That is, HTML is designed to mark up a page, or to provide instructions for how a Web page should look. HTML is written by using *tags*, which are markup instructions that tell a Web browser how to display the page. For example, to apply italic formatting to text, you (or Dreamweaver) insert the HTML tag <em>, which stands for emphasis, where you want the italics to begin and end. Most tags in HTML include both an opening tag and a close tag, indicated by the forward slash /. Thus, to make the name of this book appear in italics, I would write the code like this:

```
<em>Dreamweaver CS5 For Dummies.</em>
```

Another challenge of HTML and XHTML is that the tags have changed over time. In the early days, bold was created using the <b> tag and if you wanted italics, you used the <i> tag. Although that may seem more logical than using <em> for italic and <strong> to make text bold, these latter tags are now preferred because they give the user greater control over the display of text in the browser. That's because the formatting for the <em> and <strong> tags can be altered to use other formatting options for text that you want to emphasize or strengthen on the page.

XHTML, a stricter version of HTML, is the recommended language to use to meet the highest standards of Web design today. Among the differences between the two languages, XHTML must be written in lowercase letters; in HTML, it doesn't matter whether tags are upper- or lowercase. Similarly, XHTML requires that all tags include a close tag (more on that later in this chapter). Rest assured all templates and code examples in this book follow the XHTML standard.

You have two ways to see what the code behind a Web page looks like:

✔ In most browsers, choose View⇨Source.

✔ If you're using Dreamweaver (as shown in Figure 1-1), you can click the Split button (upper-left corner of the workspace) to see the code and the design areas of the program at the same time in *Split view.*

Split view in Dreamweaver is a useful way to keep an eye on what's going on behind the scenes — and, as a bonus, you can learn a lot of XHTML as you go along.

Dreamweaver offers three view options:

- ✔ **Code:** In Code view, you see only the XHTML and other code.
- ✔ **Split:** In Split view, the page is divided so you can see the code in one part of the workspace and a view of the how the page should be displayed in a Web browser in the other part.
- ✔ **Design:** In Design view, you see only the page as it should be displayed in a Web browser.

In Dreamweaver's Split view, Code and Design views are completely integrated. If you select something in Design view — say, the headline shown in Figure 1-1 — then you see the same text highlighted in Code view, enabling you to find your place easily in the code.

If (at first glance) you think that XHTML code looks like hieroglyphics, don't give up too quickly. With just a little training, you can start to recognize at least some common tags, such as the `<h1>` tag (heading 1 tag) used to format the headline on the page shown in Figure 1-2.

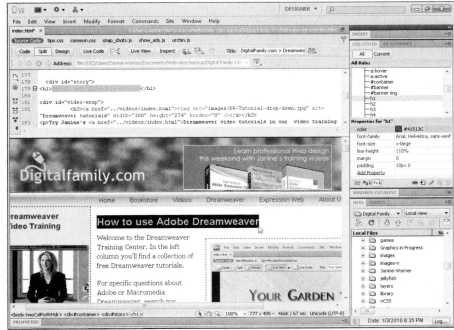

Figure 1-1: Use the Split view option in Dreamweaver to display the page design and the code behind the page.

Figure 1-2:
A
heading
1 tag high-
lighted in
Dream-
weaver
Code view.

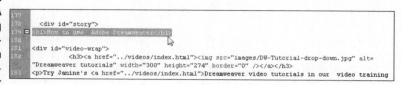

```
177
178        <div id="story">
179   ☐  <h1>How to use  Adobe Dreamweaver</h1>
180
181        <div id="video-wrap">
182              <h3><a href="../videos/index.html"><img src="images/DW-Tutorial-drop-down.jpg" alt=
      "Dreamweaver tutorials" width="300" height="274" border="0" /></a></h3>
183        <p>Try Janine's <a href="../videos/index.html">Dreamweaver video tutorials in our  video training
```

Here are a few points to help you better understand XHTML:

- **In XHTML, all tags must include the closing slash.** A few tags can stand alone — for example, the `<br />` tag, which adds a line break. As a rule, XHTML tags must have a closing tag, even if there's only one tag, and close tags always contain a forward slash (/). Thus the line-break tag looks like `<br>` in HTML and like `<br />` in XHTML.

- **XHTML includes many tags that are designed to be hierarchical.** Examples are the `<h1>` (heading 1) through `<h6>` (heading 6) tags, which are ideally suited to formatting text according to its importance on a Web page. Reserve the `<h1>` tag for the most important text on the page, such as the top headline. `<h2>` is ideal for subheads or secondary headings, `<h3>` for the third level of headings, and so on. A headline formatted with the `<h1>` tag looks like this:

  ```
  <h1>This is a headline</h1>
  ```

- **Some tags are more complex, and the open and close tags don't always match.** More complicated tags, such as the tags used to create links or insert images into pages, are more challenging to use because they include link information, and the close tag doesn't always match the open tag. For example, the code to create a link to another Web site looks like this:

  ```
  <a href="http://www.digitalfamily.com">This is a link
          to DigitalFamily.com</a>
  ```

At its heart, XHTML is just text — and believe it or not, you can write XHTML in a plain-text editor as simple as Notepad, SimpleText, or TextEdit. If you ever try it, however, you have to be careful to type all the code perfectly because there is no room for error or typos in XHTML. After writing code yourself, even to create a simple page, you're sure to quickly appreciate how well Dreamweaver writes the code for you.

How Web browsers work

Web browsers such as Internet Explorer, Firefox, Chrome, and Safari are designed to decipher HTML, XHTML, CSS, AJAX, and other code — and display the corresponding text, images, and multimedia on a computer screen. Essentially, browsers read the code in a Web page and interpret how to display the page to visitors. Unfortunately, because Web browsers are created by different companies and the code they display has evolved dramatically over the years, not all Web browsers display Web pages the same way. Differences in browser display can lead to unpredictable (and often frustrating) results because a page that looks good in one browser may be unreadable in another. For more information on browser differences and testing your pages to make sure they look good to all your visitors, see Chapter 4.

Comparing Static and Dynamic Sites

The first step to building a site is choosing what kind of site you want to build. This section introduces you to methods for building different features on the Web.

To start, know that Web sites fall into two very broad categories: *static* Web sites, which are generally built with a program like Adobe Dreamweaver, and *dynamic* Web sites, which use advanced programming to create advanced, interactive features, such as those used in a WordPress blog (covered in more detail in Chapter 13). Keep in mind that you can add multimedia, video, audio, animation, and so on to either type of site.

Static Web sites are made up of a collection of individual pages with the .html or .htm extension. You might think that all Web sites are made up of individual pages (and in a way they are), but with static sites those pages are saved as separate files. With a dynamic site, as you discover a little later in this section, the pages you view in a Web browser are created dynamically as they are delivered to the browser, so they're not saved as individual pages but as pieces of pages that can be mixed and matched. That gives dynamic sites many advantages, but it also makes them a lot more complicated to create.

The upshot is this: Because dynamic Web sites are more complicated to create, if you're just creating a simple profile or small business site, go with a static site. Dynamic sites are often not worth the extra effort, unless you're creating a site that you expect to grow to more than 100 pages or so. The big exception is a blogging site, because — thanks to specialized blogging tools like WordPress — creating a dynamic site with the common features of a blog is relatively easy. As a result, many people create both a static Web site for their profile or small business and a blog where they can easily add posts and other updates over time.

You find an introduction to using Dreamweaver's dynamic development tools and how Dreamweaver can be used to edit sites created with blogging tools and other content management programs, in Chapter 13. If you're interested in learning more about WordPress, check out *WordPress For Dummies,* 2nd Edition, by Lisa Sabin-Wilson.

Static Web pages

Static pages work well for small and medium-sized Web sites, such as a professional profile or online gallery. Because static Web pages are written in plain text, you can create them in a program as simple as Notepad or SimpleText, although tools such as Dreamweaver make designing pages a lot easier because you don't have to remember all the cryptic XHTML tags.

A static Web site offers a few advantages, especially if you're just starting out, including the following:

- ✔ **Easy to learn to develop:** Anyone who can resize a photo has a head start on the skills needed to create and arrange graphic elements on a static page.

- ✔ **Gives you complete control over design of each page:** You can tweak the size, colors, fonts, and arrangement of the elements on each page individually, and you can edit templates for these kinds of sites more easily than the templates for dynamic sites.

- ✔ **Easy to build, test, and publish to a Web server:** You can create and test static Web pages on any personal computer and then host them on any commercial Web server — and you need only FTP access (which is built-in to programs like Dreamweaver) to publish pages to the Internet.

Dynamic Web pages

The technical aspects of dynamic sites get complicated quickly. You find a more detailed introduction to creating dynamic Web sites in Chapter 13, but the gist is that instead of creating a collection of individual pages, you store all your content in a way that makes text, images, and other data easy to display in a variety of combinations. That's what enables shopping sites like Amazon.com to keep track of your last order and recommend books when you return.

A site can even gather information from different sources to create complex pages dynamically. For example, you can combine information about customers' shopping habits with a list of your overstocked items currently on sale — and create a page tailored to each visitor.

Dynamic sites are generally created on a Web server by combining CSS (Cascading Style Sheets, introduced in Chapter 5) and XHTML (HTML that complies with today's stricter standards) with more advanced technologies, such as PHP, ASP.NET, or ColdFusion. And that brings up another big challenge of working on dynamic sites: You have to build and test dynamic pages on a computer that runs a Web server and other software (for example, a database), which is a lot more complicated than simply installing a Web browser on your personal PC to test your pages. Launching a dynamic site on a commercial Web server is also far more complicated than publishing a static page site to a Web server. (You find more information about setting up your computer to create and edit dynamic Web sites in Chapter 13.)

That said, the advantages of dynamic Web sites are significant, and most big sites on the Web are created this way, but most of the big sites on the Web also have a team of experienced programmers behind them. Unless you have advanced programming skills or a big budget, the challenges of creating a dynamic Web site mean that most small- and medium-sized Web sites are still better served with static Web sites.

Most of this book is dedicated to helping you create static sites — but that doesn't mean you can't get many of the same benefits of dynamic sites, such as the capability to update pages quickly. As you find in this book, you can combine CSS (covered in Chapters 5 and 6) with Dreamweaver's .dwt template features (covered in detail in Chapter 7) and get many features of a big-budget Web site without all the complicated programming skills. (You find a general description of Dreamweaver's template features, as well as a look at the differences among templates, in the next section of this chapter.)

Blogging is one exception to the general statement that static sites are easier to create than dynamic sites. Although blogging tools (such as WordPress and Blogger) create dynamic Web sites with all advanced capabilities, they do it in a way that makes such sites relatively easy to launch and update.

Although you can use Dreamweaver to edit Joomla! and WordPress blog templates, that's not as easy as you might imagine: Either you have to set up a Web server on your local computer and install these complex programs to run along with Dreamweaver, or you have to limit yourself to using Dreamweaver to do very limited editing — and then upload the edited files to the server to test them. (You find information on setting up your computer to work on sites created with WordPress and other content management systems — such as Joomla! — in Chapter 13.)

For these reasons, if you're new to Web design, I recommend you start by creating a static site with Dreamweaver. And keep in mind: The skills you pick up in this book — in particular, creating and editing CSS and XHTML for static sties — also apply to dynamic sites. As you get more comfortable with creating and editing Web pages, you can apply skills gleaned from this book to more complex ways of creating sites.

Multimedia: You like to move it, move it

I use the catch-all term *multimedia* to describe anything that moves on a Web page, but that's a lot of different things these days. Multimedia should be considered as a topic distinct from static-versus-dynamic sites because video, audio, and images can be added to both static *and* dynamic Web pages.

You can add multimedia to a Web page in many different ways. In addition to video, there's animation — whether you add it with Adobe Flash or Microsoft Silverlight, or simply animate a series of GIF images. AJAX, one of the newest ways to add interactivity to a site, combines JavaScript and XML — and is growing in popularity.

Fortunately, you don't have to worry too much about all the technical details to add multimedia to your Web pages. As described in Chapter 10, you can easily add many different kinds of audio and video formats using Adobe Dreamweaver. Or you can upload videos to a site such as YouTube or Vimeo, and then insert them into any Web page with copy-and-paste ease. You find instructions for creating JavaScript features (such as rollover images), with Dreamweaver's Behaviors in Chapter 9, and for using Dreamweaver's Spry options to create AJAX features (such as drop-down menus) in Chapter 12.

The advantages of a dynamic site include these:

- ✔ **Easily updated:** When you want to put new content into a dynamic Web site, you can simply add a new product or image to the database and the new content automatically appears in all corresponding pages in the site.

- ✔ **Consistent look:** When you create a dynamic site, you have to use templates, which help create a consistent look across the whole Web site. No matter how you build a site, having consistent navigation buttons, banners, and other essential elements is good practice because you want your visitors to find these items no matter which page they visit.

- ✔ **Easier to redesign:** All great Web sites grow and change over time, and as they get bigger, they become even more complex to redesign. With a dynamic site, you can simply update the templates, and the content is automatically included in the new version of the site.

Working with Templates in Dreamweaver

The term *template* is used in many different ways for many different kinds of design work (on and off the Web), but essentially a template is a shortcut in the design process. By working with Dreamweaver templates, you can set or adjust just about any aspect of a site's design or functionality, including a header, logo, navigation bar, or sidebar. Whatever you include in a

Dreamweaver template, you can then apply to any new page based on the template — which automatically applies the settings you want to appear throughout your site. Moreover, if you want to adjust the overall settings in your site, you can make those updates once in the template, update your pages, and *voilà* — all pages based on the template are updated automatically.

But not all templates are created equally. Although they all share those basic characteristics, many different kinds of templates are in use on the Web today. For example, in Chapter 7, you find instructions for creating templates for static Web sites, but these are quite different from the kinds of templates you would use if you were creating a blog with WordPress.

You can download many different kinds of templates from the Web, but they don't all work in all programs. For example, if you download templates designed for Adobe Flash, you won't be able to use them at all in Dreamweaver (although you can insert Flash files in Dreamweaver, as you discover in Chapter 10). Similarly, you can't even view a WordPress template effectively in Dreamweaver unless you've set up a local server and installed WordPress.

You can edit many different kinds of templates in Dreamweaver. Before you start using Dreamweaver to create or edit templates, I think it's helpful to better understand how they are different. The following sections cover two of the most common types of templates in use on the Web today (and what you should know about how they differ). See the nearby sidebar, "So many Dreamweaver template options," for a complete list of template options.

Dreamweaver templates

Dreamweaver templates (extension .dwt) offer many advantages without requiring advanced programming skills. When you create Dreamweaver templates with the .dwt extension, you can use XHTML and CSS to create static Web sites that include many of the high-end features found on dynamic sites — such as the capability to create new pages quickly and to update every page in your site with the click of a button.

Although you can use Dreamweaver to create templates that use advanced programming (such as PHP or Java), the .dwt Dreamweaver template is a much simpler option that's ideal for small- to medium-size Web sites — which is why I've dedicated much of Chapter 7 to making the most of Dreamweaver templates.

WordPress and Joomla! templates

Templates such as the ones you get with a blogging program like WordPress use the extension .php because they're written in the PHP (Hypertext

Preprocessor) programming language. Although you can create PHP pages and templates in Dreamweaver and use them for more than just WordPress, these types of files are far more complex to create than .dwt Dreamweaver templates.

Because so many people use WordPress and so many sites offer WordPress template downloads, many people are confused about why WordPress templates don't work in Dreamweaver in the same way that .dwt Dreamweaver templates work.

So many Dreamweaver template options

Dreamweaver supports many kinds of technologies, as well as the templates that go with each. When you create new pages in Dreamweaver by choosing File➪New, you have the option of create a blank page or a blank template, as shown in this figure.

When you create a simple HTML template, Dreamweaver uses the .dwt extension (see the nearby "Dreamweaver templates" section in this chapter).

Dreamweaver also supports Microsoft ASP and ASP.NET, and you can create templates using either ASP JavaScript or ASP VBScript (both of which use the .asp extension) — or you can use ASP.NET C# or VB (which use the .aspx extension).

The templates for a site created using Java end in .jsp. And if you use Adobe's ColdFusion technology, your templates end in .cfm.

The big lesson is this: Make sure you have the right kind of template for the kind of site you're creating — and rest assured that Dreamweaver supports just about any kind of technology you can use to create a Web site today.

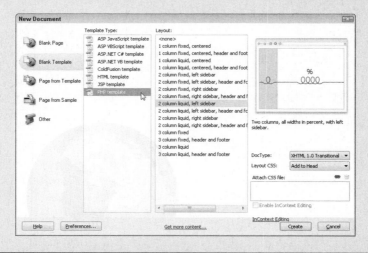

WordPress templates offer many of the same benefits as Dreamweaver templates — except that templates for blogs such as WordPress draw their content from a database. As a result, they include XHTML and CSS (as do the Dreamweaver templates), plus much more complicated code in the PHP programming language — which describes how content from the database should be displayed in a Web page. As a result, to make WordPress templates work in Dreamweaver, you must first install additional software, such as the MySQL database — as well as server software that essentially turns your computer into a Web server — so your browser can generate WordPress pages the same way a commercial Web server does. (See Chapter 13 for an introduction to how to work with WordPress blogs and other dynamic Web sites.)

Although creating a basic blog with a WordPress template is easy, editing a WordPress template is not so easy. Because that underlying technology is so complicated, changing the fonts, colors, columns in a page layout, and so on is also complicated.

The gardening Web site `www.GardenstoTables.com` (featured in Figure 1-3) was created with a program called Joomla!. Similar to WordPress, Joomla! offers many types of templates and add-ons to make creating a dynamic Web site easier. These tools are ideal if you plan to create a large, complex site — especially one that you expect to grow into hundreds (or thousands) of pages over time. But remember: You can always start your site as a static site in Dreamweaver, and then graduate to a more complicated way of building a site (such as Joomla!) as your site grows.

Figure 1-3: Dynamic sites created with content management programs make it easier to create magazine-style sites like Gardens to Tables.

Comparing Tables, Frames, and Layers

If you've already done a little Web design, you may be wondering what happened to some of the old ways of creating Web page layouts. For years, Web designers used the HTML feature called Tables to create page layouts. Then Frames came along, and many people were excited by the capability to display multiple pages in one browser window (which Frames and iFrames make possible). Then came Layers, which were especially popular among designers because they seemed to offer precise design control.

Today, most professional designers agree that the best way to create a Web page design is to use XHTML (eXtensible HyperText Markup Language, a strict form of HTML) with Cascading Style Sheets, which are covered in detail in Chapters 5 and 6.

Over the years, all these other options have become less desirable except in a few special cases. In this section, you find a quick review of when tables, frames, and layers may still be useful.

Creating page designs with HTML tables

In the early days of Web design, most page layouts were on the Web were created with tables. By merging and splitting table cells and even adding background images, designers created complex Web designs with tables. CSS expands upon this concept by adding many new design options — including the capability to add precise margins and padding around elements, which offers better control of how and where background images appear.

Figure 1-4 provides an example of an old-school site created with the HTML `table` tag. Most designers turn off table borders by setting the table border to 0 to create cleaner layouts, but in Figure 1-4, I've set the borders to 2 pixels so you can see the outline of the table. As you can see in Figure 1-4, table cells surround each of the photos and captions in this two-column layout — and I've merged the columns at the top of the design to make room for the banner image that spans the full width of the page.

Although tables are no longer recommended for creating page layouts, they're still considered the best way to format tabular data like that you'd find in a spreadsheet program. Thus you can use tables to format a consistent collection of information — such as the list of trees for sale on the Dexter Tree Farm site, as shown in Figure 1-5.

Figure 1-4:
In the old days, the only way you could create a complex Web page design was to use an HTML table to control text and image placement.

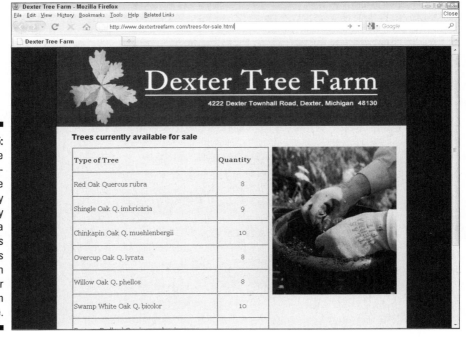

Figure 1-5:
Tables are still considered the best way to display tabular data such as this list of trees for sale on the Dexter Tree Farm site.

Although I recommend that you redesign sites like the one shown in Figure 1-4 with CSS and <div> tags, I do understand that many designers still find it easier to create layouts with tables, and not everyone has time to redesign their Web sites right away. I have to admit, I've been guilty of leaving a few sites online designed with tables long after I knew better. That said, I recommend using only CSS today for all your Web page layouts — except when you're creating a layout for tabular data. Even then, I still urge you to use CSS to add any styling (such as background colors or padding) that you might want in your tables. In Chapter 8, you discover how to create tables like the one shown in Figure 1-5.

If you visit the site at www.chocolategamerules.com, you can view the code and see how the page in Figure 1-4 was created using <div> tags and CSS. (I explain how <div> tags work with CSS in Chapter 6.)

Considering design options with HTML frames

You won't find any instructions in this book for creating Web sites that use frames, such as the Pink Flamingos site shown in Figure 1-6. Frames enable you to display multiple Web pages in one browser window. Among Web designers, frames are a little like those plastic pink flamingos stuck in the front yards of so many homes in South Florida: Some people love how kitsch they are, and others just think they're tacky. Although frames are still used on the Web, most designers don't like them because they can make navigation confusing.

Frames are also problematic because when you use frames, the URL at the top of a Web browser does not change, even when you click links and change the pages displayed within the frames. As a result, you can only *bookmark* (create a link to) the first page of a site that uses frames. Worse yet, search engines have a hard time properly indexing a site designed with frames — which can diminish your site's search-engine ranking.

Using layers (or AP Divs) to create designs

In Dreamweaver MX, MX 2004, and 8, a Layer feature offered an easy way to click and drag boxes that designers could position with precision on a page. Starting in version CS3 and continuing in version CS5, Adobe changed the name to AP Divs. *Divs* are simply XHTML <div> tags that serve as *dividers* in a page. Essentially, they create boxes around content, where the content between the opening and closing `<div>` tags is considered a box. By organizing content in this way, designers can position sections of text or images independently. Don't be confused by the fact that I (and most other Web designers today) recommend using `<div>` tags with CSS to create your page layouts. We just don't recommend that you do so *with* the AP Divs (except in a few special cases).

AP Divs, as the name implies, are `<div>` tags that include styling information that adds absolute positioning. That means when you place an AP Div in a Web page, it stays where you put it, no matter how much space you have in the browser window. This may seem like a good idea at first — and AP Divs were popular among some designers for a while because they're so easy to use and so similar to many features in desktop publishing programs (such as Adobe InDesign). But because AP Divs create such inflexible layouts, they don't adapt well to the changing environment of the Web, where different-size monitors and other display variations can lead to cut-off text and other undesirable results in AP Div–based designs.

Many designers use AP Divs on occasion to add immovable elements (such as a logo anchored to the top-left of a page) to a page layout, but creating an entire design with this feature is no longer recommended.

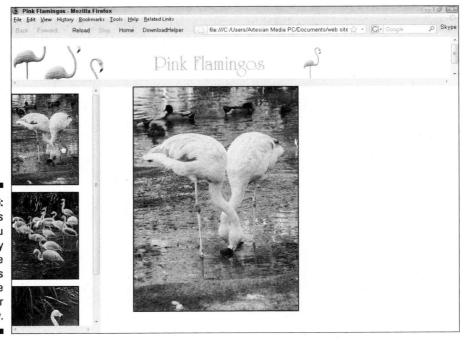

Figure 1-6:
Frames enable you to display multiple Web pages in one browser window.

Appreciating the Benefits of Cascading Style Sheets

The concept of creating styles has been around since long before the Web. Desktop publishing programs (such as Adobe InDesign) and even word processing programs (such as Microsoft Word) have long used styles to manage the formatting and editing of text on printed pages. When using styles in a word processor, you can create and save styles for common features, such as headlines and captions. In print design, styles are great timesavers because they enable you to combine a collection of formatting options (such as Arial and bold and italic) into one style — and then apply all those options at once to any selected text in your document, using only a single style. The advantage is that if you change a style, you can automatically apply the change everywhere you've used that style in a document.

On the Web, you can do all that and more with CSS — because you can use style sheets for more than just text formatting. For example, you can use CSS to create styles that align images to the left or right side of a page, add padding around text or images, and change background and link colors. You can even create more than one style sheet for the same page — say, one that makes your design look good on computers, another for cell phones, and a third for a printed page.

For all these reasons (and more), CSS has quickly become the preferred method of designing Web pages among professional Web designers. One of the most powerful aspects of CSS is that it enables you to make global style changes across an entire Web site. Suppose, for example, that you create a style for your headlines by redefining the <h1> tag to create large, blue, bold headlines. Then, one fine day, you decide that all your headlines should be red instead of blue. If you aren't using CSS, changing all your headlines could be a huge undertaking — a matter of opening every Web page in your site to make changes to the font tags around every headline. But if you're using CSS in an external style sheet, you can simply change the style that contains formatting information for the <h1> tag in the style sheet — and *voilà!* All your headlines all turn red automatically. If you ever have to redesign your site (and believe me, every good site goes through periodic redesigns), you can save hours (or even days) of work if you created your design with CSS in the first place.

A Web site designed with CSS separates content from design. Keeping the content of site (such as the text and headings) separate from the instructions that tell a browser how the content should look benefits both you as a designer and your site visitors. Here are some of the advantages:

✔ **CSS simplifies design changes.** CSS styles can be saved in the header section at the very top of an XHTML page, or they can be saved in a separate file that can be attached to multiple XHTML pages. Either way, if you use a style to format many headlines, you can make formatting changes by simply editing the style.

✔ **Separating content from design enables you to create different style sheets for different audiences and devices.** Today's Web sites are as likely to be viewed on giant, wall-size screens as they are to be seen on screens small enough to hide in the palm of your hand during a lunch date. CSS makes enables you to create Web-page designs that are more adaptable so they look good on big *and* small screens, as well as everything in between.

As you get more advanced with CSS, you can even create multiple style sheets for the same Web page. For example, you can create one that's ideally suited to a big computer monitor, another that's designed to get the best results when page is printed, and yet another designed with a larger font size for anyone who may have trouble reading the small print that's so common on Web pages.

✔ **Using CSS makes your site comply with the current standards.** Today, the *W3C,* which sets standards for the Internet, recommends using CSS for nearly every aspect of Web design because the best CSS designs are accessible, flexible, and adaptable.

✔ **Web sites designed in CSS are accessible to more visitors.** Today, a movement is growing among some of the best designers in the world to get everyone to follow the same standards, create Web sites with CSS, and make sure sites are accessible to everyone.

When Web designers talk about *accessibility,* they mean creating a site that anyone who might ever visit your pages can access — including people with limited vision who use special browsers (often called *screen readers*) that read Web pages aloud, as well as many others who use specialized browsers for a variety of other reasons.

If you work for a university, a nonprofit, a government agency, or a similar organization, you may be required to create accessible designs. Even if you're not required to design for accessibility, know that pages that meet accessibility standards also tend to score better in search-engine rankings because accessible designs also enable search engines to access and interpret site content more easily.

Understanding Browser Differences

HTML was created to share information in a way that could be displayed on every computer on the planet — it's one of the greatest advantages of the Web. However, for Web designers, this advantage is also a challenge because not all those computers use the same browsers, the same fonts, or the same monitor size. On top of that, a lot of older Web browsers that can't display the latest Web features are still in use — and the newer browsers don't all display those features in the same way. So before you start creating Web pages, know that no matter how carefully you create your designs, your pages will never look exactly the same to every possible visitor to your site.

If you want to create page designs using the latest technology, and you want to reach the broadest possible audience, pay special attention to Dreamweaver's browser preview and compatibility features — and be prepared to move on to training that's more advanced than this book. Entire books and Web sites are dedicated to creating highly complex CSS layouts that display well on various computers and browsers — and to combining CSS and other special code to make complex pages look good in older and newer Web browsers. They're not for the casual user or the faint of heart.

In Chapters 5 and 6, you find an introduction to creating styles and page designs with CSS. In Chapter 4, you find more information about browser differences, as well as Dreamweaver's testing and compatibility features, which can help ensure that your pages work well for a broad audience.

Introducing the Dreamweaver CS5 Workspace

Dreamweaver can seem a bit overwhelming at first: It has so many features, spread among so many panels, toolbars, and dialog boxes that you can easily get lost. If you prefer to build an understanding by poking around, have at it (and feel free to skip to Chapter 2, where you start building your first Web page right away). If you want a tour before you get started, the last few sections of this chapter introduce you to the interface and give you a quick overview of the features in this powerful program.

When you launch Dreamweaver, the Welcome screen, shown in Figure 1-7, appears in the main area of the program (and reappears anytime you don't have a file open, unless you close it by selecting the Don't Show Again option). After you select an option on the Welcome screen (options explained in Chapter 2), Dreamweaver creates a new blank HTML page in the main *workspace,* the main area of the program where you design your page. The workspace consists mainly of a Document window, which displays the page you're working on and is where you add text, images, and other elements that will appear on your Web pages. The Document window is surrounded by a collection of panels, toolbars, and menus that provide easy access to Dreamweaver's many features. Details of these controls follow.

Changing workspace layouts

Dreamweaver CS5 has eight preset workspace layouts to choose from. These layouts arrange the many toolbars, panels, and other features in popular configurations. You can change layouts by choosing Window➪Workspace Layout and then choosing any of the listed layouts. Or choose a layout from the drop-down list at the top of the Dreamweaver window, such as Designer (which is selected in Figure 1-7) or App Developer (shown in Figure 1-8). There are eight total options, in three categories (Designer, App, and Coder), and variations on each.

Figure 1-7: When Dreamweaver opens, the welcome screen provides easy access to commonly used items, such as recently opened pages.

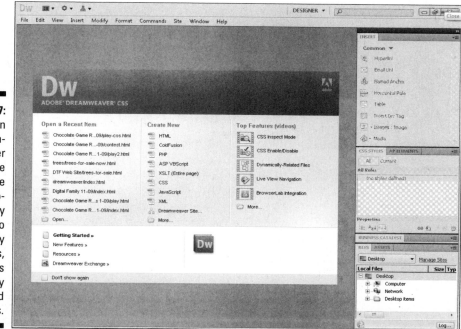

The Designer layouts were created for people who have a design background and favor the design features of the program. You can also choose the App and Coder layouts were created for programmers who are likely to prefer working in the Code view and having handy access to the coding features.

In addition to the preset workspace layouts, you can create your own by following these steps:

1. **Open, close, or move any of the panels, inspectors, or other features, as described in the following sections.**

2. **Choose Window⟹Workspace Layout⟹New Workspace.**

3. **Give your new workspace a name and click OK.**

    Your custom workspace is added to the Layout menu so you can easily reset the program to match your favorite settings.

The name that the Layout menu displays will match the last layout you chose and used. If your last choice was Designer, it says Designer; if your last choice was Coder, it says Coder.

If you move a panel or inspector and then want to return it to its original location, use the Layout menu: Choose Reset and then choose the name of the workspace layout you want to restore.

Create a collection of workspace layouts optimized for common tasks, such as creating and applying CSS, or working with database content, and save them so you can easily arrange the program to best suit your preferences.

The menu bar

As with most programs you've used, the menu at the top of the screen provides easy access to most program features, including the options you find in the Insert bar, Property inspector, and panels, as well as a few others that are available only from the menu.

The Document toolbar

Across the top of the workspace, just under the menu bar and above the workspace, is the Document toolbar, as shown in Figure 1-8. Here you find the following options:

✔ **Code, Split, and Design view buttons:** Click a button to display only the code or design in the workspace, or both the code and the design using Split view (refer to Figure 1-8).

✔ **Live Code button:** Provides a preview of the page in Live Code view, which is dynamic and provides an update of the page you're interacting with in Live View.

✔ **Live View button:** Provides a preview of the page, complete with working links and dynamic content; the page works in Dreamweaver much as it would when previewed in a Web browser.

✔ **Inspect button (new in version CS5):** Helps you identify and trouble-shoot CSS.

✔ **Preview in Browser button:** Launches the page in a Web browser.

✔ **View Options button:** Provides access to additional display features, such as the ruler and guides.

✔ **Visual Aids button:** Makes turning on special display features (such as CSS Layout Outlines) easy. The CSS Layout Outlines option adds a thin, dotted line around otherwise-invisible elements (such as <div> tags).

✔ **Title field:** Displays the *page title,* which is the text that appears at the top of a browser window when a page is displayed. This is also the text that's saved when a visitor bookmarks a page.

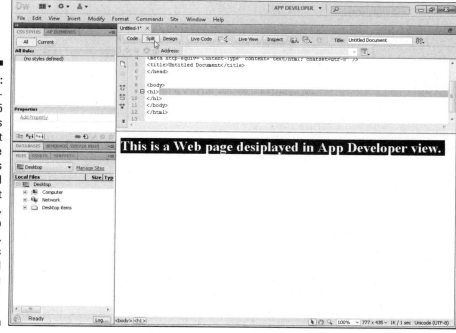

Figure 1-8:
Dream-weaver CS5 includes eight workspace layouts optimized for different work styles, such as App Developer, which is optimized for working on dynamic Web sites.

The Document window

The big, open section in the main area of the workspace is the Document window, which is where you work on new and existing pages.

 If you use the Designer workspace layout, the Document window is displayed in Split view, showing the code on the left and the Design view on the right. To change the Split view from left-right to top-bottom, choose View⇨Split Vertically to deselect the Split Vertically option (which is selected by default in version CS5). If you want to hide the code to focus only on your design, click the Design view button in the Document toolbar.

The docking panels

The docking panels are located to the right of the work area when you choose any of the Designer layouts (such as the one shown in Figure 1-7), or on the left when you choose any of the Developer layouts (such as the one shown in Figure 1-8).

The docking panels display a variety of important features in Dreamweaver, including the following:

- ✓ **The Insert panel,** described in detail in the following section.
- ✓ **The Files panel,** which displays all the files and folders in a site.
- ✓ **The CSS Styles panel,** which displays a list of all the Cascading Style Sheets available to the document.

You work with the panels in the following ways:

- ✓ **To open and close panels,** click the gray bar at the top of any panel next to the panel's name or double-click the name in the tab at the top of the panel.
- ✓ **To move panels anywhere on the screen,** click the dark gray bar at the top of the panel and drag it to the desired location.
- ✓ **To display more panels,** select the panel name from the Window menu.
- ✓ **To expand or collapse all the visible panels at once,** click the double arrow at the top-right corner of the topmost panel.
- ✓ **To expand or collapse a single panel when the panel collection is collapsed,** click the name of the panel, as shown in Figure 1-9.

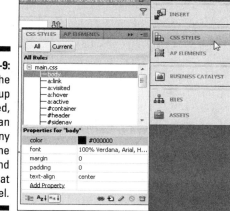

Figure 1-9:
When the
panel group
is collapsed,
you can
click any
panel name
to expand
only that
panel.

The Insert panel

The Insert panel, located at the top of the panel section, includes seven *sub-categories,* each with a different set of icons representing common features. Click the small arrow to the right of the name to access the drop-down list and switch from the buttons of one subcategory to the buttons for another. The options are

- ✔ **Common Insert panel:** Displays icons for many of the most common features, including links, tables, and images.

- ✔ **Layout Insert panel:** Displays Div, Table, and Frame options (essential for creating page layouts).

- ✔ **Forms Insert panel:** Features the most common form elements, such as radio buttons and boxes.

- ✔ **Data Insert panel:** Displays options for building dynamic Web pages powered by database material.

- ✔ **Spry Insert panel:** Features a collection of widgets that combine HTML, CSS, and JavaScript to create interactive page elements, such as drop-down lists and collapsible panels.

- ✔ **InContext Editing Insert panel:** Displays features that are handy for creating Repeating and Editable Regions, as well as managing CSS classes, when working with dynamic content.

✔ **Text Insert panel:** Displays common text-formatting features, including paragraphs, breaks, and lists.

✔ **Favorites Insert panel:** Enables you to right-click (Windows) or Control-click (Mac) to add any icons from the other Insert bar options as a favorite, so you can create your own collection of favorite features.

At the end of the drop-down list are the two options that control the display of the list of options in the Insert panels. **Color Icons** restores the color to the icons. **Hide Labels/Show Labels** enables you to display the names of the Insert panel features next to each icon, or to remove the names.

The Property inspector

The Property inspector is docked at the bottom of the workspace in Dreamweaver. If you prefer, you can click the gray bar at the top of the inspector and drag it to detach it so it floats in the workspace. You can move the inspector anywhere on the screen or you can drag and dock it in the panel group. When you dock the Property inspector with the other panels, you can expand and collapse it just as you would any other panels. To restore the inspector to its original location, choose Window⇨Workspace Layout⇨Reset. (I rather like that the Property inspector is handy, yet out of the way, at the bottom of the screen.)

The Property inspector displays the *properties,* or options, for any selected element on a page, and it changes based on what's selected. For example, if you click an image, the Property inspector displays image properties. If you click a Flash file, the Property inspector displays Flash properties.

For many elements, the Property inspector is split into two sections, one for HTML features and the other for CSS. Use the CSS and HTML buttons on the left side of the Property inspector (as shown in Figure 1-10) to switch from one to the other. (You find detailed instructions for how to use these two modes of the Property inspector in Chapters 5 and 6.)

Figure 1-10:
The Status bar and the Property inspector in CSS mode.

At the bottom-right corner of the Property inspector, you see a small arrow. Click this arrow to reduce or expand the inspector to hide or reveal additional attributes, such as the image map options when a graphic is selected. Click the gray bar at the top of the inspector to close and open the inspector.

The status bar

The status bar is located at the bottom of the Document window and just above the Property inspector, as shown in Figure 1-10. The status bar includes access to a number of features that control the display of a page in Dreamweaver's workspace:

✔ **Tag selector:** On the far left of the status bar, as shown in the top of Figure 1-10, you find the tag selector, which displays the HTML tags and CSS rules that apply to any selected element on the page. In Figure 1-10, the cursor is inside a text block that's formatted with the <h1> tag, which is inside a <div> tag with a #container ID, which is inside the <body> tag.

  • *Clicking* any tag in the tag selector selects the tag and all its contents in the workspace.

  • *Right-clicking (Control-clicking on a Mac)* a tag opens a pop-up menu with options to add or remove tags and CSS rules.

✔ **Select tool, Hand tool, Zoom tool, and Magnification pop-up menu:** You can use these tools, which are toward the middle of the status bar, to move, enlarge, or reduce the display of a page in the workspace.

✔ **Download Size/Download Time tool:** Found on the far-right side of the status bar, this tool displays the total size of the Web page, including all images and other elements on the page — and the estimated time downloading the page will take, based on the connection speed specified in Dreamweaver's preferences. By default, the connection speed is set to estimate the download time of a page over a 56K modem, but you can change it to a faster or slower speed by changing the preferences, as shown in the following section.

Changing preference settings

The more you use Dreamweaver, the more you're likely to appreciate how readily you can customize its features. Remember that you can always change the workspace to better suit the way you like to work, and you can easily alter Dreamweaver's preference settings using the Preferences dialog box.

To open the Preferences dialog box, choose Edit⇨Preferences on a Windows computer, or Dreamweaver⇨Preferences on a Mac. Dreamweaver includes 19 different categories in the Preferences dialog box and makes it possible to change the appearance, default settings, and many other options throughout the program.

Chapter 2

Opening and Creating Sites

. . . .

In This Chapter

▶ Starting with the site setup process

▶ Creating new Web pages

▶ Inserting and formatting text

▶ Creating links

▶ Adding search engine keywords to meta tags

. . . .

*W*hether you're building a new site or need to make changes to an existing site, this chapter is the place to start. Here you discover an important preliminary step: the *site setup process* that enables Dreamweaver to keep track of the images and links in your site. After you complete the site setup process, you're ready to create Web pages, insert text and images, set links, and more. (You find instructions for doing all those things in this chapter, too.) But whatever you do, don't skip the first step of defining a site — it only takes a minute or two.

Although you can use Dreamweaver without doing this initial site setup, you run the risk of breaking links when you publish your site using the built-in FTP features. Other features, such as templates, automated link checking, and the Library, won't work at all.

The best approach to Web design with Dreamweaver is to first create a Web site on your computer's hard drive, where you use Dreamweaver's preview options to test the site in any browser on your computer before you publish it on the Internet. That's why this chapter starts with setting up a folder on your hard drive where you'll keep your site files. When you're ready to publish the completed site, you transfer it to a Web server. A *Web server* is a computer with a permanent connection to the Internet and special software that enables it to communicate with Web browsers, such as Internet Explorer and Firefox. Find detailed instructions for previewing and publishing a Web site in Chapter 4.

Setting Up a New or Existing Site

To set up a site in Dreamweaver, you need to store all your site's resources in one main folder on your hard drive. Dreamweaver calls this the *local site folder,* and when you set up a new site, you essentially just identify that folder in Dreamweaver. The site setup process is a crucial first step because all the elements of your site must remain in the same relative location on your hard drive as they are on your Web server in order for your links, images, and other elements to work properly. Identifying the local site folder on your computer helps Dreamweaver set all your links properly and ensure they still work when you publish your site to a Web server (which you discover how to do in Chapter 4).

In earlier versions of Dreamweaver, the local site folder was called the local root folder and the site setup process was called the Site Definition process.

The Site Setup dialog box also contains a category called Servers (on the left side) where you can set up your site to use Dreamweaver's file transfer features, including its FTP (File Transfer Protocol) capabilities. (*FTP* is a common method of copying files to and from computers connected across a network, such as the Internet.) To keep things simple for now, you can skip all the categories except the Site category covered in the section that follows. In Chapter 4, you find detailed instructions for using Dreamweaver's publishing features as well as instructions for downloading an existing Web site hosted on a remote server.

If the site setup process seems a little confusing at first, don't worry; it's a quick, relatively painless process that you must do only once for each site, but it's a crucial first step and it's important not to skip it.

Whether you're creating a new site or working on an existing site for the first time in Dreamweaver, the following steps walk you through the process of defining the local site folder, a folder or directory, where you store all the images, text, and other files in your site.

1. **Choose Site⇨New Site.**

   The Site Setup dialog box appears.

2. **Click the Site tab.**

   When you open the Site Setup dialog box, the Site tab should already be selected by default. This dialog box contains three other tabs, as shown in Figure 2-1, but you don't need to open any of them to complete the basic site setup process.

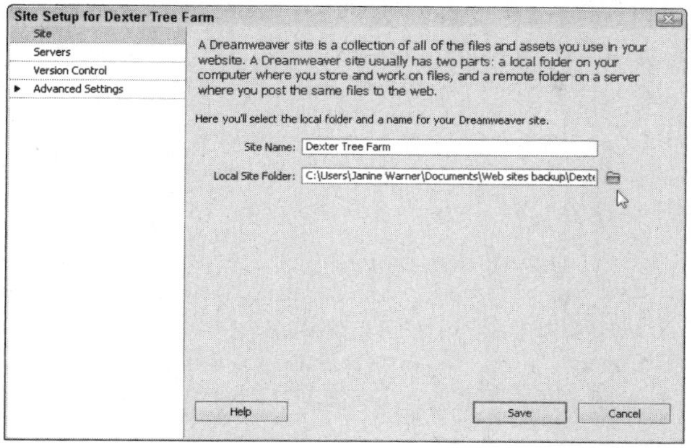

Figure 2-1:
Use the Site
Setup dialog
box to com-
plete the set
up process
and identify
the local
site folder
for any new
Web site
in Dream-
weaver.

Site Setup for Dexter Tree Farm

Site
Servers
Version Control
▶ Advanced Settings

A Dreamweaver site is a collection of all of the files and assets you use in your website. A Dreamweaver site usually has two parts: a local folder on your computer where you store and work on files, and a remote folder on a server where you post the same files to the web.

Here you'll select the local folder and a name for your Dreamweaver site.

Site Name: Dexter Tree Farm

Local Site Folder: C:\Users\Janine Warner\Documents\Web sites backup\Dextr

Help   Save   Cancel

3. In the Site Name text box, type a name for your site.

You can call your site whatever you like; this name is used only to help you keep track of your sites in Dreamweaver. Many people work on more than one Web site, and the name you enter here is the name also listed in the Files panel, where you select which site you want to work on in Dreamweaver, which is why it's helpful to use a name that will help you identify the site later. (The next section discusses moving among sites via the Files panel in more detail.)

4. Click the Browse button (which it looks like a file folder) next to the Local Site Folder text box and browse your hard drive to locate the folder you want to serve as the main folder for all the files in your Web site.

If you're working on an existing site, select the folder that already contains the files for that site. If you're creating a new site, you can create a new folder as follows:

- **In Windows:** Click the Create New Folder icon at the top of the Choose Root Folder dialog box.

- **In Mac OS X:** Click the New Folder button at the bottom of the Choose Root Folder dialog.

The goal is to simply select the folder so that Dreamweaver can identify where all the files and folders for your site will be stored. When you've completed this step, the name of the folder and the path to that folder's location on your hard drive, appear in the Local Site Folder field.

5. **Click Save to close the Site Setup dialog box and save your settings.**

   If the folder you selected as your local site folder already contains files or folders, they're automatically cached and all the files and folders in your site are displayed in the Files panel. As you see in Figure 2-2, I already had many files in my Dexter Tree Farm site, so they are listed in the Files panel. If I were creating a new site with a new empty folder, the Files panel would only contain the main site folder.

   If you haven't checked the Enable Cache option, a message box appears asking whether you want to create a cache for the site. Choose Yes to speed up Dreamweaver's site management features.

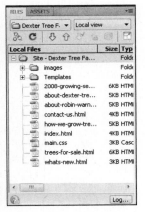

Figure 2-2:
When site setup is complete, the files and folders in an existing site are displayed in the Files panel.

Switching Among Sites

You can set up as many sites as you like in Dreamweaver and change from one site to another by selecting the site name in the Files panel. To load a different site into the Files panel, use the drop-down arrow next to the site name and choose the name of the site you want to display.

In Figure 2-3, I'm selecting the DigitalFamily.com site from a list of defined sites. When you select a site, the files in that site replace the ones of any currently open site in the Files panel. Selecting a site in the Files panel before you start working on it is always best.

Figure 2-3:
You can
define multi-
ple sites and
change the
active site
by selecting
its name
in the Files
panel.

Managing Sites in Dreamweaver

After you complete the site setup process covered in the preceding exercise, you can make changes and additions to a site setup by choosing Site⇨Manage Sites, selecting the name of the site in the Manage Sites dialog box. Use the buttons on the right to manage your site as follows:

- ✔ **New:** Click this button to define a new site. (The process is the same as choosing Site⇨New Site, as explained in "Setting Up a New or Existing Site," earlier in this chapter.

- ✔ **Edit:** Clicking Edit opens the site in the Site Setup dialog box, where you can change the name by replacing whatever you entered in the Site Name field and change the local site folder by clicking the Browse button and selecting a different folder. In Figure 2-4, I selected the DigitalFamily.com site and am about to click the Edit button to open it.

- ✔ **Duplicate:** Clicking Duplicate makes a copy of the site setup, but does not actually make a new copy of the site on your hard drive.

- ✔ **Remove:** When you remove a site from the Manage Sites dialog box, you don't delete the site's files or folders from your hard drive; you simply remove the site setup in Dreamweaver.

- ✔ **Import and Export:** These buttons are designed to make it easy to share the site setup information for a site among multiple computers. When you click Export, Dreamweaver creates a .ste file. This is not a copy of the files and folders in a site; it's a copy of the information stored in the Site Setup dialog box, including any server, FTP, or other information you have entered for the site. The Import button lets you import a .ste file to add any site that has already been set up in Dreamweaver.

Figure 2-4:
You can
edit any
site setup
by select-
ing it in the
Manage
Sites dialog
box and
clicking the
Edit button.

Manage Sites

Chocolate Game Rules
Dexter Tree Farm
Digital Family
Jasper Jahol Photography
Sandbox

New...
Edit...
Duplicate
Remove
Export...
Import...

Done
Help

Creating New Pages

Every Web site begins with a single page. Visitors are first greeted by the front page — or *home page* — of your site, and that's usually a good place to start building.

Dreamweaver makes creating new pages easy: You can work from the Welcome screen or use the New Document window, which provides more options. The following sections explain both methods, and you find details about the best names to use for new pages so that they'll work well when you publish your site to the Web.

Starting from the Welcome screen

When you open Dreamweaver, a Welcome screen greets you with shortcuts to many handy features for creating new pages in a variety of formats:

✔ **If you want to create a simple, blank Web page,** choose HTML from the Create New list in the middle column (see Figure 2-5). Remember that choosing HTML doesn't mean that you have to write the HTML code yourself. Rather, you're just telling Dreamweaver that you want to create a page written only with HTML, not of one of the more complex technologies, such as PHP or ASP.net. You still have the option to work in the code editor or the visual editor and let Dreamweaver write the underlying HTML for you.

✔ **If you're creating a dynamic site,** choose ColdFusion, PHP, or one of the other dynamic site options. (If you don't even know what those options mean, you probably won't need to use them yet, but you can find some information about these advanced options in Chapter 13.)

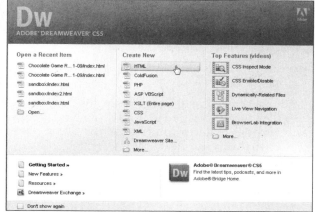

Figure 2-5:
The
Welcome
screen pro-
vides a list
of shortcuts
for creating
new files
or opening
existing
pages in
Dream-
weaver.

If you prefer not to use the Welcome screen, you can turn it off by selecting the Don't Show Again box in the bottom-left corner.

Creating an HTML page with the New Document window

You can also create a new HTML page by using the New Document window, which offers more options than the Welcome screen, including access to any templates you've created with Dreamweaver (covered in Chapter 7), as well as a collection of predesigned layouts, which can give you a head start on your designs.

You can create many different kinds of files using the New Document window, and you can mix and match some, but not all, of the options. This can be confusing at first, but essentially, if you choose an option under Page Types that creates a Web page, including HTML, HTML Template, or any of the ASP, ColdFusion, JSP, or PHP options, you can also choose one of the page layouts from the Layout list. If you choose any of the other options, such as Library, CSS, JavaScript or XMTL, the layout options are not available because you would not include a layout in any of these types of files. Also note that the layouts are all created with CSS, which Dreamweaver as it creates the new page. You read more about editing the CSS to change these layouts in Chapter 6.

To create a new, completely blank HTML file, follow these steps:

1. **Choose File⇨New.**

   The New Document window opens, as shown in Figure 2-6.

2. **From the left side of the screen, select Blank Page.**

3. **From the Page Type list, select HTML.**

4. **From the Layout section, choose <none>.**

5. **Use the drop-down list next to DocType if you want to change the document type.**

   By default, Dreamweaver creates pages using the XHTML Transitional doctype, which is the best option for most Web pages today. If you are working on a site that requires you create strict HTML pages, however, make sure to change this setting.

6. **Click Create.**

   The New Document window closes, and a new blank page is created and opened in the workspace.

   In this example, I'm creating a blank page by choosing <none>, but I often start new pages by using one of Dreamweaver's many great layouts. You find instructions for creating and editing pages with these layouts in Chapter 6.

7. **Choose File⇨Save to save your page and give it a filename.**

   In general, you should not include spaces or special characters in file names in your Web site (although the dash and underscore are okay). For more on how best to name files and folders in your Web site, see the upcoming sections "Naming new page files" and "Naming the first page index.html."

   Get in the habit of saving new Web pages in your local site folder as soon as you create them, even though the pages are still blank. As you create links or add images to your pages, Dreamweaver needs to be able to identify the location of your page within your site folder. Although Dreamweaver sets temporary links until your page is saved, saving a page first is best because many other Dreamweaver features won't work until a page is saved.

Naming new page files

Over the years, I've received many e-mail messages from panicked Web designers because of broken links caused by filename conflicts. Because these problems usually don't occur until after a Web site is published on a server, they can be especially confusing and difficult to understand. If you're publishing your Web site to a Web server that runs on Mac or Windows, the following may not apply to you; but if you're using a Web server that runs

Unix or Linux (which is what many commercial Web hosting companies use), the following instructions are especially important. If you're not sure, follow these rules when you save Web pages, images, and other files on your site to be safe:

✔ **Include an extension at the end to identify the file type** (such as .html for HTML files or .gif for GIF images). Dreamweaver automatically adds the .html file extension to the end of HTML files, which works for most Web servers. [However, in the rare case that you need to change the extension to .htm for your Web server, you can do so in Dreamweaver's Preferences dialog box by choosing Edit➪Preferences (Windows) or Dreamweaver➪Preferences (Mac).] See the "Showing file extensions in Windows" sidebar for tips on how to view file extensions, which are hidden in Windows.

✔ **Don't use spaces or special characters in filenames.** For example, don't name a Web page with an apostrophe, such as cat's meow page. html. If you want to separate words, you can use the underscore (_) or the hyphen (-). For example, meow-page.html is a fine filename. Numbers are okay in most cases, and although capital letters don't generally matter, most designers stick with lowercase to keep filenames consistent and making setting and checking links easier because the name of the file and its reference in any links must match.

Figure 2-6:
The New Document window offers more options when creating a new page, such as starting with one of Dreamweaver's predesigned CSS Layouts.

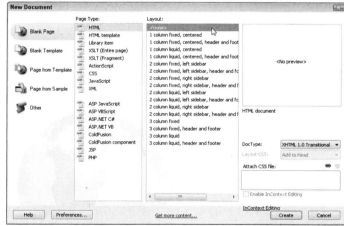

Showing file extensions in Windows

Unless you change the settings, you won't see the file extension of your GIFs, JPEGs, or HTML pages on a Windows computer (although these extensions will be displayed in the Files panel in Dreamweaver).

To change these settings, open the Folder Options dialog box, as shown in the following figure, choose the View tab, and then look through the long list of options and deselect Hide Extensions for Known File Types. How you open the Folder Options dialog box depends on which version of Windows you're using; but if you search for Folder Options in the Help section, you should find it easily.

The reason for all this fuss? Filenames are especially important in Web sites because they're included in the HTML code when you set links. Links with spaces and special characters work just fine when you test pages on a Mac or a PC computer, but many Web servers on the Internet use software that doesn't understand spaces or special characters in links. Thus, links that don't follow these rules may get broken when you publish the site to a Web server. By following these rules, you ensure that the filename and the code in the link match.

Naming the first page index.html

Another confusing rule — and one of the most important — is that the main page (or the *front page*) of your Web site must be called index.html (on some Windows-based servers, the first page should be named default.html).

That's because most servers are set up to serve the index.html or default.html page first.

Essentially, when a Web browser comes to a domain name, such as DigitalFamily.com, the first page that opens is index.html. Similarly, when a Web browser is directed to a subfolder within a site, it also displays the index page first. As a result, if you create a subfolder with the name books, for example, and inside that subfolder you create page named index.html as the main page, you can tell visitors to your site to simply enter **www. DigitalFamily.com/books** to arrive at the books page within your site. If you name the first page anything else, such as books.html, visitors have to type **www.DigitalFamily.com/books/books.html** to open the page. The rest of the pages in your site can be named anything you like, as long as the names don't include any spaces or special characters (except the hyphen or underscore).

It doesn't matter if you use upper- or lowercase letters when typing a domain name, but everything that comes after the .com (or .net, or whatever three- ending your domain name has) must match the case of the file and folder names. Thus, www.DigitalFamily.com and www.digitalfamily.com are the same, but if you create a folder named books with a lowercase b, the address typed into a browser must use a lowercase b, as in www.DigitalFamily.com/books and if someone enters www.DigitalFamily.com/Books in a browser, they will get a 404 error.

Bestowing a page title

When you create new pages, adding a page title right away is also good practice. A *page title* is the text that appears in the title bar when a visitor opens your site in a browser window.

In Dreamweaver, you can add a page title by changing the text in the Title box at the top of the workspace. This detail is easy to forget, but page titles play an important role in your site's appearance as well as behind the scenes:

✔ The title won't appear in the main part of your Web page, but it does appear at the top of a browser window, usually just to the right or left of the name of the browser. Pages on the Web look unfinished when the words *untitled document* appear at the top of the browser window.

✔ The page title is also the text that appears in a user's Favorites or Bookmarks list.

✔ Many search engines give special priority to the words that appear in the title of a Web page, so including the name of your site and a few keywords can help you score better in search results.

Changing Page-Wide Styles with the Page Properties Dialog Box

You can change many individual elements on a page in the Property inspector. If you want to make changes that affect the entire page — such as changing the background color of the entire page or changing the way links and text are formatted — use the Page Properties dialog box.

As shown in Figure 2-7, the Page Properties dialog box includes a list of categories on the left. Each of these reveals different options for specifying page settings. Some of these options are covered in other parts of the book, such as the Background Image feature, covered in Chapter 3.

Changing background and text colors

The following section focuses on changing the background and the text colors available from the Appearance categories, as shown in Figure 2-7. Note that the CSS options are recommended over HTML options. When you use the Appearance (CSS) options, Dreamweaver creates corresponding styles for the body tag automatically.

Figure 2-7:
The Appearance (CSS) category in the Page Properties dialog box enables you to specify text color, font face, font size, background, and margins.

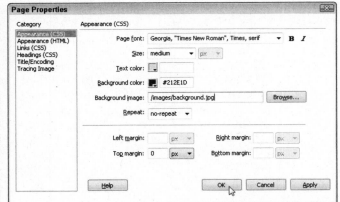

Although you can apply global settings, such as text size and color, in the Page Properties dialog box, you can override those settings with other formatting options in specific instances. For example, you could set all your text to

Helvetica in Page Properties and then change the font for an individual headline to Arial with the Font field in the Property inspector.

To change the font settings, background and text colors, and page margins for an entire page, follow these steps:

1. **Choose Modify⊏▷Page Properties.**

   The Appearance (CSS) category of the Page Properties dialog box appears (see Figure 2-7).

2. **In the Page Font drop-down list, specify the fonts you want for the text on your page.**

   In this example, I set the font face to the collection that begins with the Georgia font. If you don't specify a font, your text appears in the font specified in your user's browser, which is usually Times.

3. **If you want all the text on your page to appear bold or italic, click the B or I (respectively) to the right of the Page Font drop-down list.**

   If you select one of these options, all your text appears bold or italic in the page.

4. **In the Size drop-down list, specify the font size you want for the text on your page.**

   Again, you can override these settings for any text on the page.

5. **Click the Text Color swatch box to reveal the color palette. Choose any color you like.**

   The color you select fills the color swatch box but won't change the text color on your page until you click the Apply or OK button.

6. **Click the Background Color swatch box to reveal the color palette. Choose any color you like.**

   The color you selected fills the color swatch box. The color doesn't fill the background until you click the Apply or OK button.

7. **If you want to insert a graphic or photograph into the background of your page, click the Browse button next to the Background Image box and select the image in the Select Image Source dialog box.**

   When you insert a background image, it automatically repeats or tiles across and down the page unless you choose the No-Repeat option from the Repeat drop-down list or use CSS to further define the display.

8. **Use the margin options at the bottom of the dialog box to change the left, right, top, or bottom margins of your page.**

   Entering **0** in all four of these fields removes the default margin settings that automatically add margin space at the top and left of a Web page, enabling you to create designs that begin flush with the edge of a browser.

9. **Click the Apply button to see how the colors look on your page.**

10. **Click OK to finish and close the Page Properties dialog box.**

Changing Link Styles with Page Properties

If you're like many designers, you probably don't like the underline that automatically appears under all the linked text in a Web page. In this section, you discover how easy it is to remove that underline and change the color, font face, and size for the links with Dreamweaver's Page Properties dialog box. You can also change other page-wide settings, such as the background color and page margins, from the Page Properties dialog box.

The easiest way to alter all your link styles at once is to change them in the Page Properties dialog box. When you use this option, Dreamweaver creates the corresponding tag selector styles automatically and lists them in the CSS Styles panel. Other page-wide settings in this dialog box work similarly.

To change hyperlink and other styles with the Page Properties dialog box, open an existing page or create a new one and follow these steps:

1. **Choose Modify⇨Page Properties.**

   Alternatively, you can click the Page Properties button in the Property inspector. The Page Properties dialog box appears.

2. **Select the Links (CSS) category on the left of the Page Properties dialog box, as shown in Figure 2-8.**

Figure 2-8: Use the Links (CSS) category in the Page Properties dialog box to change the style definitions for all four hyperlink states.

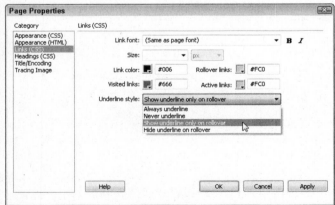

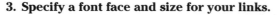

3. Specify a font face and size for your links.

If you want to use the same font size and face for your links as you use in the rest of the text on your page, it's best to leave these options blank; then, if you change the text settings for the page, you won't have to remember to change them for your links as well.

4. Specify colors for each hyperlink state by clicking in the corresponding color well and selecting a color from the Color dialog box.

You can change any or all the link color settings. If you don't specify a link color, the browser uses the default link color. Here's an explanation of each of the four link states:

- **Link Color:** The color in which your links appear when the page is first loaded and the linked page hasn't yet been visited by the browser. The corresponding HTML tag is `<a:link>`.

- **Visited Links:** The color your links change to after a browser has already viewed the linked page. The corresponding HTML tag is `<a:visited>`.

- **Rollover Links:** The color a link changes to as a user rolls a cursor over a link. The corresponding HTML tag is `<a:hover>`.

- **Active Links:** The color a link changes to as a user is actively clicking a link. The corresponding HTML tag is `<a:active>`.

5. Select a style from the Underline Style drop-down list.

Many designers prefer to remove the underline that automatically appears under linked text by choosing Never Underline. I like to give visitors the visual cue of the underline, but only as they roll a cursor over a link, so I generally prefer the option labeled "Show underline only on rollover," as shown in Figure 2-8.

6. Click OK.

The Page Properties dialog box closes, the style settings are applied automatically to any links on the page, and the corresponding styles are added to the CSS Styles panel.

To fully test link styles, preview your page in a Web browser or click the Live View button at the top of the workspace. It's good practice to test link settings in a browser when you make changes like the ones in the preceding exercise. Take a look at how your links appear; for example, do the active and visited link colors look good against the background color of the page. Remember that any styles you create using the Page Properties dialog box affect *all* links on your page unless you specifically apply a different style to an individual link that overrides the redefined tag style. If you want to use different link styles in different parts of the same page, you can create compound styles to create different link styles (see Chapter 6 for instructions on creating compound styles).

Adding and Formatting Text

Many people are pleasantly surprised by how easily they can create a basic Web page with text and images in Dreamweaver. This section focuses on text, the next section on images.

In this chapter, I use Dreamweaver's HTML formatting options, including the heading and paragraph tags. I start with basic HTML tags to keep things simple at this stage and to introduce you to what many designers consider the basic building blocks of a good Web page. In Chapters 5 and 6, you find detailed instructions for using CSS to change the size, color, and font and other style options of text formatted in HTML.

Adding text to a Web page

To add text to a page, you can simply click to insert your cursor at the top of a page and type. If you want to add text that you have somewhere else, such as file created in Microsoft Word, you can copy and paste it into Dreamweaver instead of retyping it.

Dreamweaver offers many ways to maintain formatting when you copy and paste text from another program. This is especially important when you copy text from Microsoft Word because if you just paste text in as is, you risk including a lot of extra code that is unique to Microsoft Word and can cause problems in your Web page.

You can change the default for how Dreamweaver handles formatting when you choose Edit⇨Paste by altering the Preferences in the Copy/Paste category. You can also choose Edit⇨Paste Special to display these options any time you paste new content.

Here are your four main options for inserting text when you choose Edit⇨Paste Special (and two ways to refine your choice):

- ✔ **Text Only:** Dreamweaver strips any formatting and inserts plain text.
- ✔ **Text with Structure:** Dreamweaver includes paragraphs, lists, tables, and other structural formatting options. (This choice is my favorite because it removes any code specific to a program like Word if you use the Clean Up Word Paragraph Spacing check box described a little later, while preserving basic formatting.)
- ✔ **Text with Structure Plus Basic Formatting:** Dreamweaver includes structural formatting as well as basic formatting, such as bold and italic.

✔ **Text with Structure Plus Full Formatting:** In addition to the previous options, Dreamweaver includes formatting created by style sheets in programs, such as Microsoft Word.

✔ **Retain Line Breaks:** Line breaks are preserved, even if you don't keep other formatting options. This option is not available if you choose Text Only.

✔ **Clean Up Word Paragraph Spacing:** This option removes special formatting code that is unique to Microsoft Word, and is unnecessary (and not recommended) for text on the Web.

I cover many more text formatting options in Chapter 5 because formatting on the Web is best done with CSS and you need to understand the basics of CSS before you start using styles to format text.

Formatting text with the heading tags

One of the best formatting options for headlines is the collection of heading tags. In HTML, using heading tags (<h1>, <h2>, and so forth) to format text that serves as a title or headline offers many advantages. Heading tags are designed to be displayed in relative sizes, with <h1> the largest, <h2> smaller, <h3> smaller still, and so on through <h6>. So no matter what a Web page's default text size is (and text sizes can vary due to browser settings and computer platform), any text formatted with an <h1> tag is always larger than text formatted with <h2>. (In Chapter 5, you find instructions for creating styles that can change the appearance of heading tags while still preserving these benefits.)

Popular belief is that many search engines give priority to keywords in text formatted with an <h1> tag because the most important text on a page is generally included in the largest size headline.

To format text with a heading tag, follow these steps:

1. **Highlight the text you want to format.**

2. **In the Property inspector, at the bottom of the workspace, make sure the HTML button on the left side of the inspector is selected.**

3. **Use the Format drop-down list to select a heading option (see Figure 2-9).**

   When heading tags are applied, the text automatically changes to become big and bold in design view.

Figure 2-9:
With HTML selected, the Property inspector provides easy access to common HTML formatting features, such as the heading tags.

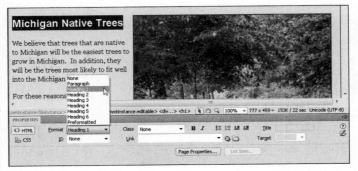

In general, I find the Property inspector the easiest way to apply basic formatting, but you can also find these HTML formatting options by choosing Format➪Paragraph Format and then selecting a heading option from the submenu that appears..

Adding paragraphs and line breaks

When you create page designs for the Web, you must work within many limitations that may seem confusing at first. Web design and print design are fundamentally different, and that can make even seemingly simple tasks more complicated than you might expect. How you create paragraph and line breaks is a good example.

If you're working in design view in Dreamweaver and press the Enter key (Windows) or the Return key (Mac), Dreamweaver inserts a paragraph tag, or <p>, in the code, which creates a line break followed by a blank line. If you want a line break without the extra blank line, hold down the Shift key while you press Enter (or Return) to tell Dreamweaver to insert the <br /> tag into the code, creating a single line break.

Best practice is to avoid using multiple paragraph or break tags to create extra space in a Web page (and not all browsers will maintain the blank space if you create it that way). If you want to add a lot of space between paragraphs or other elements on a page, your best option is to use CSS, which I cover in Chapters 5 and 6.

If you're working in code view and add space using the Enter or Return key, you add blank space within the code. Extra space in HTML code can be useful because extra space can make code easier to read, but it doesn't affect the way a page displays in design view or in a Web browser.

Setting Links in Dreamweaver

Dreamweaver is truly a dream when it comes to setting links. As you set links, remember that a link is essentially an address on the Internet (a URL or Universal Resource Locator) that tells a viewer's browser what page to open and where it is located when a viewer clicks the text or image containing the link.

To link to a page within your Web site, you can create a *relative link* that includes a path describing how to get from the current page to the linked page within your local site folder. A relative link doesn't need to include the domain name of your site, just instructions for a browser to get from one page within your site to another.

Linking to a page on another Web site — called an *external link* — is even easier than linking to an internal link. All you need is the URL of the page to which you want to link, and you're most of the way there.

In the following sections, you find step-by-step instructions for creating internal and external links, as well as e-mail links, and jump links, which make it possible to link to a specific part of a Web page.

Linking pages within your Web site

Linking from one page to another page in your Web site is easy. Just make sure to save your pages in your local site folder (as described in the "Setting Up a New or Existing Site" section, at the beginning of this chapter) before you start setting links.

Here's how you create a link from one page in a Web site to another:

1. **In Dreamweaver, open the page where you want to create a link.**

2. **Select the text or image that you want to serve as the link (meaning the text or image that a user clicks to trigger the link).**

   Click and drag to highlight a section of text or click once to select an image. In this example, I selected the text **how we grow trees** and I linked it to a page named `how-we-grow-trees.html` located in the same folder.

3. **Click the Hyperlink icon in the Common Insert panel, at the top right of the workspace, shown in Figure 2-10.**

Alternatively, you can set a link by clicking the Browse button (which looks like a file folder) just to the right of the Link field in the Property inspector. Or see the Remember icon later in this section for a great shortcut using the Point to File icon.

4. **In the Hyperlink dialog box (see Figure 2-11), click the Browse icon to the right of the Link drop-down list.**

The Select File dialog box opens.

Figure 2-10:
Click the
Hyperlink
icon in the
Common
insert panel
to create a
link.

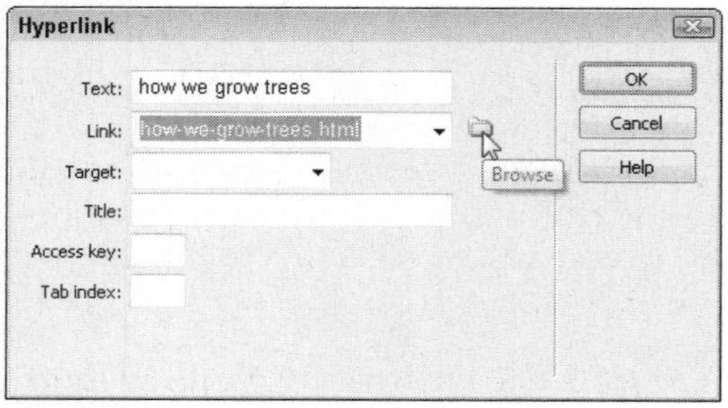

Figure 2-11:
The
Hyperlink
dialog box
includes a
number of
link settings
not avail-
able from
the Property
inspector,
including
Target
options and
accessibility
settings.

5. **(Optional) Use the Target field in the Hyperlink dialog box to set where your linked page opens.**

   For example, the _blank option causes the linked page to open in a new browser window or in a new tab within a browser, depending on the user's browser settings.

6. **Click the filename to select the page that you want your image or text to link to, and then click OK (Windows) or Choose (Mac).**

   When you click OK, the link is set automatically, and the dialog box closes. Note that to test your links, you have to view your page in a browser, a process I cover in Chapter 4.

After you become used to setting links, here's a great shortcut:

1. **Click the Point to File icon in the Property inspector.**

   It looks like a circle with a dot in the middle and is located just to the left of the folder icon.

2. **Drag your cursor across the page (without taking your finger of the right mouse button) and rest it on the name of any file in the Files panel.**

   When you click and drag from the File icon to a filename in this way, Dreamweaver extends a line to help you visualize that you're setting the link properly.

   The file must be visible in the Files panel, thus you may need to open a subfolder to reveal the file before you can set a link this way.

Setting links to named anchors in a page

Setting links to named anchors makes it possible to link to a specific place within a Web page. These kinds of links are generally used only on really long pages. A *named anchor link* is an HTML tag that can be inserted anywhere on a page to mark a specific point on the page with a name. The name can then serve as a target for a link. You can use a named anchor to link from an image or a section of text in one part of a page to another place on the same page, or to link from one page to a specific part of a different page. As you see in the following steps, to create an anchor link, sometimes called a *jump link,* you first insert a named anchor in the place you want to link to, and then add that anchor to the link code to direct the browser to that specific part of the page.

Suppose that you want to set a link from the word *Tigers* at the top of a page to a section lower on the page that starts with the headline *Lions are Cooler than Tigers.* First insert a named anchor at the *Lions are Cooler than Tigers* headline and then link the word *Tigers* from the top of the page to that anchor.

Creating multiple pages to set links

Creating a new page to start a Web site may seem obvious but consider this: Before you get too far in your development, you may want to create a few new pages and start organizing the new pages in subdirectories before you add anything to them. Doing so enables you to organize the structure of your site before you start setting links. After all, you can't use Dreamweaver's link features to link to a page that doesn't exist. If you plan to have three links on your front page that link to the three main sections of your site, go ahead and create those three main pages, even if you don't put anything but a little text on each page as you create it. (Of course, you can always change those pages later and add more pages to each section, but setting up the main links to the main sections is a great way to start designing your site.)

For example, say you're creating a site for your small business. You likely want a few main pages, such as a page about your staff, another page about your products or services, and a third page with general information and resources. At this initial stage, you could create four pages — one for the front page of the site and one for each subsection. Name the front page `index.html` and the other pages `staff.html`, `about.html`, and `general.html`.

If you expect to create many related pages in each section, consider creating subfolders for each, with a main page in the subfolder. For example, you could create a main `index.html` page inside a services subfolder and another `index.html` page inside a staff subfolder. Remember, naming the main page within a subfolder `index.html` enables you to use addresses to subpages that include the folder name, such as `www.domain.com/services`. Your site can include as many `index.html` pages as you like, as long as each is in a separate subfolder.

As you start creating your site, setting up all these main section pages helps you to organize your site and makes setting up the main links on all the site pages easier.

To insert a named anchor and set a link to it, follow these steps:

1. **Open the page on which you want to insert the named anchor.**

2. **Place your cursor next to the word or image that you want to link to on the page.**

   You don't need to select the word or image; you just need a reference point that appears when the link is selected. For this example, I placed the cursor to the left of the product listing for *White Spruce*.

3. **Choose Insert➪Named Anchor.**

   The Insert Named Anchor dialog box appears.

4. **Enter a name for the anchor.**

   You can name anchors anything you want (as long as you don't use spaces or special characters). Just make sure that you use a different name for each anchor on the same page. Then be sure that you remember the anchor's name because you have to either type it to set the link or select its name from the drop-down list in the Hyperlink dialog box, as you see in Step 8. In this example, I chose *wspruce* as the anchor name.

5. **Click OK.**

   The dialog box closes, and a small anchor icon appears on the page where you inserted the anchor name. You can move an anchor name by clicking the anchor icon and dragging it to another location on the page.

   If you're curious about what this named anchor looks like in HTML, here's the code that appears before the headline in my example:

   ```
   <a name="wspruce" id="white-spruce"></a>
   ```

   Remember that Dreamweaver creates XHTML code, which is a strict version of HTML and requires that all code be in lowercase letters.

6. **To set a link to the named anchor location, select the text or image that you want to link from.**

   You can link to a named anchor from anywhere else on the same page or from another page. In my example, I linked from the words *White Spruce* at the top of the page to the anchor I made next to the product listing for that type of tree.

7. **Click the Link icon in the Common Insert panel, at the top right of the workspace.**

8. **In the Hyperlink dialog box, use the small arrow to the right of the Link box to select the anchor.**

   Alternatively, using the Property inspector, you can set a jump link by typing a pound sign (#) followed by the anchor name.

    You can also select the text and drag a line from the Point to File icon (next to the Link text box) to the anchor icon. The anchor name automatically appears in the Link box, saving you from typing the name.

   In my example, I typed **#wspruce** in the Link text box. The HTML code for this line looks like this:

   ```
   <a href="#wspruce">White Spruce</a>
   ```

   If you want to link to an anchor named *wspruce* on another page with the filename `trees-for-sale.html`, type **trees-for-sale.html#wspruce** in the Link text box.

Linking to another Web site

To link to a page on another Web site — sometimes called an *external link* — all you need is the URL of the page to which you want to link, and you're most of the way there.

To create an external link, follow these steps:

1. **In Dreamweaver, open the page where you want to create the link.**

2. **Select the text or image that you want to act as the link.**

3. **In the Link text box in the Property inspector, type the URL of the page you want your text or image to link to.**

   The link is set automatically. In the example in Figure 2-12, I created a link using the text RootMaker® System to link to a Web site about this special way of growing trees, which is at the URL `www.rootmaker.org`.

Figure 2-12: To set a link to another Web site, highlight the text or image you want to link and type the URL in the Link text box.

Although, you don't have to type the `http://` or even the `www.` at the beginning of a Web site address to get to a site in most Web browsers, you must always use the full URL, including the `http://`, when you create a link to another Web site in HTML. Otherwise, the browser can't find the correct external site address, and the visitor will probably end up on an error page.

Setting a link to an e-mail address

Another common link option goes to an e-mail address. Visitors can send you messages easily with e-mail links. I always recommend that you invite visitors to contact you because including contact information helps establish credibility on the Web and because visitors to your site can point out mistakes and give you valuable feedback about how you can improve your site. Setting a link to an e-mail address is just as easy as setting a link to another Web page. All you need to know is the e-mail address you want to link to and what text or image you want to use when you set the link.

To create an e-mail link, select the text you want to link and then click the E-mail Link icon in the Common Insert panel. In the E-mail Link dialog box, enter the e-mail address in the Link field and then click OK. If you want to use an image as an e-mail link, select an image in Dreamweaver's main work area, then click the Hyperlink icon in the Common insert panel, and type the e-mail link into the Link field.

You can also set e-mail links using the Link field in the Property inspector, but you must enter the code `mailto:` (no `//`) before the e-mail address, as shown in Figure 2-13. For example, if you typed a link to my e-mail address into the Property inspector, you'd need to type **mailto:janine@jcwarner.com**. Here's what the full line of code behind that e-mail link would look like:

```
<a href="mailto:janine@jcwarner.com">Send a message to
        Janine</a>
```

Figure 2-13:
Create an
e-mail link in
the Property
inspector.

When visitors to your Web site click an e-mail link, their computer systems automatically launch their e-mail program and create a blank e-mail message to the specified e-mail address. Although this trick is cool, your users may find an e-mail's sudden appearance disconcerting if they don't expect it to happen, and the e-mail link won't work if your users don't have e-mail programs on their computers. That's why I always try to let users know when I use an e-mail link. For example, instead of just linking the words *Contact Janine,* I link the words *E-mail Janine.* Even better, I often link the actual e-mail address.

When you create an e-mail link on a Web page that will be displayed on the public Internet, you open yourself to spammers, some of whom use automated programs to "lift" e-mail addresses off Web pages. Spam is the reason many sites don't include e-mail links, but instead use one of the following methods to provide visitors with contact info:

✔ **Text worded for people (not bots):** An example is *Send e-mail to Janine at jcwarner.com.* Using text to describe the e-mail address instead of including the actual address can help thwart spammers, but it does make it a little harder for your visitors to send you e-mail.

✔ **Code that hides your e-mail address from bots:** The online service AddressMunger, which makes it easy for you to create special code using JavaScript to hide your e-mail address from spammers. Visit `www.AddressMunger.com` to read more about this free service.

✔ **Forms:** By setting up a form with a script that delivers the form's contents to an e-mail address, you can also require visitors to your site to include more information, such as why they are sending you an e-mail message. Using a form requires that you set up a script on your Web server, which can get complicated. You read more about form mail scripts and how to create the HTML code needed for forms in Chapter 11.

Understanding the HTML behind links

You don't have to learn HTML code to use Dreamweaver, but the ability to recognize important snippets of code behind your pages is often helpful. Because links are so important to Web pages and the Internet as whole, I include this final section to help you understand the code behind your links.

Here's an example of what the code looks like for a relative link from the home page on my Web site at `www.DigitalFamily.com` to the Dreamweaver page in the books section, which is contained within a folder named `books`. Note that essentially, you are telling the browser to enter the subfolder named books and find the page named `dreamweaver.html`:

```
<a href="books/dreamweaver.html">Dreamweaver Books</a>
```

```
<a href="/books/dreamweaver.html">Dreamweaver Books</a>
```

If you link to a page on a different Web site, the link includes the full Internet address of the other site. Here's an example of what the code would look like if you created a link from your site to the Dreamweaver page in my books section:

```
<a href="http://www.digitalfamily.com/books/
        dreamweaver.html">Janine's Books on
        Dreamweaver</a>
```

If all that `href` code stuff looks like Greek to you, don't worry. Remember Dreamweaver sets links like this for you so you don't even have to look at this code if you don't want to. (I include these final tips because I think it's helpful to have a little understanding of what's happening behind the scenes, not because you have to memorize any of this stuff or anything.)

Adding Meta Tags for Search Engines

If you've heard of meta tags, you probably associate them with search engines, and you'd be right. Meta tags are used for a variety of things, but one of the most common uses is to provide special text that doesn't appear on your page but is read by crawlers, bots, and other programs that scour the Web cataloging and ranking Web pages for Bing, Google, and a long list of other search-related sites.

In Dreamweaver you find features that help you add meta tags for keywords and descriptions. Here's a brief explanation of each tag; the steps for filling each tag with text are coming up:

- **Meta keyword tag:** A meta keyword tag enables you to include a list of keywords you would like search engines to match if someone searches for those words. Unfortunately, meta keywords have been so abused by Web designers attempting to mislead visitors about the true content of their Web pages that most search engines ignore the meta keyword tag and its contents. That said, some search engines still recognize meta keywords, and using this meta tag won't hurt your ranking with any search engines. Thus, most search engine experts consider it good practice to include them.

- **Meta description tag:** This tag, which is more widely used, is designed to let you include a written description of your Web site a worthwhile endeavor. Search engines often use the meta description tag's contents as the brief description that appears in search results pages. If you don't include your own text in a meta description tag, many search engines use the first several words that appear on your page as the description. Depending on your design, the first few words may not be the best description of your site, and you'll be better served by including your own meta description in the code.

You can include the same meta description on every page of your site, but most search engine experts will tell you that the best strategy is to include a description that is specific to the contents of each page on your site.

Follow these steps to add a meta description tag to your page:

1. **Open the page where you want to add a meta description.**

   You can use meta descriptions on any or all pages on your Web site. (Many people using search engines to find your site may end up directly at internal pages if the content matches the search.)

2. **Choose Insert⇨HTML⇨Head Tags⇨Description, as shown in Figure 2-14.**

   The Description dialog box appears.

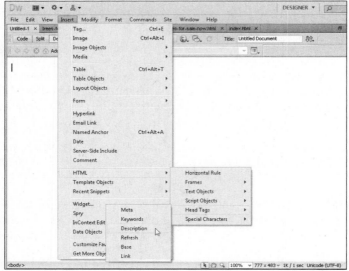

Figure 2-14:
Many
search
engines
use the text
entered into
the meta
description
field as the
descrip-
tion of your
Web page
in search
results.

3. **In the Description text box, enter the text you want for your page description.**

   Don't add any HTML to the text in this box.

4. **Click OK.**

   The description text you entered is inserted into the Head area at the top of the page in the HTML code. Meta content doesn't appear in the body of the page.

If you want to add keywords, repeat Steps 1–4, choosing Insert➪HTML➪Head Tags➪Keywords in Step 2. Type a list of keywords, separated by commas, in place of a description in Step 3.

Using the Quick Tag Editor

If you're one of those developers who likes to work in the Dreamweaver Design area — sometimes referred to as the WYSIWYG (what you see is what you get) editing environment — but still wants to look at the HTML tags once in a while, you'll love the Quick Tag Editor.

The Quick Tag Editor, as the name implies, lets you quickly access HTML tags and enables you to modify, add, or remove an HTML tag without opening the

HTML Source window. So while you're in the middle of working on a page in design view, you can view the HTML tag you're working on without switching over to code view. You can use the Quick Tag Editor to insert HTML, edit an existing tag, or wrap new tags around a selected text block or other element.

The Quick Tag Editor opens in one of three modes — Edit, Insert, or Wrap — depending on what you selected on the page before you launched the editor. Use the keyboard shortcut Ctrl+T (Windows) or ⌘+T (Mac) to change modes while the Quick Tag Editor is open.

You can enter or edit tags in the Quick Tag Editor just as you would in code view, without having to switch back and forth between code view and design view. To enter or edit tags in the Quick Tag Editor, follow these steps:

1. **With the document you want to edit open, select an image, text block, or other element.**

   If you want to add new code, simply click anywhere in the file without selecting text or an element.

2. **Choose Modify⬦Quick Tag Editor.**

   You can also press Ctrl+T (Windows) or ⌘+T (Mac). Or, you can right-click the name of the element tag in the status bar at the bottom of the workspace.

   The Quick Tag Editor opens in the mode that is most appropriate for your selection, as shown in Figure 2-15. For example, if you click an image or formatted text, it displays the current tag so that you can edit it. If you don't select anything or if you select unformatted text, the Quick Tag Editor opens with nothing in it, and you can enter the code you want to add.

Figure 2-15:
You can view and edit HTML tags in the Quick Tag Editor without switching to code view.

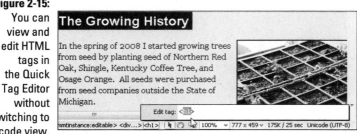

3. **To add a new tag or attribute, simply type the code into the Quick Tag Editor.**

If you aren't sure about a tag or attribute, press the spacebar, and the Hints drop-down list appears automatically, displaying all the tags or attributes available for the element you're editing. If this Hints drop-down list doesn't appear, choose Edit⇨Preferences⇨Code Hints (Windows) or Dreamweaver⇨Preferences⇨Code Hints (Mac) and make sure that the Enable Code Hints option is selected.

4. **To close the Quick Tag Editor and apply all your changes, press Enter (Windows) or Return (Mac).**

Chapter 3

Creating Web Graphics

*N*o matter how great the writing on your Web site may be, the graphics always get people's attention first. The key to making a good first impression is to use images that look great and download quickly.

If you're familiar with using a graphics-editing program, such as Adobe Photoshop or Fireworks, to create graphics for the Web, you're a step ahead. If not, you find pointers throughout this chapter on how to convert images for the Web, what image formats to use, and how to optimize images for faster download times. I use Adobe Photoshop CS5 in the examples in this chapter, but because the features I use in this chapter are nearly identical in both programs, you can use these same instructions to complete these tasks in Photoshop Elements. (See the sidebar "Comparing Adobe Web graphics programs" to learn more about the differences.)

If your images are already in GIF, JPEG, or PNG format and ready for the Web, you can jump ahead to the "Inserting Images in Dreamweaver" section, where you find out how to place and align images and use an image as a background. You also discover some of Dreamweaver's built-in image-editing features, which enable you to crop images and even adjust contrast and brightness without ever launching an external image-editing program.

Comparing Adobe Web graphics programs

Most professional designers strongly prefer Adobe Photoshop, although I have to say I've been impressed with Photoshop Elements, which is a "light" version but offers many of the same features for a fraction of the cost. The following is a list of some of the most popular image-editing programs on the market today. All these image programs are available for both Mac and Windows:

✔ **Adobe Photoshop** (www.adobe.com/photoshop): By far the most popular image-editing program on the market, Photoshop is a widely used standard among graphics professionals. With Photoshop, you can create original artwork, edit and enhance photographs, and so much more. Photoshop has a wealth of powerful painting and selection tools, special effects, and filters that enable you to create images far beyond what you can capture on film or create with many other illustration programs. In previous versions, Photoshop came bundled with a program called *Image Ready,* a companion program designed for Web graphics. In CS3, those Web features were included in Photoshop; and in CS4, they've been enhanced. Switching between Photoshop and Dreamweaver is easier than ever.

✔ **Adobe Photoshop Elements** (www.adobe.com/elements): If you don't need all the bells and whistles offered in the full-blown version of Photoshop, Photoshop Elements is a remarkably powerful program — for about a sixth of the price. If you're a professional designer, you're best served by Photoshop. But if you're a hobbyist or small business owner and want to create good-looking images without the high cost and learning curve of a professional graphics program, Elements is a great deal and well-suited to creating Web graphics.

✔ **Adobe Fireworks** (www.adobe.com/fireworks): Fireworks was one of the first image-editing programs designed to create and edit Web graphics. Originally created by Macromedia, the program is now part of the Adobe Web Suite and is fully integrated with Dreamweaver. Fireworks gives you everything you need to create, edit, and output Web graphics, all in one well-designed product. Although Fireworks lacks many of the advanced image-editing capabilities of Photoshop, Fireworks shines when creating Web graphics and is especially popular among Web designers who rave about the ability to create a design in Fireworks that can easily be sliced and converted into a Web page in Dreamweaver.

If you have an Internet connection and want to do basic image editing for free, visit http://www.gimp.org or www.photoshop.com/express. Both sites make it possible to edit and optimize images online without purchasing a software program.

Creating and Optimizing Web Graphics

The most important thing to keep in mind when creating images for the Web is that you want to *optimize* your images to make your file sizes as small as possible so that they download as quickly as possible.

How you optimize an image depends on how the image was created and whether you want to save it as a JPEG, PNG or, GIF. You find instructions for optimizing images with Photoshop in the sections that follow, but the bottom line is this: No matter what program, format, or optimization technique you choose, your biggest challenge is finding the best balance between small file size and good image quality. Essentially, the more you optimize, the faster the image will download, but the compression and color reduction techniques used to optimize images can make them look terrible if you go too far.

As a general rule, do any editing, such as adjusting contrast, retouching, or combining images before you reduce their size or optimize them because you want to work with the highest resolution possible when you're editing. Also, resize an image before you optimize it. You find instructions for resizing an image in the next exercise and instructions for optimizing in the sections that follow.

Resizing graphics and photos

Resizing is important for two reasons: The images must be small enough to display well on a computer monitor, and you want them to download quickly to a user's computer. The smaller the image is, the faster it will download.

Although you can change the display size of an image in a Web page by altering the height and width settings in Dreamweaver, you get much better results if you change the physical size of the image in editor program such as Photoshop, instead.

When you alter an image's height and width in the HTML code (via the height and width settings in Dreamweaver), you simply instruct a Web browser to display the image in a different size. Unfortunately, browsers don't do a good job of resizing images because browsers don't change the image itself, but just force it to fit in the assigned space when the browser loads the page. If you set the image to display larger than its actual size, the image is likely to look fuzzy or distorted because the image doesn't contain enough pixels for all the details to look good in a larger size. If you set the code to display the image smaller than it is, the image is likely to look squished, and you're requiring that your users download an image that's larger than necessary.

Reducing an image's size for use on the Web requires two steps. First, you reduce the resolution of an image, which changes the number of pixels in the image. When you're working with images for the Web, you want to reduce the resolution to 72 pixels per inch (or ppi). (If you're wondering why 72, see the sidebar that's appropriately named "Why only 72 ppi?") Second, you reduce the image's physical size by reducing its dimensions. You want to size your images to fit well in a browser window and to work within the design of your site.

Follow these steps to lower the resolution and reduce the size of an image in Photoshop (in Photoshop Elements or Fireworks, you follow a similar process although the specific steps may vary):

1. **With an image open in Photoshop, choose Image⇨Resize.**

   The Image Size dialog box opens, as shown in Figures 3-1 and 3-2.

   If you don't want your original image to lose quality (or you just want to play it safe), make a copy of your image and resize the *copy* for your Web site.

2. **To change the resolution of your image, first deselect the Resample Image check box at the bottom of the Image Size dialog box, as shown in Figure 3-1.**

   For best results, you always want the Resample Image check box deselected when you change the resolution.

3. **Click and drag to highlight the number in the Resolution field and replace it by typing in the number 72.**

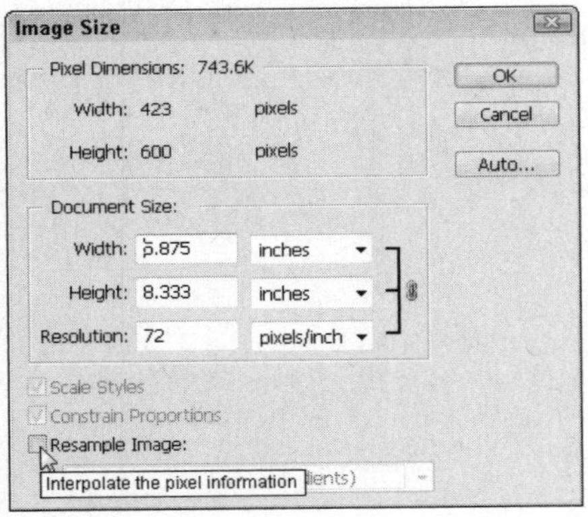

Figure 3-1:
To best prepare your images for the Web, change the resolution to 72 ppi and they will download faster.

Image Size	
Pixel Dimensions: 743.6K	
Width: 423 pixels	OK
Height: 600 pixels	Cancel
	Auto...
Document Size:	
Width: 5.875 inches	
Height: 8.333 inches	
Resolution: 72 pixels/inch	
Scale Styles	
Constrain Proportions	
Resample Image:	
Interpolate the pixel information	

4. **Click to select the Resample Image check box.**

   With the Resample Image check box deselected, you can't change the Pixel dimensions so it must be checked when you change the image size.

5. **Enter a height and width for the image in the Height and Width fields.**

   As shown in Figure 3-2, I'm reducing the size of this image to 200 pixels wide. If the Constrain Proportions check box at the bottom of the dialog box is checked (as it is in this example), any changes you make to the height automatically affect the width (and vice versa) to ensure that the image proportions remain constant. I prefer to work this way, but if you do want to change the image and not maintain the proportions, you can deselect this box.

Figure 3-2:
When you resize an image in Photoshop in the Pixel Dimensions area, you can specify the new size in pixels or as a percentage of the original size.

6. **Click OK to resize the image.**

If you want to return the image to its previous size, choose Edit⇨Undo. Beware that when you save the image, the changes become permanent.

Why only 72 ppi?

When you save images for the Web, you save them at a resolution of 72 pixels per inch (better known as *ppi*). Most computer monitors display no more than 72 ppi, so any resolution higher than that is wasted on the Web because you'd be making your visitors download more pixels than they can see. However, if you want to print an image, you want all the pixels you can get, usually at least 200 ppi or higher, which is why most images you see on the Web look terrible if you try to print them in a large size.

Choosing the best image format

One of the most common questions about images for the Web concerns when to use GIF or PNG and when to use JPEG. Table 3-1 provides the simple answer.

Table 3-1	Image Formats for the Web
Format	*Best Use*
GIF (Extension is `.gif`)	For line art (such as one- or two-color logos), simple drawings, animations, and basically any image that has no gradients or blends. GIF is also the best format when you want to display an image with a transparent background.
PNG (Extension is `.png`)	PNG generally produces better-looking images with smaller file sizes than GIF for the same kinds of limited-color images. Really old browsers, such as IE 3, don't support the PNG format, but most Web designers now choose this format over GIF because so few people use such old browsers. Browsers as recent as IE6 don't display transparent PNG files properly, which is unfortunate because PNG files tend to handle transparency better. If you're using transparency and know that many of the visitors to your site still use IE6 or earlier versions, you may want to consider using GIFs instead.
JPEG (Extension may be `.jpg` or `.jpeg`)	JPEG is the best format for colorful, complex images (such as photographs); images containing gradients or color blends; and any other images with millions of colors.

Saving images for the Web: The basics

If you're new to saving images for the Web, the following basics can help you get the best results from your files, your image-editing program, and ultimately your Web pages. You can

✔ **Convert an image from any format into the GIF, PNG, or JPEG formats.** For example, turn all your TIF, BMP, and PSD image files into a Web-friendly file format.

✔ **Optimize images that are already in GIF, PNG, or JPEG format.** Even if your files are already in a Web-friendly format, following the instructions in this chapter to optimize images with Adobe's Save for Web dialog box further reduces their file sizes for faster download over the Internet.

✔ **Use many programs to create Web graphics, but Photoshop is one of the best and easiest to use.** Under the File menu in Photoshop (and Photoshop Elements), you'll find the Save for Web option. (In Photoshop CS4 and CS5, the option is Save for Web & Devices.) Fireworks provides a similar feature, and although the dialog boxes are slightly different in each program, the basic options for compressing and reducing colors (which are covered in this chapter) are the same.

See the upcoming sections "Optimizing JPEG images for the Web" and "Optimizing images in GIF and PNG formats" for details about using the Save for Web feature.

✔ **Make image edits before you optimize.** When you're editing, using the highest quality image possible is always best. Make sure to do all your editing, sharpening, and resizing before you use the Save for Web option. Similarly, if you want to make further changes to an image after you've optimized it, you'll achieve the best results if you go back a higher resolution version of the image rather than editing the version that's been optimized for the Web. (When you use the Save for Web & Devices feature, Photoshop creates a new copy of your image and leaves the original unchanged.)

Optimizing JPEG images for the Web

The JPEG format is the best choice for optimizing continuous-tone images, such as photographs and images with many colors or gradients. When you optimize a JPEG, you can make the file size smaller by applying compression. The more compression, the smaller the image, but if you compress the image too much, the image can look terrible. The trick is finding the right balance, as you discover in this section.

If you have a digital photograph or another image that you want to prepare for the Web, follow these steps to optimize and save it in Photoshop (in Photoshop Elements or Fireworks, the process is similar although the specific steps may vary):

1. **With the image open in Photoshop, choose File⇨Save for Web & Devices (or File⇨Save for Web).**

   The Save for Web & Devices dialog box appears.

2. **In the top-left corner of the dialog box, choose either 2-Up or 4-Up to display multiple versions of the same image for easy side-by-side comparison.**

   In the example shown in Figure 3-3, I chose 2-Up, which makes it possible to view the original image on the left and a preview of the same image as it will appear with the specified settings on the right. The 4-Up option, as the name implies, displays four different versions for comparison.

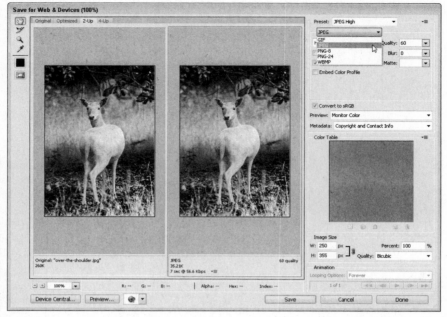

Figure 3-3:
The JPEG
format is
best for
photographs
and other
images with
millions of
colors.

3. On the right side of the window, just under Preset, click the small arrow to open the Optimized File Format drop-down list and choose JPEG (this dialog window is open in Figure 3-3).

4. Set the compression quality.

Use the preset options Low, Medium, High, Very High, or Maximum from the drop-down list. Or use the slider just under the Quality field to make more precise adjustments. Lowering the quality reduces the file size and makes the image download more quickly, but if you lower this number too much, the image will look blurry and blotchy.

Photoshop uses a compression scale of 0 to 100 for JPEGs in this dialog window, with 0 the lowest possible quality (the highest amount of compression and the smallest file size) and 100 the highest possible quality (the least amount of compression and the biggest file size). Low, Medium, and High represent compression values of 10, 30, and 60, respectively.

5. Specify other settings as desired (the compression quality and file format are the most important settings).

6. Click Save.

The Save Optimized As dialog box opens.

7. Enter a name for the image and save it into the images folder in your Web site folder.

Photoshop saves the optimized image as a copy of the original and leaves the original open in the main Photoshop work area. (Chapter 2 explains the importance of the images subfolder.)

Repeat these steps for each image you want to optimize as a JPEG.

At the bottom of the image preview in the Save for Web and Devices dialog box, Photoshop includes an estimate of the time required for the image to download at the specified connection speed. In the example shown in Figure 3-3, the estimate is 7 seconds at 56.6 Kbps. As you adjust the compression settings, the size of the image changes and the download estimate will automatically adjust. You can change the connection speed used to make this calculation by clicking on the small arrow just to the right of the connection speed and using the drop-down list to select another option, such as 256 Kbps for Cable Modem speed. Use this estimate as a guide to help you decide how much you should optimize each image.

Optimizing images in GIF and PNG formats

If you're working with a graphic, such as a logo, cartoon character, or drawing that can be displayed in 256 colors or less, your best bet is to use the PNG format and reduce the total number of colors used in the image as much as possible to reduce the file size. (If you are concerned about visitors using a very, very old Web browser, use GIF instead.)

To help make up for the degradation in image quality that can happen when colors are removed, GIF and PNG use a dithering trick. *Dithering* involves alternating pixels in a checkerboard-like pattern to create subtle color variations, even with a limited color palette. The effect can smooth the image's edges and make it appear to have more colors than it actually does.

To convert an image to a GIF or PNG in Photoshop, follow these steps (in Photoshop Elements or Fireworks, the process is similar although the specific steps may vary):

1. **With the image open in Photoshop, choose File⇨Save for Web & Devices (or File⇨Save for Web).**

   The Save for Web & Devices dialog box appears.

2. **In the top-left corner of the dialog box, choose 2-Up or 4-Up to display multiple versions of the same image for easy side-by-side comparison.**

   In the example shown in Figure 3-4, I chose 4-Up, which makes it possible to view the original image (in the upper-left corner), as well as three different previews of the same image.

3. **Select a preview image to begin changing its settings.**

Changing the preview images in the 4-Up view enables you to compare an image with up to four different color settings, as you see in Figure 3-4.

4. **On the right side of the dialog window, just under Preset, click the small arrow to open the Optimized File Format drop-down list and choose either GIF or PNG.**

5. **In the Colors box, select the number of colors, as shown in Figure 3-4.**

   The fewer colors you use, the smaller the file size and the faster the image will download. But be careful; if you reduce the colors too much (as I have in the bottom-right preview shown in Figure 3-4), you lose details. The ideal number of colors depends on your image; if you go too far, your image will look terrible.

6. **If you want to maintain a transparent area in your image, select the Transparency check box.**

   Any area of the image that was transparent when you created the image in the editor appears transparent in the preview window. If you don't have a transparent area in your image, this setting has no effect.

   Transparency is a good trick for making text or an image appear to float on a Web page. That's because a transparent background doesn't appear on the Web page. You can select transparency as a background option in the New File dialog box when you create a new image in Photoshop or Photoshop Elements.

7. **If you choose Transparency, also specify a Matte color.**

   You want the matte color to match the background of your Web page so that the dithering along the transparent edge will blend in with the background. If you don't specify a matte color, the transparency is set for a white background, which can cause a *halo* effect when the image is displayed on a colored background.

8. **Specify other settings as desired.**

   The remainder of the settings in this dialog box can be left at their defaults in Photoshop.

9. **Click Save.**

   The Save Optimized As dialog box opens.

10. **Enter a name for the image and save it into the images folder (or any other folder) in your local site folder.**

Repeat these steps for each image you want to optimize as a GIF or PNG for your site.

Trial and error is a great technique in the Save for Web & Devices dialog box. In each of the three preview windows displaying optimized versions of the cool cartoon image in Figure 3-4, I used fewer and fewer colors, which reduced the file size with increasingly degrading effect.

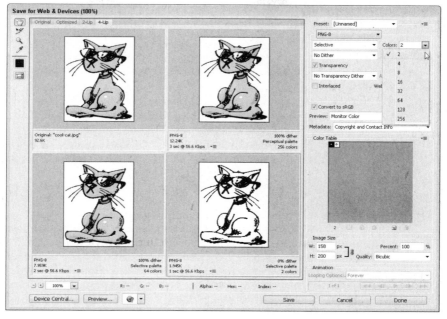

Figure 3-4:
The GIF
and PNG
formats
are best
for images
with limited
colors, such
as cartoons
and line art.

Illustration by Tom McCain

The version in the top left of the dialog box is the original, which has a file size of 92.6K. Reducing the image to 256 colors dramatically reduced the file size to 12.24K, but made little noticeable change to the image, as you see in the top right. In the bottom left, the image is reduced to 64 colors, which brought the size down to 7.959K, but still made little change to the quality of the image. In the bottom right, I reduced it to 2 colors, and the image quality suffered dramatically. Although it's harder to tell in the black-and-white reproduction in this book, all the color and details disappeared, leaving just a black-and-white outline. In this last case, the small savings in file size are clearly not worth the loss of image quality.

How small is small enough?

After you know how to optimize GIFs and JPEGs and appreciate the goal of making them as small as possible, you may ask, "How small is small enough?" The answer is mostly subjective, but the following points are good to remember:

✔ **The larger your graphics files, the longer people have to wait for them to download before they can see them.** You may have the most beautiful picture of Mount Fuji on the front page of your Web site, but if it takes forever to download, most people aren't patient enough to wait to see it.

✔ **When you build pages with multiple graphics, you have to consider the cumulative download time of all the graphics on the page.** Even if each individual image is a small file size, they can add up. Unlike most things in life, smaller is definitely better on the Web.

✔ **Most Web pros consider anything from about 75K to 150K a good maximum** *cumulative* **size for all the elements on a given page.** With the increasing popularity of DSL and cable modems, many Web sites are starting to become a bit more graphics heavy and go beyond that size limit. However, anything over 150K is pushing the limit, especially if you expect people with dialup modems (56K and under) or those surfing on mobile phones to stick around long enough to view your pages.

To make determining the total file size of the images on your page easy, Dreamweaver includes this information in the status bar at the bottom of the Document window, as shown in Figure 3-5. In the small text at the bottom of this Web page about Fallow Deer, the status bar shows that the total size of all the images, text, and code on the page adds up to 149K and will download in 10 seconds at the connection at the speed specified in Dreamweaver's preferences. In this example, the connection speed is set to 128K. (You can change connection speed by choosing Edit➪Preferences➪Status Bar➪Connection Speed. On a Mac, choose Dreamweaver➪Preferences➪Status Bar➪Connection Speed.)

Figure 3-5:
The Dream-weaver status bar indicates the total file size of all elements on a page and the estimated download time.

Inserting Images in Dreamweaver

Now for the fun part. Adding an image to your Web page may seem almost magical at first because it's so simple with Dreamweaver. The challenge with Web graphics isn't adding them to your pages but creating good-looking images that load quickly in your viewer's browser. You need another program, such as Photoshop, Photoshop Elements, or Fireworks, to create, convert, edit, and optimize images (covered in Chapter 3). *Optimizing* images makes file sizes smaller so your images download faster. Dreamweaver provides some basic image-editing tools, but mostly you use Dreamweaver to insert and position images on your page.

Dreamweaver makes placing images on your Web pages easy and provides multiple ways to do so:

- ✔ Click the Images icon in the Common Insert panel and then select an image using the Insert image dialog box

- ✔ In the Files panel, click and drag an image name onto the page where you want the image to appear.

- ✔ Use the Insert menu, as I explain the following steps.

If you don't have a Web-optimized JPEG, GIF, or PNG image handy, you can download free images that are already optimized from my Web site by going directly to www.DigitalFamily.com/free. (You find instructions for downloading the free images when you get to this special page on my Web site.)

To place an image on a Web page using the Insert menu, follow these instructions:

1. **Open an existing page or choose File➪New to create a new page.**

2. **Place your cursor where you want to insert the image on the page.**

3. **Choose Insert➪Image.**

   The Select Image Source dialog box appears, as shown in Figure 3-6.

4. **Browse to locate the image you want to insert.**

   Depending on your computer system, you can preview images as you insert them in different ways. Here are three common options:

   - **On a PC with Windows XP**, choose Thumbnails from the View drop-down list to the right of the Look In field to display thumbnail versions of all the images in any open folder. You can also view a single preview of any selected image in the far right of the dialog box.

- **On a PC with Windows Vista or Windows 7** (as shown in Figure 3-6), choose one of the icon options (small, medium, large, or extra large) from the View drop-down list just to the right of the Look In field to display thumbnail versions of all the images in any open folder. You can also view a single preview of any selected image in the far right of the dialog box.

- **On a Mac,** choose the View As Columns option from the top left of the dialog, and you can view a single preview of any selected image in the far right of the dialog.

5. **To insert the image, double-click the image name or click once and then click OK.**

   If you have Accessibility options turned on in Preferences (the default), the Image Tag Accessibility Attributes dialog box appears.

   If you insert an image into a page and the image isn't saved in your local site folder, Dreamweaver prompts you with a warning dialog and offers to copy the image into your local site folder. (Find out how to set up a local site folder in the section "Setting Up a New or Existing Site," in Chapter 2.) Many designers create a subfolder called *images* inside the local site folder where they store all the images in their site, but you can organize images in multiple subfolders if you prefer.

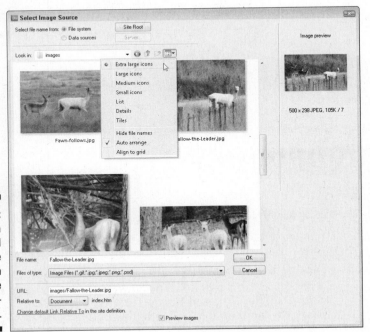

Figure 3-6: You can locate and preview the images in the Image Source dialog box.

6. **In the Image Tag Accessibility Attributes dialog box, enter text that describes the image in the Alternate Text field.**

   Adding alternate text in this dialog box is always a best practice.

   Alternate text won't appear on your Web page unless the image isn't visible, but it will appear in Internet Explorer when a user holds the cursor over the image. Alternate text is also important for Web surfers who use *screen readers,* or browsers that "read" Web pages to them, such as those with limited vision. For this reason, alternate text is required for accessibility compliance. A long description is considered optional under most accessibility guidelines. You can enter the address of a Web page with a longer description of the image in this field. You can also add or edit alternate text in the Property inspector after clicking to select the inserted image.

7. **Click OK to close the Accessibility Attributes dialog box and insert the image.**

   The image appears in the page.

8. **Click to select the image on your Web page to view image properties.**

   Image options are displayed automatically in the Property inspector at the bottom of the page when an image is selected, as shown in Figure 3-7.

Figure 3-7: When an image is selected, the Property inspector provides easy access to common image attributes, such as height and width settings.

Although you can change many settings, such as image alignment, by using the HTML attribute options available in the Property inspector, using CSS (covered in Chapter 5) is almost always a better option. For example, you can use the H Space attribute in the Property inspector to create a margin around an image, but H Space adds margin on both the left and right sides of an image. With CSS, you can create a style that applies margin space to any or all sides of an image, giving you more control of your design.

Table 3-2 describes the many image attributes available in the Property inspector when an image is selected. If you don't see all the attributes listed in the table on your screen, click the small triangle in the bottom-right corner of the Property inspector to reveal all the image options.

When you insert an image file onto a page, you don't actually add a copy of the image to the page; you create a reference to the image. The underlying code looks much like the code for a link from one page to another. Both image references and links include the name of the file (the page you link to or the image you insert) and the path from the page to that file. Essentially, you're creating an instruction for a Web browser to find the image when it displays the page.

So to display an image on your Web page, you need to upload both the page and the image when you publish your Web site. If your image files and the pages that refer to those files aren't in the same relative location on your hard drive as they are on your Web server, you break the reference to your images, and an ugly broken image icon appears on your page. The best way to make sure that your images and files stay where they're supposed to in relation to one another is to let Dreamweaver keep track of them for you. That's why it's so important to complete the site setup process at the beginning of Chapter 2 and to make sure you never move or rename an image, except in the Files panel.

Table 3-2		Image Attributes in the Property Inspector
Abbreviation	*Attribute*	*Function*
Image	N/A	Displays the file size.
ID	Name	Identifies image uniquely on the page — an important detail if you use behaviors or other scripts that target an image. Can be left blank.
Map	Map Name	Assigns a name to an image map. All image maps require a name.
Hotspot tools	Image Map Coordinates	Use the Rectangle, Oval, and Polygon icons to create image map hotspots for links. (See Chapter 3 to find out how to create an image map.)

Abbreviation	*Attribute*	*Function*
W	Width	Dreamweaver automatically specifies the width of the image based on the actual size of the image dimensions.
H	Height	Dreamweaver automatically specifies the height of the image based on the actual size of the image dimensions.
Src	Source	Required. The *source* is the filename and path from the current document to the desired image. Dreamweaver automatically sets this when you insert the image.
Link	Hyperlink	This field displays the address or path if the image is used as a link. (For more about creating links, see "Setting Links in Dreamweaver" later in this chapter.)
Alt	Alternate Text	Use this field to add or edit alternate text.
Edit	Icons for Edit, Image Editing Settings, and Update from Original	Click the Edit icon to launch the image editor associated with Dreamweaver (you can change these settings in Dreamweaver's preferences dialog box). Use the Image Editing Settings icon to launch the Image Preview dialog box where you can make basic edits to an image. Choose the Update from Original icon to ensure that edits are made using the original image. *Note:* This setting works only if you've used an associated Adobe image editor to edit the image before inserting the image into the page.
V Space	Vertical Space	Measured in pixels, this setting inserts blank space above and below the image. (You will have more control if you use the margin and padding settings in CSS, covered in Chapter 6.)
H Space	Horizontal Space	Measured in pixels, this setting inserts blank space to the left and right of the image. (You will have more control if you use the margin and padding settings in CSS, covered in Chapter 6.)
Target	Link Target	Use this option when the image appears in a page where you want to control the target, such as when a page is part of an HTML frameset. If you want a link to open a new browser window, choose _blank.

(continued)

Table 3-2 *(continued)*

Abbreviation	Attribute	Function
Border	Image Border	Measured in pixels, this attribute enables you to control the appearance of a border around an image. To prevent an automatic border being added when an image is used as a link, set the image border to 0 (zero).
Icons for	Crop, Resample, Brightness and Contrast, and Sharpen	Use any of these icons to make minor alterations to an image in Dreamweaver. ***Note:*** Any changes made using these options permanently alter the image when the page is saved.
Class	CSS Setting	The Class field enables you to apply any class styles defined in Dreamweaver. To use this option, select any element in the workspace and then select any class style you want to apply from the drop-down list.
Original	N/A	If you are using the Smart Objects features in Photoshop or Firefox, you can use this field to indentify the original version. (See your Photoshop or Firefox documentation for more on these features.)
Align	Align	Although you can align images using this option, it is far better to use the float settings in Cascading Style Sheets, covered in Chapter 6.

Why can't I place images anywhere I want them?

You can't just place your cursor anywhere on a page and insert an image where you want it. This isn't a limitation of Dreamweaver; the way HTML is displayed on the Web restricts how you can place images.

By default, all images, text, and other elements are inserted starting at the top-left corner of the browser window. To create more complex layouts and position images precisely on a page, your best option is to create a layout with CSS (which I cover in Chapters 5 and 6). You can also use an HTML table to position elements on a Web page (which I cover in Chapter 8).

Image Editing in Dreamweaver

Dreamweaver includes basic image-editing features, including the Crop, Resample, Brightness/Contrast, and Sharpen options. You find these tools next to the Border option in the Property inspector, as shown in Figure 3-8. Image-editing features in Dreamweaver enable you to make minor changes to images without opening Fireworks, Photoshop, or any other graphics-editing program.

Figure 3-8:
Use the image-editing tools to do basic image editing.

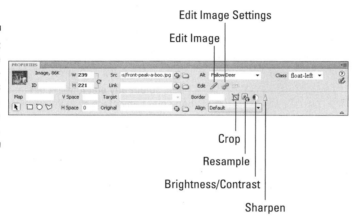

Edit Image Settings

Edit Image

Crop

Resample

Brightness/Contrast

Sharpen

Before you get carried away editing your images, remember that Dreamweaver is primarily a Web page-creation application and isn't really designed to edit graphics. Although these tools can be useful, they shouldn't take the place of doing serious work on your graphics in a graphics application, such as Fireworks or Photoshop.

When you use Dreamweaver's image-editing tools, beware that you're changing the actual image (not just a copy of it). Make sure you're happy with these changes before you save the page you're working on. You can use the Undo feature in Dreamweaver to revert back several steps, but after you save the page, you can't undo changes made to an image with these tools. To protect your original image, save a copy before editing it.

Cropping an image

Essentially, cropping an image involves trimming the edges off of it. If you're trying to fit an image into your design and need it to be just at touch smaller,

Dreamweaver's cropping tool can come in handy. To crop a graphic or photo, follow these steps:

1. **In the Document window, select the image you want to crop by clicking it.**

   The Property inspector changes to display the image's properties.

2. **Click the Crop icon (see Figure 3-9).**

   A dialog box appears, warning you that cropping changes the original image.

   Don't make the change if you're concerned about keeping the entire image available. If you're concerned, the best thing to do is to make a copy of the image before you crop it.

3. **Click OK in the warning dialog box.**

   A solid crop line with handles at the sides and corners appears over the image, as shown in Figure 3-9.

Figure 3-9:
Define the area to crop by dragging the edges of the cropping tool outline.

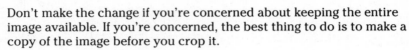

4. **Click and drag the handles to outline the area of the image you want to keep.**

   Any part of the image outside the crop line (and shaded) is deleted when the crop is completed.

5. **Double-click inside the box or press Enter (Return on a Mac).**

   The image is cropped.

You can undo cropping by choosing Edit➪Undo. However, after you save the page, changes permanently apply to the image and can't be undone.

Adjusting brightness and contrast

Adjusting an image's *brightness* allows you to change the overall amount of light in an image. *Contrast* controls the difference between the light and dark areas of an image.

Using Dreamweaver's editing tools permanently alters the image when the page is saved. If you're concerned, the best thing to do is to make a copy of the image and make your adjustments to the copy.

To adjust brightness and contrast, follow these steps:

1. **In the Document window, select the image you want to alter.**

   The Property inspector shows the image properties.

2. **Click the Brightness and Contrast icon (labeled in Figure 3-8).**

   A dialog box appears, indicating that the changes you make are made to the original file.

3. **Click OK in the warning dialog box.**

   The Brightness/Contrast dialog box appears.

4. **Use the sliders to adjust the brightness and contrast settings of the image.**

   Make sure to select the Preview check box if you want to see how the changes affect the image as you move the sliders around.

5. **Click OK.**

   The settings take effect permanently when you save the page.

Sharpening an image

When you apply *sharpening* to an image, you increase the distinction between areas of color. The effect can increase the definition of shapes and lines in an image.

Using Dreamweaver's editing tools permanently alters the image when the page is saved. If you're concerned, the best thing to do is to make a copy of the image and make your adjustments to the copy.

To sharpen an image, follow these steps:

1. **In the Document window, select the image you want to sharpen.**

   The Property inspector shows the image properties.

2. **Click the Sharpen icon (labeled in Figure 3-8).**

   A dialog box appears, warning that your change is made to the original file.

3. **Click OK in the warning dialog box.**

   The Sharpen dialog box appears.

4. **Use the slider to adjust the sharpness of the image.**

   Select the Preview check box to see how the changes affect the image as you move the slider.

5. **Click OK.**

   The image is sharpened, and changes to the image become permanent when you save changes to the page.

Optimizing images in Dreamweaver

Dreamweaver CS4 and CS5 include an Edit Image Settings icon that you can use to optimize images in the GIF, PNG, or JPEG formats by reducing the colors or increasing the compression, much as you can do in Photoshop or Fireworks. To use this feature, simply select any image in the Dreamweaver workspace and then click the Edit Image Settings icon in the Property inspector. (**Hint:** It looks like a two small gears and is labeled in Figure 3-8.)

Dreamweaver's editing tools permanently alter the image when the page is saved. If you want to protect your original image, make a copy of the image before you make any changes.

To optimize an image in Dreamweaver, follow these steps:

1. **In the Document window, select the image you want to optimize.**

   The Property inspector shows the image properties.

2. **Click the Edit Image Settings icon (labeled in Figure 3-8).**

   The Image Preview dialog box appears with the Options tab selected, as shown in Figure 3-10.

3. **In the Format drop-down list, select the image format you want.**

   If you want don't want to change the format, skip this step. You can select the GIF, JPEG, or PNG format.

4. **If you choose JPEG, use the slider that appears when you click the arrow next to Quality to select the level of compression. If you choose GIF or PNG, choose the number of colors desired.**

   The image is altered based on the settings you specify.

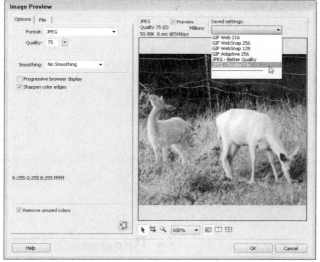

Figure 3-10:
You can
resize and
optimize
images in
Dream-
weaver
using the
Edit Image
Settings
option.

5. **Click the File tab at the top left of the Image Preview dialog box.**

   The Image Scale options are displayed.

6. **Change the height and width by altering the current size settings or by entering a percentage.**

   The image size changes based on your settings.

7. **Click OK to close the dialog and save your settings.**

   When you save the page, your changes to the image become permanent.

You can also change other settings in the Image Preview dialog box, such as transparency settings for the GIF format, much as you would in Photoshop or Fireworks.

Opening an image in Photoshop or Fireworks from Dreamweaver

The Property inspector includes an icon that enables you to easily open an image in Photoshop or Fireworks from within Dreamweaver. The Edit icon changes to the icon of the program specified in Dreamweaver's preferences. To open an image in your preferred program, simply select the image in

Dreamweaver, click the icon in the Property inspector, and watch your image appear as you've commanded.

Adobe has done great work integrating the Photoshop and Fireworks programs into Dreamweaver. When you save changes to the image in Fireworks or Photoshop, they're automatically reflected in the version you've already inserted into a page in Dreamweaver.

To specify the image editor you want to associate with a file type in Dreamweaver's preferences, follow these instructions:

1. **Choose Edit⇨Preferences (Windows) or Dreamweaver⇨Preferences (on a Mac).**

   The Preferences dialog box opens.

2. **On the left, select the File Types/Editors Category, as shown in Figure 3-11.**

3. **In the Extensions pane, click to select** `.gif`**.**

   Dreamweaver lists a wide variety of file types here, and you can associate any or all of them with your favorite editors. To associate image editors with these graphic formats, select the GIF, PNG, and JPEG options one at a time and then continue with these steps.

4. **In the Editors pane, click to select the editor you want associated with the** `.gif` **format.**

   In the example shown in Figure 3-11, Photoshop is listed already, so you can simply click Photoshop to select it. If you want to associate an editor that isn't on this list, such as Fireworks, click the plus (+) sign just above the Editors pane, browse to find the program on your hard drive, and select it to make it appear on the list.

5. **With the file type and program name selected, click the Make Primary button to associate the editor with the file type.**

   The editor specified as Primary is launched automatically when you select an image in Dreamweaver and click the Edit button in the Property inspector.

6. **Click to select** `.jpeg` **from the Extensions pane and repeat Steps 4 and 5.**

   You can continue with this process for any or all the other formats listed.

   To add additional file formats to Dreamweaver, click the plus (+) sign over the Extensions pane and type the extension beginning with a dot (.).

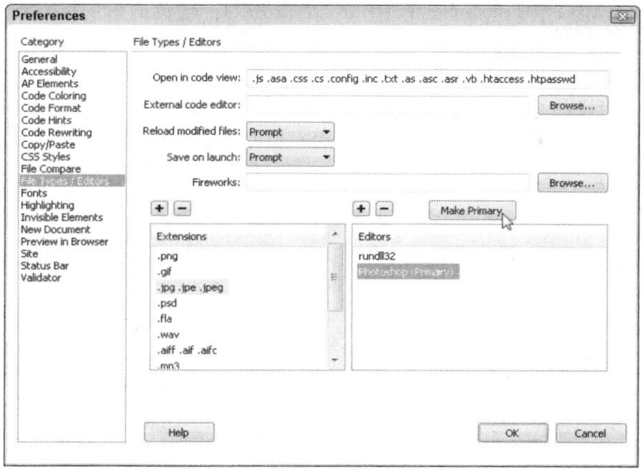

Figure 3-11:
Use Dreamweaver's preferences settings to associate your favorite image editor.

Inserting a Background Image

Background images can add depth and richness to a page design by adding color and fullness. Used cleverly, a background image helps create the illusion that the entire page is one large image while still downloading quickly and efficiently. The trick is to use an image with a small file size that creates the impression of a large image. One way this works on the Web is to use the default settings for a background image, which cause the image to *tile* (repeat) across and down the page (see Figure 3-12).

Beware that certain backgrounds (such as the one shown in Figure 3-12) can make it difficult to read text placed on top. Choose your background images carefully and make sure your background and your text have plenty of contrast. Reading on a computer screen is hard enough.

With CSS, you can have far greater control over the display of a background image. When you create a CSS background style, you can insert a background image that doesn't repeat or that repeats only across the Y axis or down the X axis of the page.

To insert a background image in Dreamweaver, choose Modify➪Page Properties, click the Browse button to the right of the Background Image field (see Figure 3-13), and select the image you want to use as your background. If the image isn't already in your local site folder, Dreamweaver offers to copy it there when you click OK.

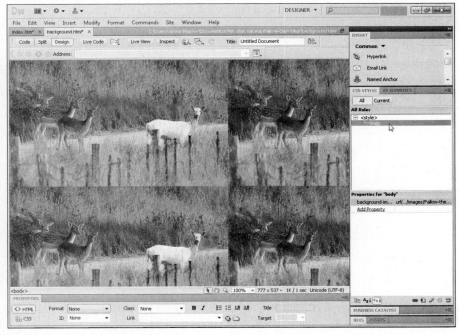

Figure 3-12:
This back-
ground
example
shows how
an image
repeats
across and
down a
page when
inserted
into the
background
using the
default
HTML
settings.

When you insert an image using Dreamweaver's Page Properties feature,
you can use the Repeat drop-down list to specify how the image repeats
on the page, as shown in Figure 3-13. When you specify a repeat option,
Dreamweaver automatically creates a style for the page with these background settings. If you use the CSS Definition dialog box to further edit the
background options in the body style (covered in Chapter 5), you can also
specify where the background image is displayed on a page.

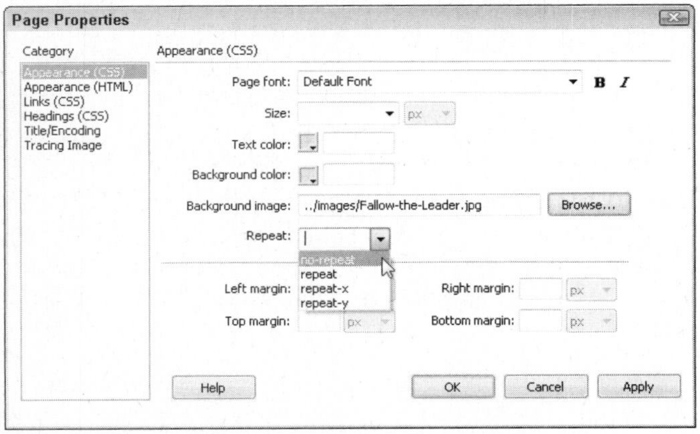

Figure 3-13:
The Page
Properties
settings
control
how a
background
image is
repeated on
a page.

Creating Image Maps

Image maps enable you to create *hotspots* (clickable areas) in an image and link each area to a different Web page. An image map is commonly used with a geographic map, such as the map of Northern California shown in Figure 3-14. Hotspots on the map link to different locations, depending on the section of the map a visitor clicks. For example, if you work for a national bank and want customers to find a local branch or ATM machine easily, you can create hotspots on an image map of the United States and then link each hotspot to a page listing banks in that geographic location.

Dreamweaver makes creating image maps easy by providing a set of simple drawing tools that enable you to create hotspots and set their corresponding links. To create an image map, follow these steps:

1. **Place the image you want to use as an image map on your page.**

2. **Select the image.**

   The image properties are displayed in the Property inspector.

3. **To draw your hotspot, choose a shape tool from the image map tools in the lower left of the Property inspector (labeled in Figure 3-14).**

   The shape tools (a rectangle, a circle, and an irregular polygon) allow you to draw the hotspot regions on your images, each with a specific link. In the example shown in Figure 3-14, I'm creating hotspots on each county in this map of Northern California.

4. **With a shape tool selected, click and drag over an area of the image that you want to make *hot* (link to another page).**

   Here's how the different hotspot tools work:

   • **Rectangle:** When you click and drag, a light blue highlight appears around the region that you're making hot; this highlighted area indicates the active region. If you need to reposition the hot area, select the Pointer hotspot tool (labeled in Figure 3-14) and then select and move the region to the location you want. You can also resize the hotspot by clicking and dragging any corner.

   • **Circle:** The Circle tool works much like the Rectangle tool — just click and drag. To resize a circle hotspot, select the Pointer hotspot tool, and click and drag one of the small square boxes on its edges.

   • **Polygon:** The Polygon tool functions a little bit differently than the other two tools. To make a polygon selection, click the tool once for each point of the polygon shape you want to draw. The shape automatically connects the points while you click. When you're finished, switch to another map tool or click outside the image. You can change the size of the polygon or move any of its points by using the Pointer hotspot tool.

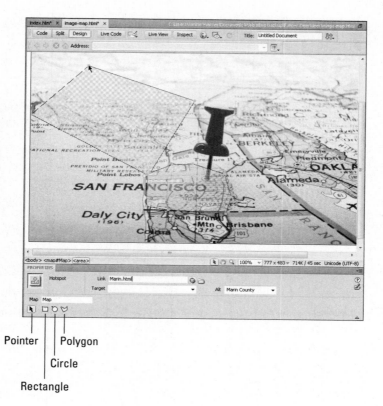

Figure 3-14:
Use the
image map
tools in the
Property
inspector
to create
hotspots on
an image
that can
be linked
to different
pages.

Pointer | Polygon

Circle

Rectangle

When prompted to describe the image map in the Alt field on the Property inspector, click OK to close the dialog box and then add a text description of the link in the Alt field in Hotspot properties of the Property inspector. The Alt field is for *alternative text* that doesn't appear on the page itself. Screen readers and other devices that *read* the code behind a page need these hotspot descriptions to better understand the image map.

5. **To link a selected hot area:**

   a. **Click the Browse icon next to the Link text box (at the top of the Property inspector).**

   The Select File dialog box opens.

   b. **Browse to find the HTML file that you want to link to the hotspot on your image.**

   c. **Double-click the file to which you want to link.**

   The hotspot links to the selected page, and the Select File dialog box automatically closes.

   You can also type the path directly in the Link text box.

6. **To add more hotspots, choose an image and a shape tool, and repeat Steps 4 and 5.**

7. **To give your image map a name, type a name in the Map text field, just above the shape tools.**

   Giving your map (and all the hotspots it includes) a name helps to distinguish it in the event that you have multiple image maps on the same page. You can call the map anything you want, as long as you don't include spaces or special punctuation.

   When you finish, a light blue highlight indicates where all your image map hotspots are.

At any time, you can edit the image map. Simply click and highlight the blue region on your image and drag the edges to resize the hotspot or enter a new URL to change the link.

Chapter 4

Managing, Testing, and Publishing a Web Site

In This Chapter

▶ Previewing your site in different Web browsers

▶ Testing your site with the Dreamweaver site reporting features

▶ Fixing broken links

▶ Moving and changing filenames and links

▶ Setting up FTP and other file transfer options

▶ Publishing your site to a Web server

*T*he scenario is shocking: You create a page design that looks just perfect in your favorite Web browser on your own computer. You publish it on the Internet and tell all your friends. And the next thing you know, your cousin in Chicago and your friends in Italy are telling you that it looks terrible, the text is unreadable, and your video files won't play at all.

Don't let this happen to you. Take time to test your work before you publish it to ensure your site works well in the many different Web browsers, operating systems, and monitor sizes that your visitors are likely to use on today's increasingly international Internet. You also want to use Dreamweaver's tools to check that your site code is valid, the links all work, and everything is in tip-top shape before you publish it on the Web. As you work with the files in your site, you may appreciate that Dreamweaver includes tools for managing files and folders so that your links stay up-to-date as your site grows. And when you're ready to publish or update your site on the Web, Dreamweaver has tools to help you transfer files, too. In this chapter, you discover how to use these features, as well as a few tips I've learned along the way.

If you're looking for information about where to host your Web site, how to choose a Web-hosting service, or how to register a domain name, you find recommendations and tips for choosing the best services on my Web site at www. DigitalFamily.com/dreamweaver.

Why Can Web Pages Look Bad on Different Computers?

A confusing and frustrating aspect of Web design is that different browsers and computer systems impact a page's appearance. You can create a page that looks great in Dreamweaver and test it in a browser to confirm that it looks fine only to discover later that it looks terrible in another Web browser or on a different computer system. Web pages can look different from one system to another for many reasons, but the following issues are the most common culprits:

- **Browser differences:** Today, dozens of browsers are in use on the Web, not counting the different versions of each browser. For example, at the time of this writing, Internet Explorer (IE) 8 is the newest release from Microsoft, but a significant percentage of Web users haven't upgraded yet and are still using IE7 or even earlier versions. (More on browser differences in the next section.)

- **Hardware differences:** Another challenge comes from the differences between Macintosh and Windows computers. For example, most fonts appear smaller on a Macintosh than on a PC. (Times 12 on a PC looks like Times 10 on a Mac, which makes text harder to read and can change the layout of a page.) Image colors and brightness can also vary from one computer to another.

- **Individual preferences:** Most Web browsers include preference settings that individual users can adjust to suit their needs. For example, someone may increase the text size in his browser settings to make text more readable, which may cause text to wrap your carefully designed pages to look overly crowded page designs and text wrapping changes that may make your look terrible.

- **Monitor resolution settings:** In addition, the same Web page may look very different on a 21" monitor than it does on a 15" monitor. And even on the same monitor, different resolution settings can alter the way a page looks. On a PC, a common resolution is 1024 x 768; on a Mac, the resolution is generally set much higher, making the design look much smaller, even if the monitor sizes are the same.

As a result of all these differences, the same Web page can look very different to the many people who visit a Web site. For example, Figure 4-1 shows a Web page in Internet Explorer on a PC, and Figure 4-2 shows the same page in Safari on a Macintosh. Notice that the text displays in a larger font size on the PC, changing how the text wraps around the photo in the left column.

This challenging aspect of the Web is at the root of many of the limitations and complications of creating good Web designs. With patience, testing, and an understanding of the tags and styles that are most problematic, you can create great Web sites that look good to most, if not all, of the people who visit your Web site.

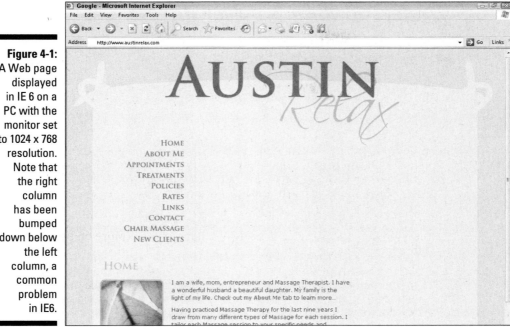

Figure 4-1:
A Web page displayed in IE 6 on a PC with the monitor set to 1024 x 768 resolution. Note that the right column has been bumped down below the left column, a common problem in IE6.

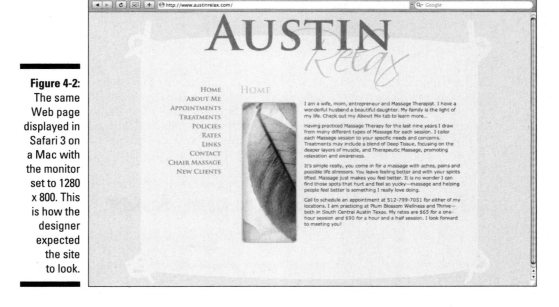

Figure 4-2:
The same Web page displayed in Safari 3 on a Mac with the monitor set to 1280 x 800. This is how the designer expected the site to look.

Understanding browser differences

Of the many reasons why Web pages can look different from one browser to another, it boils down to this:

- ✔ Over the years, Web browsers have evolved to support new Web technologies. Thus, many older browsers still in use have trouble displaying some newer, more advanced features that you can use on your Web pages today.

- ✔ Compounding this problem, the companies that make Web browsers — including Microsoft, Google, and Apple — don't all agree or follow the same rules (although most are getting better at complying with the same set of standards in their latest browser versions).

- ✔ Dozens of browsers are now in use on the Web, not counting the different versions of each browser. For example, Firefox has become increasingly popular and is one of the best for supporting pages designed to follow modern Web design standards, but a significant percentage of Internet users haven't yet changed or upgraded and are still using the browser that came with their computer. If that browser is IE6, it's especially unfortunate because IE6 is notoriously bad at displaying CSS (Cascading Style Sheets) and other modern Web features.

Browser limitations and differences are the root of many limitations and complications of creating Web sites. Appreciating these challenges as you learn to create pages is helpful. HTML was designed to create simple text documents that could be viewed on any computer on the planet. As you learn Web design, some of the rules may seem strange or limiting at first. But if you understand the reasons for working within these limitations, creating sites can go more smoothly for you.

Entire books and Web sites are dedicated to how best to design for the differences among browsers. I can't possibly cover all the issues or tricks to working around them in this book. However, in this chapter, I do include tips and testing sites to help you ensure your pages look their best, and throughout this book, I try to stick to design strategies and techniques that most browsers in use today support.

Targeting browsers for your design

Some Web designers have decided to ignore users with older browsers or to simply include a warning message, such as: "This page looks best in the latest version of Firefox, upgrade now." Other designers carefully test their pages in browsers such as IE 6 to make sure they look good even to the least sophisticated users on the Internet. As you decide how to approach this issue, I suggest taking your audience into account. For example, consider the following scenarios:

- **Your visitors are advanced computer users.** In this case, you may not need to concern yourself as much with older browsers but watch out for niche browsers. Advanced computer users are much more likely to update their computers and also to customize their computer with a browser like Firefox (initially a niche browser that's very popular today) or Chrome (a newer player on the Web, with increasing popularity).

- **Your audience attracts users mostly from large corporations.** These users often cannot update their own software, so they're stuck with older browsers until the company policy changes, which can take a notoriously long time. That said, if you're designing a site only for use by people within the company, you can often find out exactly what software they are using and design specifically for their systems.

- **Your audience is made up of people with older computers who are unlikely to have upgraded their Web browsers.** For this audience, design Web pages with older browsers in mind. Although Web browsers are generally free, and relatively easy to install, some people are afraid to download any software over the Internet, and many don't appreciate the benefits of using a newer browser.

Today there is a growing movement toward more standardized Web development, but getting your pages to look exactly the same on every computer on the planet today is still difficult if not impossible. As a result, most designers strive to create pages that look as good as possible on as many browsers as they consider important, even if the same pages don't look *exactly* the same on all browsers.

Which browsers you should design for depends on your audience. If you have the luxury of having accurate reports on the visitors to your site, you can see a list of all browsers that visitors to your site use. (In Chapter 15 you find a list of Web-statistic services that include browser usage information.)

The statistics in this list are from the trends page at www.w3schools.com/browsers/browsers_stats.asp. (The site is updated monthly, so check the site for the most recent stats.) Assume for now that your Web statistics reveal that your audience's browser usage follows the trend and breaks down as follows:

- **IE8:** 13.5 percent
- **IE7:** 12.8 percent of your audience uses

✔ **IE6:** 10.9 percent

✔ **Firefox 3:** 46.4 percent

✔ **Chrome:** 9.8 percent

✔ **Safari:** 3.6 percent

✔ **Opera:** 2.3 percent

With those numbers in mind, you may decide to design pages so that that they look best in Firefox, and you'll settle for them not looking quite as good in Safari and Chrome because such a small percentage of your visitors use those browsers.

Previewing Your Page in a Browser

Although Dreamweaver displays Web pages much like a Web browser, not all interactive features work in Dreamweaver. To test links, for example, preview your work in a Web browser.

The simplest way to preview your work is to save the page you're working on and then click the Preview/Debug in Browser icon located at the top right of the workspace, as shown in Figure 4-3 (it looks like a small globe). You can also choose File➪Preview in a Browser.

When you install Dreamweaver, it should automatically find all the browsers installed on your computer and set them up so that you can easily select them to preview your pages.

Figure 4-3:
Use the
Preview/
Debug in
Browser
icon at the
top of the
workspace
to open
any page
displayed
in Dream-
weaver
in a Web
browser.

Testing your pages in more than one Web browser is always a good practice, because page display can vary (sometimes dramatically) from one Web browser to another. How many browsers you should test your pages in depends on the audience you expect to visit your Web site and your access to browsers and different operating systems. Most good Web designers test their pages in many different browsers, including the latest two or three versions of Internet Explorer, Firefox, Chrome, and Safari. It's also good practice to preview your pages on both Macintosh and Windows computers because the page display differs from one operating system to another.

To help you test your pages, Dreamweaver includes a few special features, including the ability to add more browsers to the preview option as you install them on your hard drive. You can also use Adobe's BrowserLab option, which tests a Web page in multiple Web browsers and returns images of the page as it looks in each browser. BrowserLab, discussed later in this section, can help you quickly identify potential problems in the way a page looks in different browsers. The following sections explain the many tools available to you in more detail.

Adding Web browsers to Dreamweaver

Before you can preview your Web pages in different browsers, you need to set up Dreamweaver to support them. The first step is to download and install a variety of browsers on your hard drive (see the sidebar "Downloading new browsers").

After you've installed one or more new browsers on your computer, follow these steps to add them to Dreamweaver's browser preview list:

1. **Choose File➪Preview in Browser and then choose Edit Browser List from the fly-out menu.**

   The Preferences dialog box opens with the Preview in Browser settings displayed. ***Note:*** You must have a page open in Dreamweaver for these menu options to be accessible.

2. **Click the plus (+) sign next to the word Browsers, at the top of the Preferences dialog box.**

   The Add Browser dialog box opens.

3. **Enter a name for the browser.**

   I like to include the version number as well as the name, as I have in the example shown in Figure 4-4 for Firefox 3.

4. **Click the Browse button.**

   The Add Browser dialog box opens.

5. **Navigate your hard drive until you find the browser you want to add. Look for the browser's executable or application file (indicated with an** .exe **extension on Windows and stored in the Applications folder on a Mac) rather than a shortcut on your desktop.**

   You can add a browser to Dreamweaver only if the browser is on your hard drive. (See the nearby sidebar, "Downloading new browsers," for more about finding and downloading new browsers for testing.)

6. **Click the name of the** .exe **file to select it, and then click Open to add the browser to the Application field in the Add Browser dialog box.**

7. **Select the Primary Browser check box if you want this browser to be the browser that's listed first in the Browser drop-down list (see Figure 4-4). Select the Secondary Browser check box to make a browser second on the list.**

   You can also launch the designated primary browser by pressing the F12 key. To launch the secondary browser, press Ctrl+F12 in Windows or ⌘+F12 on a Mac.

8. **Repeat Steps 2–7 to add more browsers to the list.**

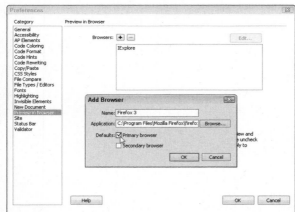

Figure 4-4:
Dream-
weaver
makes it
easy to add
additional
Web brows-
ers to the
Preview in
Browser
list.

Previewing pages in many Web browsers

When you preview pages, preview in a variety of Web browsers. Then make any necessary adjustments to the designs based on what you find. This way, you make sure that your site looks suitable to at least most of your visitors. The following steps walk you through the process of previewing the same Web page in multiple browsers:

1. **Open a Web page that you want to preview in Dreamweaver. Then, choose File⇨Preview in Browser, and select a Web browser from the list of browser options.**

   You find out how to add more browsers to the Preview in Browser list in the preceding section, "Adding Web browsers to Dreamweaver."

2. **Study the page carefully, testing all the links, rollovers, and any other special effects to make sure that the page appears the way you want it to in this browser.**

3. **Close the browser window and return to Dreamweaver to make any necessary changes to the page.**

   Often, making minor changes, such as swapping the position of an image with a block of text, or adding a paragraph return using a <p> tag after a video, can make the page look much better.

4. **Preview the same page again in the same browser to make sure the changes you made had the desired effect.**

   Return to Dreamweaver to make further changes as necessary.

5. **Preview the same page in another Web browser.**

   If you're not happy with the way the page looks in this browser, make further adjustments to the design in Dreamweaver.

Downloading new browsers

So how do you put new browsers on your hard drive so that you can preview your pages with them? The simplest way is to visit the Web sites of the companies that create the most popular browsers. You can download the latest version for free from each of these sites, and all four browsers are available for Mac and Windows computers:

Microsoft Internet Explorer: `www.microsoft.com/ie`

Mozilla Firefox: `www.firefox.com`

Apple Safari: `www.apple.com/safari`

Google Chrome: `www.google.com/chrome`

If you're not sure what may be causing the problems among browsers, try using the Browser Compatibility testing features, covered later in this chapter. When you do this test, Dreamweaver gives you list of any known issues it finds in your page design, a handy reference that can help you find and solve common problems that affect the display of pages in different Web browsers.

Sometimes, a workflow different from one outlined in the preceding steps works better. You may find that previewing the same page in a few browsers in rapid succession, noting any differences among them, works best. Then, you can make any necessary changes in Dreamweaver, and preview the same page again in all the same browsers. This strategy can help ensure that you create a page that looks as good as possible in the most browsers and reduces the risk that changes you make to improve the design in one browser make the page look worse in another browser without your realizing it.

Testing sites with Adobe's BrowserLab and other online browser emulators

Unless you own a dozen computers with different operating systems and a vast collection of Web browsers, you can't fully test your Web site — at least not on your own. Fortunately, a growing number of online services are available to help you preview your pages on many different operating systems and browsers — without your having to manage multiple computers and browsers yourself.

Like many professional Web designers, I have three computers on my desk (Macs and Windows) and many different browsers installed on each. I like having several options handy so that I can test my pages as I'm developing a design, especially because you have to upload your pages to a Web server before you can use the online services listed here.

After a page design looks good in all the browsers and systems I have on my desk, I upload the site to a server and do a final test in even more browsers using these online services.

Here are some of the best places to test your Web site online:

✔ **Adobe BrowserLab:** (`https://browserlab.adobe.com`) In Dreamweaver CS5, Adobe BrowserLab is integrated into the browser preview options in Dreamweaver. You can choose it from the list of options when you choose Edit➪Preview in Browser. *Note:* Your computer must be connected to the Internet for this feature to work, and you can also use BrowserLab to test any page that's already published on the Internet.

Adobe BrowserLab enables you to test any Web page in the most common browsers on the Web simultaneously. At the time of this writing, that includes IE versions 6, 7, and 8; Mozilla Firefox versions 2 and 3; Chrome 3; and Apple Safari versions 3 and 4.

You can also test pages on different operating systems, such as Windows XP and Mac OS X. When you use this service, the result is a screenshot with a preview of the page taken in each browser. Although the screenshots enable you to spot differences quickly, be aware of a small downside: You can't test interactive features, such as dropdown menus or rollover effects. You must have an Adobe ID to use BrowserLab, but at the time of this writing it was free to anyone using Dreamweaver.

✔ **Browser Sandbox:** (`http://spoon.net/browsers/`) With Browser Sandbox, you can easily test a site using any of the eight most popular browsers without installing them all on your system. You simply download and install a plug-in from the Web site and then click the browser you want to use. After the selected browser launches, you can surf the Web as if the browser were installed on your computer. The service is free (at the time of this writing). And because you can surf through the browsers, you can interact with Web sites, testing all your pages, as well as JavaScript, AJAX, and other interactive features.

✔ **Cross Browser Testing:** (`www.crossbrowsertesting.com`) The Cross Browser Testing site takes Web site–testing to another level. Instead of simply providing screenshots of a Web page in different browsers, or letting you launch a few browsers to test pages in, this site lets you take over other computers connected to the Internet so that you can test interactive features using a variety of browsers and operating systems. For example, if you use a computer that runs Windows Vista and you want to see what your site will look like on a Mac, you can choose to use a computer with the Mac OS and then view your site in any of a dozen browsers on the Mac system. The advantage is that you get more than snapshots, and you also can test interactive features, such as JavaScript, AJAX, forms, and more. This service requires that you purchase a monthly subscription.

✔ **Browsershots:** (`www.browsershots.org`) Browsershots is a popular online testing tool. You simply enter a page's URL and choose the options you want to use for testing. Browsershots then tests the page you submitted on each computer system selected with the specified browser and takes a screenshot. Although you can't test interactive features with this service, it's one of the easiest options and provides the largest collection of browsers to choose from. The basic service is free, but it can take a few minutes or a few hours to complete testing. If you don't like waiting, you can upgrade to "priority processing" for a fee.

Using Dreamweaver's Browser Compatibility feature

In addition to being able to preview a Web page in any Web browser on your hard drive, Dreamweaver also includes a Browser Compatibility feature that can help you test for known issues among different browsers automatically.

To use this feature, open a page in Dreamweaver and choose File➪Check Page➪Browser Compatibility. You can also access this feature by clicking the Check Page drop-down arrow at the top right of the workspace and selecting Check Browser Compatibility from the drop-down list. Any recognized conflicts display in a report at the bottom of the workspace.

You can specify which browsers and browser versions you want to target by doing either of the following to open the Target Browser dialog box, as shown in Figure 4-5:

✔ Click the small menu icon at the top-left corner of the Browser Compatibility Check dialog box and choose Settings from the drop-down list.

✔ From the Check Page drop-down list, choose Settings.

Figure 4-5:
Specify the browsers and versions you want to target when you run a browser compatibility check.

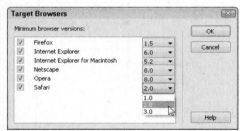

Testing your designs in mobile phone emulators with Adobe Device Central

Device Central, which was included in previous versions of Dreamweaver, is increasingly important as more and more people are surfing the Web with cell phones and other mobile devices.

Device Central works much like the other preview options but with a few extra features, including the ability to add new phone profiles.

Follow these steps to preview your pages using Device Central:

1. **Open a Web page that you want to preview in Dreamweaver. Then, choose File⇨Preview in Browser, and select Device Central from the list of options.**

   The page opens in Device Central, which displays the page in one of the many mobile emulators installed in the program, as shown in Figure 4-6.

2. **In the Test Devices panel on the left, click to select any device.**

   The page you're previewing is displayed in that device. In the Test Devices panel, you can click one device after another in the list to view the page in multiple devices.

3. **Study the page carefully, testing all the links, rollovers, and any other special effects to make sure that the page appears the way you want it to in this mobile device.**

   You navigate around the Web page that appears in a test device much like you would if you had the real mobile device. For example, use your mouse to click on the navigation arrows just above the keypad (see Figure 4-6) to scroll up, down, left, and right in the Web page.

4. **Close Device Central and return to Dreamweaver to make any necessary changes to the page.**

   See the nearby sidebar, "Designing for mobile devices," for tips about creating a design that displays well on cell phones.

You can add more devices to Adobe Device Central on a Windows computer by choosing Devices⇨Download Device Profile, but your computer must be connected to the Internet for this feature to work. On a Mac, choose Add to Test Devices.

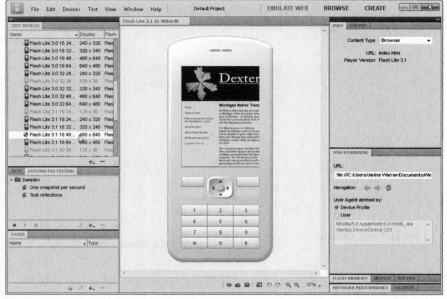

Figure 4-6:
Adobe Device Central makes it possible to view your Web pages as they will appear in a variety of mobile devices.

Designing for mobile devices

A new audience of Web page visitors has emerged. Some high-end mobile devices (think iPhone and BlackBerry Storm) are capable of loading even complex Web pages and do so reasonably well. However, the screen is much smaller, and interaction with the Web browser is much different. Site visitors navigate by touch or with input devices more challenging than a mouse. Lower-end mobile devices that make up the vast majority of the market often have even smaller screens, reduced color display, and allow only minimal interaction.

To best manage the dramatic differences on mobile devices, my best recommendation is that you create a second, very simplified version of your Web site designed to best serve the limited display options of mobile devices and then link your main Web site to the alternate mobile design. If you have experience writing server scripts (or can hire someone to do it for you), you can create an autodetect script that can determine whether a visitor to your site is using a mobile phone or a computer and then direct them to the best version of your site automatically.

Here are a few important tips to consider when designing a version of your Web site for mobile devices:

✔ Because download times are much slower on mobile devices, adjust the number of features you offer to mobile devices, and keep the number of images and style minimal.

✔ Use CSS for the design and layout of the Web page, but limit the design to internal style sheets, not external. (See Chapter 5 for more on CSS.)

✔ Avoid outdated HTML styling and layout options, such as frames and iframes, which may not display at all on mobile devices.

✔ Screen size on a mobile device is extremely limited, with less width or height than traditional computer monitors. (The view is more rectangular than square on most mobile screens.) Optimize your content and design accordingly.

✔ Users don't point with a mouse on a mobile phone. They use up and down arrows, and at best a touch screen. Adjust your design to require as little scrolling and user movement as possible and make sure links are big and well separated from each other so they are easy to click.

✔ Always validate your Web page code (numerous validation services are available for free online, such as the popular one at `http://validator.w3.org`). Mobile browsers are even less forgiving than traditional Web site browsers about errors in your code.

✔ Very few mobile devices support JavaScript, so don't use it in the mobile version of a Web site. That means try to avoid drop-down menus or rollover images in the mobile version of your site.

✔ Most mobile devices don't support Flash, Flash video, or most other multimedia formats so avoiding them is best. If you do use Flash, phones that don't support it will display a blank screen. Use multimedia sparingly and make sure to include links to alternative content for visitors who may not be able to view these features.

You also need to test a mobile site in addition to your main Web site. Test with mobile phone emulators, such as Dreamweaver's Device Central (featured in this chapter), as well as the online emulators available at `http://ready.mobi` and `http://mtld.mobi/emulator.php`. Test interactive features on a variety of mobile phones. If you can't afford to buy several phones (and who can?), ask your friends, family, and coworkers to test your site on their phones. Visit stores that sell mobile phones and ask for a demo of the phone's Web browser capabilities; then make sure to view your own site while you're testing each phone. Although it can take some time to run around town visiting mobile phone stores and doing demos, it's a cheap way to test in a variety of modern devices, and you might even find your new favorite phone.

To read more about designing for mobile devices, check out my book *Mobile Web Design For Dummies*.

Testing Your Work with the Site Reporting Features

Before you put your site online for the world to see, check your work using the Dreamweaver Site Reporting feature. You can create a variety of reports and even customize them to identify problems with external links, redundant and empty tags, untitled documents, and missing alternate text. You can easily miss things — especially when you work on a tight deadline — and what you miss can cause real problems for your viewers.

Before Dreamweaver added this great feature, finding these kinds of mistakes was a tedious, time-consuming task. Now you can run a report that identifies these errors for you in a matter of moments, and then use Dreamweaver to correct mistakes across your entire site automatically.

Follow these steps to produce a Site Report of your entire Web site:

1. **In the drop-down list at the top of the Files panel, select the site you want to work on.**

   If you already have the site you want to test open in Dreamweaver, you can skip this step. *Note:* Your site appears in the Files panel list only if you've completed the site setup process covered in Chapter 2.

2. **Make sure any documents you have open in Dreamweaver's workspace are saved by choosing File⇨Save All.**

3. **Choose Site⇨Reports.**

   The Reports dialog box appears (see Figure 4-7).

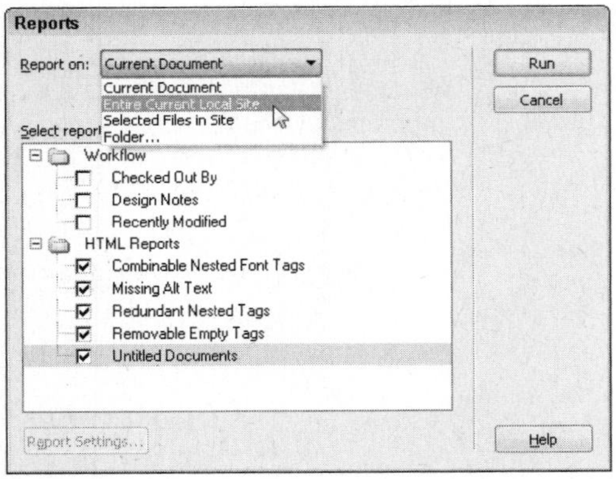

Figure 4-7: In the Reports dialog box, you can select any and all options and run reports on a single page or the entire site.

4. **In the Report On drop-down list, choose Entire Current Local Site.**

   I most commonly use this feature to test an entire site just before publishing it to the Web, but you can choose to check only a single page by opening the page in Dreamweaver and then choosing Current Document in the Report On drop-down list. You can also run a report on selected files or on a particular folder. If you choose Selected Files in Site, you must first click to select the pages you want to check in the Files panel.

5. **In the Select Reports section, click the check boxes to select the reports you want.**

   Table 4-1 describes the kind of report you get with each option. You can select as many reports as you want.

6. Click the Run button to create the report(s).

If you haven't already done so, you may be prompted to save your file, set up your site, or select a folder. (See Chapter 2 for more information on setting up a site in Dreamweaver.)

The Results panel appears, as shown in Figure 4-8, displaying a list of problems found on the site. To sort the list by category (filename, line number, or description), click the corresponding column heading.

Figure 4-8: The Results panel displays a list of problems on your site.

7. Double-click any item in the Results panel to open the corresponding file in the Document window.

The file opens, and the error is highlighted in the workspace.

You can also right-click (Windows) or Control+click (Mac) on any line of the report and choose More Info to find additional details about the specific error or condition.

8. Use the Property inspector or another Dreamweaver feature to correct the identified problem and then save the file.

Table 4-1	Site Report Options
Report Name	*What It Does*
Checked Out By	Lists files checked out of the site and identifies the person who checked them out. This feature is used only if you've set up the site to also work with Adobe Contribute.
Design Notes	Lists Design Notes used in the site.
Recently Modified	List files that have been edited within a specified time period. You can set the time period for the report by selecting the Recently Modified check box and then clicking the Report Settings button at the bottom of the dialog box.

(continued)

Table 4-1 *(continued)*

Report Name	What It Does
Combinable Nested Font Tags	Lists all instances where you can combine nested tags. For example, `<font color="#000000"><font size="2">Great Web Sites You Should Visit</font></font>` is listed because you can simplify the code by combining the two font tags into `<font color="#000000" size="2">Great Web Sites You Should Visit</font>`.
Missing Alt Text	Lists all the image tags that do not include Alt text. Alt text is a text description for an image tag included in the HTML code as an alternative if the image is not displayed. Alt text is important to anyone who uses a special browser that reads Web pages.
Redundant Nested Tags	Lists all places where you have redundant nested tags. For example, `<h1>Good headlines <h1>are harder to write</h1> than you might think</h1>` is listed because you can simplify the code by removing the second `<h1>` tag to make the code look like this: `<h1>Good headlines are harder to write than you might think</h1>`.
Removable Empty Tags	Lists the empty tags on your site. Empty tags can occur when you delete an image, text section, or other element without deleting all the tags applied to the element.
Untitled Documents	Lists filenames that don't have a title. The `title` tag is easy to forget because it does not appear in the body of the page. The `title` tag specifies the text that appears at the very top of the browser window and also the text that appears in the Favorites list when someone bookmarks a page. You can enter a title for any page by entering text in the title field just above the work area or in the title field in the Page Properties dialog box.

Finding and Fixing Broken Links

If you're trying to rein in a chaotic Web site or if you just want to check a site for broken links, you'll be pleased to discover the Link Checker. You can use this feature to verify the links in a single file or an entire Web site, and Link Checker can automatically fix all the referring links at once if a link is broken. (You find instructions for creating links in Chapter 2.)

Here's an example of what Link Checker can do. Assume that someone on your team (because you would never do such a thing yourself) changed the name of a file from `new.htm` to `old.htm` without using the Files panel or any of Dreamweaver's automatic link update features. Maybe this person changed the name using another program or simply renamed it in Explorer (Windows) or the Finder (Mac). Changing the filename was easy, but what this person may not have realized is that if he or she didn't change the links to the file when the file was renamed, the links are now broken.

If only one page links to the file that your clueless teammate changed, fixing the broken link isn't such a big deal. As long as you remember which file the page links from, you can simply open that page and use the Property inspector to reset the link the same way you created the link in the first place.

But many times, a single page in a Web site is linked to many other pages. When that's the case, fixing all the link references can be time-consuming, and forgetting some of them is all too easy. That's why the Link Checker is so helpful.

If you're working on a dynamic, database-driven site or if your site was altered with programming that was performed outside Dreamweaver, the Link Checker may not work properly. The Link Checker works best for sites with static HTML pages and sites created using `.dwt` Dreamweaver templates.

You must have the entire site on your hard drive and you must have completed the site setup process, covered in Chapter 2, for the Link Checker to work properly.

Checking for broken links

To check a site for broken links, follow these steps:

1. **In the drop-down list at the top of the Files panel, select the site you want to work on.**

   If you already have the site open in Dreamweaver, you can skip this step. For more information on how to set up a new site or import an existing one, see Chapter 2.

2. **Choose Site⇨Check Links Sitewide.**

   The Link Checker tab, shown in Figure 4-9, opens in the Results panel at the bottom of the page, just under the Property inspector. The tab displays a list of internal and external links. The tab also lists any pages, images, or other items not linked from any other page in the site — dubbed *orphans*. Unused images can waste space on your server, so this list is handy if you want to clean up old images or other elements you no longer use on the site.

Most service providers limit the amount of space on your server and charge extra if you exceed that limit. You can save valuable server space by deleting unused files, especially if they're image or multimedia files. But remember, just because you delete them from your hard drive doesn't mean they're deleted from the server. Make sure you remove them from the Remote Site window in the Files panel as well as the Local Site panel. (For more on using FTP and synchronization to update or delete files on your server, see the section "Publishing Your Web Site," later in this chapter.)

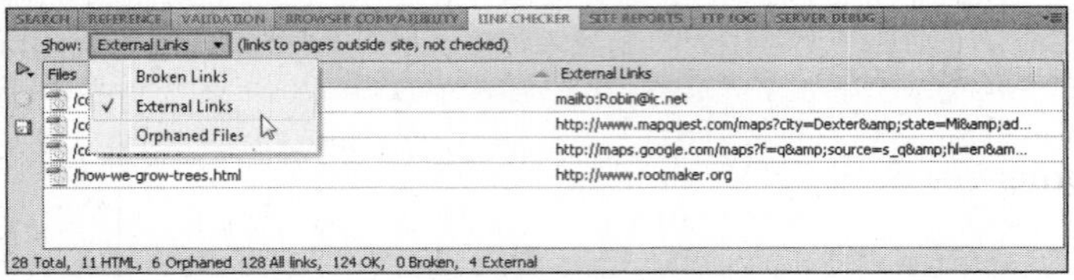

Figure 4-9:
The report can be organized by broken links, external links, and unused files.

Fixing broken links

Broken links are one of the worst problems you can have on a Web site. After you identify a broken link in a site, fix it as soon as possible. Nothing turns off visitors faster than clicking a link and getting a `File Not Found` error page. Fortunately, Dreamweaver makes fixing broken links simple by providing quick access to files with broken links and automating the process of fixing multiple links to the same file.

After using the Link Checker tab described in the preceding section to identify broken links, follow these steps to fix them by using the Results panel:

1. **With the Results panel open at the bottom of the page, double-click a filename that Dreamweaver identifies as a broken link.**

   The page and its corresponding Property inspector open. The Results panel remains visible.

2. **Select the broken link or image on the open page.**

   For example, you can fix a broken image by selecting the broken image icon on the page and then reinserting the image using the Property inspector to find the correct image file.

3. **In the Property inspector, click the Browse button (which looks like a folder) to the right of the Src text box.**

(Alternatively, you can type the correct filename and path in the text box instead of using the Browse button to find the correct image.) The Select Image Source dialog box appears.

You fix links to pages just as you fix links to images, except you type the name of the correct file into the Link text box or click the Browse button (which looks like a folder) next to the Link text box to find the file in your site folder.

4. **Click to select the filename of the correct image and then click OK.**

The link automatically changes to reflect the new filename and location. If you replace an image, the image file reappears on the page.

If the link that you correct appears in multiple pages and you fix the link using the broken link's Results panel, Dreamweaver prompts you with a dialog box asking whether you want to fix the remaining broken link references to the file. Click the Yes button to automatically correct all other references. Click the No button to leave the other files unchanged.

Finding files by their addresses

If you're not sure where you saved a file or what you called it, but you can get to it with your browser, you can determine the filename and location by looking at the URL in the browser's address bar. Each folder in a Web site is included in the address to a page within that folder. Folder names are separated by the forward slash, /, and each filename can be distinguished because it includes an extension. For example, the URL in the browser's address bar of the About the Farm page in the Dexter Tree Farm site tells me that the file is named `about-dexter-tree-farm.html`. (See the top of the figure in this sidebar.)

Similarly, you can identify the name and location of any image you're viewing on a Web page. If you're using Internet Explorer or Firefox, place your cursor over the image and right-click (Windows) or Control+click (Mac) and then choose Properties. The Element Properties dialog box includes the specific URL of the image, which has the name and folder (path). In the Element Properties dialog box shown in this example, you can see the

path to the logo on this site is `http://www.dextertreefarm.com/images/Dexter-Tree-Farm.jpg`, which tells me that the logo that appears in the top of the page is named `Dexter-Tree-Farm.jpg` and is stored in an `images` folder. If you're using the Safari browser on a Mac, it works a little differently: Control+click an image and choose Open Image in New Window. In the new window, the image URL appears in the location bar.

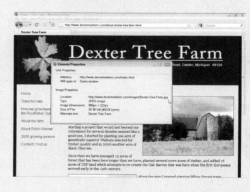

Managing Files and Folders in Your Site

Dreamweaver includes a variety of tools that help you manage the files, folders, and subfolders within a site without breaking links or image references. You can use the Files panel to rename and rearrange files and folders, as well as create new folders, all with drag-and-drop ease.

You need to complete the simple site setup process for Dreamweaver's Files panel features to work. If you haven't already set up your site, turn to the instructions at the beginning of Chapter 2. (If you're getting tired of my reminding you of this point throughout this book, I'm sorry, but I'm guessing you'd be even more annoyed if you didn't know this was necessary and couldn't get these features to work.)

Moving and renaming files

To move or rename files in a Web site, follow these steps:

1. **Open the site you want to work on (if it's not already open in Dreamweaver) by selecting the site name from the drop-down list at the top of the Files panel.**

   When you select a site by clicking the site name, the folders and files in that site appear in the Files panel.

2. **Click the plus (+) sign (Windows) or the small arrow (Mac) to open the local site folder or any subfolder to display the files within the folder.**

   Click the minus (–) sign to close a folder or subfolder.

3. **In the Files panel, select the file or folder you want to move or rename.**

   To *move* a selected file or folder:

   a. **Drag the selected file or group of files onto a folder.**

      Dreamweaver automatically moves the files into the folder and changes all the related links. The Files panel works much like the Explorer window on a PC or the Finder on a Mac, except Dreamweaver tracks and fixes links when you move files through the Files panel.

      If you move or rename files or folders in the Finder or Explorer on your computer instead of in the Files panel, you will break any links set to or from those files and any image references within them.

      When you move a linked file into a new folder in Dreamweaver, the Update Files dialog box appears, listing any linked pages that need to be updated, as shown in Figure 4-10.

   b. **To adjust the links so they don't break, choose Update.**

If you choose Don't Update, any links to or from that file are left unchanged. Of course, you can always move the file back to its original location to restore the links.

To *rename* a selected file:

a. Click twice on any filename or folder name.

Much like the Finder or Explorer on your computer, you need to click twice with a slight pause between clicks to select the name (instead of double-clicking, which opens the file).

b. When a box appears around the name, edit it by typing in new text, just as you would change a filename in the Finder or Explorer. Press Enter (Return on a Mac) to complete the change.

Again you're prompted with the Update Files dialog box to update any links affected by the filename change.

c. Choose Update to adjust the links.

To create a new folder in the Files panel:

a. Right-click (Option-click on a Mac) on the main site folder or any subfolder where you want to create a new folder.

A list of options appears.

b. Choose New Folder from the list.

A new, untitled folder appears inside the folder you selected in Step a.

c. Name the new folder by typing new text to replace the word Untitled**.**

After you've created a new folder, you can click and drag to move files or other folders in the Files panel into the folder.

To delete a folder or file from the Files panel:

a. Click to select the file or folder.

b. Press the Delete or Backspace key.

This will permanently delete the file from your hard drive.

Figure 4-10:
The Update Files dialog box lists all the files that will be changed during the update process.

Making global changes to links

If you want to globally change a link to point at a new URL or to some other page on your site, you can use the Change Link Sitewide option to enter the new URL and change every reference automatically. You can use this option to change any kind of link, including mailto, ftp, and script links. For example, if an e-mail address that you use throughout your site changes, you can use this feature to fix it automatically — a real timesaver. You can use this feature also when you want a string of text to link to a different file than it currently does. For example, you can change every instance of the words *Enter This Month's Contest* to link to /contest/january.htm instead of /contest/december.htm throughout your Web site.

To change a collection of links with the Change Link Sitewide feature, follow these steps:

1. **Make sure the site you want to work on is displayed in the Files panel.**

   See the preceding exercise for instructions on selecting a site.

2. **Choose Site⇨Change Link Sitewide.**

   The Change Link Sitewide dialog box appears.

3. **Enter the old address and then enter the new address, or click the Browse button to identify files where you want to change the links.**

   You can use this feature to change any link, including e-mail links, links from one page to another within a site, or links to a different Web site.

4. **Click OK.**

   Dreamweaver updates any documents that include the specified links.

Any changes you make to links using Dreamweaver's automated link features occur only on the local version of your site on your hard drive. Make sure you upload all affected files to your Web server to ensure that all changes are included on your published site. To automatically reconcile changes on your local and remote sites, use Dreamweaver's Synchronize Files feature, which I describe later in this chapter.

Publishing Your Web Site

If you're looking for the section where you find out how to upload your site (or any or all of the pages in your site) to your Web server, you've found it.

After you create and test your Web site so that it's ready to publish on the Web, you can put Dreamweaver's publishing tools to work. Which features you use depends on the kind of Web server you use. If you're using a commercial service provider, you'll most likely need Dreamweaver's FTP features, which I cover in detail in the following section.

Note that you need the following information from your Web hosting service before you can configure Dreamweaver's FTP features. Most service providers send this information in an e-mail message when you first sign up for an account. If you don't have this information, you will need to contact your service provider for it, because it's unique to your account on your Web hosting service. Here's what you need:

- The FTP host name
- The path to the Web directory (optional but highly recommended. It should look similar to this: `/web/htdocs/jcwarner`)
- Your FTP login or user name
- Your FTP password
- Any special instructions from your server, such as if you need to use Passive FTP, or any of the other advanced settings covered in Step 11 in the exercise that follows. This varies from server to server, so you need to ask your Web hosting service. (If you're having trouble connecting and you're not sure about these options, you can always experiment by checking and unchecking these options to see whether a setting enables you to connect.)

Setting up Dreamweaver's FTP features

After you gather all your FTP information, you're ready to set up Dreamweaver's FTP publishing features. This process can seem daunting and often takes a few tries to get right, but the good news is that you have to do it only once. (Dreamweaver saves these settings for you so you don't have to set them up every time you want to upload new pages to your site.)

Follow these steps to set up Dreamweaver's FTP features and publish files to a Web server:

1. **Choose Site⇨Manage Sites.**

   The Manage Sites dialog box opens.

2. **In the list of defined sites, select the site you want to publish and then click the Edit button.**

   The Site Setup dialog box opens. If your site is not listed in this dialog, that means you haven't set up your site. Refer to the instructions for this important initial site setup process at the beginning of Chapter 2 and then return to complete these steps.

3. **Select Servers from the categories listed in the left panel of the Site Setup dialog box.**

   The server list appears. If you haven't yet set up any Web servers in Dreamweaver, this list is blank, as it is in Figure 4-11. Any servers you have set up properly are listed in this dialog box.

Figure 4-11:
Click the small plus sign at the bottom of the Server Setup dialog box to open the Basic server configuration dialog box where you can enter your FTP information.

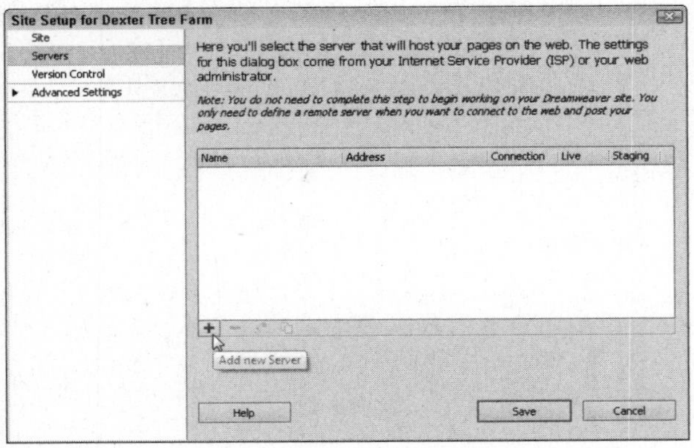

4. **Click the small plus sign at the bottom left of the server list area, as shown in Figure 4-11.**

   The Basic category opens in the servers dialog box and FTP is automatically selected, as shown in Figure 4-12. (If you need to use an option other than FTP, you find a list explaining all the Dreamweaver options under the Technical Stuff icon at the end of these steps.)

5. **Enter a name in the Server Name field.**

   You can name your server anything you like. Choose a name that will enable you to easily choose among the servers you've set up. (If you use only one Web server to host your site, the choice doesn't matter as much as it does if you host your site on multiple servers — something generally done only by very large or international sites.)

6. **Enter the FTP address for your Web server account.**

   Again this information depends on how your Web server is set up, but most use one of the following: `ftp.`*`servername`*`.com`, `ftp.`*`your domainname`*`.com`, or simply: *`yourdomain`*`.com` without anything at the beginning of the domain.

7. **In the Username and Password fields, type your username (sometimes called a login name) and password.**

Again, this information is unique to your account on your Web server.

8. **Check the Save box to the right of the Password field if you want Dreamweaver to store your access information.**

   This is handy because you can then automatically connect to the server anytime you want to upload or download pages. However, checking Save could enable anyone with access to your computer to gain access to your Web server.

9. **Click the Test button to make sure you've entered everything correctly.**

   Making a mistake is so easy, so the ability to test the connection and make any needed adjustments before you close this dialog is helpful. If you connect with no problems, Dreamweaver responds with a box saying Dreamweaver connected to your Web server successfully. (***Note:*** You must save the password to use the test feature, but you can deselect the Save Password box after you test if you prefer not to save the password in the program.)

   If you do have trouble connecting to your site, skip ahead to Step 11 for a few advanced options that may help.

10. **In the Root Directory field, type the directory on the remote site in which documents visible to the public are stored (also known as the local site folder).**

    The root directory usually looks something like this: `public_html/` or `www/htdocs/`. Again, this depends on your server.

    If you upload your files to the wrong directory on your server, they won't be visible when you view your site through a browser. The nearby sidebar, "Finding the root directory on your Web server," helps you work around this potentially frustrating problem with tips on identifying where to upload your Web site after you log into your server and finding the root directory to enter in this field if you can't find it in the information you get from your Web hosting company.

11. **Click the small arrow to the left of More Options.**

    You may not need to change any of these settings, but if you're having trouble connecting to your server, and you're sure you've entered your user name, password, and FTP address correctly, adjusting these settings may enable you to connect.

    I recommend checking and unchecking each of these options in turn, and then clicking the Test button after each change, to see if any of these adjustments makes the difference and enables you to connect to your server.

    A little experimentation with settings before waiting on hold with tech support is usually worth the effort. But if you're really having trouble establishing a connection with your server, call or e-mail the tech support staff at your Web server. The only people who can help you are those who run your Web server, because the settings are specific to your service provider and can vary dramatically from one hosting company to another. I've done my best to give you the most common options here, and with a little trial and error, the suggestions here should help you connect to most Web hosting companies, but if you're really stuck, it's okay to ask for more help from the people who run your server.

 12. **After you fill in everything and clicking Test successfully connects to your server, click Save to save your settings.**

Dreamweaver saves all your FTP settings (assuming you opted to save the password). The beauty of all this is that once you enter these settings properly and know the connection works, you never have to enter them again. You can then access your Web server from the Files panel in Dreamweaver, as you discover in the exercise that follows.

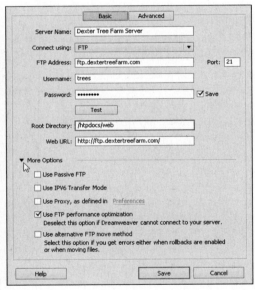

Figure 4-12:
Enter all of the information from your Web hosting company, including your name and password, in the Basic Server Setup dialog box.

Dreamweaver provides six Access options. If you work at a large company or university, you are likely to use one of these options rather than FTP. The options available from the Connect Using drop-down list in the Server Setup dialog box, are:

 ✔ **FTP:** Select this option to use Dreamweaver's built-in File Transfer Protocol features, which I cover in detail in the following section. You're most likely to need these settings if you're using a commercial Web hosting service.

- **SFTP:** Provides a more secure FTP connection. If you have the option of using a secure connection, it's definitely the preferred choice, and it's required by some Web servers to maintain higher levels of security.

- **Local/Network:** Select this option if you're using a Web server on a local network, such as your company or university server. For specific settings and requirements, check with your system administrator.

- **WebDAV (Web-based Distributed Authoring and Versioning):** Select this option if you're using a server with the WebDAV protocol, such as Microsoft IIS.

- **RDS (Rapid Development Services):** Select this option if you're using ColdFusion on a remote server.

Finding the root directory on your Web Server

Including the root directory in Dreamweaver's FTP settings is optional, but doing so does make transferring files using Dreamweaver's Upload and Download options easier. Thus, you reduce your chances of uploading your files to the wrong directory on your server, where they won't be visible when you try to view your site through a browser.

To find the root directory and the path to that directory on your server, you may need to complete the steps in the sections "Setting Up Dreamweaver's FTP Features" and "Publishing files to a Web server with FTP." That's because you may need to log into your Web server and do a little experimenting before you can figure out exactly what the path to the root directory is, but trust me, it's worth the effort. Here's why.

When you log into most commercial Web servers using the login information they provide you, you access your main folder on their server. This folder often includes several subfolders, such as a folder where your e-mail is stored on the server, another folder that stores log reports of traffic to your site, and possibly several others for things like CGI scripts. Among all these subfolders, finding the one in which you need to upload your pages can be tricky, but the

subfolder you need is usually named something like `htdocs`, or `web`, or `webfiles` (depending on what they decided to name it on your server). You have to upload your Web pages to the right folder so that your Web site becomes public on the Internet and your pages are visible when you open your domain name in a Web browser.

If you're not sure which folder you should use, try uploading just one file to any folder that looks like a good candidate (using the instructions in the "Publishing files to a Web server with FTP" section in this chapter). Then visit your domain with a Web browser to see if the page is visible (remember to click the Refresh button in your browser to see any changes each time you try uploading another page). After you figure out which folder corresponds to your domain name, upload all the rest of your site to that same subfolder, making sure that you mirror the local site folder on your hard drive with the main root folder on your server.

Also note that if you want to use Dreamweaver's synchronization features, also covered in this chapter, you need to include the root directory in the FTP folder.

Publishing files to a Web server with FTP

You can upload pages to your server and download pages from your server using the built-in FTP capabilities of Dreamweaver.

To transfer files between your hard drive and a remote server (after you've successfully set up the FTP features covered in the previous section of this chapter), follow these steps:

1. **Make sure the site you want to work on is selected in the Files panel.**

2. **In the top left of the Files panel, click the Connects to Remote Host icon (this is a tiny icon that looks like a blue electrical cable plugging into itself).**

   If you're not already connected to the Internet, the Connects to Remote Host icon starts your Internet connection. If you have trouble connecting this way, try establishing your Internet connection as you usually do to check e-mail or surf the Web, and then return to Dreamweaver and click the Connects to Remote Host icon after you're connected to the Internet. When your computer is online, Dreamweaver should have no trouble automatically establishing an FTP connection with your host server.

   If you still have trouble establishing a connection to your Web server, refer to the preceding section, "Setting up Dreamweaver's FTP features," and make sure that you specified the server information correctly.

3. **After you establish a connection between your computer and your Web server, click Expand/Collapse (the tiny icon that looks like a box within a box at the far right of the top of the Files panel).**

   When you click this icon, Dreamweaver displays both the local folder with your site on your hard drive and the remote folder with the site on your server. I prefer this dual view, because seeing both side by side makes moving files from one place to another easier. It also helps me visualize the structure of the site on the server.

   You can also view your local site folder by choosing Local View from the drop-down list at the top right (visible in Figure 4-13). Or choose Remote View to see only the files on the server.

4. **To *upload* a file (transfer a file from your hard drive to your Web server), select the file from the Local View panel (which displays the files on your hard drive) and click the Put Files icon (the up arrow) in the Files panel.**

   The files are copied automatically to your server when you transfer them. You can select multiple files or folders to be transferred simultaneously.

Get Files   Expand/Collapse

Figure 4-13: Connects to Remote Host   Put Files
The row
of icons
across the
top control
FTP func-
tions makes
it easy to
Connect to
your Web
server, as
well as
upload and
download
files.

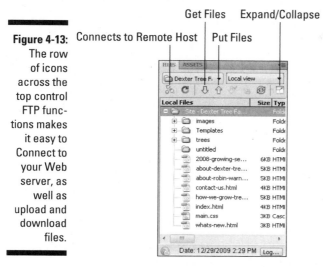

After you upload files to you server, test your work by using a Web browser to view them online. Sometimes things that look and work fine on your computer (such as links) won't work on the server.

5. **To *download* files or folders (transfer files or folders from your Web server to your hard drive), select the files or folders from the Remote View panel (which displays the files on your server) and click the Get Files button (the down arrow) in the Files panel.**

   The files are copied automatically to your hard drive when you transfer them.

Be aware that when you copy files to or from your server, the files you're transferring overwrite the files already at the destination. Dreamweaver notifies you about the overwriting if it notices you're replacing a newer file with an older one, but it can't always correctly assess the proper time differences. Take note of these warnings, but keep in mind that you can get warnings that aren't always accurate when they're based on the age of a file, especially if you use more than one computer to work on your Web site.

When the transfer is complete, you can open the files on your hard drive.

6. **To close this dual-panel dialog and return to Dreamweaver's main workspace, simply click again on the Expand/Collapse icon (the one that looks like a box within a box shown in Figure 4-13).**

Downloading an existing Web site

If you want to work on an existing Web site and you don't already have a copy of it on your computer's hard drive, you can use Dreamweaver to download any or all the files in any Web site (that you have the login information to access) so that you can edit the existing pages, add new pages, or use any of Dreamweaver's other features to check links and manage the site's further development. The first step is to get a copy of the site onto your computer by downloading it from the server.

To download an existing Web site, follow these steps:

1. **Create a new folder on your computer to store the existing site.**

2. **Specify this folder as the local site folder for the site with Dreamweaver's site setup features.**

   Follow the instructions at the beginning of Chapter 2 to set up a site, if you're not sure how to do this yet.

3. **Enter the FTP settings in the Basic server dialog box (refer to Figure 4-12).**

   I explain how to do this in this chapter, in the "Setting up Dreamweaver's FTP features" section.

4. **Connect to the remote site by clicking the tiny Connects to Remote Host button, which looks like the ends of two cables, in the Files panel.**

5. **Click the Get Files button, which looks like a down arrow, to download the entire site to your local drive.**

Sometimes your Web host has files on the remote server that you don't need to download. If you want to download only specific files or folders from the site, select only those files or folders in the Remote Site pane of the Files panel and click the Get Files button. (See the sidebar "Finding the root directory on your Web server" to find the folder on your Web server that corresponds to the local site folder on your hard drive. Re-creating the folder structure on your local computer is important because Dreamweaver needs to know the relative location of all the files in your site in order to set links properly. The safest option is to download the entire site; but if you're working on a large Web project, downloading a part of the structure will enable you to work on a section of the site without downloading it all.

If you're working on only one page or section of a site, I recommend you choose to include *dependent files,* meaning any files linked from those pages, as you download them to ensure that the links are set properly when you make changes and that all related files are downloaded to your hard drive.

6. **After you download the site or specific files or folders, you can edit them as you do any other file in Dreamweaver.**

Synchronizing local and remote sites

One of the most valuable features in Dreamweaver's FTP options is the capability to automatically synchronize the files on your hard drive with the files on your server. This is cool because it helps you keep track of which pages you've edited and ensures that they've been updated on the server. This may not matter much to you the first time you upload your site, or if you have only a few pages in your site. But if you have a large site and make frequent updates, this feature is a wonderful way to make sure you upload all the changes you make to your server. Dreamweaver also confirms which files are updated after you complete the synchronization.

Follow these steps to synchronize your Web site:

1. **Make sure the site you want to work on is selected and displayed in the Files panel.**

2. **Click the Connects to Remote Host icon, in the top left of the Files panel, to log on to your remote site.**

3. **Click the Expand/Collapse icon (labeled in Figure 4-13) to expand the dialog box and view the remote and local sites simultaneously.**

   The Site dialog box displays both the remote and local views of the site. (To collapse this dialog box, click the Expand/Collapse icon again.)

4. **Choose Site➪Synchronize.**

   The Synchronize Files dialog box appears.

5. **In the Synchronize drop-down list, choose whether to synchronize the Entire Site or Selected Files Only.**

6. **In the Direction drop-down list, choose which option you want to use to copy the files:**

   • **Put Newer Files to Remote:** This option copies the most recently modified files from your local site to the remote site. Click the Delete Remote Files Not on Local Drive box if you want those files removed from your Web site.

   • **Get Newer Files from Remote:** This option copies the most recently modified files from your remote site to the local site. Click the Delete Local Files Not on Remote Server box if you want to remove those files from your local copy.

   • **Get and Put Newer Files:** This option updates both the local and remote sites with the most recent versions of all the files.

Make sure the Delete Remote Files Not on Local Drive box is not selected. Be careful of this feature when using Get or Put. As a general rule, I recommend you leave it deselected because you may have folders and files on the server, such as log files, that don't exist on your hard drive, and you don't want to delete them inadvertently.

7. **Click the Preview button.**

The Site FTP dialog box displays the files that are about to be changed.

Now you have the option to verify the files you want to delete, put, and get. If you don't want Dreamweaver to alter a file, deselect it from the Site FTP dialog box now or forever live with the consequences.

8. **Click OK.**

All approved changes are automatically made, and Dreamweaver updates the Site FTP dialog box with the status.

9. **When the synchronization finishes, you can choose to save or not save the verification information to a local file.**

I recommend that you save the verification information because it can be handy if you want to review your changes after synchronization is complete.

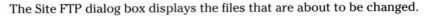

Using a dedicated FTP program

If you prefer to use a dedicated FTP program instead of Dreamweaver's built-in features, you can download FTP programs for the Mac and PC at the following Web addresses:

✔ `http://fireftp.mozdev.org/`: Fire FTP is a nifty little FTP program is an add-on to Firefox and a great alternative to Dreamweaver's FTP features. Ideal for fixing things when you're on the road and don't have Dreamweaver handy, or just want to view the files on your server without using Dreamweaver, this program can be added to any version of Firefox (for free).

✔ `http://filezilla-project.org`: A popular open source option that works on computers running the Windows, Mac, and Linux operating systems.

✔ `www.ipswitch.com`: A popular FTP program for the PC, WS_FTP is such a sophisticated FTP program many Web designers are willing to pay the cost of this program, which offers a free trial version you can use to try it out.

✔ `www.cuteftp.com`: A popular Windows program, CuteFTP, can be downloaded from the Web site.

✔ `www.fetchsoftworks.com` and `www.panic.com/transmit`: If you use a Macintosh computer, popular options are Fetch, available for download at the former Web address and Transmit, available for download at the latter address.

Setting cloaking options

The Dreamweaver Cloaking option enables you to exclude folders or files from the site publishing features, meaning they won't be uploaded to the live site when you're synchronizing or uploading a batch of files to the server. If you're wondering why you might want to prevent files from uploading to your Web server, consider this: The Cloaking feature is a handy way to prevent large graphics, such as Photoshop files, from being uploaded and taking up room on your server, while still storing your high-resolution graphics in your local site folder so you can easily keep track of them. This is useful, for example, if you have a layered .psd or .tiff file that you want to store near the optimized JPEG versions you use in your site. (You find information about converting images into JPEG and other Web-friendly formats in Chapter 3.)

You can use the Cloaking feature to save any type of files in your local site folder, with the assurance that no one can accidentally publish the files with Dreamweaver until you uncloak them and publish them. This feature is best used for large files you don't want on your Web server, such as .psd, .tiff, .avi, and other high-resolution image or video formats.

To use the Cloaking feature, follow these steps:

1. **Choose Site⇨Manage Sites.**

2. **Select the name of the site you want to work on and then click Edit.**

   The Site Setup dialog box opens and displays the site.

3. **Click the small arrow next to Advanced Settings in the left panel, and then click the Cloaking tab.**

   The Cloaking options are displayed in the main area of the dialog box.

4. **Click to Select the Enable Cloaking check box.**

   The cloaking options become active.

5. **Click to select the Cloak Files Ending With check box.**

6. **Enter the extension(s) of any file types you want to cloak in the text field, as shown in Figure 4-14.**

   For example, if you want to cloak any original Photoshop files that may be saved in your local site folder so they don't upload and take up space on your server, enter the .psd extension. If you want to cloak more than one file type, separate each file extension with a space. Do not use a comma or other delimiter.

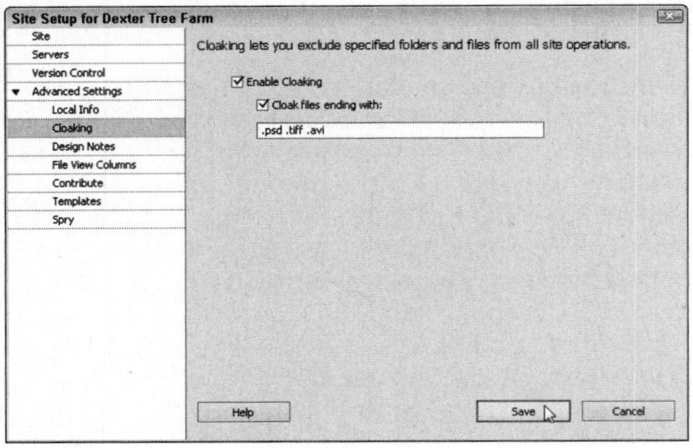

Figure 4-14:
The
Cloaking
feature
enables you
to specify
file types
that you
don't want
uploaded to
your server,
such as
.psd files.

7. **Click Save to close the Site Setup dialog box.**

   Files matching the extensions specified, if any, are now cloaked and will not be uploaded to your Web server even if you upload the folder that contains those files to the server.

   To uncloak files, repeat Steps 1–6 and delete the corresponding file extensions in the Cloaking text field.

Enabling Adobe Contribute

Adobe Contribute is a program that was created so that people who don't know much about Web design can easily *contribute* to a Web site. Think of Contribute as sort of a Dreamweaver Light, except it doesn't work very well as a standalone program. Contribute was designed to work on sites designed in Dreamweaver, and a number of features have been carefully integrated to make that collaboration work smoothly.

Using Dreamweaver's `.dwt` template features you can designate areas of each page that can be edited by users of Contribute. In this way, you can protect common elements, such as logos and navigation links, while making it easy for contributors to edit text and images in designated areas of each page.

If you're working with other developers of a site who use Contribute, make sure you select the Enable Contribute Compatibility check box in the Contribute category of the Site Setup dialog box, as shown in this figure.

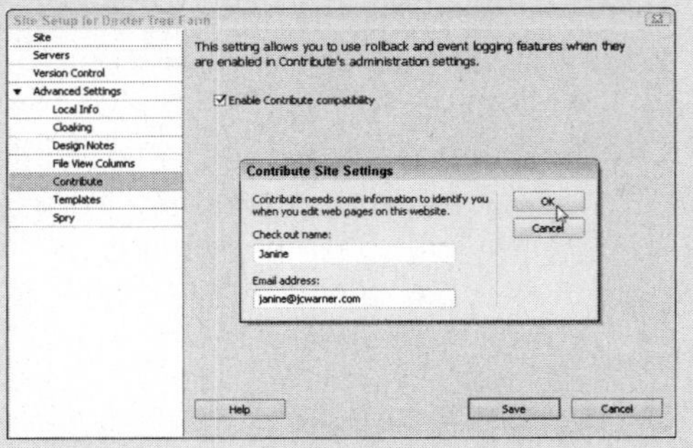

Using Design Notes to Keep in Touch

If you sometimes forget the details of your work or neglect to tell your colleagues important things about the Web site you're all working on, the Dreamweaver Design Notes feature may save you some grief. If you're the only person working on a Web site, you probably don't need the features described in this section because they are intended for use on sites developed by a team of people who need to communicate with each other and make sure they don't overwrite each other's work.

Design Notes are ideal if you want to hide sensitive information from visitors, such as pricing structures or creative strategies, but make it available to members of your development team. Information saved as a Design Note in Dreamweaver can travel with any HTML file or image, even if the file transfers from one Web site to another or from Fireworks to Dreamweaver.

Essentially, Design Notes enable you to record information (such as a message to another designer on your team) and associate it with a file or folder. Design Notes work a lot like the *comment tag* (HTML code that enables you to embed in a page text that won't appear in a browser) but with a bit more privacy. Unlike the comment tag, which is embedded directly in the HTML code of a page (and can be seen if someone views the source code behind a page on the Web), Design Notes are never visible to your visitors. The only way for a visitor to view Design Notes is to deliberately type the path to your notes subdirectory and view the notes files directly. You can even explicitly block this from being allowed, but only if you have administrative access to your server. To be even more secure, you can keep the notes on your hard drive and prevent them from ever being uploaded to your server — though, of course, your team members won't see your witty remarks.

To access the Design Notes page, choose Design Notes in the Category list in the Site Setup dialog box (see Figure 4-15). The settings on this page enable you to control how Dreamweaver uses Design Notes:

 ✔ **Maintain Design Notes:** Select this option to ensure that the Design Note remains attached to the file when you upload, copy, or move it.

 ✔ **Upload Design Notes for Sharing:** Choose this option to include Design Notes when you send files to the server via FTP.

 ✔ **Clean Up:** Use the Clean Up button, also shown in Figure 4-15, to delete any Design Notes that are not associated with any files in the site.

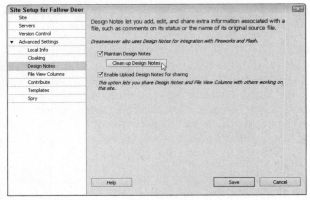

Figure 4-15:
You can
include
Design
Notes when
sending files
to the Web
server.

When you create graphics in Adobe Fireworks, you can save a Design Note for each image file that is also available in Dreamweaver. To use this integrated feature, create a Design Note in Fireworks and associate it with the image. Then when you save the Fireworks image to your local Web site folder, the Design Note goes with it. When you open the file in Dreamweaver, the Design Note appears when you right-click the image (Control+click on the Mac). This feature is a great way for graphic designers to communicate with other members of the Web development team.

To activate the Design Notes feature, follow these steps:

1. **Choose Site⇨Manage Sites.**

   The Manage Sites dialog box opens.

2. **Select the site you want to work on and then click the Edit button.**

   The Site Setup dialog box opens.

3. **Select the Advanced tab.**

4. **In the Category list at the left, choose Design Notes.**

   The Design Notes page appears (refer to Figure 4-15).

5. **Select the Maintain Design Notes option.**

   With this option selected, whenever you copy, move, rename, or delete a file, the associated Design Notes file is also copied, moved, renamed, or deleted with it.

6. **If you want your Design Notes to be sent with your files when they are uploaded to your server, select the Upload Design Notes for Sharing option.**

   If you're making notes only to yourself and don't want them to be associated with the page when you upload it to the server, deselect this option and the Design Notes will be maintained locally but not uploaded with your file.

7. Click OK in the Site Setup dialog box and then click the Done button in the Manage Sites dialog box.

The Manage Sites dialog box closes.

To add Design Notes to a document, follow these steps:

1. Open the file you want to add a Design Note to and then choose File⇨Design Notes.

The Design Notes dialog box opens. You need to have a file checked out to add or modify a Design Note, but not to read a note.

2. In the Status drop-down list box, choose the status of the document.

Your options are Draft, Revision 1, Revision 2, Revision 3, Alpha, Beta, Final, and Needs Attention. You can choose any status, and you should set a policy with your design team about what each status means and how you use these options to manage your development.

3. In the Notes text box, type your comments.

4. If you want to insert the current local date, click the Insert Date icon, which is just above the Notes text box.

The current date is inserted automatically.

You can also select the Show When File Is Open check box. If this box is selected, the Design Notes appear whenever the file is opened so that they can't be missed.

5. Click the All Info tab.

You can add other information that may be useful to developers of your site. For example, you can name a key designer (in the Name field) and define the value as the name of that person or the priority of the project (in the Value field). You may also define a field for a client or the type of file that you commonly use.

6. Click the plus (+) button to add a new information item; click the minus (–) button to remove a selected item.

7. Click OK to save the notes.

The notes you entered are saved to a subfolder named *notes* in the same location as the current file. The filename is the document's filename plus the extension .mno. For example, if the filename is art.htm, the associated Design Notes file is named art.htm.mno. Design Notes are indicated in Site View by a small yellow icon that looks like a cartoon bubble.

Part II
Appreciating Web Design Options

In this part . . .

The best way to design Web sites today is with Cascading Style Sheets (CSS). This part introduces you to the power and advantages of CSS, with two chapters on creating and using styles.

In Chapter 5, you find an introduction to CSS and a review of the CSS features in Dreamweaver. In Chapter 6, you move on to creating CSS layouts, using <div> tags and other block-level elements to create accessible, flexible designs.

In Chapter 7, you discover how the Dreamweaver templates can make creating Web pages faster, and best of all, how templates can save you time when you want to make changes to your page designs. In Chapter 8, you find out how to create tables, split and merge cells, and use table attributes. You also find tips about when to use tables and when CSS is the preferred option.

Chapter 5

Cascading Style Sheets

*W*ant to add a little style to your pages? *Cascading Style Sheets (CSS)* are all the rave on the Web, and with good reason: CSS is *the way* to create Web sites today if you want to follow the latest standards and develop sites that are accessible, flexible, and designed to work on a wide range of screen sizes and devices.

Unfortunately, most people find working with styles far more complicated and confusing than other approaches to design. In my experience, this confusion fades after you learn the basics and start working with styles. This chapter is designed to introduce you to how styles work, the different kinds of styles (and what they're best used for), and how to use the features in Dreamweaver that are designed for creating and editing CSS.

The concept of creating styles has been around since long before the Web. Desktop publishing programs, such as Adobe InDesign, and even word processing programs, such as Microsoft Word, have long used styles to manage the formatting and editing of text on printed pages. Using styles in a word processor, you can create and save styles for common features, such as headlines and captions. In print design, styles are great timesavers because they enable you to combine a collection of formatting options, such as Arial, bold, and italic, into one style and then apply all those options at once to any selected text in your document using a single style. You also have the advantage that if you change a style, you can apply the change automatically — everywhere you've used that style in a document.

On the Web, you can do all that and more with CSS because you can use style sheets for more than just text formatting. For example, you can use CSS to create styles that align images to the left or right side of a page, add padding around text or images, and change background and link colors. For all these reasons (and more), CSS has quickly become the preferred method of designing Web pages among professional Web designers. If you haven't jumped on the CSS bandwagon yet, this chapter is designed to help you understand the basics of CSS.

If you have been working with CSS for a while, you may appreciate this review of CSS and an introduction to Dreamweaver's style features.

In this chapter, you learn the basics of CSS, including how best to use the different types of style selectors and when to use external versus internal style sheets.

Chapter 6 builds on the topics in this chapter, showing you how to design page layouts by combining `<div>` and other XHTML tags with styles. You also find instructions for creating class styles, tag styles, and compound styles, which enable you to create styles that apply only to specific sections of a page. To give you a head start on your designs, I also include instructions for customizing the predesigned CSS layouts included in Dreamweaver in Chapter 6.

Introducing Cascading Style Sheets

CSS is a powerful tool because you can use it to make global style changes across an entire Web site. Suppose, for example, that you create a style for your headlines by redefining the `<h1>` tag to create large, blue, bold headlines. Then one fine day, you decide that all your headlines should be red instead of blue. If you aren't using CSS, changing all your headlines could be a huge undertaking — a matter of opening every Web page in your site to make changes to the font tags around your headlines. But if you're using CSS in an external style sheet, you can simply change the style that controls the headline in the style sheet, and *voilá!* Your headlines all turn red automatically.

If you ever have to redesign your site (and believe me, every good site goes through periodic redesigns), you can save hours or even days of work if you've created your design with CSS.

Understanding the basics of styles

Many people find CSS confusing at first because it's such a different approach to design than what you may be used to if you've worked in print. The following are three of the more confusing aspects of CSS for beginners:

> ✔ **Getting used to thinking about the styles on your site separate from your text, images, and other content:** For example, you want to avoid simply applying formatting directly to a heading to make it bold, green, and 24 point. In CSS, you create a style for your heading that includes

bold, green, and 24 point; save that style in a separate place in your document or in a separate file called an external style sheets; and then apply the style to the heading text. As a result, if you want to change the way your headline looks later, you don't go to the headline text in your page to make the change. Instead, you edit the style in the style sheet, and it automatically changes any heading text formatted with that style.

✔ **Understanding all the different kinds of style selectors you can choose from, such as class, ID, and tag selectors:** No matter how you create your styles, each style definition, or *rule,* contains a selector and a declaration. The *selector* identifies the name and type of style — `#container` or `.caption` for example. The *declaration* defines the style and describes its properties, such as bold, blue, or 300 pixels wide. If that doesn't mean much to you yet, don't worry. Dreamweaver's four selector types are described in detail later in this chapter, and as you discover how styles work, new terms like selectors and declarations begin to make a lot more sense.

✔ **Understanding when it's best to create external style sheets, internal style sheets, or inline styles:** The section "Using Internal versus External Style Sheets" explains how to use the different types of style sheets.

✔ **Understanding how you combine CSS and XHTML to create Web pages:** For example, you can control the size and positioning of a `<div>` tag by applying an ID style to the tag, or you can redefine a tag, such as the `<h1>` tag to change the way headlines look on a page.

If you're starting to feel baffled already, hang in there. I'm just trying to give you an overview as I take you further and further down the rabbit hole. Keep reading through the basic concepts covered in the sections that follow and then continue to the step-by-step instructions in this and the next chapter (even if you're not quite sure you understand everything yet).

Combining CSS and XHTML

Most professional Web designers today recommend creating Web page designs by combing XHTML (a stricter version of HTML) and CSS. Here's the simplified version of how the two work together:

1. Use XHTML to create the structure of a page with tags, such as division (`<div>`), heading (`<h1>`, `<h2>`, and so on), and paragraph (`<p>`).

2. Create styles in CSS that specify the size of these elements, where they appear on a page, and a variety of other formatting options.

Similarly, you use XHTML to insert images and create links, and then add styles to change formatting options, such as removing the underline from your links or changing the color that appears when someone rolls a cursor over a link.

Understanding style selectors

When you create new styles, you need to understand which selector to use for which job. The selector determines the kind of style you will create. Each selector option has different naming restrictions and purposes. If you're completely new to working with styles, this may not make much sense yet, but this is a fundamental part of working with styles. I encourage you to read through all these descriptions of selectors so you can appreciate your options before you move on.

Don't feel you have to memorize all this. Instead, consider folding down the corner on this page so you can refer to this list of selectors as you create and edit styles later.

The following sections offer descriptions of each of the four selection types, which are available from the New CSS Rules dialog box (as shown in Figure 5-1) when you create.

Class selectors

The class selector is the most versatile selector option. *Class styles* can format any element (from text to images to multimedia), and you can use them as many times as you like on any page in a Web site.

Class style names always begin with a period, and you can create class styles with any name as long as you don't use spaces or special characters. (Hyphens and dashes are okay.) Thus, you could create a style called *caption* for the text that appears under your pictures.

```
.caption
```

Dreamweaver helps you with the opening period (or a dot). If you choose class as the selector type and forget to include a dot at the beginning of the name, Dreamweaver adds one for you. Just don't include any space between the dot and the style name.

However, the dot appears only in your style sheet code. When you *apply* a class style to text or another element, the dot doesn't appear in the name in your XHTML code. Thus, if you applied the `.caption` style to a paragraph tag to format the text under an image, the XHTML code would look like this:

```
<p class="caption">This is a photo of a family of Fallow
          deer was taken in Northern California.</p>
```

Class styles must be applied to an element, such as the paragraph tag shown in this example. Class tags can even be added to elements that other styles already define.

When you create a class style in Dreamweaver, the style is displayed in the CSS Styles panel on the right side of the workspace (shown in Figure 5-1). You can apply class styles by using the CSS drop-down list, also shown in Figure 5-1.

Figure 5-1: Styles created with class selectors are available from the CSS drop-down list and can be applied to any element and used as many times as you like on any page.

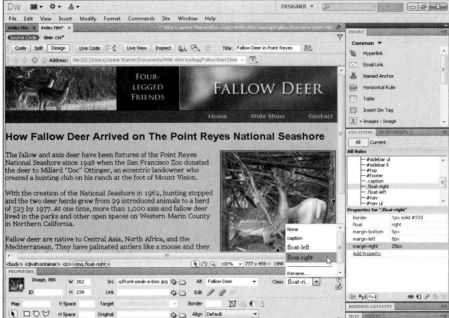

For more details and step-by-step instructions for creating and applying styles with class selectors, see Chapter 6.

ID selectors

Think of ID styles as the building blocks of most CSS page layouts. What's special about ID styles is that they must be unique. Each ID style can be used only once per page. This makes them ideally suited to formatting `<div>` tags and other block-level elements that are used to create distinct sections, like a sidebar or the header or footer. You can create as many ID styles as you want for each page, but you can only use each one once in each page design.

ID styles must begin with a pound (#) character. Similar to class styles, Dreamweaver adds # to the beginning of the style name automatically if you forget to include it. And, like with a class style, don't include a space between # and the style name.

The ID selector option was a new addition to the CSS Rule dialog box in Dreamweaver CS4 and remains this way in version CS5. In version CS3, you had to choose the Advanced option to create an ID style.

Similar to class styles, you can name ID styles anything you like as long as you don't use spaces or special characters (again hyphens and underscores are okay). An ID style used to identify the sidebar section of a page could look like this:

```
#sidebar
```

Similar to class styles, # isn't used in the XHTML code. When a style is applied to an element, such as a `<div>` tag, the XHTML code looks like this:

```
<div id="sidebar">Between these tags with the sidebar ID
         style, you would include any headlines, text,
         or other elements in your sidebar.</div>
```

In the predesigned CSS layouts included in Dreamweaver, all the designs are created by combining a series of `<div>` tags with ID styles using names like `#container`, `#header`, and `#footer` to identify the main sections of the design. In Figure 5-2, you can see how a collection of ID and compound styles are displayed in the CSS Styles panel.

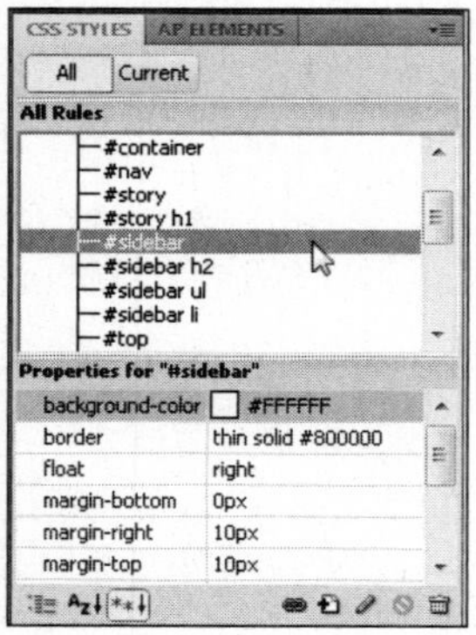

Figure 5-2:
Styles created with the ID selector should only be used only once per page and are ideal for creating a CSS layout with div tags.

Tag selectors

The tag selector is used to redefine existing XHTML tags. Select this option if you want to change the appearance of an existing XHTML tag, such as the `<h1>` (heading 1) tag or the `<ul>` (unordered list) tag.

In many cases, redefining existing XHTML tags with your desired formatting using CSS has advantages over creating new styles. For example, content formatted with the heading 1 tag is well recognized on the Web as the most important text on a page. For that reason, many search engines give priority to text formatted with the heading 1 tag. Similarly, the hierarchical structure of the <h1>–<h6> tags helps ensure that, even if a visitor to your site changes the text size in his Web browser, text formatted with the heading 1 tag is still larger relative to text formatted with an heading 2 tag, which is larger than text formatted with the heading 3 tag, and so on.

When you use the tag selector, the style definition is applied automatically to any text or other element that's been formatted with the corresponding tag. Thus, if you've formatted a heading with an <h1> tag and then create a new <h1> style, the formatting you used to define the style will apply automatically to the heading as soon as the style is created.

When you choose the tag selector type, all the XHTML tags become visible in a drop-down list in the New CSS Rule dialog box. You simply choose the tag style you want to create, as shown in Figure 5-3, where I've selected h1.

Figure 5-3:
You can redefine the appearance of any XHTML tag by creating a style with a tag selector.

Creating compound styles

The compound selector can be used to combine two or more style rules to create a style definition that displays only when one style is contained within another. Compound styles are useful when you want to do something like use the heading 1 tag multiple times to format headlines in different ways on the same Web page. For example, you could create one style for headlines that appear in the main story area of a page and then create another style for headlines that appear in the sidebar on the page and still use the heading 1 tag to format both.

Compound styles are created by combining ID, class, or tag styles and look like this:

```
#sidebar h1
```

See Figure 5-4 for an example of how an `<h1>` style defined like this within a `#sidebar` ID style looks in the New CSS Rule dialog box. For a compound style, you must

✔ Include a space between each name or tag in a compound style.

✔ Leave off the brackets around tag in a style name.

In this example, the style definition will apply only to `<h1>` tags that appear within another element, such as a `<div>` tag with an ID style `#sidebar`.

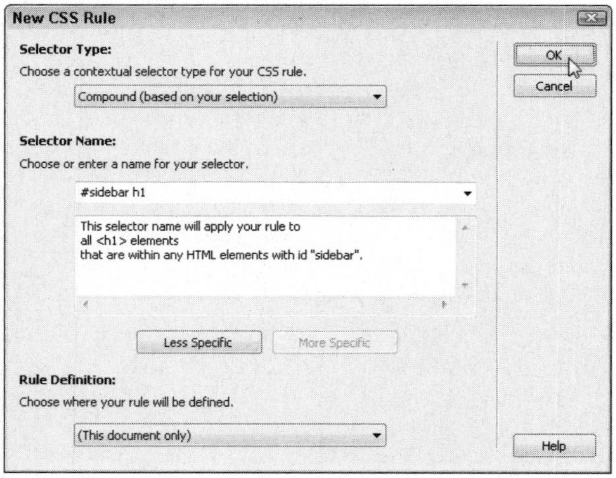

Figure 5-4:
Use the compound style selector to combine styles.

If a compound style combines more than one tag, it's written like this:

```
#sidebar h1 a:link
```

Again, you must include a space between each name or tag. In this example, you see a style that defines the appearance of the active link tag only when the link is located inside an element formatted with the `<h1>` tag that's also inside an element formatted with the `#sidebar` ID. A compound style like this enables you to create links in a sidebar headline that look different than links in another part of the sidebar.

After you figure out the differences among these style selector options and when they're best used, you're well on your way to mastering the art of creating and applying styles in Dreamweaver, which is covered in Chapter 6.

Using internal versus external style sheets

In CSS, you have the option of creating internal, external, or inline styles. You can even use a combination of these options, or attach multiple external style sheets to the same Web page. Here's an explanation of these options:

✔ **Internal styles:** If you create internal styles, the CSS code is stored in the `<head>` area at the top of the XHTML page, and you can apply the styles only that page. If you're just creating a one-page Web site or styles used on only one page, an internal style sheet is fine, but for most sites, external style sheets offer many advantages.

✔ **External styles:** If you save your styles in an external style sheet, they're stored in a separate file with a `.css` extension. You can attach external style sheets to any or all of the pages in a Web site in much the same way that you can insert the same image into multiple pages. You can also attach multiple external style sheets to the same page. For example, you can create one style sheet for styles that format text and another for layout styles. You can also create external style sheets for different purposes, such as one for print and one for screen display. For a Web designer, external style sheets offer two big advantages: They enable you to create new pages faster and more easily and to update styles across many pages at once.

✔ **Inline styles:** Inline styles are created within a document at the place that a style is used and only apply to the element to which they're attached in the document. Inline styles are generally considered the least useful of the three style sheet options, because to change the defined style, you must change the code that contains the element, which means you lose the benefits of making global updates and creating clean, fast-loading code. For example, creating one style for all your headlines and saving it in an external style sheet is more efficient than applying the style formatting options to each headline separately.

At the bottom of the New CSS Rule dialog box, shown in Figure 5-5, you find a Rule Definition drop-down list. Use this list to specify where and how you want to save each new style that you define. The options are

- **This Document Only:** Create an internal style for the open document only.

- **New Style Sheet file:** Create the new style in an external style sheet and create a new external style sheet simultaneously.

- **An existing external style sheet:** Choose any existing external style sheet attached to the page by selecting the name of the style sheet from the Rule Definition drop-down list. In Figure 5-5, I am selecting an existing style sheet with the name `slides.css`.

If you're creating a style that you're likely to use on more than one page in your site, saving the style to a new or existing external style sheet is your best choice. If you save a style in an internal style sheet and later want to add it to an external style sheet, you can move the style by clicking and dragging the style into the external style sheet list in the CSS Styles panel.

Figure 5-5:
Save a new
CSS rule in
an internal
or external
style sheet.

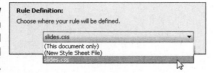

Looking at the code behind the scenes

Even if you *prefer* not to look the code behind your Web pages, it's helpful to have at least some familiarity with different kinds of tags, CSS, and other code that Dreamweaver creates for you when you design Web pages. The following examples show what the CSS code in an internal or external style sheet would look like in Dreamweaver for the following styles:

- An ID style that's created with the ID selector, named `#container`, and defined as 780 pixels wide with the left and right margins set to auto (a cool trick for centering a CSS design, covered in Chapter 6).

- A style that's created with a class selector, named `.caption`, and defined as Verdana, Arial, Helvetica, sans serif, small, italic, and bold.

✔ A style created with a tag selector to redefine the HTML tag <h1> as follows: Arial, Helvetica, sans serif, large, and bold. (**Note:** Because the heading tags already include bold formatting, it's not necessary to include bold in the style definition.)

```
#container {
        width: 780px;
        margin-right: auto;
        margin-left: auto;
}
.caption {
        font-family:  Verdana, Arial, Helvetica, sans-
        serif;
        font-size: small;
        font-style: italic;
        font-weight: bold;
}
H1 {
        font-family: Arial, Helvetica, sans-serif;
        font-size: large;
}
```

Comparing CSS Rule Options

After you determine what selector type is best for your style — and decide whether you want to save it in an external or internal style — you're done with the New CSS Rules dialog box (described in the previous sections). You are ready to move on to the CSS Rule Definition dialog box and define the formatting and other options you want to include in your style. You find step-by-step instructions for creating new style rules later in this chapter. This section continues the overview to help you better understand your choices before you start creating a new style.

The CSS Rule Definition dialog box includes eight different categories, each with multiple options. All these choices can seem a bit daunting at first, which is why I've included in this section a general overview of the options in each category. Again, don't feel you have to memorize all these options; you can always refer to this section when you're creating new styles.

Before you get overwhelmed by all the options, here's a tip. You don't *have* to specify any of the settings in the dialog boxes that follow when you create a new style in Dreamweaver. When you leave an option blank, you let the default browser settings (or other styles) already applied to the page take control. For example, if you don't specify a text color in a class style named .caption, the text formatted with the style remains black — the default color in most Web browsers, unless another style contains formatting instructions for the color of that text. (You find instructions for changing the text color for an entire page in Chapter 6.)

In most cases, you select only a few options from one or two categories for each new style you create. I've included the full list here so you can appreciate all the options.

Not all the options in the CSS Rule Definition dialog box are supported by all the Web browsers in use on the Web today; the way styles are displayed on a Web page can vary depending on the browser. Similarly, some CSS options aren't included in Dreamweaver because they're not commonly supported. The following section describes the options in each of the categories offered in the CSS Rule Definition dialog box (shown in Figures 5-6 through 5-14).

The Type category

The Type category features a collection of options that control the display of (you guessed it) the text in your pages. With the Type category selected (see Figure 5-6), you have the following formatting options:

✔ **Font-Family:** Specifies a font, a font family, or a series of families. You can add fonts to the list by choosing Edit Font List in the drop-down list. (For an explanation of why Dreamweaver includes font collections — and a look at how to create new ones — see the upcoming section, "Why so many fonts?")

Figure 5-6:
The Type category in the CSS Rule Definition dialog box.

✔ **Font-Size:** Defines the size of the text. You can choose a specific numeric size or a relative size. Use the drop-down arrow to select from a list of options that includes pixels, picas, and percentages. (For more on these options, see the sidebar "Understanding CSS size options.")

✔ **Font-Style:** Enables you to choose whether the text appears as normal, italic, or oblique. (Italic and oblique are rarely different in a Web browser, so stick with italic unless you have a specific reason not to.)

✔ **Line-Height:** Enables you to specify the height of a line on which the text is placed (graphic designers usually call this *leading*). You can specify line-height in a variety of ways, including pixels, picas, and percentages. (For more on these options, see the upcoming section, "Understanding CSS size options.")

✔ **Text-Decoration:** Enables you to specify whether text is underlined, *overlined* (a line appears over the text), displayed with a strikethrough, or displayed with the *blink effect* (which makes text appear to flash on and off). You can also choose None, which removes all decorative effects.

None is the option that removes the underline from linked text. And please, use the other decoration options sparingly, if at all. Links are underlined automatically; if you underline text that isn't a link, you risk confusing viewers. Overlined and strikethrough text can be hard to read. Use these options only if they enhance your design. And by all means, resist the blink effect; it's distracting and can make the screen difficult to read.

✔ **Font-Weight:** Enables you to control how bold the text appears by using a specific or relative boldness option.

✔ **Font-Variant:** Enables you to select small caps. Unfortunately, this attribute isn't supported by most browsers.

✔ **Font-Transform:** Enables you to globally change the case of selected words, making them all uppercase, all lowercase, with initial caps, or with no capitalization.

✔ **Color:** Defines the color of the text. You can use the color well (the square icon) to open a Web-safe color palette in which you can select predefined colors or create custom colors.

After you select the Type options for your style sheet, click Apply to apply them, and click OK to save the settings and close the CSS Rule Definition dialog box.

Why so many fonts?

Although you can specify any font you want for text on your Web pages, you don't have complete control over how that font appears on your visitor's computer because the font you apply is displayed properly only if your visitors have the same font on their hard drives. To help ensure that your text appears as you intend, Dreamweaver includes collections of the most common fonts on Windows and Macintosh computers, grouped together in families, such as

- ✔ Arial, Helvetica, sans serif
- ✔ Georgia, Times New Roman, Times, and serif

When you apply a collection of fonts, the browser displays the formatted text in the first font available in the list. For example, if you choose the font collection that starts with Georgia and your visitors have Georgia on their hard drives, they see your text in Georgia. If they don't have Georgia, the text is displayed in the next font on the list that your visitors do have — in this case, Times New Roman. If they don't have that font either, the text is displayed in Times. And if they don't even have Times (which would be very unusual), the browser looks for any serif font. (In case you're not familiar with font terms, *serif* describes fonts, such as Times, that have those little curly things on the edges of letters; *sans serif* means no curly things, which is what you get with a font like Arial.)

You can create your own font collections by selecting the Edit Font List option from the bottom of the Font-Family drop-down list in the Property inspector or the Type category of the CSS Rule Definition dialog box. In the Edit Font List dialog box, shown in Figure 5-7, you can do the following:

- ✔ **To add or remove a font collection,** use the plus and minus buttons at the top of the Edit Font List dialog box.

- ✔ **To add individual fonts to a collection,** select the font name from the bottom right of the dialog box and use the double-left arrows to add it to a font list.

- ✔ **To remove a font from a collection,** use the double-right arrows.)

The only way to ensure that text appears in the font you want is to create the text in a graphic in a program, such as Photoshop or Fireworks, and then insert the graphic with the text into your page. That's not a bad option for special text, such as banners or logos; but it's usually not a good option for all your text because graphics take longer to download than text and are harder to update later.

Figure 5-7:
The Edit
Font List
dialog box.

Understanding CSS size options

With CSS, you can specify sizes for fonts and other elements in so many ways that confusion can set in. If you're familiar with print, you'll probably recognize point sizes and pixel sizes, but these aren't necessarily the best options when you're designing for the Internet. On the Web, where display windows can vary from giant monitors to tiny cell-phone screens, using relative sizes can help you create more flexible and adaptable deigns, something you can't do as well with fixed pixel or point sizes. As you work in Dreamweaver to create Web pages, be sure to get familiar with the following sizing options:

✔ **Small, medium, and large relative sizes:** Many Web designers prefer to use relative sizes, such as the small, medium, and large. The advantage of this method is that the font size adjusts in response to your visitor's settings while maintaining its relative relationship. If text is formatted as large (for example), it appears on-screen as larger than text formatted as small — no matter what the default font size. Thus, you can maintain the hierarchy of text elements on a page, even if your user alters the default text size (an option available to users in most Web browsers).

✔ **Percent-based relative sizes:** A variation on the small-medium-large approach is to specify a page-wide base font size as medium (which is the default in most browsers), and then use percentages to make text larger or smaller, relative to that base size. For example, you could define the text in a caption style as 90 percent and your caption text would appear at 90 percent of the size of the rest of the text on the page. You could then make headlines 150 percent (for example) and subheads 125 percent.

✔ **Em and ex:** Another size option is *em,* which refers to the space taken up by a capital letter *M* in the font face specified in a style. The *ex* option is similar, but it's based on the size of a lowercase *x* in the specified font face. Although these two options may seem complex (especially when you're new to Web design), these two sizes are popular for line spacing, as well as for other settings; that's because the size is adjusted relative to the displayed text size. Although this can get confusing, em and ex work much like percentages — and adapt even better to different user settings and monitor sizes.

The Background category

Using the Background category in the CSS Rule Definition dialog box (see Figure 5-8), you can specify a background color or image for a style — and control how the background is displayed on the page. You can use background style settings for any element of your Web page that can display a background — including <div> tags and heading tags. For example, you could alter the <body> tag to include background settings that apply to the entire page, or you could create an ID style with a background setting that would add a background color only to an individual <div> tag. By including the background in the ID style of a <div> tag, you can limit the background to appear on-screen only where the <div> tag is used.

In the example shown in Figure 5-8, I've defined the rule for an ID style named #mainContent to include a background image, which I'm further defining with the No-Repeat option. Another advantage of CSS is that it includes more precise control of background images than is possible with HTML — which, by default, repeats a background image across and down a page.

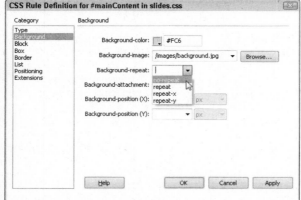

Figure 5-8:
The Background category in the CSS Rule Definition dialog box.

You can choose from these Background options:

✔ **Background-Color:** Specifies the background color of a defined style. You can use the color well to open a Web-safe color palette in which you can select predefined colors or create custom colors.

✔ **Background-Image:** Enables you to select a background image as part of the style definition. Click the Browse button to select the image.

✔ **Background-Repeat:** Determines how and whether the background image tiles across and down the page. In all cases, the image is cropped if it doesn't fit behind the element to which the style is applied. The Repeat options are

- **No-Repeat:** The background is displayed once at the top, left of the element.

- **Repeat:** The background image repeats vertically and horizontally in the background of the element.

- **Repeat-X:** The background repeats horizontally, but not vertically, in the background of the element.

- **Repeat-Y:** The background repeats vertically, but not horizontally, in the background of the element.

✔ **Background-Attachment:** This property determines how the background behaves when the page is scrolled.

- **Fixed:** The background remains glued to one place in the viewing area and doesn't scroll out of sight, even when the Web page is scrolled.

- **Scroll:** The background scrolls along with the Web page.

✔ **Background-Position (X):** Enables you to align the image left, center, or right, or to set a numeric value to determine the precise horizontal placement of the background. You can use horizontal positioning only with No-Repeat or with Repeat-Y.

✔ **Background Position (Y):** Enables you to align the image top, center, or bottom, or to set a numeric value to determine the precise vertical placement of the background. You can use vertical positioning only with No-Repeat or Repeat-X.

The Block category

The Block category (see Figure 5-9) defines the spacing and alignment settings and is commonly used for styles that will define the display of text on a Web page.

You can choose from these Block category options:

✔ **Word-Spacing:** Defines the amount of white space inserted between words in points, millimeters (mm), centimeters (cm), picas, inches, pixels, ems, and exs. (See the later section "Understanding CSS size options.")

✔ **Letter-Spacing:** Defines the amount of white space inserted between letters in points, millimeters (mm), centimeters (cm), picas, inches, pixels, ems, and exs.

✔ **Vertical-Align:** Aligns inline elements, such as text and images, in relation to the elements that surround them. Your options are Baseline, Sub, Super, Top, Text-Top, Middle, Bottom, and Text-Bottom, or you can set a numeric value. *Note that not all Web browsers support all these options and results can vary among browsers.*

✔ **Text-Align:** Enables you to left, right, center, or justify your text. You can (for example) use this setting as part of the definition of an ID style when you want to align the contents of a `<div>` tag, as when you center the text in a footer. (You can find details about styling `<div>` tags in Chapter 6.)

✔ **Text-Indent:** Specifies how far the first line of text is indented. Negative numbers are allowed if you want the first line to begin off the page.

✔ **White-Space:** Tells the browser how to handle line breaks and spaces within a block of text. Your options are Normal, Pre (for preformatted), and Nowrap, which prevents elements from being separated if they must wrap to fit within a browser window or other container.

✔ **Display:** Indicates how to render an element in the browser. For example, you can hide an element by choosing None and change the positioning of an unordered list from horizontal to vertical, by choosing Inline.

Figure 5-9:
The Block category in the CSS Rule Definition dialog box.

The Box category

The Box category (see Figure 5-10) defines settings for positioning and spacing. As you can read in Chapter 6, these settings are ideal for creating page layouts with ID styles to position `<div>` tags.

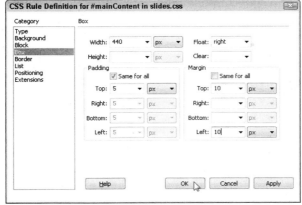

You can use the Box category properties to set these values:

- **Width:** Enables you to specify a width for any element that can have its dimensions specified, such as a `<div>` tag. You can use pixels, points, inches, centimeters, millimeters, picas, ems, exs, or percentages for your measurements. (See "Understanding CSS size options" earlier in this chapter for the basics of sizing with ems, exs, and percentages on the Web.)

- **Height:** Enables you to specify a height for any element that can have its dimensions specified.

  The Height field is often left empty to enable elements (such as `<div>` tags) to expand to fit their contents.

- **Float:** Enables you to align elements, such as images and `<div>` tags, to the left or right of a page or other container causing text or other elements wrap around it.

- **Clear:** Prevents floating content from overlapping an area to the left or right, or to both sides of an element. This is a useful option for preventing overlapping of elements, especially when the Float option is used.

- **Padding:** Sets the amount of space within the borders of an element. For example, you can use padding to create space between the borders of a `<div>` tag and its contents. You can set padding separately for the top, right, bottom, and left. Padding is measured in pixels, points, inches, centimeters, millimeters, picas, ems, exs, and percentages.

- **Margin:** Sets the amount of space around the outside of an element. Margins can be used to create space between the edge of an element and other elements on the page, such as between an image and text or between two `<div>` tags. You can set the margin separately for the top, right, bottom, and left. Padding is measured in pixels, points, inches, centimeters, millimeters, picas, ems, exs, and percentages.

Setting padding and margin spacing can be tricky because they add to the overall size of your image, div, or other element. For help on setting these options to best fit your design, see Chapter 6.

The Border category

The Border category defines settings — such as Width, Color, and Style — and is commonly used to define borders around images, tables, and <div> tags. As shown in Figure 5-11, you can specify border settings on all four sides of an element or create borders only on one, two, or three sides of an element. With this technique, you can use the border settings to create dividing lines between <div> tags that create columns or add separating lines above or below elements.

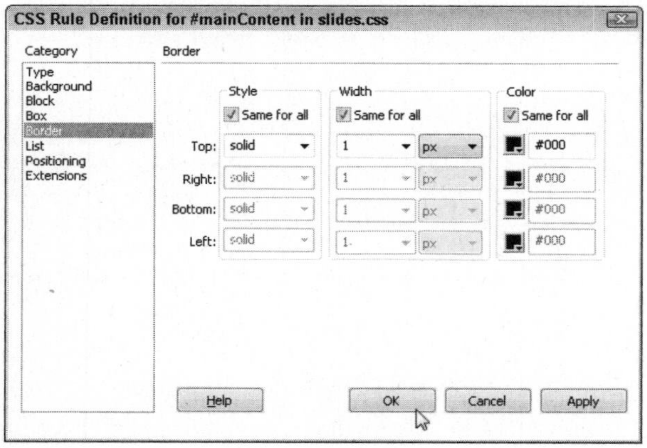

Figure 5-11: The Border category in the CSS Rule Definition dialog box.

CSS Rule Definition for #mainContent in slides.css

Category	Border		
Type	Style	Width	Color
Background	☑ Same for all	☑ Same for all	☑ Same for all
Block			
Box	Top: solid	1 ▼ px ▼	#000
Border	Right: solid	1 ▼ px ▼	#000
List	Bottom: solid	1 ▼ px ▼	#000
Positioning	Left: solid	1 ▼ px ▼	#000
Extensions			

Help   OK   Cancel   Apply

The List category

The List category defines settings, such as the size and type of bullets for list tags. You can specify whether bullets are Disc, Circle, Square, Decimal, Lower-Roman, Upper-Roman, Lower-Alpha, Upper-Alpha, or None (see Figure 5-12). Choose None if you want to use the list tag with no bullet. If you want to use a custom bullet, you can use the Browse button to insert an image to be used as the bullet. You can also control the location of the list bullet in relation to the list item. In Chapter 6, you find instructions for redefining the unordered list tag to create rollover effects for links, a popular option for creating navigation rows and other collections, or lists, of links.

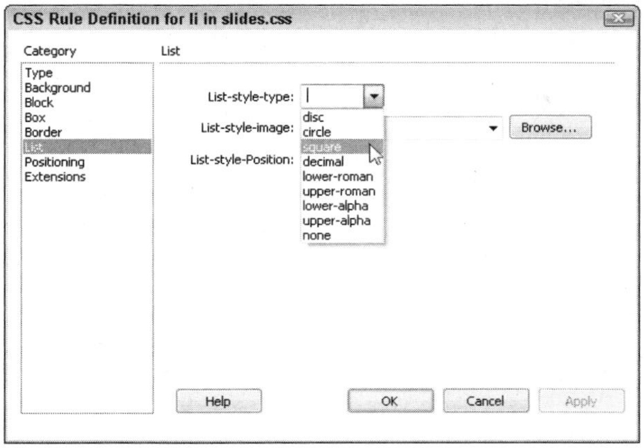

Figure 5-12:
The List
category
in the CSS
Rule
Definition
dialog box.

The Positioning category

The Positioning category (see Figure 5-13) enables you to alter the way elements are positioned on a page. As you can read in Chapter 6, positioning can dramatically change the way block-level elements appear in a browser. *Block-level elements* include table, list, header, paragraph, and <div> tags. For example, AP Divs in Dreamweaver are simply <div> tags that use absolute positioning to place elements in a specific part of a page.

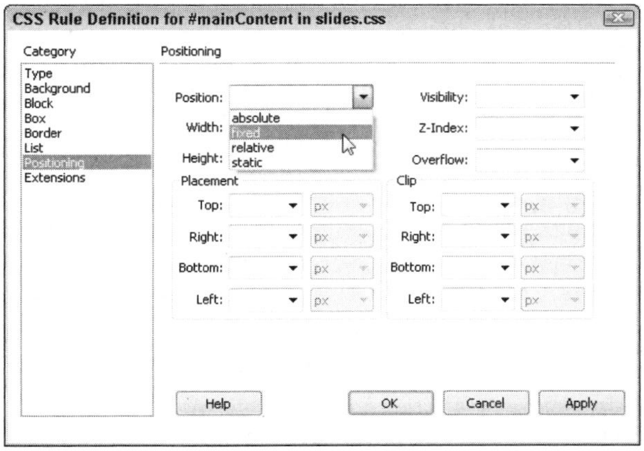

Figure 5-13:
The
Positioning
category
in the CSS
Rule
Definition
dialog box.

To understand how positioning works, it's important to know that positioning is always determined relative to something else, such as another element on the page or the browser window. How you set up positioning depends on where your element is on the page — and on whether the element is inside another element (such as a `<div>` tag). Here are the Positioning options:

✔ **Position:** Enables you to specify the position of an element, such as a `<div>` tag. Options include

- **Absolute:** Uses the top and left coordinates to control the position of an element relative to the upper-left corner of the browser window or the upper-left corner of an element that contains the element. (For example, the positioning of an AP Div contained within another AP Div is based on the position of the first AP Div.)

- **Fixed:** Positions an element relative to the top-left corner of the browser. The content of an element using fixed positioning remains constant even if the user scrolls down or across the page.

- **Relative:** Uses a position relative to the point where you insert the element into the page or relative to its container.

- **Static:** This option simply places the content at its location within the flow of the document. By default, all HTML elements that *can* be positioned are static.

✔ **Width, Height:** Enables you to specify a width and height that you can use in styles you apply to images, `<div>` tags, or any other element that can have its dimensions specified. These settings serve the same function as the Width and Height in the Box category. Entering a value in either category causes the same value to appear in the other.

✔ **Placement:** Defines the size and location of an element within its containing element. For example, you can set the right edge of the element to line up with the right edge of the element that contains it. You can specify the Top, Right, Bottom, and Left options separately and you can use pixels, points, inches, centimeters, millimeters, picas, ems, exs, or percentages for your measurements. (See "Understanding CSS size options," earlier in this chapter, for basics about ems, exs, and percentages.)

✔ **Visibility:** Enables you to control whether the browser displays the element. You can use this feature, combined with a scripting language (such as JavaScript), to change the display of elements dynamically. For example, you can cause an element to appear on a page only when a user clicks a button — and then make it disappear when the button is clicked again. The Visibility options are

- **Inherit:** The element has the visibility of the element in which it's contained. This is the default.

- **Visible:** The element is displayed.

- **Hidden:** The element isn't displayed.

✔ **Z-Index:** Controls the position of an element, such as an AP Div, on the Z-coordinate, which controls the stacking order in relation to other elements on the page. Higher-numbered elements overlap lower-numbered elements. (Note: This setting only works on elements that use absolute or relative positioning settings.)

✔ **Overflow:** Tells the browser how to display the contents of an element if the container, such as a `<div>` tag, can't fit the element's entire size.

- **Visible:** Keeps content, such as an image or text, visible, even if it expands beyond the defined height or width of a container.

- **Hidden:** Cuts off the contents if they exceed the size of the container. This option doesn't provide scroll bars.

- **Scroll:** Adds scroll bars to the container regardless of whether the contents exceed the element's size.

- **Auto:** Makes scroll bars appear only when a container's contents exceed its boundaries.

✔ **Clip:** When the content of an element overflows the space allotted and you set the Overflow property to Scroll or Auto, you can set the Clip settings to specify which part of the element is visible by controlling which part of the element is cropped if it doesn't fit in the display area.

The Extensions category

Extensions (see Figure 5-14) include filters and cursor options:

✔ **Page-Break:** Can be set for before or after an element to insert a point in a page where a printer sees a page break. This option enables you to better control the way a page is printed.

✔ **Cursor:** Defines the type of cursor that appears when a user moves the cursor over an element.

✔ **Filter:** Enables you to apply special effects, such as drop shadows and motion blurs.

Filters are visible only in Microsoft Internet Explorer, which is now used by a minority of the Web audience so most Web designers avoid these options.

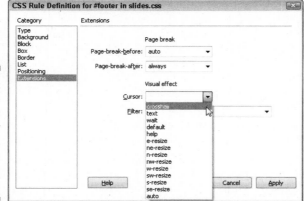

Figure 5-14:
The
Extensions
category
in the CSS
Rule
Definition
dialog box.

Using the CSS Styles Panel

The CSS Styles panel, as shown in Figures 5-15 and 5-16, provides a great place to create, attach, view, manage, organize, and edit CSS Styles. To open the CSS Styles panel, choose Window⇨CSS Styles or click the small double-arrow at the top of the panel group and then double-click CSS Styles.

When you work with the CSS Styles panel, you can switch between two modes, accessible by clicking the All or Current tabs at the top-left of the panel. The next two sections explain each mode in more detail.

Looking for conflicts in Current mode

When you select the Current tab at the top left of the CSS Styles panel, you can view the styles *currently* applied to any selected element on a page, as shown in Figure 5-15.

Current mode is useful for identifying how styles are applied to a particular element and for troubleshooting when styles conflict. Although I do most of my design and development work in the All mode, described in the next section, Current mode is great place to test styles, especially when you're not sure which styles may be affecting a particular element on your page.

The *cascade* part of Cascading Style Sheets refers to the fact that multiple styles can apply to the same element in much the same way wave after wave of water might cascade over a series of rocks. Using Current mode, you can see how multiple styles can work together — or cause conflicts. For example, the text in a heading may get its font from the body style and its color and size from a heading style. When I place your cursor in the heading and the click Current mode in the CSS Styles panel (as shown in Figure 5-15), you can see both styles displayed — as well as how the rules in each style affect the same heading.

Figure 5-15:
The Current mode of the CSS Styles panel, showing the styles applied to a headline selected in the open document.

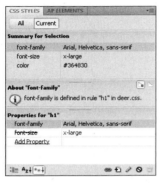

The Current mode has three sections: the Summary for Selection pane, the About pane, and the Properties pane.

✔ **In the Summary for Selection pane,** you see the rules currently defined for the selected style. This pane is especially useful when you've created a complicated layout and are trying to understand how different styles may be affecting the same element.

✔ **In the About pane,** you see a text description of where a formatting option is defined for any rule selected in the Summary of Selection. (Note that this pane has two small icons in the bottom right corner. Click the icon on the left to "show information about the selected property," as shown in Figure 5-15. Click the small icon to the right of that, to "show cascade of rules.")

✔ **In the Properties pane,** you can edit, add, or delete style rules just as you can in All mode.

Working with the big picture in All mode

The All tab, which is selected by default, displays a list of *all* the CSS rules defined in a document's internal style sheet *and* in any attached external style sheets. I do most of my CSS designing and development in this mode because I like to see all the styles that affect my site as I work on creating new ones and editing existing styles.

When the CSS Styles panel is in All mode, you can do the following:

✔ **See the styles in a style sheet:** To view the styles in an internal or external style sheet in the CSS Styles panel, click the plus sign (the triangle on the Mac) to open the style sheet within the panel. You'll find the arrow (or triangle) next to the `<style>` tag if the page includes an internal style sheet. If the page includes one or more external style sheets, click the arrow next to the name of any style sheet to view the style rules included in it. Figure 5-16 shows a Web page with an external style sheet (named `deer.css`) and an internal style sheet identified by the `<style>` tag in the CSS Styles panel.

✔ **View style properties:** Select a style in the CSS Styles panel, and its properties are displayed in the Properties pane at the bottom of the CSS Styles panel. (Note: You may need to click and drag the bottom of the CSS Styles panel down to reveal the pane at the bottom.) Notice in Figure 5-16 that the `#container` style is selected in the CSS Styles panel, and the definition of the style is displayed in the Properties pane at the bottom of the panel.

Figure 5-16:
The CSS Styles panel, showing the styles associated with the open document.

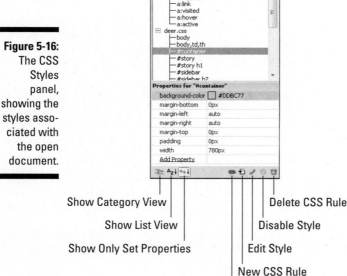

Show Category View

Show List View

Show Only Set Properties

Delete CSS Rule

Disable Style

Edit Style

New CSS Rule

Attach Style Sheet

✔ **Edit styles:** You can edit any selected style in the Properties pane by typing to change settings or selecting an option from the drop-down lists. (These handy lists appear when you place your cursor in a field and are great for making quick changes.)

I generally find it easier to edit a style — especially if I'm making a lot of changes — in the CSS Rule Definition dialog box because the all options are so well organized in the categories described in the preceding section. To open a style so you can edit in the CSS Rule Definition dialog box, double-click any style name in the CSS Styles panel.

If you don't see any styles listed in the CSS Styles panel, you probably haven't defined any styles for the document or attached an external style sheet with styles. Occasionally, however, the styles in an external style sheet won't appear on-screen, even if the name appears in the CSS Styles panel. (I've seen this happen sometimes when I open a file that was created in a previous version of Dreamweaver or a site that was moved from one computer to another.) In this case, an easy solution is to simply reattach the style sheet the same way you would attach a style sheet to a new page (see the next section for details).

Creating and listing styles

At the bottom-left of the CSS Styles panel (shown in Figure 5-16), you see three small icons that make it easy to change among the Show Category, Show List, and Show Only Set Properties views. These options apply to the Properties pane in both Current and All modes. Here's how they work:

✔ **Show Category View:** Dreamweaver displays all the properties available for a selected rule organized by the category to which they belong. For example, all the font properties are grouped into a Font category.

✔ **Show List View:** Dreamweaver displays all the properties alphabetically.

✔ **Show Only Set Properties:** In this view, Dreamweaver displays only the properties you've defined for a selected rule. This is the default setting — and the option shown in Figure 5-16. I prefer this option because it makes identifying the settings for any selected style quick and easy.

The second set of icons, on the bottom right of the CSS Styles panel (also shown in Figure 5-16) aren't dependent on the view settings. From left to right, these icons represent

✔ **Attach Style Sheet:** When you click this icon, you can browse to find any existing external style sheet in a site and attach it to the open page. (See "Attaching an external style sheet to a page," later in this chapter, for help.)

 ✔ **New CSS Rule:** Click this icon to open the New CSS Rule dialog box and create a new style.

 ✔ **Edit Style:** Click this icon to open any style selected in the CSS Styles panel in the CSS Rule Definition dialog box where you can edit it.

 ✔ **Enable/Disable Style:** Click this icon to temporarily turn off any style. This is handy if you want to see how the style is affecting elements on the page.

 ✔ **Delete CSS Rule:** Select any style name in the CSS Styles panel and click this Trash icon to delete it.

You can also rename styles in the CSS Styles panel, but be careful. You can rename styles in the CSS Styles panel in two ways — and only one changes the corresponding HTML code automatically. If you change the name of a style in the style sheet, you must also change the name *wherever the style is used in your Web-page code* or the style will no longer work. See the section "Moving, copying, and editing styles," later in this chapter. See Chapter 6 for details.

Switching between CSS and HTML Mode in the Property Inspector

The Property inspector is split into two sections: HTML and CSS. In Figure 5-17, you see the HTML mode of the Property inspector; Figure 5-18 shows the CSS mode. Notice that buttons on the left side of the Property inspector make switching between these two modes easy.

Figure 5-17:
The HTML mode of the Property inspector.

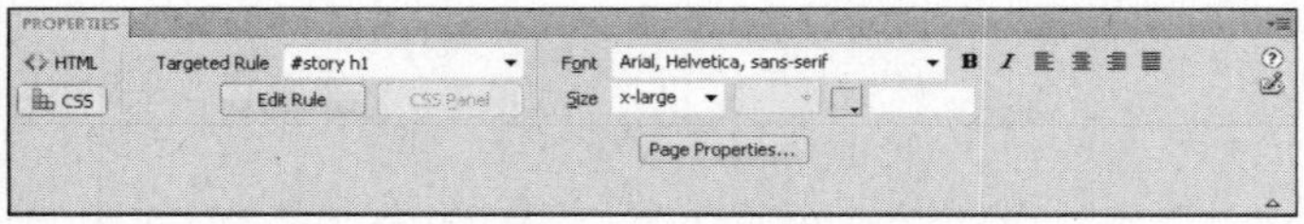

Figure 5-18:
The CSS mode of the Property inspector.

If you're new to CSS and HTML, understanding the differences between these two modes can be a little confusing. Essentially, if you use the formatting icons, such as bold and italic, in HTML mode, Dreamweaver adds HTML tags and attributes. If you use these same icons in CSS mode, Dreamweaver launches the New CSS Rule dialog box so you can create a style that includes these formatting options.

In CSS mode, you can also choose to edit existing styles to add new formatting options to styles that are already applied to text, images, or other elements on a page. Thus you can edit existing styles by simply selecting the style from the Targeted Rule drop-down list and then using the Font, Size, and other fields in the Property inspector to make any changes or additions.

Any time you edit an existing style that has already been applied to elements on a page, the changes you make to the style are applied automatically anywhere the style is used. That's wonderful when you want to change several things at once — but it can be problematic if you want to make a heading appear one way on one page and another way somewhere else.

Anytime you want to create or edit a style, use the Property inspector in CSS mode. On the other hand, if you want to apply an existing style to an element on the page, make sure you're in HTML mode first. For example, if you want to align an image with a class style or apply an ID style to a `<div>` tag, you need to be in HTML mode. To apply a style in HTML mode, select the image, text, or other element in the page where you want to apply the style and then use the Class or ID drop-down lists to select the style; Dreamweaver automatically applies it.

Similarly, if you want to apply an HTML tag, such as the `<h1>` tag, you want to be in HTML mode, but if you want to create or edit a CSS rule for the `<h1>` tag, you want to do that from the CSS mode. Of course, you don't have to create or edit styles with the Property inspector. Consider this a shortcut method; you may still prefer the CSS Rule Definition dialog box (covered in the previous section) when you want to make significant changes to a style.

The ability to see HTML and CSS in the Property inspector was new in Dreamweaver CS4 and continues in CS5. In earlier versions of Dreamweaver, the Property inspector displayed only HTML properties.

Organizing Style Sheets

External style sheets (or *linked style sheets*) offer the greatest advantages with CSS, but you also need to manage these style sheets separately from your HTML Web page. The following sections introduce you to the external style sheets that come with Dreamweaver, as well as tips for attaching, moving, copying, and editing styles in external style sheets.

Saving time with ready-made style sheets

Adobe includes several sample style sheets for you to use in your Web sites. These come in the form of external style sheets that have been created with some popular styles to give you a jump-start in designing your pages. You can use these styles as-is or modify them to suit your needs.

To create a new external style sheet using one of the sample style sheets provided by Adobe, follow these steps:

1. **Choose File⇨New.**

   The New Document dialog box opens, as shown in Figure 5-19.

2. **Choose Page from Sample.**

3. **In the Sample Folder list, select CSS Style Sheet to display the list of CSS style collections.**

4. **Select any of the sample styles listed under Sample Page.**

   A preview of styles is displayed at the far right of the New Document dialog box, as shown in Figure 5-19.

5. **Select a set of styles you like and click Create.**

   A new, untitled style sheet opens in code view. You can always edit these styles further to change any or all of the defined rules.

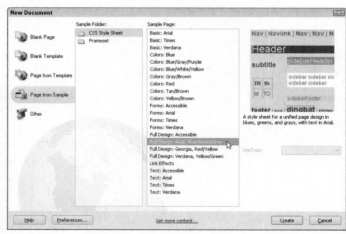

Figure 5-19:
You can preview sample style sheets in the New Document dialog box.

6. **Choose File⇨Save (or Save As) give the style sheet a name and save it in the local site folder of the site where you plan to use it.**

   You can name the style sheet anything you like — just don't use spaces or special characters — and you can save it in the main local site folder or any subfolder within it. (In Chapter 2, you find instructions for setting up a site and defining a local site folder.)

To use the styles in your new external style sheet, you need to attach it to an open file by following the instructions in the next section "Attaching an external style sheet to a Web page."

When you do save a CSS file created from a sample style collection, Dreamweaver leaves the original style collection unchanged. That means you can make edits to the new style sheet without affecting the original — and can always create a new copy by repeating the steps just given.

Attaching an external style sheet to a page

After you've created an external style sheet, you can attach it any Web page. In the step-by-step instructions that follow, you can use any of the style sheets included in Dreamweaver (covered in the previous section), or you can use these instructions to attach any style sheet you create. (You find detailed instructions for creating your own style sheets in Chapter 6.) Begin by opening the page to which you want to attach the style sheet and then follow these steps:

1. **Choose Window⇨CSS Styles.**

   The CSS Styles panel appears.

2. **Click the Attach Style Sheet icon in the CSS Styles panel (the first button in the lower-right area).**

   The Attach External Style Sheet dialog box appears (as shown in Figure 5-20).

3. **Click the Browse button and locate the CSS file in your local site folder.**

   You can also enter a URL if you want to use a remote CSS file located on another Web site, but it's most common to use a style sheet contained within the Web site you're working on. Either way, Dreamweaver sets the link to the style sheet automatically, includes the code for the style sheet's link at the top of the HTML file, and lists all the styles in the external style sheet in the CSS Styles panel.

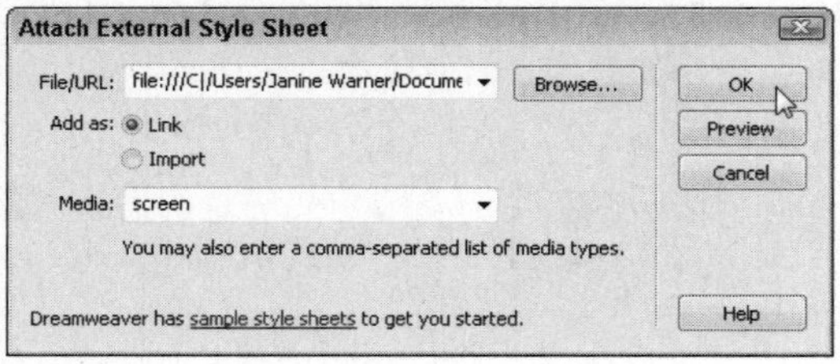

Attach External Style Sheet

File/URL: file:///C|/Users/Janine Warner/Docume ▾ | Browse... | OK

Add as: ⦿ Link
         ○ Import   Preview

Media: screen   ▾   Cancel

You may also enter a comma-separated list of media types.

Dreamweaver has sample style sheets to get you started.   Help

Figure 5-20:
The Attach
External
Style Sheet
dialog box.

4. **Select the Link or Import option.**

   If you're attaching a style sheet to an HTML file, your best choice is almost always to choose Link, which is the default option. Choose Import if you want to create one master external style sheet that contains references to other style sheets, an advanced option that enables one style sheet to refer to another.

5. **In the Media drop-down list, choose an option.**

   With the Media drop-down list, you can specify the intended use for the style sheet. For example, if you've created a style sheet that formats your page for printing, choose the Print option. You can leave this option blank if you're attaching a style sheet to control the way the page appears in a browser.

6. **Click OK.**

   The dialog box closes, and the external CSS file is automatically linked to the page. Any styles you've defined in the external style sheet appear in the CSS Styles panel, listed under the name of the style sheet, and all the styles automatically become available for use on the page.

You can attach multiple style sheets to the same HTML page. For example, you can save all your text styles in one style sheet, save all your layout styles in another, and then attach both to the same document — which makes all the defined styles available to the page. Similarly, you create different style sheets for different purposes, such as one for printing the file and another for browser display.

Moving, copying, and editing styles

After you attach an external style sheet to a document, you can move, copy, and edit styles as follows:

✔ **Moving styles:** Move any internal styles into the external style sheet by simply clicking the name of a style in an internal style sheet in the CSS Styles panel and dragging it onto the name of an external style sheet. In Figure 5-21, you can see that I'm moving a body style from the internal style sheet, which by default is `<style>`, into the external style sheet `layout.css`. If you have attached more than one external style sheet to a document, you can also move styles from one external style sheet to another using click and drag.

✔ **Copying styles:** You can copy styles from one document to another by right-clicking (Control-clicking on a Mac) a style name in the CSS Styles panel and choosing Copy. Then open the document where you want to add the style, right-click (Control-click on a Mac) the name of an internal or external style sheet in the CSS Styles panel, and choose Paste.

✔ **Editing styles:** You edit styles in an external style sheet the same way you edit styles in an internal style sheet: by clicking or double-clicking the style name in CSS Styles panel. (For more detailed instructions, see the sections in Chapter 6 about editing class styles and editing styles in Dreamweaver's CSS layouts.) Any changes you make to a style in an external style sheet are applied automatically to all the files to which the external style sheet is attached. (Remember: You must upload the style sheet to your Web server for the changes to take effect on the published version of the site.)

Figure 5-21:
Click and drag to move styles from an internal to an external style sheet.

If you want to edit a remote CSS file, download the file to your hard drive before you open it in Dreamweaver. In Dreamweaver, you open `.css` files by double-clicking them or choosing File➪Open, both of which open the style sheet in code view. Code view is the only view available for CSS files because they're text files and have no layout components. When you view an external style sheet this way, you can still use the CSS Styles panel to edit any defined styles — even if the style sheet isn't linked to an HTML page. Be sure to save it when you finish editing it!

If you prefer, you can also edit the code by hand directly in code view. Figure 5-22 shows an example of a style sheet opened directly in Dreamweaver. Notice that the CSS Styles panel displays all relevant style information and gives you access to the CSS editing tools.

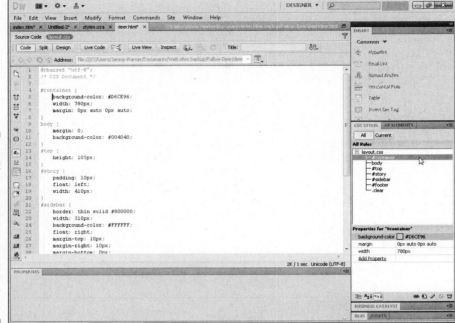

Figure 5-22:
You can edit external style sheets (files with a .css extension) by opening them as you would any other document.

When you edit an external style sheet, you must upload it to your server before you can apply the style changes to pages on your live Web site.

Chapter 6

Creating and Editing CSS Styles

*W*hether you're new to CSS or you've been struggling (I mean *designing*) with styles for years, Dreamweaver's many CSS features offer welcome assistance to even the most experienced designers.

This chapter walks you through the process of creating and applying styles using the class, tag, and ID selectors. You also find instructions for customizing the CSS layouts that are included with Dreamweaver. And you discover not only how to create styles for text, but also how to position and align images, text, and other elements on a Web page (even how to center text and other elements, which is not as easy as you might imagine with CSS).

Finally, you discover how Dreamweaver makes it easy to edit, rename, and even remove styles.

If you're new to CSS or Dreamweaver, before you start this chapter, I recommend that you at least skim through Chapter 5, where you find an introduction to CSS, and a review of the many panels, dialog boxes, and inspectors you can use to create, apply, and edit styles in Dreamweaver.

Brace yourself: You're getting into some of the most complex Web-design features that Dreamweaver has to offer, but I think you'll find the power and precision of these options well worth the effort. If you want to create Web designs that are efficient to create and maintain, display well in a variety of screen sizes, and you want to ensure that your pages meet the latest Web standards — CSS is clearly your best option.

Creating Styles with Class and Tag Selectors

Get ready to create your first styles. I start out with the class and tag selectors in the following sections because they are among the easiest to understand.

As you go through the steps to create a new style in Dreamweaver, you may be surprised by the number of options in the many panels and dialog boxes available for creating CSS. However, you use only a few of the available options to create most styles.

You can always refer to Chapter 5 for more detailed descriptions of the different selector types, as well as the many options in the New CSS Rule and CSS Rule Definition dialog boxes that you can use when you create or edit styles.

Creating styles with the class selector

The class selector can be used to create styles that you can apply to any element on a page and that can be used as many times as you like on the same page. Thus class styles are ideal for defining the formatting of things like photo captions, which may appear in many places in a Web site.

Using styles created with the class selector is a relatively straight-forward process. First, you create a new style using the class selector and give it a name; then you apply it to an element on the page by selecting that style name from the Class drop-down list in the Property inspector. In this section, you find step-by-step instructions for creating a style with the class selector, and in the next section, you see how to format text by applying a style created with the class selector. These same instructions can be used to create and apply any class style in Dreamweaver.

You can always refer to Chapter 5 for a general description of each style selector type (class, ID, tag, and compound) as well as tips about how and when each is best used.

To define a new class style, create a new document or open an existing file, and then follow these steps:

1. **Choose Format➪CSS Styles➪New.**

   Alternatively, you can click the New CSS Rule icon at the bottom of the CSS Styles panel.

   The New CSS Rule dialog box appears, as shown in Figure 6-1.

Figure 6-1: The New CSS Rule dialog box.

2. **Choose a selector type.**

   To create a class style, choose (you guessed it) Class from the Selector Type drop-down list.

3. **In the Selector Name field, type a new name for the style beginning with a dot (.).**

   For this example, I type **.caption**.

   You can name a class style anything you like, as long as you don't use spaces or punctuation, but class style names must begin with a dot (.). If you choose the Class option and neglect to enter a dot at the beginning of the name, Dreamweaver adds one for you when you click OK.

4. **From the Rule Definition drop-down list, choose where you want to create the selector.**

   Choose This Document Only (which is what I choose in this example) to create the new style in an internal style sheet. An internal style sheet applies only to the current page, which means the style can only be used to format elements in the document you have open in Dreamweaver. When you select this option, the style is created and added to the top of the open HTML page in the `<head>` section.

If you prefer, you can choose the New Style Sheet File option to create a new external style sheet as you create the style, or you can use the drop-down list to select any existing external style sheet already attached to the page and add the new style to it.

Note: If you create a style as an internal style, you can move it to an external style sheet later. (You find instructions for editing and moving styles at the end of Chapter 5.)

5. **Click OK.**

   The CSS Rule Definition dialog box opens, as shown in Figure 6-2.

6. **Choose a category from the left of the CSS Rule Definition dialog box.**

   For this example, I chose the Type category, as shown in Figure 6-2. (For a detailed description of each category, refer to the section about comparing CSS rule options in Chapter 5.)

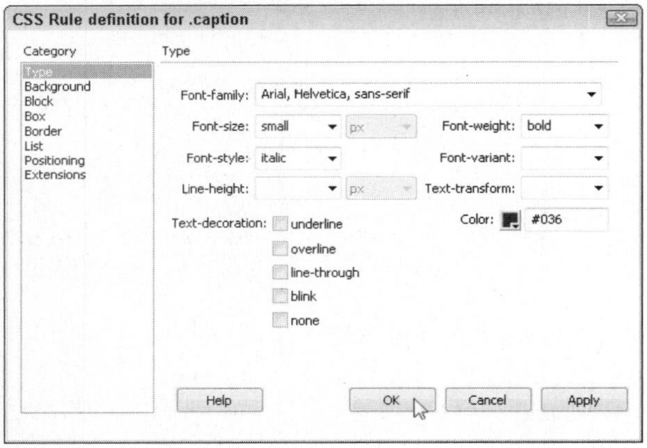

Figure 6-2:
The Type category of the CSS Rule Definition dialog box.

7. **Choose the formatting options you want to include in your class selector.**

   For my sample style, I made the following choices:

   • **In the Font-Family field, you can choose a font list collection from the drop-down list or enter the name of a font.** As you see in Figure 6-2, I chose Arial, Helvetica, sans-serif. To use a font that isn't included, choose the Edit Font List option from the drop-down list and create a new font list using your own fonts. Just beware that your visitors will see the font only if that font is installed on their computers, which is why Dreamweaver includes collections of commonly used fonts. (For more on using fonts on the Web, see the section, "Why so many fonts?" in Chapter 5.)

- **In the Font-Size drop-down list, I chose the size for my caption style.** For this example, I chose Small to create a style that will make the text appear smaller than the rest of the text on the page (which is set to Medium by default). You can specify text sizes in pixels, picas, mm, and several other measurements. (For an explanation of options, see the section "Understanding CSS size options," in Chapter 5.)

- **In the Font-Style drop-down list, I chose Italic as the font style.**

- **In the Font-Weight drop-down list, I chose Bold for the weight.**

- **To choose a color for the style, I clicked the color well.** Sticking to the default color swatches in the color well (the square icon) is certainly the quickest way to choose a color, but you can also create custom colors by clicking the icon that looks like a rainbow-colored globe in the upper-right corner of the color well and selecting a color from the System Color Picker. For this example, I chose a dark blue color.

8. **Click OK.**

   The new style name is added to the CSS Styles panel (as shown in Figure 6-3, a little later in this chapter). If the new style isn't visible, click the plus sign (+) (or triangle on the Mac) next to the `<style>` tag to reveal the rules in the current style.

When you create a class style, such as the `.caption` style in this example, it's also added to the Class drop-down list in the Property inspector, as you see in the following section.

Applying class styles in Dreamweaver

Defining class styles in Dreamweaver is the time-*consuming* part. Applying them after you define them is the time-*saving* part. How you apply a style depends on the kind of style you've created. To apply a class style in Dreamweaver, follow these steps:

1. **Open an existing document or create a new one. After you add some text, click and drag to select the text or other element to which you want to apply a style.**

   In this example, I've selected the text under the photograph in the page shown in Figure 6-3.

2. **In the Property inspector (with the HTML features displayed), select the style from the Class drop-down list.**

Figure 6-3:
To apply a class style, select the text or other element in the main workspace, and then choose the style from the Class drop-down list in the Property inspector.

Notice that Dreamweaver provides a preview of the style by formatting the name in the drop-down list based on the specified options in the style definition (in this example, the .caption style is displayed as bold, italic, and green). When you choose a style, the selected text or other element changes automatically in the Document window to reflect the application of the style. Figure 6-3 shows the caption style created in the previous section applied to the text below the photograph.

Creating styles with the CSS tag selector

In addition to creating new class styles, you can create styles that add or alter the rules of existing HTML tags. These styles are created using the tag selector, which is also known as the element selector. When you create a style in the New CSS Rule dialog box using the tag selector option, you can alter the appearance, position, and other features of an existing HTML tag.

Many HTML tags already include formatting options. For example, the heading tags include formatting to style text in large and bold. So, when you create a style with a tag selector, you have to consider the formatting options already associated with that tag. Any options you specify in the CSS Rule Definition dialog box will either be added to the existing formatting, or will override the formatting. For example, in the steps that follow, I create a CSS rule for the <h1> tag by changing the font to Georgia, which will take the place of the default font Times — but I don't need to include bold in the style definition to make the text bold because bold is in the default style of the <h1> HTML tag.

When you create a style for an existing HTML tag, you don't need to apply the style for the formatting to change the way you do with class styles. Wherever you've used the HTML tag, the style definition settings are applied automatically. Thus, when you create a style and define the font for the <h1> tag as Georgia, any text formatted with the <h1> tag will change to Georgia.

You may ask, "Why would I redefine the <h1> tag instead of just creating a new headline style as a class style?" Although you can define a new class style instead of redefining and HTML tag, sometimes using an existing HTML tag is better. Heading styles are especially important on the Web because text formatted in an <h1> tag is well recognized as the most important text on a page. Among other things, text formatted in an <h1> tag may get special consideration from search engines.

To redefine an HTML tag (such as the <h1> tag) with the tag selector, create a new file or open an existing one and then follow these steps:

1. **Choose Format⇨CSS Styles⇨New.**

   Alternatively, you can right-click (Control-click a Mac) anywhere in the CSS Styles panel and choose New, or you can click the New CSS Rule icon at the bottom right of the CSS Styles panel. The icon looks like a small plus (+) sign.

   The New CSS Rule dialog box opens, as shown in Figure 6-4.

2. **Choose Tag from the Selector Type drop-down list.**

3. **Choose the HTML tag you want to redefine from the Selector Name drop-down list.**

   You can also type to enter the name of a tag into the Selector Name field. In this example, I typed **h1** to redefine the <h1> heading tag.

4. **From the Rule Definition drop-down list, choose to add the style to an internal or external style sheet.**

   In this example, I choose to add the new style to an external style sheet. In this case, I've already attached a style sheet named slides.css to this page so it's easy to add the new style. In Figure 6-4, you can see that I'm selecting the slides.css file from the Rule Definition drop-down list at the bottom of the dialog box. You can choose the New Style Sheet File option to create a new external style sheet as you create the style, or you can select This Document Only to add the new style to an internal style sheet.

You can attach an external style sheet to any or all of the pages in a Web site. When you select this option, the style is created and added to a separate CSS file. If you edit a style in an external style sheet, any changes you make will be applied to all the pages that style sheet is attached to where that style (or HTML tag) is used.

5. **Click OK.**

The CSS Rule Definition dialog box opens.

6. **Choose a category and specify the options you want to use to redefine the new tag style.**

For this example, I redefined the <h1> tag to use the Georgia font instead of the default browser font, changed the size to extra large, and changed the text color to dark green.

7. **Click OK.**

Any text or other element you've formatted with the HTML tag immediately changes to reflect the formatting in the new definition of the tag's style.

If you want the ability to use the same HTML tag with different formatting in different parts of the same page, you can create compound styles, as described in Chapter 5. This works well, for example, if you want text formatted with the <h2> tag to look different in the main part of your page than it does in a sidebar.

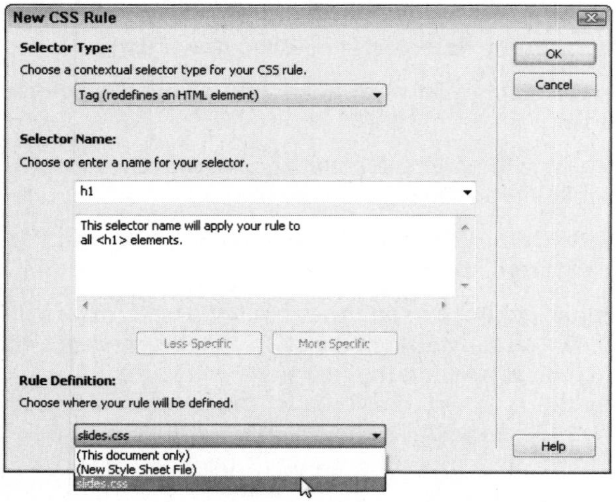

Figure 6-4:
Use the tag selector to redefine an existing HTML tag (such as <h1>) and to save the new style to an external style sheet.

Creating Layouts with CSS and Div Tags

The key to understanding how CSS works in a page layout is to think in terms of designing with a series of infinitely adjustable containers, or *boxes*. Indeed, this approach to Web design is commonly called the *box model*.

Think of the box model this way: First you use XHTML tags, such as the `<div>` (*div*ision) tag or `<p>` (*p*aragraph) tag, to create boxes around each section of your content. Then you use CSS to style each box, using CSS rules to control the position and alignment of each box by specifying such settings as Margin, Padding, Float, and Border. The combined effect is one beautiful page, created by combining CSS styles with XHTML tags.

Although you can use any XHTML tag as part of your page layout, the `<div>` tag is used most often to create the boxes for main sections of a page, such as the banner area, commonly used at the top of a page, the main content area, sidebars, and footer. Think of `<div>` tags as generic containers designed to contain text, images, or other content. Essentially, `<div>` tags create divisions on the page, separating one section of content from another. Unlike other HTML tags, `<div>` has no inherent formatting features. Unless CSS is applied to a `<div>` tag, it's invisible on a page when viewed in most Web browsers; yet the tag has a powerful purpose because you can easily format with CSS any content surrounded by opening and closing `<div>` tags.

Adobe uses the box model to create all the CSS layouts included in Dreamweaver. In these layouts, each `<div>` tag in the page has a corresponding style. As a result, to change the size or positioning of the header, footer, or any of the other main areas of the page separated by `<div>` tags, you need to edit the corresponding style. You find detailed instructions for how to identify and edit these styles in the sections that follow.

Splitting the view

If you're creating a series of `<div>` tags to position content on a Web page, you may find it easier to keep track of the `<div>` tags if you use Dreamweaver's split view, as shown in this figure. Split view enables you to see the code view and design view simultaneously. To split the workspace area, choose View⇨Code and Design or click the Split View button, located just under the Insert panel at the top of the workspace.

If you select an image, text, or another element on a page in design view, it's highlighted automatically in code view — a great feature that makes it easier to find your place in the code

(continued)

(continued)

when you're trying to troubleshoot what's happening behind the scenes.

I like to use split view to keep an eye on the code as I create page designs — especially when I'm

inserting `<div>` tags. When you're using only design view, keeping track of how `<div>` tags are arranged and nested can be hard.

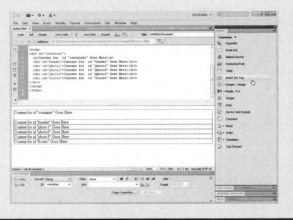

Using Dreamweaver's CSS Layouts

Dreamweaver includes a collection of CSS layouts you can customize to create a seemingly infinite variety of page designs. These layouts give you a head start when you create a new page; they're designed to work well in a variety of Web browsers, so they can help you avoid common problems caused by the different ways Web browsers display CSS. For all these reasons, I almost always recommend starting your design work in Dreamweaver with a CSS layout chosen in the New Document window.

One of the challenges with CSS is that it's still a relatively new addition to the world of Web design, and it continues to change. Unfortunately, browser support — which can make the difference between a beautiful Web page and a jumbled, unreadable design — hasn't always kept up, and the companies that make browsers haven't always agreed on how to display CSS. (You find more about browser differences and testing in Chapter 4.)

To help you get around the problems caused by browser differences, Adobe dedicated the equivalent of decades of time (at least in Internet years) to designing a collection of CSS layouts designed to display well in many different Web browsers. Whether you're creating a simple XHMTL page, using Dreamweaver's templates, or designing advanced database-driven sites with PHP, you're sure to appreciate the benefits of starting your page designs with one of Dreamweaver's prestyled layouts.

Before you rush off to check out all the cool CSS layouts included in Dreamweaver, let me warn you: They're not much to look at when you first open them. They're intentionally designed with the most basic of formatting options and a dull color scheme — but fortunately color styles are some of the easiest to alter in CSS.

No matter what your experience level, the following sections are designed to help you appreciate how Dreamweaver's CSS layouts work, and to help you create your own page designs by customizing the layouts step by step. You find out how to change the width of columns, the formatting styles for text, and the alignment of any element on the page in one of Dreamweaver's layouts. If you're new to CSS, altering one of these layouts may seem confusing at first, but trust me: it's certainly easier than creating a design from scratch. (If you haven't read Chapter 5 yet, you can skim that chapter to get a handle on the basics before you begin working with Dreamweaver's CSS layouts.)

Comparing CSS layout options

Dreamweaver includes a variety of CSS layouts, designed with two distinct approaches to CSS. When you create a new page with one of these layouts, the first thing you must do is decide which type you want to use. Essentially, you have two options:

- ✔ **Liquid layouts** are designed to expand and contract depending on the size of the browser window.

- ✔ **Fixed layouts** are centered within the browser and set to a width of 960 pixels. (As you discover in the next section, you can change the width by editing the corresponding style.) In the examples shown in the upcoming Figure 6-6, I've selected a design that creates a two-column, fixed layout, with a left sidebar, header, and footer.

In general, fixed layouts give you greater control over your design and are an easier option to start with because you have better control of positioning the elements on a page. However, liquid designs do have advantages. Because liquid designs are designed to be flexible, they adapt to fit many different screen sizes.

Creating a new page with a CSS layout

To create a new page using one of Dreamweaver's CSS layouts, follow these instructions:

1. **Choose File⊏>New.**

   The New Document dialog box appears (see Figure 6-5).

2. **Choose Blank Page from the left column and HTML from the Page Type column in the middle.**

   Alternatively, you can choose an option in the bottom part of the Page Type section that corresponds to the programming language used on your site, such as ASP.NET, PHP, or ColdFusion, and then progress to Step 3. (If you're not familiar with these programming options, stick with HTML.)

3. **Select any of the CSS layouts listed in the Layout section.**

   For this example, I chose 2 Column Fixed, Left Sidebar, Header and Footer.

   Notice in Figure 6-5, that when you select a CSS layout, a preview of the layout is displayed at the top right of the dialog box.

Figure 6-5:
When you select the name of a CSS layout in the New Document dialog box, a preview appears in the top-right corner.

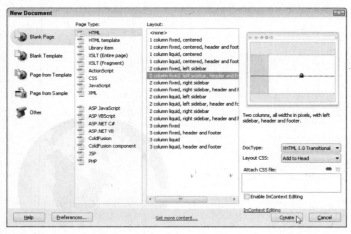

4. **From the Layout CSS drop-down list, choose the type of style sheet you want to create as you design the page.**

   • Choose Add to Head to create an internal style sheet and include all the styles for the layout in the Head area of the new document.

   • Choose Create New File to create a new external style sheet with all the page styles as you create the new document with the design.

   • Choose Link to Existing File to add the style sheet information for the new document to an existing external style sheet.

   Note: You can always change how the style sheet is set up later by moving styles from an internal style sheet to an external one or from one external style sheet to another. (You can find instructions for creating external style sheets and moving styles at the end of Chapter 5.)

5. **Click Create.**

   The new page is created and opened in the main workspace.

Why Dreamweaver's CSS layouts use class styles instead of ID styles with <div> tags

Although there's no hard and fast rule, the common practice is to combine ID styles with <div> tags to create the main sections of a page when you create a layout using CSS. The differences among style selectors are covered in more detail in Chapter 5, but essentially, ID styles are best used for elements that will only appear once per page, such as the main sections of a page, which are commonly identified as the container, header, and footer of a page.

In contrast, class styles can be used multiple times on each page so they are more versatile and ideal for styles you want to use over and over, such as a style for the caption under a photo, or a style that adds alignment to elements.

If you study the code behind Web pages on the Internet (you can do this by choosing View⇨Page Source in Firefox, or View⇨Source in Internet Explorer), you'll quickly discover that Web pages are created in many, many different ways; not everyone follows the same rules.

The designer who created the CSS layouts in Dreamweaver decided that it was simpler and more versatile to create these layouts using class styles, so you won't see ID styles in the style sheets at all.

Again, it's not wrong to use only class styles, but that's different from the approach many people use on Web sites these days. To help you appreciate both approaches, this chapter shows you how to edit the class styles used for the main content areas in the Dreamweaver CSS layouts, and how to use ID styles for this purpose when you create a custom CSS layout.

6. **Choose File⇨Save to save the page and styles.**

If you saved the styles in an external style sheet, a second box prompts you to save the style sheet separately. If the styles are contained in an internal style sheet, they're saved automatically when you save the page.

It's important to save all the pages of a Web site, including external styles sheets, in your local site folder. (For more about defining a Web site and specifying a local site folder in Dreamweaver, see Chapter 2.)

Editing the styles in a CSS layout

After you create a new page with a CSS layout, you have a seemingly infinite number of options for editing it, but first you have to determine which styles in the style sheet correspond to the elements you want to edit.

In this example, I've chosen a fixed-width layout, so I know I need a style that specifies the fixed width for the entire layout. Following a common practice of using `<div>` tags to contain elements on a page and using styles to describe how they should be displayed, every CSS layout in Dreamweaver includes a `<div>` tag with a style named `.container`. To change the width of a design, change the corresponding `.container` style, as shown in this section.

The steps in the following sections explain how to edit the overall design of a page created with a Dreamweaver CSS layout. I've broken the process into several step lists to help you following along more easily. *Note:* The steps assume you're proceeding through the sections in order.

As you can probably imagine, you can edit the styles in a CSS layout in many ways to create your own designs, but the process I explain in the following sections should serve you well as you get started with any of these layouts.

After you adjust the existing styles to get the basic page design the way you want it, you can create as many additional styles as you desire. For example, in my example in this section, I delete the `<div>` tags and styles in the sidebar that are included in this layout to create a row of vertical links. Instead, I want links across the top of the page, just under the banner (which you learn to create in the section "Creating a Navigation Bar from an Unordered List of Links," later in this chapter).

Checking out the available styles and making basic edits

You can use these same basic instructions with any CSS layout included in Dreamweaver. To edit styles in a CSS layout, follow these steps:

1. **Open a page file that's based in a Dreamweaver CSS layout, and choose Window⇨CSS Styles (or click the CSS Styles button to expand the panel).**

   The CSS Styles panel opens or expands, as shown in Figure 6-6.

2. **Click the plus (+) sign (or a triangle on a Mac) next to the style sheet name to open the list of styles.**

   All the styles associated with the new page are listed.

   To change any element in the design of this page, you edit the corresponding style.

3. **Select the name of any style listed in the CSS Styles panel.**

   The corresponding CSS rules defined for the style are displayed in the Properties pane at the bottom of the CSS Styles panel, as shown in Figure 6-6. Clicking through the list of styles and reviewing their corresponding rules is a good way to get a quick overview of the design and to see where the various page-formatting options are stored.

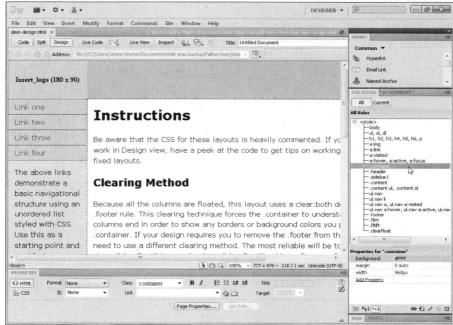

Figure 6-6:
Alter any
style in a
CSS layout
by editing a
style defini-
tion in the
CSS Styles
panel.

The styles named `.container`, `.header`, `.sidebar1`, `.content`, and `.footer`, are the styles that control the main sections of the page. For example, the style named `.container`, which is shown in Figure 6-6, includes a rule that makes the entire design area 960 pixels wide. Thus, to change the width of the page, you'd change that setting. (You find detailed instructions for editing the `.container` and other main styles in this CSS layout in the section, "Customizing the content areas" later in this chapter.) As explained in the nearby sidebar "Why Dreamweaver's CSS layouts use class styles instead of ID styles with `<div>` tags," Dreamweaver CS5 includes no ID styles in the CSS layouts.

Editing page-wide settings

To edit page-wide settings — such as the background color of the page, or the main font face, size, and color of the text used throughout the page — follow these steps:

1. **Double-click the style for the `<body>` tag in the CSS Styles panel.**

   The CSS Rule Definition dialog box opens with the rules for the `<body>` tag style displayed, as shown in Figure 6-7.

2. **Select the Type category from the options at the left in the dialog box, and change or add your desired Font settings.**

You can change the font face, size, style, and weight. To change the space between lines of text, change the line height.

3. **Select the Background category and use the color well in the Background-Color field to specify a color for the entire background of the page.**

   Alternatively, you can enter any hexadecimal color code manually in the Background-Color field. To add a background image, click the Browse button to the right of the Background-image field and select the image you want to serve as the background. Use the Background-repeat drop-down list to specify how the background image should repeat (if at all) on the page.

4. **Click the Apply button to preview your changes and then click OK to save the changes and close the dialog box.**

Figure 6-7:
Defining
page-wide
settings
(such as
background
color, main
font face,
size, and
color) in the
style for the
<body> tag.

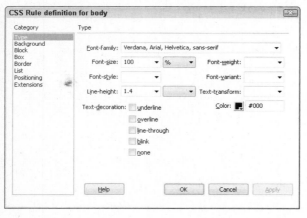

Customizing the content areas

To change the width or other settings of the main content areas, which control the overall size of the page, as well as the header, footer, and sidebar, follow these steps:

1. **To change the width of the entire main design area, double-click the** `.container` **style in the CSS Styles panel.**

   You open the `.container` style in the CSS Rule Definition dialog box. If you click once to select a style (such as the `.container` style), your choice's style definition appears in the Properties pane (refer to Figure 6-6), where you can also edit the style.

2. **Select the Box category on the left of the CSS Rule Definition dialog box.**

   The box settings open in the dialog box, as shown in Figure 6-8.

3. **Select a size in the width field or type a new number for your desired page width.**

   In this example, I selected the width, which was set to 960, and I changed it to 780. When you alter the width of the `.container` style, as I did here, you change the width of the entire design because all the other `<div>` tags are contained within the `<div>` that's formatted with the `.container` style — and they're all set to expand to fill the `.container <div>`. (For more on the best width for a Web page, see the nearby sidebar "How wide should I make my Web page's design?")

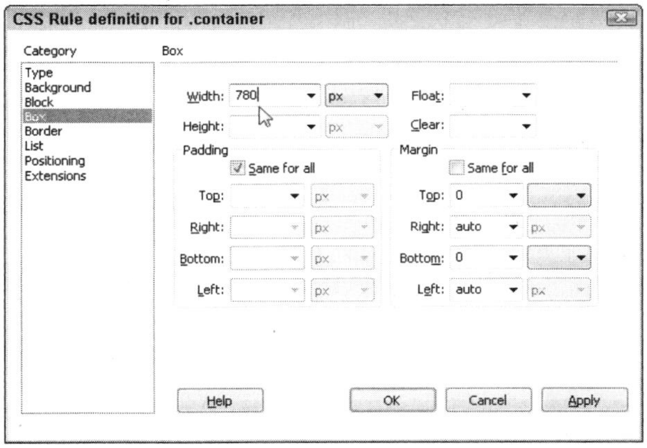

Figure 6-8:
To change the width of the design, use the Box category in the CSS Rule Definition dialog box to the edit the style `.container`.

4. **Click Apply to preview the changes. Click OK to save the changes and close the dialog box.**

   The new size is applied automatically to the `.container <div>` — and the page layout changes.

   Reducing the width of the `.container <div>`, causes the `.content <div>` to drop below the sidebar because the `.content <div>` is now too wide for the space created by the `.container`. This is a common problem, because when you change one style, you often affect elements controlled by other styles. The next step explains how to fix the problem.

5. **Double-click the** `.content` **style in the CSS Styles panel.**

   The `.content` style opens in the CSS Rule Definition dialog box. Choose the Box category again; this time, reduce the width of the `.content` style.

   If you're wondering what size to make the width of the content style, consider this: It's set to 780 pixels wide. You've just reduced the overall layout of the page from 960 to 780 — by 180 pixels. So if you reduce the size of the `.content` style by 180 pixels, it should fit and pop right back into place. That means setting the width to 600 pixels — assuming you don't want to change the width of the left sidebar.

6. **To change the background color of any style on the page, double-click the corresponding style and select the Background category in the CSS Rule Definition dialog box.**

   In the CSS layout I'm using in this example, the sidebar is defined in a style named `.sidebar1`. Thus, to change the background color, I double-clicked `.sidebar1` in the CSS Styles panel to open it in the CSS Rule Definition dialog box. Then I selected the Background category and clicked the color well (as shown in Figure 6-9) to change the color. (***Note:*** Changing the background color of the sidebar will not change the color of the links at the top of the sidebar in this layout. Move on to the next step to find out how to edit those.)

Figure 6-9:
Changing background color for part of the design by opening the corresponding style, selecting Background, and choosing a color from the color well.

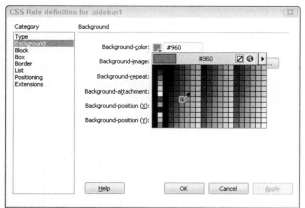

7. **To change the links in the top of the left sidebar, double-click the compound style** `ul.nav a, ul.nav a:visited` **to open it in the CSS Rule Definition dialog box.**

   Again, select the Background category and use the color well to change the color. Select the Box category to change the width or adjust the padding. (See "Comparing Margins and Padding in CSS," later in this chapter, for more on these design elements.)

8. **To edit the section at the top of the page, double-click the** `header` **style in the CSS Styles panel.**

   Select the Background category and use the color well to change the color. Select the Box category to change the width or adjust the padding.

9. **To add an image to the banner, simply double-click the placeholder image labeled Insert Logo and select any image using the Select Image Source dialog box, shown in Figure 6-10.**

10. **Replace text and insert images in the sidebar and main content areas.**

    You can add or replace text and insert images in any page created from a CSS layout, just as you would in any other Web page.

11. **Choose File➪Save to save the page and styles.**

    If you saved the styles in an external style sheet, you're prompted by a second dialog box to save the style sheet separately. If the styles are contained in an internal style sheet, they're saved automatically when you save the page.

You can combine CSS layouts with Dreamweaver's template features to create a template — a page design you can use to create additional pages without repeating all the steps to customize the styles for each page. (As you discover in Chapter 7, Dreamweaver's template features offer many advantages when you're designing a site with more than a few pages; for example, you can make changes that affect many pages at once.)

Here's a related tip: If you intend to use the design as a template, make sure you save your styles in an external style sheet so you can edit the style rules outside the template. (Find instructions for creating external style sheets and for moving internal styles into an external style sheet in Chapter 5.)

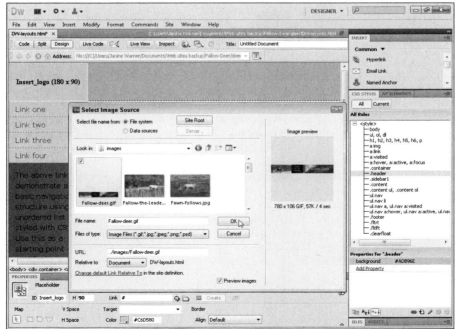

Figure 6-10:
The Select
Image
Source
dialog box.

Creating compound styles

Compound styles make it possible to create more specific styles. These have many uses, but one of my favorites is the ability to create tag styles that appear differently in different parts of the same page.

When you redefine a tag (as with the unordered list and link tags), the new style applies to all uses of that tag within a page, unless you define the tag as a compound style by including the name of its container in the style name.

For example, in the "Creating a Navigation Bar from an Unordered List of Links" section, instead of creating a new tag style with just the name of the `<ul>` tag, I created a compound style called `#navbar ul` to redefine the `<ul>` tag *only* when it's contained within a `<div>` tag with an ID of `navbar`.

When you create compound styles like this, make sure you separate each style name by a single space. In this example, I also created styles for the `<li>` and `<link>` tags in the same way, creating styles with names like `#navbar a:link`, `#navbar a:hover`, and `#navbar ul li`. You can create compound styles with multiple tags and style names to create more specific CSS rules.

Creating a Navigation Bar from an Unordered List of Links

Here's a great CSS trick for turning a bulleted list (or unordered list) into a navigation bar with a simple rollover effect. Using a bulleted list for navigation bars is a well-accepted convention for Web sites that meet current accessibility standards. A bulleted list is a logical choice for navigation elements; even if the style rules are removed, the links still stand out from the rest of the elements on the page and are clearly grouped together in a list. In Figures 6-11 and 6-12, you see how the same page appears with and without the styles applied to the content. In Figure 6-11, you see links contained in an unordered list. In Figure 6-12, those same links are still contained in the unordered list, but the CSS styles change their appearance dramatically.

Thanks to CSS, you can gain the benefits of styling a list of links with the unordered list tag and still format your links with any style you choose. That way you don't have to keep those boring bullets and can align your links horizontally or vertically. Using CSS instead of images to create a rollover effect (like the one featured in the following steps) not only makes your page more accessible, but also helps your page load faster.

As you figure out different design tricks, like the navigation bar I explain in this section, you may find it helpful to see other pages without the styles applied, as you do in Figure 6-11. In Firefox, you can turn off the styles on any page that uses CSS by choosing View⇨Page Style⇨No Style. As you see in Figure 6-11, when the styles are turned off, the page looks very different. In Figure 6-12, you see how the styles cause the `<div>` tags to align so the three photos appear side by side in three columns. Similarly, the styles make the navigation links appear as a horizontal row instead of an unordered list.

You can use the following steps to add a list of links to any CSS layout included in Dreamweaver, as well as to any custom CSS layout you create yourself.

To create a navigation bar using CSS to redefine the unordered list and link tags, follow these steps:

1. **Click to place your cursor where you want to create your navigation bar in the page.**

   When you're creating a list of links to serve as your navigation bar, it's good practice to position those links at the top or side of the page where visitors to your site can find them easily.

Figure 6-11:
To view the same Web page with styles turned on or off, choose View⇨Page Style⇨No Style the Firefox browser. Here the styles are turned off.

Figure 6-12: This is the same page shown in Figure 6-11, but the styles are turned on.

2. **Enter the text you want to serve as the links, separated by paragraph returns.**

   Be sure you use a paragraph return to separate each text block that you want to link; each link will be on a separate line and easy to format as an unordered list.

   You can type any text you want, but it's generally recommended that you keep the main navigation links in your site very short. For example, use a single word when possible (such as "Home") instead of something longer (such as "The front page of the site").

3. **Create links by selecting each piece of text in turn, clicking the Hyperlink icon in the Common Insert panel, and then selecting the page you want to link to, or entering any URL.**

   Essentially, you set these links as you would set any other links in your site. (You find more detailed instructions for creating a variety of different types of links, including links to other Web sites and e-mail links, in Chapter 2.)

4. **Click and drag to select the entire set of links, and then click the Unordered List icon in the Property inspector, as shown in Figure 6-13.**

   A bullet point appears at the beginning of each link. If any link isn't set off with a separate bullet, click to delete the space between it and the link before it, and then press Return or Enter to separate the links with a paragraph return (which will be automatically converted into a bullet in the unordered list).

5. **To add a `<div>` tag around a list of links (or any other content that is already on a page, click to select the content and then click the Insert Div Tag icon in the Common Insert panel.**

The Insert Div Tag dialog box opens.

Adding a `<div>` tag around the unordered list of links is helpful if you want to add formatting, such as the background color that fills the entire navigation row in this example.

6. **Choose Wrap Around Selection from the Insert drop-down list, as shown in Figure 6-14.**

For more precise control over where you add a new `<div>` tag, you can choose options from the Insert drop-down list at the top of the Insert Div Tag dialog box. Choosing the Wrap Around Selection option, for example, adds open and close `<div>` tags to the code before and after the content you've selected. In this case, that's the bulleted list of links.

7. **Enter a name in the Class field or the ID field and click OK.**

A `<div>` tag with the class or ID name you entered is added automatically to the page surrounding the list of links.

In this example, I chose to create a class style with the name `.navbar` (as shown in Figure 6-14) by choosing Wrap Around Selection as described in Step 6.

You can create a class or ID style to format the `<div>` tag that surrounds your list of links. If you plan to have only one navigation bar on the page, an ID style is a good option. If you plan to repeat the navigation bar in more than one place (as I've done in this example by adding a navigation bar to the top and bottom of the page), it's a good idea to create a class style so you can use it twice on the same page. (***Remember:*** ID styles can be used only once per page, but if you create a class style, the navigation bars will be formatted exactly the same each time you use that class style.)

Figure 6-13:
Formatting a collection of links as an unordered list.

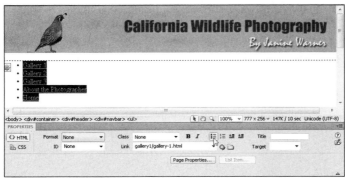

Figure 6-14:
Adding a
<div> tag
around
content to
create a
class style.

Insert Div Tag

Insert: Wrap around selectior ▾

Class: .navbar ▾

ID: ▾

New CSS Rule

OK

Cancel

Help

8. **Click the New CSS Rule button at the bottom of the CSS Styles panel to define the new style name you entered when you added the <div> tag.**

    The New CSS Rule dialog box opens.

9. **Choose the option from the Selector Type drop-down list that corresponds with the type of style you want to create.**

    In this example, I'm creating a class style to go with the class name (.navbar) that I gave to the new <div> tag. If I had chosen to add an ID instead of a class in Step 7, I would choose ID from the drop-down list to create a corresponding style.

10. **Enter the name of the style and click OK.**

    The CSS Rule Definition dialog box opens.

    Note: You must enter the name exactly as you typed it when you created the <div> tag. In this example, I entered **.navbar**.

    If your cursor was in the <div> when you clicked the New CSS Rule button, the name is already entered in the Selector Name field. Unless you want to be very specific with this style, I suggest you delete any other code that might appear and enter only the name of the style: **.navbar** if it's a class style or **#navbar** if it's an ID style.

11. **Specify your desired settings for color, background, size, margins, and padding.**

    For the .navbar style shown in this example, I set the font size to small, and the background color to dark blue. I also added 5 pixels of padding to the top and bottom so the dark blue background would extend above and below the links.

12. **Click Apply to preview the style. Click OK to save the style and close the dialog box.**

    The formatting options you specified are applied automatically to the <div> tag around the links.

13. **To create a style that will affect only this unordered list, you create a compound style that includes the class name** .navbar. **To do so, follow these steps:**

    a. **Choose Format⇨CSS Styles⇨New.**

    b. **Under Selector Type, choose Compound.**

    c. **In the Selector Name field, enter** .navbar ul, **as shown in Figure 6-15, and then click OK.**

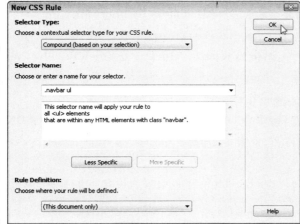

Figure 6-15: Create a compound style to redefine any existing HTML tag in only a specified area of the page.

    d. **In the CSS Rule Definition dialog box, choose the Box category and set margins and padding to** 0.

    e. **Select the Same for All check box for both margins and padding to remove the margins and padding included in the** <ul> **XHTML tag.**

    f. **Click OK to save the style and close the dialog box.**

    The spacing around the list of links that was formatted as an unordered list disappears.

14. **Create a new compound style to redefine the list item tag by following these steps:**

    a. **Choose Format⇨CSS Styles⇨New.**

    b. **Under Selector Type, choose Compound.**

    c. **In the Selector Name field, enter** .navbar ul li **(make sure to include spaces between each name) and then click OK.**

    d. In the CSS Rule Definition dialog box, select the Block category and set Display to Inline.

    This changes the style of the `<li>` tag from vertical to horizontal.

    e. Select the List category and set Type to None to remove the bullet.

    f. Select the Box category and set margins left and right to 20 pixels.

    This separates the list items from one another in the horizontal list. You can change the setting to any measurement to create the amount of space between links that best fits your design.

    g. Click OK to save these settings and close the dialog box.

15. **Create a new style to redefine the link tag by following these steps:**

    a. Choose Format⇨CSS Styles⇨New.

    b. Under Selector Type, choose Compound.

    c. In the Tag field, enter .navbar a:link and then click OK.

    You can make this style as specific as you choose. For example, the style `.navbar a:link` will change the appearance of any links in the `.navbar <div>`. However, if you create the style `.navbar ul li a:link`, that style will apply only to links that appear in the `.navbar <div>` and inside the unordered list tags. Because these are the only links I use in the `.navbar <div>`, I don't need to be so specific; both styles will work the same in this example.

    d. In the CSS Rule Definition dialog box, select the Type category and set Text-decoration to None by selecting the None check box.

    This removes the underline from linked text.

    e. While still in the Type category, choose a color from the color well to specify what color the links will be when they're first loaded on a page.

    Here I set the text color to an off-white.

    f. Click OK to save these settings and close the dialog box.

16. **Create a new style to redefine the hover-link tag so that the link color will change when a user rolls a cursor over the link:**

    a. Choose Format⇨CSS Styles⇨New.

    b. Under Selector Type, choose Compound.

    c. In the Tag field, enter .navbar a:hover and then click OK.

    Again, I could create a more specific compound link by entering **.navbar ul li a:hover**, but it's not necessary here.

d. In the CSS Rule Definition dialog box, select the Type category and set Text-decoration to None by clicking the check box.

This removes the underline from linked text. If you prefer to have the underline appear when a user rolls a cursor over a link, check Underline.

e. While still in the Type category, choose a color from the color well to specify what color a link will be when users roll their cursors over the link.

Here I set the text color to a bright yellow. The more dramatic the color difference between the a:link and a:hover colors, the more dramatic the rollover effect.

f. Click OK to save these settings and close the dialog box.

17. **Create a new style to redefine the visited link tag so the link color changes after a user clicks a link:**

a. **Choose Format⇨CSS Styles⇨New.**

b. **Under Selector Type, choose Compound.**

c. **In the Tag field, enter** .navbar a:visited **and then click OK.**

d. **In the CSS Rule Definition dialog box, choose the Type category and set Text-decoration to None by clicking the check box.**

e. **While still in the Type category, choose a color from the color well to specify a link's color after it's been visited.**

Here I set the text color to a light gray. If you want the color to remain the same, set the a:visited link to the same color as the a:link.

f. **Click OK to save these settings and close the dialog box.**

18. **Click the Live View button at the top of the workspace or click the Preview button to view the page in a browser to see the effect of the link styles, as shown in Figure 6-16.**

Figure 6-16:
To preview your links, click the Live View button, or preview the page in a Web browser.

Comparing block and inline elements

As a general rule, HTML tags can be divided into block elements and inline elements. *Block elements,* such as the `<div>` tag, interrupt the flow of the page, creating a box or block around which other page elements align. In HTML, block elements include the paragraph (`<p>`) tag, which creates a line break before and after it's used and doesn't allow anything to appear alongside it. Heading tags, such as `<h1>`, `<h2>`, and `<h3>`, and list tags, such as `<ul>` and `<ol>`, are also block elements.

In contrast, *inline elements* follow the flow with text. For example, the `<strong>` and `<em>` tags, which apply bold and italics respectively, are inline elements. You can place these elements one after another, and a new line break doesn't appear between each element. They simply flow with the text. For that reason, the `<span>` tag, which is an inline element, is a good choice for applying styles that you want to affect a small amount of text within a block, such as when you want to add a little color to text contained within `<p>` tags. Because of this, Dreamweaver often adds `<span>` tags when you apply a class style to text in the middle of a paragraph.

Comparing Margins and Padding in CSS

When creating or editing CSS styles, new Web designers are often confused by how and when to use margins and padding. Both of these settings add space between elements — for example, a margin between text and an image or a little padding between the border of a `<div>` tag and its contents. Here's how margins and padding work:

- **Padding** adds space inside an element. Think of padding as a way to add a cushion around the inside of a box so your content doesn't bump into the sides of your box.

- **Margins** add space outside an element. Think of margins as a way to add space between boxes, on the sides of images, or around any other element on a page, so things don't bump into each other.

Figure 6-17 shows a `<div>` tag with a corresponding ID style that creates the thin black border around the `<div>` tag and defines it as follows:

500 pixels wide

25 pixels of padding inside the `<div>` tag border

50 pixels of margin spacing outside the `<div>` tag border

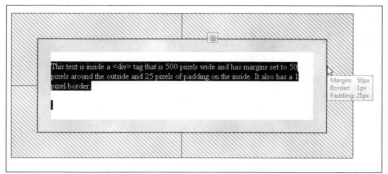

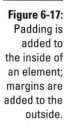

Figure 6-17:
Padding is
added to
the inside of
an element;
margins are
added to the
outside.

Here's the confusing part:

✔ **Padding adds to the specified width.** If you specify a width for a `<div>`
tag (or any other box element) — as I have in Figure 6-12 — the padding increases the total width. In my example, the `<div>` tag will fill 550
pixels of space on the page: 500 pixels for the width plus 25 pixels on
each side of padding.

✔ **Margins add to the total space taken up by an element in a page.** The
margins of the `<div>` tag style are set to 50 pixels, so the `<div>` tag is
positioned 50 pixels from the top and left of the page and no other element will appear on-screen closer than 50 pixels on the right or at the
bottom. This prevents the display of any other element in that space; it
means the `<div>` tag effectively takes up all that space on the page.

✔ **Borders add to the specified element width.** The ID style for the `<div>`
tag also includes border settings, which cause the dark border to surround the `<div>` tag. In this example, I created a 1-pixel border, which
adds two pixels to the width. If you choose the thin border setting, it
adds 2 pixels to each side of the `<div>` tag (4 pixels total).

Thus the `<div>` tag fills a total space on the page of 652 pixels:

500 pixel width

50 pixels total of padding

2 pixels of border

100 pixels for the 50-pixel margin on each side

Further complicating all this is a little-understood rule of HTML called Margin Collapse. This is not specific to CSS, but it does affect how margins in CSS are displayed in a Web browser. Margin Collapse causes top and bottom margins between elements to overlap. The goal of Margin Collapse is to keep elements that appear one above the other, such as paragraphs created with <p> tags, from displaying with twice as much space as you'd want between them. That's useful with the paragraph tag, but it can cause confusing problems when you set margin space above and below adjacent elements and the total margin space doesn't add up the way you'd expect. For example, imagine you have two <div> tags, one above the other. Now imagine that you've set the bottom margin of the top <div> to 10 pixels, and the top margin of the <div> below it to 20 pixels. You'd expect those to combine to create 30 pixels of space between the two <div> tags (because you'd get 30 pixels of space if those same margins were set on the left and right and the <div> tags that were side by side). However, with <div> tags that are stacked on top of each other, the Margin Collapse rule causes the margins to overlap, resulting in a space that is equal to the largest of the two margins. In this case, the 10 pixel and 20 pixel margins would combine to take up 20 pixels of space between the <div> tags, not the 30 pixels of space you might expect because 20 pixels is the largest of the two margins.

The exception to the Margin Collapse rule? (Of course, there's an exception to this rule. . . .) If you add a border or padding to the <div> tags, the Margin Collapse rule is ignored and the margin space will be the total of the two margins, plus the padding or border size. In that case, it will all add up just like you'd expect.

How wide should I make my Web page's design?

Although you can set the width of your Web page's design to any size, most Web designers create pages that are 780 pixels wide or 960 pixels wide. These sizes are based on the most common screen resolutions. If you want your Web pages to look good to computers with monitors set to 800 by 600, design your pages to be 780 pixels wide (to leave room for the borders of a Web browser). In the early days, most Web pages were designed for that resolution — but increasingly designers feel it's safe to design for the higher resolution of 1024 by 768. As of this writing, the W3Schools Web site reports that only 3 percent of the users of the Internet still have monitors set to a resolution of 800 x 600. If you design for the more popular 1024 x 768 setting, creating a page that is 960 pixels wide seems to be a good choice. Although I generally design my own Web sites with a width of 960 pixels, I use Web designs that are 780 pixels wide for the purposes of this book; they fit better in the settings recommended by my publisher that make the screen captures included in this book easier to read on these printed pages.

Aligning and Centering Elements in CSS

In addition to formatting text, you can use CSS to align elements and position them in relation to one another on a page. In this section, you find out how to use floats to align images and other elements, how to use margin settings to center an element, such as a <div> tag on a page, and how to use the text alignment option to center text or other elements contained in a <div> tag.

Centering a page layout with CSS margins

Many Web page designs are centered on the page so they seem to float between the sides of the browser window no matter how wide or narrow the window becomes. This helps create the illusion that the design fills the page, even if the browser window is much wider than the design of the page.

Most Web page designs created with CSS achieve this effect by creating one <div> tag that surrounds all the contents of the page and then applying a style to that<div> tag. This is commonly done with an ID style named something like #wrapper or #container, but you can achieve the same effect with class styles and can name the style anything you like, as long as you don't use spaces or special characters.

I generally name the style I use for this purpose #container because it *contains* all the other tags and contents on the page.

Thus if you want to center the design of a page, a common technique is to first surround all the content with a <div> tag and then create a style for that <div>. This technique works well whether you want to center a simple page or a complex page with multiple columns, images, and multimedia.

 If your page isn't already set up with a <div> tag around all your content, here's a tip for adding one. First click and drag to select all of the text, images, and other contents of the page. Then choose Insert➪Layout Objects➪Div Tag. In the Insert Div Tag dialog box, make sure the Wrap Around Selection option is selected from the Insert drop-down list. Leave the rest of the fields blank and click OK to add a <div> tag around all the contents of your page, and you're ready for the steps that follow.

To center an entire page design, make sure that a <div> tag surrounds all of the contents of the page, and follow these steps:

1. **Click the New CSS Rule icon (it looks like a small piece of paper with a plus sign (+) over it) at the bottom of the CSS Styles panel.**

   Alternatively, you can choose Format➪CSS Styles➪New.

   The New CSS Rule dialog box opens.

2. **Choose ID from the Selector Type drop-down list.**

   Although you can use a class style selector instead of an ID selector, the ID option is generally recommended for styles such as this one that you use only once per page.

3. **Enter a name for the style.**

   You can name ID styles anything you like, just don't use spaces or special characters. Also ID style names must begin with a # sign. If you don't enter a # sign before the name, Dreamweaver adds one for you as it creates the new ID style.

   In this example, I named the style #container.

4. **Select a style sheet option from the Rule Definition drop-down list.**

   To add the style to an internal style sheet, which makes the style available only to the page you have open, choose This Document Only.

   To add the style to any existing external style sheet in the site, choose the name of the style sheet from the drop-down list.

   To create a new external style sheet as you create the style, choose New Style Sheet File.

5. **Click OK.**

   The New CSS Rule dialog box closes and the CSS Rule Definition dialog box opens. The name you entered appears at the top of the CSS Rule Definition dialog box.

6. **Choose the Box category from the left of the dialog box and then specify the formatting settings.**

   As shown in Figure 6-18, for the container <div> tag in this example, I set the width to 780 pixels. Here's the trick to centering a <div> tag like this: Set the left and right margins to Auto. That way, a browser automatically adds an equal amount of margin space to each side of the <div> tag, effectively centering it on the page.

7. **Click the Apply button to preview the style and then click OK to close the CSS Rule Definition dialog box and save the style.**

8. **Click to select the ID that surrounds all the content on the page.**

   To make sure you've selected the right <div> tag, click to place your cursor anywhere in the main part of the page, then click the <div> tag that is listed to the farthest left in the Quick Tag Selector at the bottom of the workspace. The outline of the <div> tag and all of its contents will be highlighted when you select it.

9. **With the** `<div>` **tag selected, click to select the name of the style you created from the ID drop-down list in the Property inspector.**

    The style rules you defined when you created the style are automatically applied to the `<div>` tag. In this example, the result is that the size of the `<div>` tag is changed to 780 pixels wide and the `<div>` tag and all its contents are centered on the page.

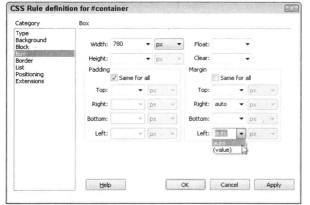

Figure 6-18: Set the left and right margins to Auto in the Box settings to center an element, such as a `<div>` tag, on a page.

Aligning the contents of an element

If you want to align the contents of an element, you can do that by using the Block category in the CSS Rule Definition dialog box, as shown in Figure 6-19. This technique is useful for centering the text in a `<div>` tag, for example, or for aligning a list of navigation links to the right side of a page. A common approach to using this option is to create an ID or class style that you will apply to an entire `<div>` tag and include the text alignment option as part of the style rule. In Figure 6-19, you see that I'm setting the text-align field to center as part of an ID style named `#footer` that I plan to apply to the `<div>` tag at the bottom of the page to center the copyright information.

In this example, I also used the Text category to change the size and font of the text in the same style named `#footer`. This enables me to apply all of these formatting options at once when I assign this ID to the `<div>` tag that surrounds the copyright information.

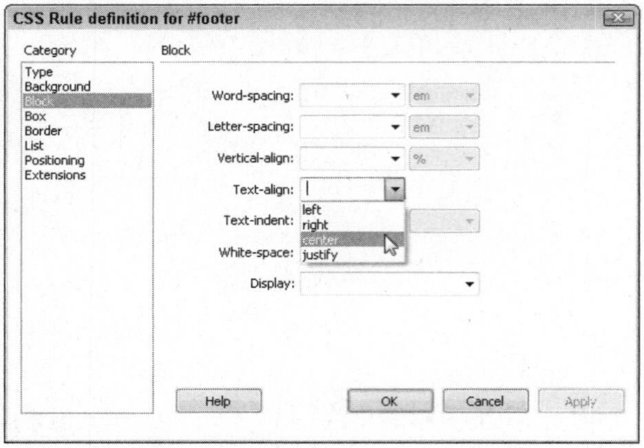

Figure 6-19: Use the Text-align drop-down list in the Box category to center the contents of a <div> tag.

Aligning elements with floats

Designers often align an image, <div> tag, or other element to the left or right of a Web page and then wrap any text or other content around that element. In Figure 6-20, you see how I've used a style to align the image to the right of the column so that the text wraps up next to it on the left. In the steps that follow, you find out how to create styles like this one.

Figure 6-20: You can apply Class styles by selecting an element and then using the drop-down list in the Property inspector.

CSS offers many advantages when it comes to aligning elements like this, but the way you set up these styles is not as obvious as you might expect at first because you use the float option.

After you understand that you can float elements, such as images, to the left or right side of a page, it's pretty easy to create styles that accomplish this goal. In this exercise, you learn to create two styles that are ideal for aligning images to the left and right of a page, complete with a little margin just where you need it.

To create two class styles that you can use to align images and other elements to the left and right of a page, follow these steps.

1. **Click the New CSS Rule icon (it looks like a small piece of paper with a plus sign over it) at the bottom of the CSS Styles panel.**

   Alternatively, you can choose Format⇨CSS Styles⇨New.

   The New CSS Rule dialog box opens.

2. **Choose Class from the Selector Type drop-down list.**

   In this case, the class selector is ideal because you're likely to use your alignment styles more than once on a page.

3. **Enter a name for the style.**

   You can name class styles anything you like; just don't use spaces or special characters. Class style names must begin with a dot (.). If you don't enter a dot before the name, Dreamweaver adds one for you as it creates the new class style.

   In this example, I named the style `.float-left`.

4. **Select a style sheet option from the Rule Definition drop-down list.**

   To add the style to an internal style sheet, which makes the style available only to the page you have open, choose This Document Only.

   To add the style to any existing external style sheet in the site, choose the name of the style sheet from the drop-down list.

   To create a new external style sheet as you create the style, choose New Style Sheet File.

5. **Click OK.**

   The New CSS Rule dialog box closes, and the CSS Rule Definition dialog box opens. The name you entered appears at the top of the CSS Rule Definition dialog box.

6. **Choose the Box category from the left of the dialog box.**

   The Box options open.

7. **Choose an option from the Float drop-down list.**

   To create a style that will align images or other elements to the left of a page, chose Left from the Float drop-down list. To create a style that will align images or other elements to the right of a page, chose Right from the Float drop-down list.

   In all my sites, I create two styles like this, one to align images and other elements to the left, and another to align to the right. ***Note:*** Most (but not all) of the CSS layouts that are included in Dreamweaver CS5 already have float styles that you can use to align elements to the right and left. These class styles are named `.fltlft` (for, you guessed it, float left) and `.fltrt` (for float right).

8. **Add margin space to create a margin around the floated element.**

   It's good practice to add margin space to the opposite side from the float setting. For example, if you are creating a style to float an image to the left, add 5 or 10 pixels of space to the Right margin field. Then, when you use the style to align an image to the left side of the page, a margin will also be created between the image and any text or other element that wraps next to the image.

9. **Click OK to close the CSS Rule Definition dialog box and save the style.**

   The style name and definition appear in the CSS Styles panel and become available in the Class drop-down list in the Property inspector.

10. **Click to select the image or other element you want to align in the page.**

11. **Click to select the name of the style you created from the Class drop-down in the Property inspector.**

    The style rules you defined when you created the style are automatically applied. If you had selected an image in a page of text, the image would move to the left side of the page and the text would wrap around it with a margin between the image and text.

    Repeat Steps 1-9, once with the float set to Right and 5 to 10 pixels of margin space in the Left margin field in the Box category and again with the Float set to Left and 5 to 10 pixels of margin space in the Right margin field in the Box category.

Editing, Renaming, and Removing Styles

After you create and apply a few styles, you're likely to want to go back and edit some of them. Fortunately, Dreamweaver makes it easy to rename, edit, and even remove styles, as you learn in the sections that follow.

Editing an existing style

You can change the attributes of any style after you create it by editing its style definition. This is where some of the biggest advantages of Cascading Style Sheets come into play. You can make global changes to a page (or even to an entire Web site) by changing a style; when you edit the style, the changes are applied automatically to every element that uses the style.

This is one of the reasons that external style sheets are so valuable: You can create styles that are used on any *or* all pages in a site. Beware, however, that this capability can also lead to problems. If you decide to edit a style when you use it on a new page, don't forget that you'll be changing the formatting everywhere else you've already used that style.

You can create new styles by duplicating an existing style, giving it a new name, and then altering the style definitions. This is a time-saving trick when you want to create a new style that's similar to an existing one.

To edit any existing style (whether it was created using the class, tag, or ID selector), follow these steps:

1. **Open the CSS Styles panel by choosing Window⇨CSS Styles.**

2. **Double-click the name of an existing style in the CSS Styles panel.**

   The style is opened in the CSS Rule Definition dialog box.

   Alternatively, you can click once to select any style in the CSS Styles panel and then edit that style in the Properties pane at the bottom of the panel, as shown in Figure 6-21.

3. **Edit the settings for the style to your liking.**

   • **If you edit a style in the CSS Rule Definition dialog box,** changes are applied automatically when you click the Apply button or when you click OK.

   • **If you edit a style definition in the Properties panel,** the changes are applied automatically as soon as you press the Return or Enter key or click outside the formatting field in the panel.

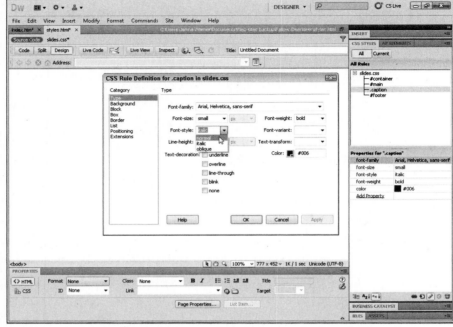

Figure 6-21:
To edit a style, double-click the name of the style in the CSS Styles panel; it opens in the CSS Rule Definition dialog box.

Renaming existing styles

You can rename a style in the CSS Styles panel in much the same way you'd rename a filename in the Files panel, by clicking to select the name and then typing a new name. Take care, however, that renaming a style this way doesn't change its corresponding reference in the HTML code for your Web pages.

If you change a name in the CSS Styles panel, you must also change the name in the corresponding page code, or reapply the style using the Property inspector — which can get complicated if you've used the style in many places.

For example, let's say you create a class style and name it .caption and then apply it to the text under the photos in your Web page using the Property inspector (as I did in the first exercises in this chapter). Then suppose you decide later on to change the name of the style to .imagecaption. Changing the name in the CSS Styles panel is easy enough, but then you have to make sure that every place you've used that style in your site is updated — either by reapplying the style using the Property inspector or by changing the name in the code wherever the style has been applied.

If you want to change the name of a class style, Dreamweaver includes a feature that updates the corresponding code automatically, but only if you change the name using the right-click or (Control-click) option — and only for class styles. If you change the name of an ID style or a compound style, you must reset the style using the Property inspector, or change the corresponding references in the code manually using code view or the Quick Tag Editor.

To rename a class style and update the style references in the code at the same time, open any page where the style is used and follow these instructions:

1. **Open the CSS Styles panel by choosing Window➪CSS Styles.**

2. **Right-click (Control-click) the name of the class style in the CSS Styles panel.**

3. **Choose Rename Class, as shown in Figure 6-22.**

   The Rename dialog box opens.

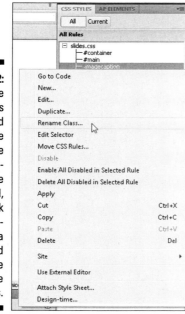

Figure 6-22: To rename a class style and change the style name automatically in the page codel, right-click (Control-click on a Mac) and choose Rename Class.

4. **Type a new name in the New Name field and click OK.**

   If you've already applied the style and the style is saved in an external style sheet, a dialog box opens, offering to "Use Find and Replace to fix the documents that use this style?"

   If the style you want to rename is saved in an internal style sheet, the name will change automatically anywhere the style is applied in the code. With internal style sheets, the Find and Replace dialog box does not open; then you don't have all the options shown in these steps. However, any changes appear in the Results panel, which opens automatically at the bottom of the workspace.

5. **Click Yes to automatically update references to the style in the code with the new style name.**

   The Find and Replace dialog box opens (see Figure 6-23) with the name of the style already filled in. Don't change these settings unless you know what you're doing with these advanced search strings and want to alter the way Dreamweaver renames the style.

Figure 6-23:
Dream-
weaver
sets up the
needed
search
strings in
the Find and
Replace
dialog box
when you
use the
Rename
Style option
to change
the name
of a class
style.

6. **Click Replace All to automatically update all references to the style in the code.**

Dreamweaver warns you that this operation can't be undone, but you can always rename the style again by repeating these steps if you change your mind.

Removing a style

If you want to remove a style from any text, image, or other element on your page, here are two options:

✔ Click to select the text, image, or other element. Then open the Class or ID drop-down lists in the Property inspector and choose None, as you see in Figure 6-24.

✔ Click to select the element, and then right-click (Control-click on a Mac) the tag the style is applied to in the Quick Tag Selector at the very bottom of the workspace, as shown in Figure 6-25. When you right-click a tag in the Quick Tag Selector, a list opens with many options, choose the corresponding option for the selected style. In the example shown in Figure 6-25, it's Set ID — which reveals a list of all of the ID styles in the site. Using this list, you can change or remove any style.

If you don't see the tag that you want to edit in the tag selector, click to select the corresponding image, text, or other element in the Web page: The tag will appear in the Quick Tag Selector, where you can edit it.

Figure 6-24: To remove a style, select the element that the style is applied to; then choose None from the Class drop-down list in the Property inspector.

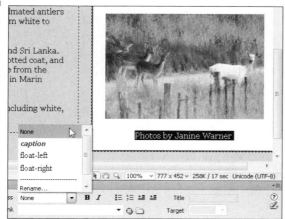

Figure 6-25:
You can
use the
Quick Tag
Selector at
the bottom
left of the
Dream-
weaver
workspace
to change
or remove
any style or
HTML tag.

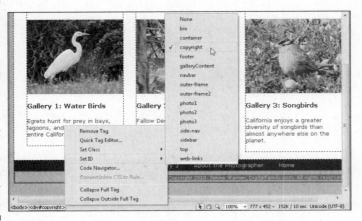

Using Design-Time Style Sheets

As you get increasingly savvy about using style sheets, you'll find that work-ing with external style sheets affords the most power because you can link to them from multiple pages in your site rather than having to create a new inter-nal style sheet for each page in your site. You have an added advantage: You can easily alter your styles in just one place if you need to make changes after styles are applied. Even better, you can create multiple external style sheets as part of the design process, using a Dreamweaver feature — *Design-Time Style Sheets* — to switch between them as you work on your document.

One benefit of the Design-Time Style Sheets feature is that you can view how different external style sheets affect your page without linking to them. This feature is a great way to switch quickly between style sheets in a document and explore various what-if scenarios with the style sheets you create — before you apply them. You may begin to like this feature because you can play around with and explore the full power of CSS. After you decide you like a particular style sheet, you can apply it to your page as you would any other style sheet.

Design-Time Style Sheets affect the appearance of styles only in Dreamweaver. Because they're not real links, they show up only at runtime when a Dreamweaver document is open. Design-Time Style Sheet info is also stored in a Design Note file. If you want to preserve your Design-Time Style Sheet info, be careful not to delete the corresponding Design Note file.

To set up Design-Time Style Sheets, follow these steps:

1. **Choose Format⇨CSS Styles⇨Design-Time.**

   The Design-Time Style Sheets dialog box appears.

2. **To work with a specific style sheet, click the Add Item button (+) above the Show Only at Design-Time field.**

   The Select File dialog box appears, and you can select a CSS file. Remember that CSS files usually end with a .css extension. You can also add multiple CSS files by clicking the Add button again.

3. **To hide a specific style sheet, click the Add Item button (+) above the Hide at Design-Time field and select, from the Select File dialog box, the style you want to hide.**

4. **To delete a listed style sheet from either category, select the style sheet and click the Remove Item button (–) to delete it.**

For a list of more advanced CSS training resources online and off, visit www. DigitalFamily.com/dreamweaver and look for the article on "Where to learn advanced CSS tips and tricks."

Chapter 7

Saving Time with Dreamweaver Templates (And More)

Strive for consistency in all your designs — except when you're trying to be unpredictable. A little surprise here and there can keep your Web site lively. But, most Web sites work best and are easiest to navigate when they follow a consistent design theme. Case in point: Most readers take for granted that books don't change their designs from page to page, and newspapers don't change headline fonts and logos every day. Publishers of books and newspapers want to make life easier for their readers, and consistency is one of the primary tools for making sure readers find publications familiar. That doesn't mean you should limit modern Web design to what's possible in print, but it does mean we can all learn a thing or two from hundreds of years of print design.

Dreamweaver offers several features to help you develop and maintain a consistent look and feel across your site. In this chapter, you discover four of my favorite Dreamweaver features — templates, Library items, History panel, and the Tracing Image feature.

Both the Templates and Library item features help you work more efficiently and make changes to a site faster and easier. These features work well with CSS, and as you discover in this chapter, you can work even more efficiently by combining CSS with templates and library items. After you discover how these features make creating and managing Web sites faster and easier, you're well on your way to simplifying your work even before you start.

Templates in Dreamweaver not only make it easy to create pages with consistent design elements, they make it easy to update those pages later when things change — and things always change.

The History panel also offers a number of timesaving features, from replaying steps that are repetitive to easily jumping back to an earlier state in your design.

Tracing images are handy design tools, which you can insert into the background of a page to guide your design work. As you discover at the end of this chapter, tracing images don't display in a Web browser, but they are useful if you like to first create your designs in a program like Photoshop and then recreate your page designs as Web pages in Dreamweaver.

Templating Your Type

You can choose from many different kinds of templates to create Web sites; and you can find many places on the Web where you can buy them or even download them for free. At its simplest, a *template* is a ready-made page design, usually created in a way that makes it easy to add your own text and images. Some templates are customizable so that you can change design elements, such as colors, images, or fonts.

Keep in mind that many different kinds of templates are available, and templates designed for a program like WordPress or Flash won't work in Dreamweaver using the instructions in this chapter. (See Chapter 1 for more about the different kinds of templates that can be used in the many different ways you can create Web sites.)

In this chapter, I focus on Dreamweaver's .dwt templates, which you can use to create new pages quickly as well as to make global changes across all the pages created from a template.

Dreamweaver templates are best used in the following scenarios:

✔ **Templates are definitely the way to go when you're creating a number of pages that share the same characteristics, such as the same background color, navigation elements, or logo.** I recommend that you use a template anytime you create a site with more than a few pages. For example, you might create a template that includes your logo, a row of links at the top and bottom of each page, and styles for the text colors and fonts. After you create a template with all these features, you can use it as the basis for all the other pages in your site. This approach enables you to quickly and easily create a series of pages that share the same navigation, logo, and so on. If you ever decide to change one of these elements, such as your logo, you can change it once in the template and automatically update all the pages created from the template in your site.

✔ **If you want to use different design elements in different sections, you can even create more than one template for a site.** For example, if you're creating a Web site for a bed-and-breakfast inn, you might create one template for all the pages where you want to show off the rooms in the inn and another for a collection of pages that features great places to hike in the area.

When creating multiple templates for a Web site, you may benefit from a *nested* template, a template whose design and editable regions are based on another template.

For example, you can create a main template for elements that appear on every page across an entire site, such as a navigation bar. Then for secondary templates, start with the main template and add nested templates that have design variations for a section (or sections) of a site.

✔ **Templates are valuable when you're working with a team of people with varying skill levels.** For example, say you're building a site for a pet store and want to let the employees update their own pet stories without messing up the page design. The fact that templates have locked regions can protect the most important elements of a page, making it easy for sales staff to add new information without accidentally breaking navigation elements or other consistent features.

The most powerful aspect of Dreamweaver's template feature is the capability to make global changes to every page created from a template. Even if you're working alone on a site, this aspect of templates can save hours (or even days) of time as the site grows and changes over time.

Creating Templates

Creating a template is as easy as creating any other file in Dreamweaver. You can start by creating an HTML Template page much as you would any other page. You can also choose File⇨Save As to turn any existing page into a template. The main difference is that the extension for a template file is .dwt (Dreamweaver Web Template), and template files are stored in a special Templates folder. When you create your first template in a Web site, Dreamweaver automatically creates a Templates folder in your local site folder and stores all your .dwt template files in this folder. Templates must be kept in this common Templates folder and the folder must be kept at the top level or root level of your Web site (meaning you can't move the Templates folder into another folder) for the automated features in Dreamweaver to work properly.

The template features work only if you set up your Web site in Dreamweaver. If you haven't gone through the setup process to define your local site folder yet, see Chapter 2 and complete those setup steps first.

Creating editable and uneditable regions

Perhaps the most difficult concept to grasp when it comes to templates is how editable and uneditable regions work and why they're important. Here's the short answer (I get into the details later in this chapter).

When you create a template design, every aspect of the design is locked automatically, or uneditable, until you designate some part of the page as an *editable region* — an area of the template page that can be changed in any page created from the template. The steps for making a region editable are relatively simple (you find detailed instructions in the sections that follow). When you create a new page from a template, *only* the areas you've designated as editable regions can be altered. If you want to make global changes with a template, only the areas that you've left uneditable can be used to make changes across multiple pages.

For example, suppose you create a design for an online magazine with the logo and navigation bar at the top of the page and the copyright and navigation links at the bottom, and you leave all these areas uneditable. Then you create a design area in the middle of the page where a story and photo can be added to each page created from the template and you designate that area as an editable region. When you create new pages from the template, you can replace the photo and story on each page because they're in editable regions, but you can't change the logo, navigation links, or copyright because they're in uneditable regions.

Now imagine that you've used this template to create many pages that are exactly the same, except that each features a different story and photo in the middle area designated as the editable region. Then one day you decide to change the logo for your company, so you need to change that section of the page on all the pages you've created. If the logo is in an uneditable region of the template, no problem. You simply open the template file and edit the logo on that one page. When you save the template, the new logo is applied automatically to all the pages created from that template. That saves a ton of time because you don't have to replace the logo on each page separately. You could make the same kinds of global changes to the navigation links at the top and bottom of the page because they're also in uneditable regions.

In contrast, if you make changes to the editable region in the template, those changes aren't applied to the pages created from the template. This is important because you wouldn't want to make a global change that overwrites all the individual stories and photos you've inserted into each page. It comes down to this: *Locked* areas of a template (areas you don't designate as editable) can be changed only in the template itself, and those changes can then be applied automatically to all the pages created from that template. Areas of a template designated as editable can be changed in any page created from the template, but those areas can't be updated automatically by changing the template.

If you're still a little confused after all this theory, don't worry; you see all this in action in the sections that follow.

Why the head section is editable by default

In a new template, all elements are locked by default except for the document head section, which is indicated by the `<head>`, `</head>` tags at the very top of any HTML page. Within the head tags you find `<title>` tags. The `<title>` tags enable you to change the title in any page created from a template, which is good practice.

When you create a new template, Dreamweaver creates two editable regions in the head area of the page, one for the title, and the second for any scripts, links to CSS files, or other elements that must be added to the head section. For example, when you use behaviors on a page (covered in Chapter 9), Dreamweaver inserts JavaScript in the page at the place the script is used as well as in the head section of the page. Similarly, if you add multimedia files, such as Flash or Flash video, to a page, Dreamweaver adds special code to the header at top of the page to make the multimedia files play properly. For all these reasons, editable regions are automatically added to the head area when you create a template or save a page as a template.

In previous versions of Dreamweaver, if you created a template from an existing HTML page using the File➪Save As feature to save the file as a .dwt template file, editable regions were not added to the head section automatically. If you're working with a template created in a previous version of Dreamweaver, you may run into this problem. You'll know if you do because you won't be able to edit the title of any page created from the template or add features that use JavaScript. To solve this problem you can

✔ Re-create the template from a new file in Dreamweaver CS5.

✔ Manually add the template code to the head region of the existing file by copying it from the head region of a new template.

Creating a new Dreamweaver template

If you're working on a new site or haven't yet defined your site, read Chapter 2 for information on defining the site before you create a template.

To create a Dreamweaver template that you can use to create new pages, follow these steps:

1. **Choose File⇨New.**

   The New Document window opens.

2. **In the list on the left, click the Blank Template option, as shown in Figure 7-1.**

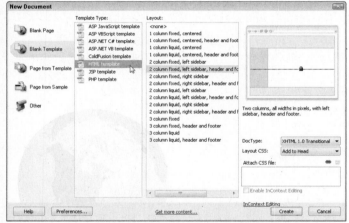

3. **In the Template Type list, choose HTML Template.**

   In this example, I'm creating a new HTML page template, which will enable me to take advantage of template features without using the programming code required in the other template options. You can also choose from a variety of template options, including templates for ASP (Active Server Pages), ColdFusion, JSP (Java Server Pages), and PHP (a recursive acro- nym for Hypertext Preprocessor). These file types are used when creating dynamic Web sites and require more advanced programming than HTML. Find an introduction to creating dynamic Web sites in Chapter 13.

4. **In the Layout area, choose <none> to create a blank page or select any of the predesigned CSS layouts.**

   Dreamweaver's many CSS layout options, covered in Chapter 6, pro- vide a great head start to creating a new page design. In this example, I selected a CSS layout as the basis for my page design.

5. Click the Create button.

A new blank template is created and opens in the main work area, and the New Document dialog box closes.

6. Choose File➪Save.

If you haven't disabled the dialog box, a warning appears stating that the template doesn't have any editable regions and asking whether you really want to save it. Click Yes to continue. You find instructions for creating editable regions in Step 10.

7. Click OK to save the page as is for now.

The Save window appears with the Templates folder open. If you don't already have a folder named Templates in your local site folder, Dreamweaver will create one for you when you create your first template.

For Dreamweaver templates to work properly, they must be saved in a folder named Templates in your local site folder. If you change the folder name or move the Templates folder into a subfolder, your templates will no longer work properly.

8. Give the template a name and click Save.

The template is saved automatically with a .dwt extension, which designates the file as a Dreamweaver template.

9. Create a design for the page by adding images, text, and other elements as you would in any other Dreamweaver file.

You find instructions for adding all these features to your pages throughout this book. Again, remember, you create a page design in a template just like you would in any other Web page.

10. To create an editable region:

a. Select any image, text block, or content area.

Often the best option is to select an entire area of a page so that everything in that section becomes editable. If you've designed your pages with `<div>` tags and CSS, as covered in Chapter 6, a good option is to select the `<div>` tag for an entire section, such as the mainContent div I've selected in this example (see Figure 7-2).

A handy way to select a section surrounded by a `<div>` tag is to place your cursor anywhere in that area of the page, and then use the tag selector at the bottom of the workspace to select the div, as shown in Figure 7-2.

b. Choose Insert➪Template Objects➪Editable Region (as shown in Figure 7-3).

The New Editable Region dialog box opens.

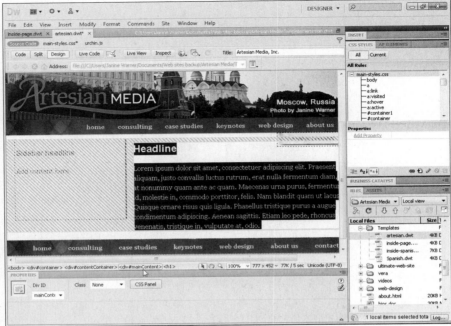

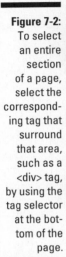

Figure 7-2:
To select an entire section of a page, select the corresponding tag that surround that area, such as a <div> tag, by using the tag selector at the bottom of the page.

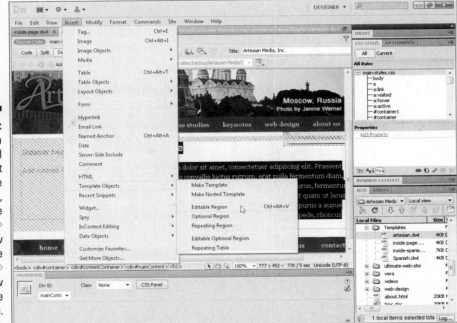

Figure 7-3:
To make a selected element an editable region, choose Insert⇨ New Template Object⇨ New Editable Region.

c. Give the new editable region a name.

I recommend something that identifies the type of content it is, such as *headline* or *main-content*.

The region you define as editable becomes an area that can be changed in any page created from the template. You can have multiple editable regions in one template. In the site shown in this example, I also made the big banner photo at the top of the page an editable region so that I could use different banner images on each page. Each editable region must have a different name. Also, editable region names can't use spaces or special characters, but underscores and hyphens are okay.

d. Click OK.

A light blue box (with a light blue tab at the top left of the box) surrounds the editable region. The name you entered into the New Editable Region dialog box appears on the tab.

11. **When you finish designing the page and add all the editable regions you want, choose File➪Save to save your template.**

When you save a new template page or you save an existing page as a template, Dreamweaver automatically adds the `.dwt` extension and saves the file into a Templates folder.

If you save a template before you specify any editable regions, Dreamweaver gives you a warning because templates aren't useful without editable regions. You don't have to create editable regions before you save a template, but you can't make any changes in any pages created from a template until you create one or more editable regions. You can always go back and add editable regions later, so it's not a problem if you want to save your work before you create editable regions, which is generally good practice.

Saving any page as a template

Sometimes you get partway through designing a page before you realize that you're likely to want more pages just like it and should create a template to avoid re-creating the same page design over and over. Similarly, you may want to turn a page that someone else created into a template. No matter the page's origin, creating a template from an existing page is almost as easy as creating a new template from scratch.

To save a page as a template, follow these steps:

1. **Open the page that you want to turn into a template.**

Choose File➪Open and browse to find your file. Or open the site in the Files panel and double-click the file to open it.

2. Choose File⇨Save as Template, as shown in Figure 7-4.

The Save dialog box appears.

3. In the Site drop-down list, choose a site.

The menu lists all the sites you've set up in Dreamweaver. By default, the site you've set up and opened in the Files panel is selected when the dialog box opens. If you're working on a new site or haven't yet set up your site, flip to Chapter 2 for information on the site setup process.

You can use the Save as Template option to save a page as a template into any defined site, which makes it easy to save a page design from one site as a template for another site.

4. In the Save As text box, type a name for the template.

Although you don't have to add a description, if you're working on a big site with many templates, descriptions can be very helpful for keeping track of which templates go with which sections of your site.

5. Click the Save button.

If you haven't disabled the dialog box, a warning appears stating that the template doesn't have any editable regions and asking whether you really want to save it. Click Yes to continue.

Notice that the file now has the .dwt extension, indicating that it's a template.

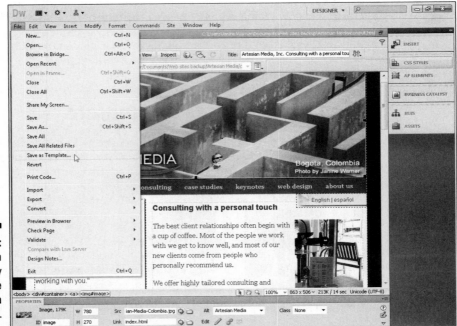

Figure 7-4:
You can save any HTML page as a template.

6. **Click OK in the Dreamweaver dialog box that appears to update links in the template.**

   Because your original file probably wasn't saved in the Templates folder, any links to other pages or images must be updated when the file is saved. After you click OK, Dreamweaver corrects any links in the file as it saves the file in the Templates folder.

7. **Make any changes that you want and then choose File⇨Save.**

   You edit a template just as you edit any other page in Dreamweaver.

8. **To create an editable region:**

   a. **Select any content area, image, or text.**

   b. **Choose Insert⇨Template Object⇨Editable Region (refer to Figure 7-3).**

      The New Editable Region dialog box opens.

   c. **Give the new region a name.**

      You can name the region anything you like — just don't use spaces or punctuation. The region you define as editable becomes an area that can be changed in any page created from the template. You can create multiple editable regions in any template.

   d. **Click OK.**

      The editable region is enclosed in a highlighted area with a tab at the top left, identified by the name you gave the region.

9. **When you finish designing the page, choose File⇨Save to save your completed template.**

Making attributes editable

In addition to making any element in a page editable, you can also make the attributes of any element editable. This step is only necessary if you want to make an attribute editable when the tag itself is not editable (for example, when you want the ability to change the background image of a <div> tag, but not the <div> tag itself).

Editable attributes are especially handy for making the color of a link editable. When you set up a list of navigation links so that you can alter the color of any one link on any page without losing the advantage of the template, you can still update all the links throughout the site by editing the template. By making only the color attribute of the link editable, you can change the color of that link when a visitor is on the corresponding page and use the color to identify the section a visitor is currently viewing.

To create editable attributes in a template, follow these steps:

1. **In any Dreamweaver template, select an item that you want to give an editable attribute.**

   In the example shown in Figure 7-5, I selected the navigation link About Us and am in the process of making one of the its attributes editable.

   To make sure you've selected a link and not just the text, click anywhere in the linked text and then use the Quick Tag Selector at the bottom of the workspace to select the <a> tag.

2. **Choose Modify⇨Templates⇨Make Attribute Editable.**

   The Editable Tag Attributes dialog box appears, as shown in Figure 7-6.

3. **From the Attribute drop-down list, choose the attribute you want to make editable.**

   The attribute options vary depending on whether you select an image, link, text, or other element on the page.

   In this example, I selected HREF to be able to change the color of the link, as shown in Figure 7-6. The link tag is one of the most confusing HTML tags because it's known as the anchor tag, displayed as just an <a> in the Quick Tag Selector. But the full tag is <a href>, and in the Editable Tag Attributes dialog box, it's identified as HREF.

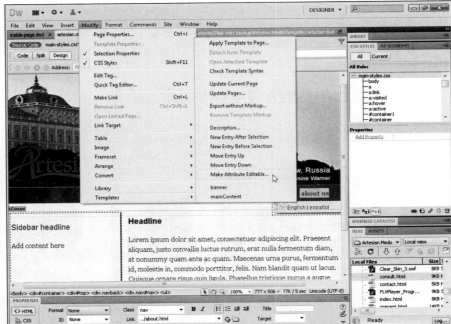

Figure 7-5: Select any link, image, or other tag and use the Modify menu to make the attributes of that tag editable.

If the attribute you want isn't listed, click the Add button and then enter the name of any attribute.

4. Click to select the Make Attribute Editable check box.

The options for that attribute become active in the bottom of the dialog box.

5. In the Type drop-down list, select an attribute type.

As shown in Figure 7-6, the link tag has several attributes. I selected Color in this example.

6. Click OK to make the attribute editable and close the dialog box.

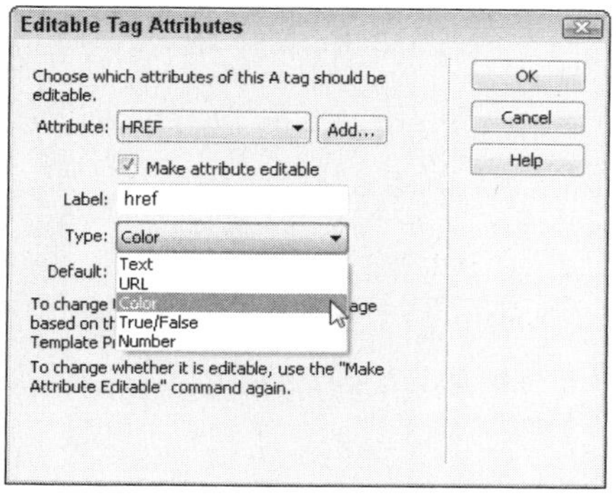

Figure 7-6:
In the
Editable Tag
Attributes
dialog box,
identify
which attri-
butes you
want to be
editable.

To change an editable attribute in a page created from a template, follow these steps:

1. Create a new page from the template, or open any page that was created with the template.

2. Choose Modify⇨Template properties.

The Template Properties dialog box opens, listing any editable attributes, as shown in Figure 7-7.

3. Select the attribute you want to edit in order to see your options in the bottom of the dialog box.

To change the color of the link, which I set up as an editable attribute in the preceding steps, I selected href to display the options shown in Figure 7-7. I then clicked the color swatch in the bottom left of the Template Properties dialog box and selected a color.

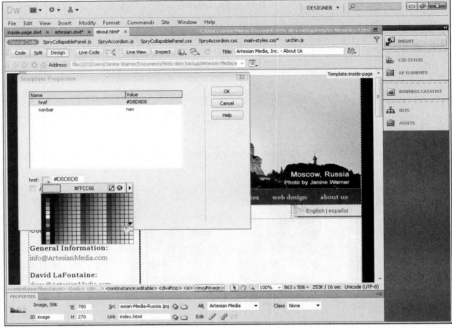

Figure 7-7:
You change
alter
Editable
Attributes
in the
Template
Properties
dialog box.

4. **Click OK to close the dialog box and save the setting.**

    The new setting is applied when the dialog box closes. In this example, the color of the About Us link changed to the new color after the dialog box closed.

Creating a New Page from a Template

After you create a template, it's time to put it to use. You can use one template to create all the pages in your Web site or create different templates for different sections. For example, in a site, such as my consulting firm site at www.ArtesianMedia.com shown in these examples, I created one template for the English version of the site, and a second template for the Spanish version. After you create a template or a collection of templates, using a template to create a new page is similar to creating any other XHTML page.

To use a template to create a new page, follow these steps:

1. **Choose File⇨New.**

   The New Document window opens.

2. **In the list on the left, click the Page from Template option, as shown in Figure 7-8.**

3. **In the Site list in the middle of the page, choose the name of the site that contains a template you want to use.**

   The templates in the selected site appear in the Template for Site section just to the right of the Site list in the New Document window (see Figure 7-8).

4. **In the Template for Site list, select the template you want to use.**

   Notice that when you click the name of a template, a preview of the selected template appears on the far right of the New Document window. In the example shown in Figure 7-8, I selected the artesian template from the Artesian Media site.

Figure 7-8: From the New Document window, you can preview and select any template saved in any defined Web site to create a new page.

5. **Click the Create button.**

   A new page is created from the template and appears in the main work area.

6. **Edit any region of the page that's editable with Dreamweaver's regular editing features and save the file as you would save any other HTML page.**

When you create new pages from a template, you can change only the editable regions in each file created from the template. When you edit a template, only the regions that aren't defined as editable can be used to make global changes to all the pages created from the template. In the template shown in this example, both the main content area of the page and the big banner image at the top of the page can be edited in the page created from the template.

Making Global Changes with Templates

The great advantage of templates is that you can automatically apply changes to all the pages created with a template by altering the original template. For example, say the navigation links are an uneditable region in a template, and I decide to add a new section to the site. I can add a new navigation link to that section by editing the row of links at the top of the page in the template, and the new link is added to all the pages in the site created from that template.

To update files in a site that were created from a template, follow these steps:

1. **Open the template file.**

   Note that template files are distinguishable by the .dwt extension and are saved in the Template folder.

   If you're not sure which template was used to create a page, its name appears in the top-right corner of the page (see the upcoming Figure 7-10). If you don't see the template name, choose View⇨Visual Aids⇨Invisible Elements to turn on the feature that displays the template name. Alternatively, you can open a template from any page created from a template, by following the steps in the next section.

2. **Use Dreamweaver's editing features to make any changes you want to the template.**

   Remember that only changes to uneditable regions are updated automatically. In this example, the logo and navigation elements are locked regions and can be edited to make global changes. Thus, if I add a new link to the row of links at the top of the page, it will be added to all the pages created from the template.

3. **Choose File⇨Save.**

   The Update Template Files dialog box appears, as shown in Figure 7-9. The Update Template Files dialog box lists all the pages created from the template.

4. **Click the Update button to modify all pages listed in the Update Template Files dialog box. Click the Don't Update button to leave these pages unchanged.**

   If you click Update, Dreamweaver automatically changes all the pages listed in the Update Template Files dialog box to reflect any changes made to uneditable regions of the template.

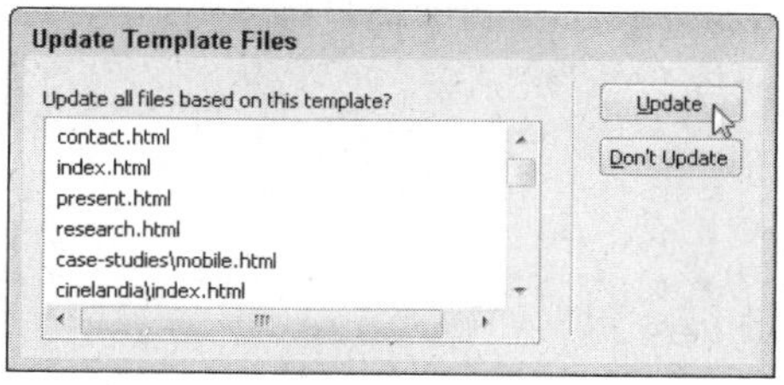

Figure 7-9:
You can update all files created from a template automatically.

Update Template Files

Update all files based on this template?

contact.html
index.html
present.html
research.html
case-studies\mobile.html
cinelandia\index.html

Update

Don't Update

Opening a template from any page created from a template

If you're not sure which template was used to create a page, you can open the template while you have the page open, make changes to the template, and update all the pages created with it by following these steps:

1. **Open a document that uses the template that you want to change.**

2. **Choose Modify⇨Templates⇨Open Attached Template, as shown in Figure 7-10.**

   The template opens.

3. **Use Dreamweaver's regular editing functions to modify the template as you would edit any page or template.**

4. **Choose File⇨Save.**

   The Update Template Files dialog box appears (refer to Figure 7-9).

5. **Click the Update button to modify all the pages listed in the Update Template Files dialog box. Click the Don't Update button to leave these pages unchanged.**

   If you choose Update, Dreamweaver automatically changes all the pages listed in the Update Template Files dialog box.

If you have a page that was created from the template open, the changes are automatically applied, but you need to save the page before closing it to save the changes.

You can also apply changes to all the pages created from a template with the Update Pages option. To do so, open the template, and then make and save your changes without applying those changes to pages created with the template. Anytime later, you can choose Modify⇨Templates⇨Update Pages to apply the update.

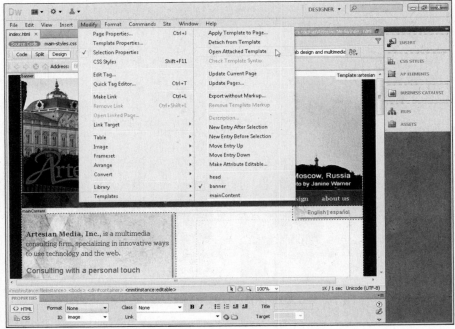

Figure 7-10:
Open an
attached
template
from within
any page
created
from a
template.

Attaching and detaching templates

You can remove a template from any page by detaching it, and you can apply a template to an existing page by attaching it, although the page layout must match the template for it to work.

You can apply a template to an existing page by using one of the following techniques:

- ✔ Choose Modify➪Templates➪Apply Template to Page and then double-click the name of a template to apply it to the page.

- ✔ Drag the template from the Template Assets panel into the Document window. To open the Template Assets panel, click the Assets tab behind the Files panel tab and then click the Templates icon. You can also choose Window➪Assets.

When you apply a template to an existing page, Dreamweaver automatically searches the page and attempts to match each editable region in the template with a section of the page. If sections don't match, you need to reconcile them using the Inconsistent Region Names dialog box (see Figure 7-11).

In the Inconsistent Region Names dialog box, you need to match each region name with a region in the page. If the new template doesn't use some of the regions that were included in the previously applied template, you can use Nowhere from the drop-down list, and the older elements are not affected. After the region conflicts are resolved, click OK. If the page design is too different from the template, it may not be possible to reconcile the regions effectively. In that case, your best option is to re-create the page by creating a new page from the template and then copy and paste the content from the existing page into the new page created from the template.

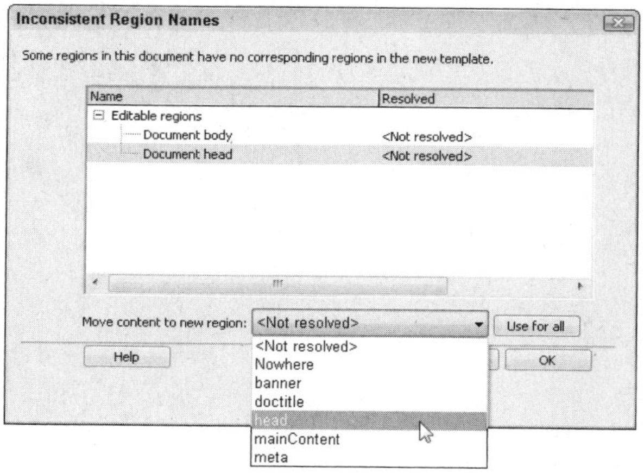

Figure 7-11: Match each region in the template with a corresponding section in the page.

You can remove or detach a template from a page if you no longer want changes to the original template to affect the page created with the template. Detaching a template also unlocks all regions of a page, making it completely editable. You can detach a template by choosing Modify⇨Templates⇨Detach from Template. This action makes the file fully editable again, but any future changes you make to the template aren't reflected on the detached page.

Reusing Elements with the Library Feature

The Library feature isn't a common feature in other Web design programs, so the concept may be new to you even if you've been developing Web sites for a while. The Library feature is handy when you have a single element you want to reuse on many pages, such as a copyright statement you want to appear at the bottom of each page or even something as complex as a row of navigation links.

A *Library item* is a snippet of code that can contain almost anything, including images, videos, text, and links. You can't, however, use features created with Dreamweaver's Behaviors or Spry menu, which use JavaScript.

After you save a section of code in the Library, you can insert it into any page with drag-and-drop ease. If you ever need to change a Library item (by adding or changing a link, for example), simply edit the stored Library item, and Dreamweaver automatically updates the contents of the Library item on any or all pages where it appears throughout the site.

Like templates, Library items are a great way to store frequently used items and make global changes to those items if you need to update them in the future. You have more flexibility with Library items than templates because they're elements you can place anywhere on any page, even multiple times. Libraries aren't shared among sites the way templates are, but you can copy and paste the same Library item from one site into another.

Library items can't contain their own style sheets because the code for styles can appear only as part of the head area of an HTML file. You can, however, attach an external style sheet to a Library item to see how the styles affect the display of the Library item, but the same styles must be available on each page where the Library item is used for the styles to be applied. (For more on style sheets, see Chapters 5 and 6.)

Creating and Using Library Items

The following sections show you the steps for creating a Library item, adding one to a page, and editing and updating a Library item across multiple pages. For these steps to work properly, you must do them in sequential order. Before creating or using Library items, you must first set up the site and open it in the Files panel. (See Chapter 2 for instructions on setting up a site in Dreamweaver.)

Creating a Library item within an existing page works well because you can see how the item looks before you add it to the Library. You can edit an item after it's in the Library, but it may not look just as it will on a Web page. For example, Library items don't include <body> tags when they're saved in the Library, so link colors are displayed as default blue when viewed in the Library, even if the link colors have been changed to, say, purple in the `<body>` tag of the page.

Creating a Library item

To create a Library item that you can use on multiple pages on your site, follow these steps:

1. **Open any existing file that has images, text, or other elements on the page that you want to save as a Library item.**

2. **From this page, select an element or collection of elements that you want to save as a Library item, such as the copyright information that appears at the bottom of this page.**

3. **Choose Modify⇨Library⇨Add Object to Library.**

   The Library Assets panel opens and displays any existing Library items. Your new Library item appears as *Untitled*.

4. **Click to select Untitled and replace it by typing a new name as you would name any file in Explorer on a PC or the Finder on a Mac.**

   In the example shown in Figure 7-12, I've named the Library item *copyright*.

   When you create a Library item, Dreamweaver automatically saves it to the Library. Naming Library items makes them easier to identify when you want to use them. You can then easily apply Library items to any new or existing page in your site by following the steps in the next section.

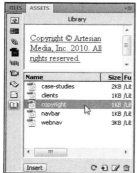

Figure 7-12:
The Assets Library panel.

Adding a Library item to a page

You can easily add elements from the Library to your pages by simply dragging them from the Assets panel to the page. When you add a Library item to a page, the content is inserted into the document and a relationship is established between the content on the page and the item in the Library. This is important because it enables you to edit the Library item later and apply the changes to all pages where the item appears, but it also means that you can't edit the item on the page where it's inserted. You must edit Library items from within the Library, as you see in the following section.

To add a Library item to a page, follow these steps:

1. **Create a new document in Dreamweaver or open any existing file.**

2. **From the Files panel, click the Assets tab, and then click the Library icon.**

   The Library opens in the Assets panel (refer to Figure 7-12).

3. **Drag an item from the Library to the Document window.**

   Alternatively, you can select an item in the Library and click the Insert button. The item automatically appears on the page. After you insert a Library item on a page, you can use any of Dreamweaver's formatting features to position it on the page.

Highlighting Library items

Library items are highlighted to distinguish them from other elements on a page. You can both customize the highlight color for Library items and show or hide the highlight color in the Preferences dialog box. To change or hide Library highlighting, follow these steps:

1. **Choose Edit⇨Preferences (Windows) or Dreamweaver⇨Preferences (Mac).**

   The Preferences dialog box appears.

2. **In the Category section on the left, select Highlighting.**

3. **Click the color box to select a color for Library items and then select the Show box to display the Library highlight color on your pages.**

   Leave the box blank if you don't want to display the highlight color.

4. **Click OK to close the Preferences dialog box.**

Making global changes with Library items

The Dreamweaver Library feature saves time because you can make changes to Library items and automatically apply those changes to any or all pages where the Library item appears. To edit a Library item, follow these steps:

1. **From the Files panel, click the Assets tab and then click the Library icon.**

   The Library opens in the Assets panel (refer to Figure 7-12).

2. **Double-click any item listed in the Library to open it.**

   Dreamweaver opens a new window where you can edit the Library item.

   Because the Library item is just a snippet of code, it won't have a `<body>` tag in which to specify background, link, or text colors. Don't worry about this: The Library item acquires the right settings from the tags on the page where you insert it.

3. **Change the Library item as you would edit any element in Dreamweaver.**

   For example, you can change a link, edit the wording of text, change the font or size, and even add images, text, and other elements.

4. **Choose File⇨Save to save changes to the original item.**

   The Update Library Items dialog box opens, displaying a list of all the pages where the Library item appears.

5. **To apply the changes you made to the Library item on all the listed pages, click the Update button. If you don't want to apply the changes to all the pages where the Library item appears, click the Don't Update button.**

   If you clicked the Update button, the Update Pages dialog box appears and shows the progress of the updating. You can stop the update from this dialog box, if necessary.

If you want to create a new Library item based on an existing one without altering the original, follow Steps 1–3, and in place of Step 4, choose File⇨Save As and give the item a new name.

Editing one instance of a Library item

If you want to alter a Library item on a specific page where you've inserted it, or if you want to make changes to just a few pages, you can override the automated Library feature by detaching it, or breaking the link between the original item in the Library and the item inserted into the page.

After you break a connection, you can no longer update that page's Library item automatically.

To make an instance of a Library item editable, follow these steps:

1. **Open any file that contains a Library item and select the Library item.**

   The Property inspector displays the Library item options, as shown in Figure 7-13.

Figure 7-13:
You can detach a Library item in the Property inspector.

2. **Click the Detach from Original button.**

   A warning message appears, letting you know that if you proceed with detaching the Library item from the original, you can no longer update this occurrence of it when the original is edited.

3. **Click OK to detach the Library item.**

Remembering Your History

With the History panel, you can keep track of what you're doing and even replay your steps. The History panel also lets you undo one or more steps and create commands to automate repetitive tasks.

To open the History panel, choose Window➪History. As soon as you open a file, the History panel starts automatically recording your actions as you work in Dreamweaver. You can't rearrange the order of steps in the History panel, but you can copy them, replay them, and undo them. Don't think of the History panel as an arbitrary collection of commands; think of it as a way to view the steps you've performed, in the order in which you performed them.

The History panel offers a great way to let Dreamweaver do your work for you if you have to repeat the same steps over and over. It's also a lifesaver if you make a major mistake and want to go back one or more steps in your development work.

Here's a rundown of how you can put the History panel to use:

✔ **To copy steps you already executed:** Use the Copy Steps option in the lower right as a quick way to automate steps you want to repeat. You can even select steps individually, in case you want to replay some (but not all) actions exactly as you did them.

✔ **To replay any or all steps displayed in the History panel:** Highlight the steps you want to replay and click the Replay button at the bottom of the History panel.

✔ **To undo the results of the replayed steps:** Choose Edit⇨Undo Replay Steps.

✔ **To apply steps to a specific element on a page:** Highlight that element in the Document window before selecting and replaying the steps. For example, if you want to apply bold and italic formatting to just a few words on a page, you can replay the steps that applied bold and italics to selected text.

You can also set the number of steps displayed in the History panel by choosing Edit⇨Preferences (Windows) or Dreamweaver⇨Preferences (Mac) and selecting General from the Category list on the left. The default is 50 steps, more than enough for most users. The higher the number, the more memory the History panel uses.

Repeating your steps with Recorded Commands

You can automate repeat tasks using Dreamweaver's Recorded Commands feature, available from the Commands menu. Simply start the record option, execute any series of actions in Dreamweaver, stop, and save them. Then, you just replay the recording to repeat the actions automatically. To use the Recorded Commands option, choose Commands⇨Start Recording, and then carefully execute a series of steps that you want to be able to repeat. When you complete the steps you want to record, choose Commands⇨Stop Recording and name the command to save it. To play back the actions, choose Commands⇨Play Recorded Command and select your new command. Then kick back and watch the action; or better yet, take a break and get out of your office for a change.

Using a Tracing Image to Guide Your Design Work

The Tracing Image feature is especially popular among designers. The concept dates back to the earliest days of design. The Tracing Image feature enables you to use graphics as guides for your page designs, much as you might copy a cartoon through thin transparent paper.

The Tracing Image feature is ideal for people who like to first create a design in a program, such as Photoshop or Fireworks, and then model their Web page after it. By using the Tracing Image feature, you can insert any Web-ready image into the background of any Dreamweaver page. Then you can position <div> tags or insert tables or other elements on top of the tracing image, making it easier to re-create your design in Dreamweaver. You can use JPG, GIF, or PNG images as tracing images and you can create them in any graphics application that supports these formats.

Although the tracing image appears in the background of a page, it doesn't take the place of a background image and won't appear in a browser.

To add a tracing image to your page, follow these steps:

1. **Create a new page or open an existing page in Dreamweaver.**

2. **Choose View⇨Tracing Image⇨Load.**

   The Select Image Source dialog box opens.

3. **Select a JPEG image you want to serve as your tracing image and click OK.**

   The Page Properties dialog box opens with the Tracing Image options category selected, as shown in Figure 7-14.

4. **Click the Browse button to locate the image you want to use as a tracing image.**

   The Select Image Source dialog box appears.

5. **Click the image you want to trace from and then click Apply to preview how the image looks behind the page.**

6. **Set the opacity for the tracing image with the Transparency slider.**

   Lowering the transparency level causes the tracing image to appear faded, which makes distinguishing between the tracing image and content on the page easy. You can set the transparency level to suit your preferences, but somewhere around 50 percent works well with most images.

7. **Click OK.**

   The tracing image appears in the Document window, and the dialog box closes.

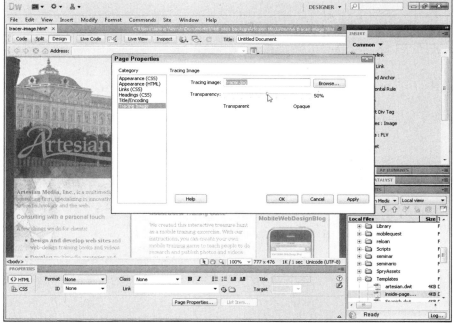

Figure 7-14:
The Page Properties dialog box lets you set the options for a tracing image, which you can use as a guide when design your page.

You have a few other options with the Tracing Image feature. Choose View⇨Tracing Image to reveal the following options:

- ✔ **Show:** Hides the tracing image if you want to check your work without it being visible but don't want to remove it.

- ✔ **Align with Selection:** Enables you to automatically line up the tracing image with a selected element on a page.

- ✔ **Adjust Position:** Enables you to use the arrow keys or enter X, Y coordinates to control the position of the tracing image behind the page.

- ✔ **Reset Position:** Resets the tracing image to 0, 0 on the X, Y coordinates.

- ✔ **Load**: Enables you to add or replace a tracing image.

After you have the tracing image in place, you can use it as a guide while you design your page. Because the tracing image is behind the page, it won't interfere with your design work, and you can add any elements over the tracing image that you could add to any other Web page. Use the tracing image as a reference as you insert and position <div> tags, images, and other elements.

Chapter 8

Coming to the HTML Table

- -

- -

*I*n the early days of Web design, HTML tables offered one of the only options for creating complex page layouts. By splitting and merging table cells and using them as containers for text and images, Web developers could create intricate page designs despite the limits of HTML.

Using tables to create designs was far from ideal, and most of us found this solution frustrating. But because tables were all we had, we had to be clever, and we often resorted to imperfect tricks, such as

✔ Using a clear GIF to control spacing (see the sidebar "The transparent, or clear, GIF trick," later in this chapter).

✔ Using carefully designed background images to add graphic elements and the illusion of layers to specific parts of a page.

✔ Inserting tables within tables to create ever-more elaborate designs.

If you pulled out all these tricks, you could you could use tables to position text, images, and other elements, anywhere you wanted on a page (well, almost anywhere). For example, you could use a table to align two columns of text side by side and then merge the cells at the top to create a wider space for a headline across the top like the format you might see in a newspaper or magazine. Because you could make the borders of a table invisible, you could use tables to create page layouts without the table itself being visible on the page. Back in the day, we were all rather proud of ourselves for figuring out these clever work-arounds.

Today CSS has completely changed the way designers create Web pages, and tables are no longer the recommended solution for creating page layouts, except when you need to format tabular data, such as content you could display in a spreadsheet or columns and rows of data exported from a database.

Today, most professional designers use CSS to create overall page designs because pages designed with CSS download faster, are easier to update, and are more flexible and accessible than tables ever were. Chapters 5 and 6 are dedicated to CSS and the latest developments in Web design.

In this chapter, you discover how to create and edit tables in Dreamweaver in the few cases where tables are still the best solution — when you need to format and sort tabular data. Even though tables are no longer *recommended,* I've also included a few tips for working with tables for page layouts, in case you are still working on a site that was designed the old-fashioned way.

Creating HTML Tables

Tables are made up of three basic elements: rows, columns, and cells. If you've ever worked with a spreadsheet program, you're probably familiar with tables. Working with tabular data in HTML tables is quite similar to working with a spreadsheet: In most cases, you'll want to create a row of headings along the side or top of a table and then columns and rows that can be populated with text, images, and other data.

The code behind an HTML table is a complex series of <tr>, <th>, and <td> tags that indicate table rows, table header, and table data cells, respectively. Figuring out how to type those tags so that they create a series of little boxes on a Web page was never an intuitive process. If you wanted to merge or split cells to create rows or columns with varying numbers of cells, you faced a truly complex challenge.

Thank the cybergods that you have Dreamweaver to make this process easy. With Dreamweaver, you can easily

✔ Create tables and modify both the appearance and the structure of a table by simply clicking and dragging its edges.

✔ Add any type of content to a cell, such as images, text, and multimedia files — even nested tables.

✔ Use the Property inspector to merge and split cells, add color to the background or borders, and change the vertical and horizontal alignment of elements within a cell.

You can create tables in Standard or Expanded mode in Dreamweaver:

✔ **Expanded mode,** shown in Figure 8-1, literally expands the borders and table cells. The added space makes editing content within tables easier: You can easily select inside and around tables. However, the added space also changes the way the table appears in Dreamweaver, which can be confusing because the space isn't visible when you view the page in a browser.

✔ **Standard mode,** as shown in Figure 8-2, is more consistent with how tables will appear in a browser, so generally do most of your table editing, especially resizing and moving tables, in this mode.

You can switch between these two modes by clicking the Standard and Expanded mode buttons in the Layout menu bar at the top of the work area, as shown in Figures 8-1 and 8-2.

Alternatively, you can switch between modes by choosing Choose View➪Table Mode➪Standard Mode or Choose View➪Table Mode➪Expanded Tables Mode.

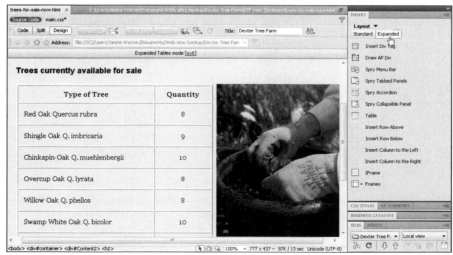

Figure 8-1: When you choose Expanded mode, Dreamweaver adds space around table cells, making it easier to select and edit the content within a table.

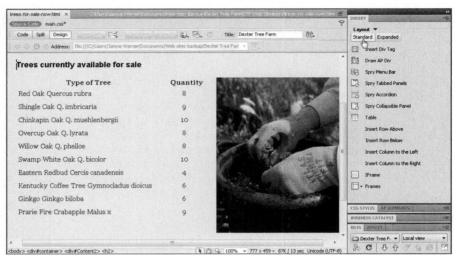

Figure 8-2:
In Standard
mode,
Dream-
weaver's
table display
is more con-
sistent with
how the lay-
out will look
in a Web
browser,
such as
Firefox or
Internet
Explorer.

Creating Tables in Standard Mode

Although Expanded mode is useful for selecting and editing the contents of a table, Standard mode is best for creating tables and editing table properties, such as the width of cells and the borders that surround them. The following tips can help you create a table, and the sections that follow explain how to further refine it:

- ✔ **You can insert a table by choosing Insert⇨Table or by clicking the Table icon in the Common or Layout Insert panel.**

- ✔ **When you insert a new table, the Table dialog box, as shown in Figure 8-3, makes it easy to specify many table settings at once.** Don't worry about perfecting the settings; you can always change these options later.

- ✔ **You can edit all the table options, except the Accessibility options, in the Property inspector.** When you select a table or cell, the attributes appear in the Property inspector at the bottom of the work area. Click the border of any table to select the entire table, and the Property inspector displays the table options, as shown in Figure 8-4. To view all the options, click the expander arrow in the lower-right corner of the Property inspector. (All these options are described in the next section.)

- ✔ **Select a table with the Select Table command.** Sometimes selecting the entire table and not just an individual cell is tricky. If you're having trouble selecting the table, simply place your cursor anywhere inside the table and choose Modify⇨Table⇨Select Table.

To create tables without missing any important steps, check out "Following a workflow for creating tables," at the end of this section. The steps there give you a framework for using Dreamweaver's table options from start to finish.

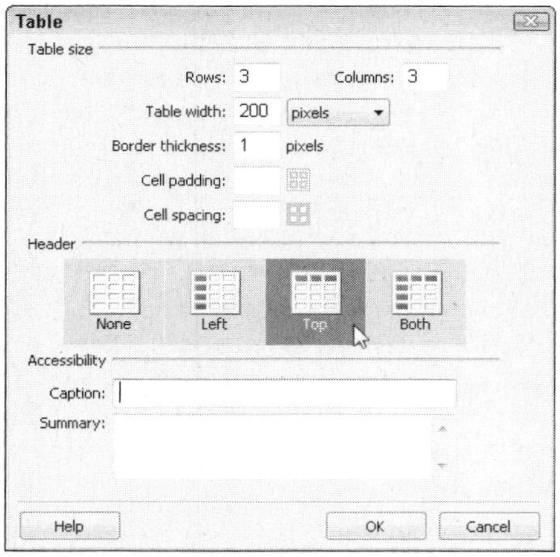

Figure 8-3:
When you insert a table into a Web page, you can specify many table settings in this dialog box.

Figure 8-4:
The Property inspec-tor when a table is selected.

Choosing your table's appearance

When you select a table in Dreamweaver, the Property inspector gives you access to the following options for customizing your table's appearance:

- ✔ **Table:** Provides a text area where you can enter a name for a table. This name, or ID, is useful for targeting the table in scripts.

- ✔ **Rows:** Displays the number of rows in the table. You can alter the size of the table by changing the number. Be careful, though: If you enter a smaller number, Dreamweaver deletes the bottom rows — contents and all.

✔ **Cols:** Displays the number of columns in the table. You can alter the size of the table by changing the number. Again, if you enter a smaller number, Dreamweaver deletes the columns on the right side of the table — contents and all.

✔ **W (width):** Displays the width of the table. You can alter the width by changing the number. You can specify the width as a percentage or a value in pixels. Values expressed as a percentage increase or decrease the table's size relative to the size of the user's browser window or any enclosing container, such as another table or a `<div>` tag.

Table dimensions expressed as a percentage enable you to create a table that changes in size when the browser window is resized. For example, if you want a table to always take up 75 percent of the browser window, no matter how big the user's monitor or display area, set the size as a percentage. If you want a table to always be the same size — that is, to remain the same size regardless of the browser window size — choose pixels rather than percentages for your table width. See the nearby sidebar "How wide should you make a table?" for more help selecting a width that displays well on most browsers.

If a table is inserted inside another container, such as a `<div>` tag or a table with a fixed width, it doesn't change size based on the browser window but is sized based on the container.

Note: Beginning in Dreamweaver CS4 and also in CS5, you no longer find an H (height) field. As a best practice, most designers don't specify table height, because the table's contents may change from one visitor to another. For example, the font size of text depends on a user's system and settings.

✔ **CellPad:** Specifies the space between the contents of a cell and its border.

✔ **CellSpace:** Specifies the space between table cells.

✔ **Align:** Controls the alignment of the table on the Web page. The options are Default, Left, Center, and Right. As a general rule, the Default setting aligns the table from the left side of the browser window or other container.

✔ **Border:** Controls the size of the border around the table. The larger the number, the thicker the border. If you want the border to be invisible, set it to 0.

✔ **Class:** Provides easy access to style sheet options. (See Chapters 5 and 6 for more on CSS.)

✔ **Clear and Convert:** The icons in the lower-left area of the Property inspector (click the expander arrow in the lower-right corner to view them) provide these formatting options:

• **Clear Row Heights** and **Clear Column Widths** enable you to remove all height and width values at one time.

- **Convert Table Widths to Pixels** and **Convert Table Widths to Percents** enable you to automatically change Width settings from percentages to pixels. Pixels specify a fixed width; a percent setting means the browser automatically adjusts the specified percentage of the browser display area.

You can also apply formatting options and change the attributes of any element — such as text, an image, or a multimedia file — within a table cell. To do so, click to select the element and then use the options in the CSS or HTML Property inspector to make your desired changes, just as you would if the element weren't in a table cell. See "Specifying cell options," later in this section, for more details.

Making tables more accessible

A few simple, behind-the-scenes elements can make your tables more accessible to people who are blind or have limited sight and view Web pages with screen readers. *Screen readers* are special browsers that read the contents of a Web page aloud.

One important element is the table header (`<th>`) tag for table headings. The `<th>` tag adds bold formatting and centering to content, and identifies the content as the header of the row or column.

For example, say you have a table like the one in the Dexter Tree Farm Web site that includes a list of trees and the number available of each kind (refer to Figures 8-1 and 8-2). Identifying text in the top row with the table header tag tells the screen reader to repeat the heading before each tree name and number. Thus instead of just reading a long list of names and numbers, the screen reader will identify each cell by the name of the header as it reads through the contents.

You don't have to make all your table headings bold and centered just because you use the table header tag. Like any other HTML tag, you can alter the formatting of the `<th>` tag by creating a tag style (as I explain in Chapter 5).

Dreamweaver also includes Accessibility options at the bottom of the Table dialog box when you first insert a new table (refer to Figure 8-3). Here's what those options do:

- ✔ **Caption:** If you enter a table caption, it's displayed within the table. You can specify where the caption appears with the Align Caption option.
- ✔ **Summary:** The Table Summary doesn't appear in a Web browser but prompts a screen reader to describe the table for visitors who can't *see* the contents of the table. This gives your visitors overall context before they hear the entire table read out loud.

Make sure the table fits the contents

Be aware that table cells automatically adjust to accommodate whatever you insert into them. For example, if you create a cell that's 100 pixels wide and then insert a 300-pixel-wide image, the table cell expands to fit the image. This can cause problems if the overall size of the table isn't set wide enough to accommodate all the objects within the table cells. When you build your tables, be aware of the size of the images and multimedia files you're inserting into cells or you may end up with a mess on your hands.

For example, if you set a table to a total width of 400 pixels and then insert 600 pixels worth of images, the table is forced to adjust in a way that contradicts the settings. When it does, some content may get cut off or expand beyond the desired width of the page layout. Worse yet, the table may not appear the same in all browsers as different browsers try to accommodate these errors in different ways, which can lead to unpredictable results.

If you don't include these Accessibility settings as you insert your table, there is no way to get back to these options in Dreamweaver. To add a label and summary to a table after you insert it into a page in Dreamweaver, you either have to re-create the table or add the code manually in code view.

Specifying cell options

In addition to changing overall table settings, you can specify options for individual cells within a table. When you select a cell, which you can do by clicking to place the cursor anywhere inside the cell area, the Property inspector changes to display the individual properties for that cell (see Figure 8-5), such as the formatting and alignment of the contents of a particular cell.

Beginning in Dreamweaver CS4, the Property inspector features both HTML and CSS settings. CSS settings are generally preferred and work the same for the contents of a table cell as they do for content anywhere else on a Web page. (See Chapters 5 and 6 for more on using CSS.)

You can also change multiple cells at the same time. For example, suppose that you want to format some (but not all) cells in your table with a certain background color and style of text. You can apply the same properties to multiple cells by selecting more than one cell at a time before choosing the settings in the Property inspector. Any properties you change in the Property inspector apply to all selected cells. Here are tips for selecting cells:

✔ **To select adjacent cells,** press the Shift key while clicking to select cells.

✔ **To select multiple cells that aren't adjacent,** press the Ctrl key (the ⌘ key on the Mac) and click each cell you want to select.

✔ **If you're having trouble selecting an individual cell because it contains an image,** click the image and then use either the ← or → key on your keyboard to move the cursor and deselect the image, which activates the Property inspector and displays the options for that cell.

Figure 8-5:
The
Property
inspector (in
CSS mode)
displays cell
properties
when <td>
or <th>
tags are
selected.

When one or more cells are selected (they have to be adjacent for this to work), the top half of the Property inspector controls the formatting of text and URLs within the table cells. The lower half of the Property inspector provides these table cell attribute options (refer to Figure 8-5):

Although the alignment, color, and formatting options in the Property inspector are handy, using CSS is the preferred option. You learn more about working with CSS and creating styles to alter the appearance of HTML tags, such as the table tags, in Chapters 5 and 6.

✔ **Merge Cells icon:** Merges two or more cells. To merge cells, you must first select two or more cells by clicking and dragging or by pressing either the Shift or Ctrl key while selecting multiple cells.

✔ **Split Cell icon:** Splits one cell into two. When you select this option, a dialog box lets you specify whether you want to split the row (you split the cell horizontally) or the column (you split the cell vertically). You can then specify the number of columns or rows, which controls how many times the cell divides. Note that you can apply the Split Cell option to only one cell at a time.

See the section, "Merging and splitting cells" later in this chapter for more details about working with these options.

✔ **Horz:** Controls the horizontal alignment of the cell contents.

✔ **Vert:** Controls the vertical alignment of the cell contents.

See "Aligning table content in columns and rows" later in this section for tips on working with the Horz and Vert alignment options.

- ✔ **W:** Controls the width of the cell.

- ✔ **H:** Controls the height of the cell.

- ✔ **No Wrap:** Prevents word wrapping within the cell. The cell widens to accommodate all text while you type or paste it into a cell. (Normally, the excess text just moves down to the next line and increases the height of the cell.)

- ✔ **Header:** Formats a cell's contents by using a header tag, which displays the text in bold and centered by default in most Web browsers.

- ✔ **Bg (color):** Click in the color well to select a background color from the color palette or enter a hexadecimal color code into the text field. If you use the color palette, the hexadecimal code is entered automatically into the Bg color field. Make sure you include the # sign if you add your own hexadecimal color or the color will not display properly in many browsers.

Aligning table content in columns and rows

Clean alignment of elements in columns and rows makes your table neat and easy to read. Achieving that look can be tricky, however, because you don't have as much control in HTML as you have in a program such as Excel, where you can align numbers to the decimal point, for example. In an HTML table, you can align the content of columns to the left, right, or center. The following steps explain the basics of aligning rows and columns in your table (and you find tips for solving common alignment problems, too):

1. **Select the column or row for which you want to change the alignment.**

   Place the cursor in the first cell in the column or row you want to align; then, click and drag your mouse to highlight all the columns or rows that you want to change.

2. **Choose an alignment option from the Horz (horizontal) or Vert (vertical) drop-down lists in the Property inspector (refer to Figure 8-5).**

   The content of the cell adjusts to match the selected alignment option.

   Alternatively, you can access many formatting options, including alignment options, by selecting a table and then right-clicking (Windows) or Control-clicking (Mac).

If you follow the preceding steps but table contents still aren't aligning, try the following tips:

- ✔ **If you use the same number of digits after the decimal point in all your numbers, you can get them to line up in a column.** For example, if one price is $12.99 and another is $14, express the latter as $14.00; then, when you right align, the numbers line up properly. (If your columns still aren't lining up the way you want them to, consider using a monospace font, such as Courier, which lines up better.)

✔ **If you're having trouble aligning the contents of adjacent cells, set the vertical alignment to Top.** A common frustration when you're building tables is that you have two or more rows side by side with text in one and images in the other, and you want the top of the image and the top of the text to line up. Often they don't line up because they're different lengths, and the table is trying to adjust the contents to best use the space within their respective cells. The solution is simple: Select all the cells you want to align, and in the Property inspector, change vertical alignment to Top. Seemingly like magic, all the content jumps right to the top of the cells and lines up perfectly. This is such a common problem that I routinely set the vertical alignment of table cells to Top.

✔ **Make sure you use the same formatting, paragraph and break tags if you want the contents of adjacent cells to line up.** Another situation in which the contents of adjacent cells don't line up properly occurs when you include paragraph tags around the text or an image in one cell and not in another. Use split view (by clicking the Split button at the top of the workspace) and make sure that the code in both cells matches. If you have <p> tags around the contents in one cell and not in another, make sure to include them in the second cell or remove them from the first so that both cells match.

Merging and splitting table cells

Sometimes, the easiest way to modify the number of cells in a table is to *merge* cells (combine two or more cells into one) or *split* cells (split one cell into two or more rows or columns). With this technique, you can vary the space in table sections and customize table structures. For example, you may want a long cell space across the top of your table for a banner and then multiple cells below it so that you can control the spacing between columns of text or images. The following two sets of steps show you how to merge and split cells in a table.

To merge cells, in an existing table:

1. **Highlight two or more adjacent cells by clicking and dragging the mouse from the first cell to the last.**

   You can merge only cells that are adjacent to one another and in the same row or column.

2. **Click the Merge Selected Cells icon, in the lower-left region of the Property inspector (as shown in Figure 8-6), to merge the selected cells into a single cell.**

The cells are merged into a single cell by using the `colspan` or `rowspan` attributes. These HTML attributes make a single cell merge with adjacent cells by spanning extra rows or columns in the table.

Figure 8-6:
The
Property
inspector
includes
small icons
that merge
and split
cells.

To split a cell, create a new table or open a page with an existing table and follow these steps:

1. **Click to place the cursor inside any cell you want to split.**

2. **Click the Split Selected Cell icon, in the lower-left region of the Property inspector.**

   The Split Cell dialog box appears.

3. **Select Rows or Columns in the dialog box, depending on how you want to divide the cell.**

   You can split a cell into however many new rows or columns you want.

4. **Type the number of rows or columns you want to create.**

   The selected cell is split into the number of rows or columns you entered.

Following a workflow for creating tables

If you're starting from scratch, create a new, blank HTML page and follow these steps from the beginning:

1. **Make sure that you're in Standard mode. (Choose View⇨Table Mode⇨Standard Mode.)**

2. **Click to place the cursor where you want to create a table.**

   In both Standard and Expanded modes, tables are created automatically in the top-left area of the page, unless you insert them after other content.

3. **Click the Table icon on the Common or Layout Insert panel.**

   Alternatively, you can choose Insert⇨Table. The Insert Table dialog box appears.

4. **In the appropriate boxes, type the number of columns and rows you want to include in your table.**

   Remember you can always add or remove cells later with the Property inspector.

5. **Specify the width, border, cell padding, and cell spacing.**

   See "Choosing your table's appearance" earlier in this chapter for specifics about each of these options.

6. **Choose the header option that best corresponds to the layout you want for your table to create a row of header cells across the top, side, or both.**

7. **Add a caption and summary in the Accessibility section and click OK.**

   The table automatically appears on the page.

   If you're not familiar with the header, caption, and summary options, see "Making tables more accessible" earlier in this chapter for details.

8. **Click to place the cursor in a cell and then type the data you want in that cell. Repeat for each cell.**

   Alternatively, you can use Edit⇨Paste Special to insert columnar data from another program, such as Excel.

   If you want to import data from a table you've created in a program, such as Word or Excel, see the section "Importing Table Data from Other Programs," later in this chapter.

9. **Apply formatting options, such as bold or italic, to selected cells and their contents by choosing the option from the from the Property inspector.**

   The sections "Specifying cell options," "Aligning table content in columns and rows," and "Merging and splitting table cells" explain the basics of table formatting.

Sorting Table Data

When you're working with lots of columnar data, you want to be able to sort that data just as you do in a spreadsheet program, such as Excel. In Dreamweaver, you can sort data even after you format it in HTML. You still don't have as many options as you do in Excel. For example, you can sort an entire table based on a specified row, but you can't sort different rows individually.

To use the Sort Table Data feature, create a new, blank HTML page, add a table with several rows and columns, and add some content. (I explain how in the preceding section.) You may also open an existing page with a table of columnar data. Then, follow these steps:

1. **Select the table you want to sort.**

    To select a table for sorting, you can simply place the cursor in any cell of the table you want to sort.

2. **Choose View⇨Table Mode⇨Standard Mode.**

3. **Choose Commands⇨Sort Table.**

    The Sort Table dialog box appears, as shown in Figure 8-7.

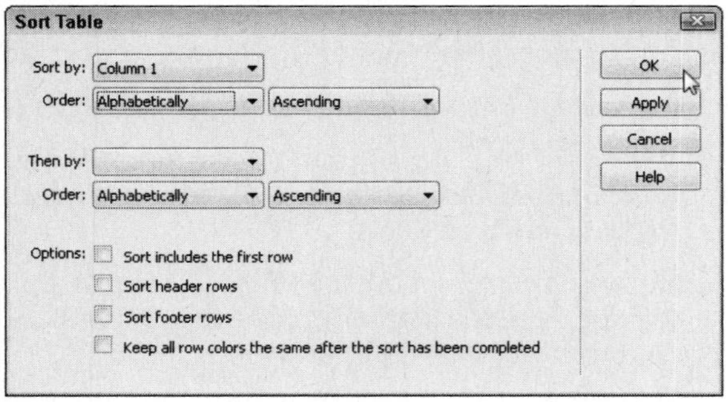

Figure 8-7: You can sort cell contents alphabetically or numerically, even after they're formatted in HTML.

4. **Specify which column you want to sort by and then choose Alphabetically or Numerically and Ascending or Descending.**

    You can set up one or two sorts to happen simultaneously and opt whether to include the first row and whether to keep the `<tr>` (table row) attributes with a sorted row by selecting Keep All Row Colors the Same.

5. **Click OK.**

    The selected cells are sorted, just as they are in a program, such as Excel. (Pretty cool, huh?)

Importing Table Data from Other Programs

Manually converting financial data or other spreadsheet information can be tedious. Fortunately, Dreamweaver includes a special feature that enables you to insert table data created in other applications, such as Word or Excel. To use this feature, the table data must be saved from the other program in a *delimited* format — the columns of data are separated by tabs, commas, colons, semicolons, or another type of delimiter. Most spreadsheet and database applications, as well as Microsoft Word, enable you to save data in a delimited format; files with a CSV (Comma Separated Values) file extension are one example. Consult the documentation for the application you're using to find out how to convert your data into a delimited format, and then you can import the data into Dreamweaver.

To import table data into Dreamweaver after it's been saved in a delimited format (such as CSV) or in its native application (such as Access or Excel), create a new, blank HTML page or open an existing file and follow these steps to import the data:

1. **Choose File➪Import➪Tabular Data.**

   The Import Tabular Data dialog box appears (see Figure 8-8).

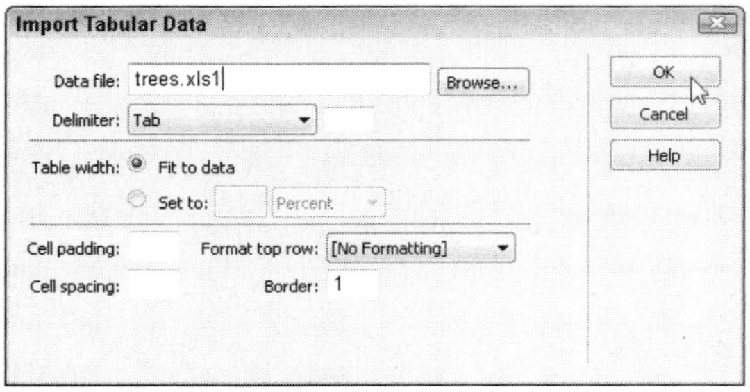

Figure 8-8:
You can import tabular data into Dreamweaver from other programs, such as Excel.

2. **In the Data File text box, type the name of the file you want to import or use the Browse button to locate the file.**

3. **In the Delimiter drop-down list, select the delimiter format you used when you saved your file in the native application.**

   The delimiter options are Tab, Comma, Semicolon, Colon, and Other. You should have made this choice when you exported the data from the original program in which you created it, such as Excel or Access. If you don't remember what you chose, you can always go to the original program and export the data again. You must select the correct option for your data to import correctly.

4. **Select the table width.**

   If you choose Fit to Data, Dreamweaver automatically creates the table to fit the data being imported. If you choose Set, you must specify a percent or pixel size.

5. **(Optional) Specify the cell padding and cell spacing only if you want extra space around the data in the table to be created.**

6. **(Optional) Choose an option from the Format Top Row drop-down list only if you want to format the data in the top row of the table.**

   Your options are Bold, Italic, or Bold Italic.

7. **Specify the border size.**

   The default is 1, which puts a small border around the table. Choose 0 if you don't want the border to be visible. Choose a larger number if you want a thicker border.

8. **Click OK to automatically create a table with the imported data.**

Dreamweaver also enables you to export data from a table into a delimited format. This capability is useful if you want to export data from a Web page so that you can import it into another program, such as Word or Excel, or into a database program, such as FileMaker or Access. To export data from Dreamweaver, place the cursor anywhere in the table and choose File➪Export➪Table. In the Export Table dialog box, choose from the options on the Delimiter drop-down list (you can choose Tab, Space, Comma, Semicolon, or Colon). From the Line Breaks drop-down list, specify the operating system (you can choose Windows, Mac, or UNIX).

Using Tables for Spacing and Alignment

Tables have long been used on the Web to create page layouts that require more than basic alignment of elements on a page. In the early days of Web design, using tables was one of the only ways you could get around many of the limitations of basic HTML and accomplish some otherwise impossible design feats, such as evenly spacing bullets, creating columns side-by-side on a page, and spanning headlines or images across multiple columns.

Today, CSS offers a much better option for these kinds of designs, but many people are still using tables and you may have Web sites that you created in this way (or you may inherit a design that uses them). If you're working on a site that's designed with tables to create a page layout for any content that isn't tabular, such as the Chocolate Game Rules page, as shown in Figure 8-9, consider redesigning the page layout with `<div>` tags and CSS, which are covered in detail in Chapter 6.

Figure 8-9:
Many two-column page layouts, such as the one shown here, were created with HTML tables.

Nesting Tables within Tables

Placing tables within tables, or *nested tables,* can help you create extremely complex designs. For example, with a table that contains scores of all the baseball games in a season, you could add a smaller table inside one cell to include detailed stats of an exceptional game. You create nested tables by inserting a table within a cell of another table.

The best Web designs communicate the information to your audience in the most elegant and understandable way and are easy to download. To make sure that your designs don't get too messy, remember these guidelines:

✔ A table within a table within a table is nested three levels deep. Anything more than that gets hairy.

✔ Pages that use nested tables take longer to download because browsers have to interpret each table individually before rendering the page. For some designs, the slightly longer download time is worth it, but in most cases, you're better off adding or merging cells in one table, as I explain in the section "Merging and splitting table cells," earlier in this chapter. One situation that makes a nested table worth the added download time is when you want to place a table of financial or other data in the midst of a complex page design.

To place a table inside another table, follow these steps:

1. **Click to place the cursor where you want to create the first table.**

2. **Choose Insert⇨Table.**

   The Insert Table dialog box appears.

3. **Type the number of columns and rows you need for your design.**

4. **Set the Width option to whatever is appropriate for your design and then click OK.**

   The table is sized automatically to the width you set.

5. **Click to place the cursor in the cell in which you want to place the second table.**

6. **Repeat Steps 2–4, specifying the number of columns and rows you want and the width of the table.**

   The new table appears inside the cell of the first table.

7. **Type the information that you want in the nested table cells as you would enter content in any other table.**

Part III
Making It Cool with Advanced Features

The 5th Wave   By Rich Tennant

"Evidently he died of natural causes following a marathon session animating everything on his personal Web site. And no, Morganstern — the irony isn't lost on me."

In this part . . .

Dreamweaver's behaviors, covered in Chapter 9, make it easy to use JavaScript to create rollover images and pop-up windows, as well as more complex image swaps. In Chapter 10, you find out how to add multimedia files, such as sound, video, and Flash animations, to your Web pages. In Chapter 11, you discover that Dreamweaver has all the tools you need to create forms for your Web site. In Chapter 12, you discover how to use Dreamweaver's Spry menu to create advanced features for your site, such as drop-down menus and collapsible panels using AJAX. Chapter 13 introduces you to creating dynamic sites in Dreamweaver, and Chapter 14 walks you through the steps of setting and using InContext Editing with site contributors as well as introducing the new Business Catalyst feature.

Chapter 9

Adding Interactivity with Behaviors

*W*ant to add cool effects like rollovers and pop-up windows? Dreamweaver's behaviors make it easier than ever to create these kinds of interactive features with a JavaScript scripting language.

Behaviors are ready-to-use scripts that you can customize to create a variety of features. You can apply behaviors to almost any element on an HTML page and even to the entire page itself. For example, you can use the Swap Image behavior to create an interactive slide show or the Open Browser Window behavior to play a video in a small, separate browser window.

In this chapter, I introduce you to the Behaviors panel and show you how to use some of Dreamweaver's most popular options.

Brushing Up on Behavior Basics

When you start working with behaviors in Dreamweaver, you can get up and running more easily if you start with this basic introduction to how behaviors work and the terminology they use. When you set up a behavior, you can choose from a number of *triggers,* or *events,* such as OnMouseOver or OnClick. Consider this slightly corny example: If you tickle someone and make the person laugh, you used an event to trigger an action. Dreamweaver would call the tickling the *event* and the laughter the *action*. The combination is a Dreamweaver *behavior*.

You may already be familiar with the *rollover* behavior, when one image is switched for another. In a rollover, putting your mouse over an image is the *event*. The *action* is the switching of the original image for another image, as shown in Figure 9-1. Rollovers are common in navigation, and you can create one with simple effects that use two images, as long as the images are exactly the same size. Alternatively, you can use the Swap Image behavior to create much more complex effects, such as causing any or all the images on a page to change when any other element is triggered.

The rollover behavior used to be a great way to create rollover effects on links, but with the advent of CSS, a better option has emerged. The rollover behavior is still a cool feature when you want to swap two images, but as you learn in Chapter 6, you can now create links with rollover effects using CSS, an option that's more search engine friendly and more accessible to people who use screen readers.

Figure 9-1:
When a
cursor rolls
over the
main image
on this
page, a sec-
ond image
of equal size
is displayed
in its place.

Dreamweaver includes about 20 behaviors, and you can download and install more. (You find instructions in the "Installing New Extensions for Behaviors" section, at the end of this chapter.)

Creating a Rollover Image

Rollover images, as the name implies, are designed to react when someone rolls a cursor over an image. The effect can be as dramatic as a picture of a dog being replaced by a picture of a lion, or as subtle as the color of a word changing as one image replaces another. Either way, this is one of the most common JavaScripts in use on the Web, and it's such a popular feature that Dreamweaver includes a special dialog box just for rollovers.

In the section that follows, you find instructions for using the Behaviors panel, where Dreamweaver stores most of the Behaviors included in the program. In this section, you find instructions for using the Insert Rollover Image dialog box, which makes creating a simple rollover effect one of the easiest behaviors to apply.

You can create more complex rollover image effects with the Swap Image option from the Behaviors panel. The Swap Image option enables you to change multiple images at the same time.

To create a simple rollover effect with Dreamweaver's Insert Image Rollover dialog box, follow these steps:

1. **Place your cursor on the page where you want the rollover to appear.**

   Rollover effects require at least two images: one for the initial state and one for the rollover state. You can use two different images or two similar ones, but both should have the same dimensions. Otherwise, you see strange scaling effects because both images must be displayed in exactly the same space on the page.

2. **Choose Insert⇨Image Objects⇨Rollover Image.**

   Alternatively, you can use the drop-down list available from the images icon in the Insert panel and select Rollover Image.

   The Insert Rollover Image dialog box appears, as shown in Figure 9-2.

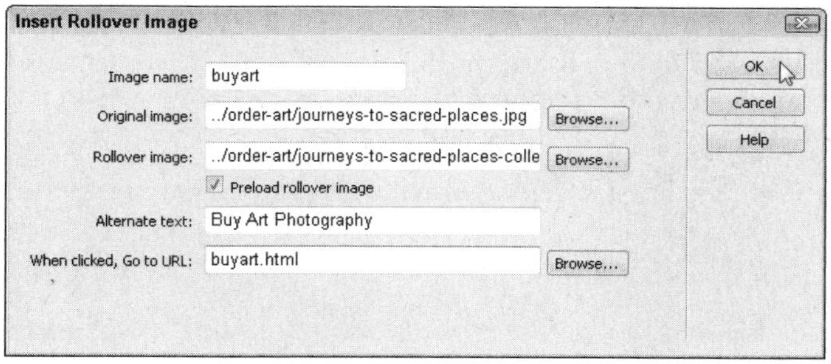

Figure 9-2: Select the original and rollover images.

Insert Rollover Image

Image name:	buyart
Original image:	../order-art/journeys-to-sacred-places.jpg Browse...
Rollover image:	../order-art/journeys-to-sacred-places-colle Browse...
	☑ Preload rollover image
Alternate text:	Buy Art Photography
When clicked, Go to URL:	buyart.html Browse...

OK   Cancel   Help

3. **In the Image Name box, name your image.**

   Before you can apply a behavior to an element, such as an image, the element must have a name so that the behavior script can reference it. You can name elements anything you like as long as you don't use spaces or special characters.

4. **In the Original Image box, specify the first image you want visible. Use the Browse button to locate and select the image.**

If the images aren't already in your local site folder, Dreamweaver copies them into your site when you create the rollover. (If you haven't already set up your site in Dreamweaver, see Chapter 2 for more on this important preliminary step.)

5. **In the Rollover Image box, enter the image you want to become visible when visitors move their cursors over the first image.**

Again, you can use the Browse button to locate and select the image.

6. **Select the Preload Rollover Image check box to load all rollover images into the browser's cache when the page first loads.**

If you don't choose to do this step, your visitors may experience a delay because the second image won't be downloaded until a mouse is rolled over the original image.

7. **In the When Clicked, Go to URL box, enter any Web address or browse to locate another page in your site that you want to link to.**

If you don't specify a URL, Dreamweaver automatically inserts the # sign as a placeholder in the code.

The # sign is a common technique for creating links that don't link anywhere. Because rollover images that don't link to another page have many great uses, this is a useful technique. Just remember that if you do want your rollover to link, you need to replace the # sign with a link to another page. See Chapter 2 for details about setting links.

8. **Click OK.**

The images are set up automatically as a rollover.

9. **Click the globe icon at the top of the workspace to preview your work in a browser where you can test how the rollover works.**

Peeking at the JavaScript code

JavaScript is the code behind Dreamweaver behaviors. Writing JavaScript is more complex than writing HTML code, but not as difficult as writing in a programming language, such as C# or Java. (No, Java and JavaScript aren't the same.) Dreamweaver takes most of the challenge out of JavaScript by giving you a graphic interface that doesn't require you to write the complicated code yourself. When you use behaviors, Dreamweaver automatically writes the code for you behind the scenes.

To fully appreciate what Dreamweaver can do for you, you may want to switch to code view after setting up a behavior just to see the complex code required when you use JavaScript. If you don't like what you see, don't worry: Go back to design view and you can continue to let Dreamweaver take care of the code for you. (I just want you to see how lucky you are that Dreamweaver includes these features.)

Adding Behaviors to a Web Page

Dreamweaver offers a number of behaviors you can choose from, including the Swap Image behavior and the Open New Browser Window behavior covered in detail in the next two sections. The process of adding other behaviors is similar to these two, but each behavior has its quirks. The tips and tricks you find here can help you get started with behaviors, find out where the majority of the behavior features are in the program, and how you match behaviors with triggers using the Behaviors panel.

Creating swaps with multiple images

Before you start creating a more complex page design with Dreamweaver's Swap Image behavior, first take a look at the finished page so you can see the result before you get into the details. Notice in Figure 9-3 that a collection of thumbnail images is on the bottom of the page and a larger version of one of those images is displayed in the main area of the page.

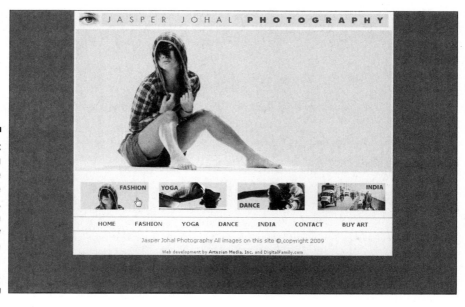

Figure 9-3:
When you use the Swap Image behavior, you can replace any or all the images on a page.

Notice in Figure 9-4 that when the page is displayed in a browser and I roll my cursor over a different thumbnail image on the bottom, the larger image displayed above it changes. With the Swap Image behavior, you can replace any or all the images on a page.

TIP

When you use the Swap Image behavior, it's important to make all of the images that you will 'swap' the exact same size (height and width).

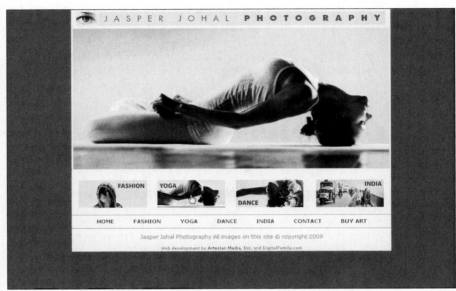

Figure 9-4: When you preview a behavior in a browser, you can see the effect of the Swap Image behavior when the cursor is rolled over an image.

Follow these steps to use the Swap Image behavior:

1. Create a page design with all the images you want displayed initially.

In the page design I created for these photos by Jasper Johal, the initial page design includes all thumbnail images positioned on the bottom of the page, and the first of the big images displayed in the main area just above them.

TECHNICAL STUFF

You can use the Swap Image behavior to change images on any Web page no matter how the layout is created. In the design featured in this section, I used CSS to create a layout with separate `<div>` tags for the row of thumbnails on the bottom and another `<div>` tag for the bigger image above the thumbnails. These divs are positioned with CSS. (Find instructions for creating CSS layouts in Chapter 6.)

2. Name your images in the Property inspector, as shown in Figure 9-5.

To target your images with JavaScript, which is how behaviors work, first give each image a unique ID. The image ID isn't the same as the image filename, although you can use the same or similar names. In this example, I gave each thumbnail image an ID that matched the text on the small image, to make indentifying the thumbnails easy. You can name images anything you like as long as you don't use spaces or special characters. I find it helpful to use names that correspond to the image or its order.

Using the same or similar IDs for your images as you use for the image file-names helps make it easier to match them when you create the behavior.

In contrast, I usually name the main image something simple and distinctive, such as `display_photo` or `mainImage`, to make it easier to keep track of which image I'm replacing each time.

Although Dreamweaver automatically assigns a name to each image you insert into a Web page, I find it easier to keep track when I set up the Swap Image behavior if I use names that describe the images or correspond to their order.

3. **Choose Window⟳Behaviors.**

The Behaviors panel opens. You can drag the Behaviors panel elsewhere on the page, and you can expand it by dragging its bottom or side. You may also want to close any other open panels to make more room by clicking the dark gray bar at the top of any panel.

4. **Select an image and choose the Swap Image behavior.**

First click to select the image in the page that will serve as the trigger for the action. In this example, I'm using the thumbnail images as triggers, so I select them one at a time. I started with the fashion thumbnail, but because it triggers the image that appears when the page is first displayed, I'm going to use the second one as the example here. You repeat this same process for each thumbnail.

Figure 9-5:
In the top left of the Property inspector, enter an ID for each image.

Figure 9-6:
With a thumbnail image selected, use the drop-down list in the Behaviors panel to specify an action, such as Swap Image.

In the example shown in Figures 9-6 and 9-7, I've selected the second thumbnail image named `yoga`. With that trigger image selected in the workspace, I then click the Add Behavior arrow in the Behaviors panel (the small arrow under the plus sign) to open the drop-down list of actions, and then select the action I want to apply. In the example shown in Figure 9-6, I selected the Swap Image action, which opens the Swap Image dialog box shown in Figure 9-7.

5. **Specify the images to swap.**

   a. **In the Swap Image dialog box, select the ID for the image that will be replaced.**

   In Figure 9-7, I selected the image with the ID `main Image`. Note that you don't want to choose the image you selected; you want to choose the image you want to replace. In this case I'm replacing the main fashion image with the main yoga image using the yoga thumbnail as the trigger.

   b. **Click the Browse button to select the image that replaces the main image.**

I selected the `main-yoga.jpg` image, which I carefully named to correspond to the matching thumbnail, which is named yoga. Now when a user rolls a cursor over the yoga thumbnail image, the big photo from the fashion gallery will be replaced with the big photo from the yoga gallery.

Note: If the image is not already saved in the local site folder, Dreamweaver will offer to copy it there for you.

Figure 9-7:
Use the Browse button to select the image you want to swap.

6. **At the bottom of the Swap Image dialog box, select Preload Images to instruct the browser to load all the images into the cache when the page is loaded.**

   If you don't select this option, a delay may occur when the image swap is used.

7. **Deselect the Restore Images OnMouseOut option if you wish.**

   The Restore Images OnMouseOut option means that when an event is completed (such as the mouse is moved off the triggering thumbnail), the original image is replaced. By default, Dreamweaver preselects this option for the Swap Image behavior, but in the example shown here, I deselect it because I found that replacing the original image each time I rolled the cursor over another thumbnail was distracting.

8. **After you specify all the settings for the behavior, click OK.**

   The new behavior appears in the Behaviors panel.

9. **Specify an event for the behavior.**

   After the action is applied, you can go back and specify which event will trigger the action (as shown in Figure 9-8). By default, Dreamweaver applies the `OnMouseOver` event when you use the Swap Image action, but you can change that to any available event, such as `OnClick`, which requires that the user click the image to trigger the Swap Image action. In this example, I leave it set to `OnMouseOver`.

The list of Behaviors and Events varies depending on the element selected and the applied behavior. For more information about events and what each one accomplishes, see the "Choosing an event for a behavior" sidebar, elsewhere in this chapter.

Figure 9-8:
When you set up a behavior, you can specify any available action to trigger an event.

You can display or hide events by clicking the Show All Events icon in the top left of the Behaviors panel. Note that if you're using Windows, you also see a collection of events that begin with an <a> and are for elements that are linked.

10. **Apply additional behaviors.**

    To apply the Swap Image behavior to other images on a page, repeat Steps 5–9, clicking to select the image you want to serve as a trigger and then specifying the corresponding image that should be swapped. In this example, I selected each of the thumbnails in turn and set up a Swap Image behavior that replaced the `mainImage` with the corresponding larger version of the photo in the thumbnail.

For best display, make sure that the images that are swapped, such as the large photos shown in the main display area of this site, are all the same size.

11. **Test your work in a browser.**

    You can't see the effects of behaviors like this one until you click the Live View button at the top of the workspace in Dreamweaver or preview your page in a browser, such as Firefox or Internet Explorer.

Choosing an event for a behavior

Events, in interactive Web-speak, are things a user does to trigger a behavior or an action in a Web page. Clicking an image is an event, as is loading a page into a browser or pressing a key on the keyboard. Different browser versions support different events (the more recent the browser, the more events available). Some events are available only for certain kinds of objects or behaviors. If an event can't be used with a selected element or behavior, it appears dimmed. This list describes the most common events:

✔ onBlur: Triggered when the specified element stops being the focus of user interaction. For example, when a user clicks outside a text field after clicking in the text field, the browser generates an onBlur event for the text field. onBlur is the opposite of onFocus.

✔ onClick: Triggered when the user clicks an element, such as a link, a button, or an image.

✔ onDblClick: Triggered when the user double-clicks the specified element.

✔ onError: Triggered when a browser error occurs while a page or an image is loading. This event can be caused, for example, when an image or a URL can't be found on the server.

✔ onFocus: Triggered when the specified element becomes the focus of user interaction. For example, clicking in or tabbing to a text field of a form generates an onFocus event.

✔ onKeyDown: Triggered as soon as the user presses any key on the keyboard. (The user doesn't have to release the key for this event to be generated.)

✔ onKeyPress: Triggered when the user presses and releases any key on the keyboard. This event is like a combination of the onKeyDown and onKeyUp events.

✔ onKeyUp: Triggered when the user releases a key on the keyboard after pressing it.

✔ onLoad: Triggered when an image or the entire page finishes loading.

✔ onMouseDown: Triggered when the user presses the mouse button. (The user doesn't have to release the mouse button to generate this event.)

✔ onMouseMove: Triggered when the user moves the mouse while pointing to the specified element and the pointer doesn't move away from the element (stays within its boundaries).

✔ onMouseOut: Triggered when the pointer moves off the specified element (usually a link).

✔ onMouseOver: Triggered when the mouse pointer moves over the specified element. Opposite of onMouseOut.

✔ onMouseUp: Triggered when a mouse button that's been pressed is released.

Using the Open Browser Window behavior

You can use behaviors in Dreamweaver to create many interactive features, such as opening a new browser window when someone clicks a link. As you can see in Figure 9-9, this is a great way to make supplemental information available without losing the original page a visitor was viewing. The Open Browser Window behavior enables you to specify the size of the new window and to display it over the existing window.

Figure 9-9:
A larger
version of
the photo
of pilgrims
crossing
the Ganges
River is
displayed
in a new
browser
window
when a user
clicks the
thumbnail
version of
the image.

To add the Open Browser Window behavior to a selected image (or any other element) on a page, follow these steps:

1. **Create the page that will open in the new browser window.**

   For this example, I created a new blank HTML page and inserted a larger version of the image that corresponds to the thumbnail I'll be using as a trigger. The goal is that when a user clicks the trigger image, a browser window will open that is sized exactly to fit the larger image but much smaller than the full browser window.

   When you name files that will be used in behaviors, such as a page that will open when the Open Browser Window behavior is used, avoid using slashes anywhere in a filename or numbers at the beginning of a filename (you can use numbers anywhere else in the name). You can use hyphens and underscores.

2. **Select the image, text, or other element you want to serve as the trigger for the action.**

   You can select any image, text, or other element on a page and apply a behavior to it the same way.

3. **Choose Window➪Behaviors to open the Behaviors panel.**

4. **Click the plus sign (+) and choose the behavior you want from the drop-down list.**

   In this example, I selected the Open Browser Window behavior.

   If a behavior appears dimmed, it can't be associated with the selected element. For example, the Swap Image behavior can be applied only to an image, so it appears dimmed if you've selected text or another element.

5. **In the Open Browser Window dialog box, as shown in Figure 9-10, specify the settings.**

   You can set a number of options that control how the new browser window appears:

   • **Use the Browse button to the right of the URL to Display box to select the page you want to open in the new browser window.** (You can also enter a URL in this box to open a page in another Web site.)

   • **Set the window width and height to specify the exact pixel size of the new browser window that will open.** In this example, I set the width to the exact size of the image.

   • **Select the options Navigation Toolbar, Location Toolbar, Status Bar, Menu Bar, Scrollbars as Needed, or Resize Handles if you want the new browser window to include any of these features.** I selected Scrollbars as Needed in case my visitor's browser window is smaller than the size I specified for the photo, but I left all the others deselected because I want a clean, simple browser window without any menus or other features.

   • **Name the new window, which is important if you want to target that same window to load other pages into it.**

Figure 9-10:
Specify settings for the display of the window.

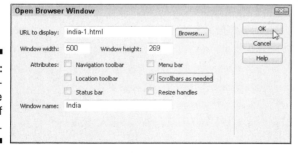

6. **After you specify all the settings for the behavior, click OK.**

   The new behavior appears in the Behaviors panel.

7. **To change the event that triggers your behavior, select the current event from the left side of the Behaviors panel.**

   In the Events drop-down list, select any available event to serve as the trigger for the behavior. For more information about events and what each one accomplishes, see the "Choosing an event for a behavior" sidebar, elsewhere in this chapter.

8. **To test the action, choose File⇨Preview in Browser.**

   Click the image to test whether a new browser window opens.

Attaching Multiple Behaviors

You can attach multiple behaviors to the same element on a page (as long as they don't conflict, of course). For example, you can attach one action that's triggered when users click an image and another when they move their cursors over the image. You can also trigger the same action by using multiple events. For example, you can open the same page in a new browser window when a user triggers any number of events.

To attach additional behaviors to an element, click the plus sign in the Behaviors panel and select another option from the pop-up list. Repeat this process as many times as you want.

Editing a Behavior

You can always go back and edit a behavior after you create it. You can choose a different event to trigger the behavior, choose a different action, or remove behaviors. You can also change behavior options after a behavior is applied.

To edit a behavior, follow these steps:

1. **Select an object with a behavior attached.**

2. **Choose Window⇨Behaviors to open the Behaviors panel.**

   Here are some options you can choose in the Behaviors panel:

   • **Change a triggering event:** Choose a different event in the Events drop-down list in the Behaviors panel.

- **Remove a behavior:** Click the action in the Behaviors panel to select it and then click the minus sign at the top of the pane. The behavior disappears.

- **Change parameters for an action:** Double-click the gear icon next to the action and change the parameters in the dialog box that opens.

- **Change the order of actions when multiple actions are set:** Select an action and then click the Move Event Value Up or Move Event Value Down buttons to move the action to a different position in the list of actions.

Installing New Extensions for Behaviors

Even with all the cool features in Dreamweaver, a day will almost certainly come when you'll want to do things that Dreamweaver can't do with the features that shipped with the program. Fortunately, the programmers who created Dreamweaver made it possible for other programmers to add features with the Extension Manager. The result? You can add new functionality by adding extensions from a variety of third-party sources.

You can find extensions that do everything from adding highly customizable drop-down and fly-out menus to full-featured shopping cart systems. Keep in mind, however, that not all extensions are well supported and few come with good instructions. They're not all free, either. Some cost hundreds of dollars, but most are in the $20–$50 range. When you visit the Dreamweaver Exchange site, you find reviews and rankings to help you sort through the best options.

In the following steps, I explain how you find, download, and install a free Dreamweaver extension. Although how extensions work after they're installed can differ dramatically, the basic process of adding them to Dreamweaver is nearly the same.

1. **Visit the Dreamweaver Exchange site.**

   Get to the Dreamweaver Exchange site by

   - Choosing Get More Behaviors from the bottom of the Behaviors drop-down list in the Behaviors panel.

   - Visiting www.adobe.com/exchange and following the link to the Dreamweaver section.

   - Clicking the link in the bottom right of the Dreamweaver Welcome screen.

Note: If you launch Dreamweaver and find a link to download an update for Dreamweaver instead of the link to the Exchange site, by all means download and install the update first. After you're finished, the update link is replaced by the link to the Exchange site.

 2. **Sort through the many available extensions.**

You'll find a wide range of extensions on the Dreamweaver Exchange site. You can search through extensions by category, keyword, and ranking options. Many of the extensions featured on the Exchange site include links to their creators' sites, where you'll often find even more extensions.

 3. **Select an extension and review its features.**

When you click a link to an extension on the Exchange site, you'll find more information about the extension, including system requirements and the version of Dreamweaver that the extension was designed for. In general, you can use extensions designed for earlier versions of Dreamweaver in more recent versions. Be aware, however, that extensions designed for later versions of Dreamweaver usually won't work in earlier versions of the program.

Before you leave the extension's page, I highly recommend that you take the time to read the special instructions in the middle of the page.

Some extensions include important instructions, such as where you find the new feature in the Dreamweaver interface after it's installed and warnings that some functionality of an extension will work only when previewed on a live Web server (this is true for the random image extension, for example).

 4. **To download an extension, click the Download button (for free extensions) or the Buy button next to the extension name and save the extension to your hard drive.**

 5. **Install the new extension after it's downloaded by choosing Help➪ Manage Extensions to open the installation dialog box.**

Most extensions require that you close Dreamweaver before installation, and most install with the click of a button. Dreamweaver's Extension Manager launches automatically to install most extensions.

 6. **In the Extension Manager dialog box, choose File➪Install Extension and then browse your drive to select the extension file you downloaded.**

After the installation is complete, Dreamweaver displays instructions for using the extension. These are usually the same as the instructions included in the middle of the page on the Exchange site.

Pay special attention to the part of the instructions that tells you where you'll find your newly installed extensions. Extensions may be added to menus, dialog boxes, and other parts of Dreamweaver depending on their functionality and how the programmer set them up. Finding them can be hard if you don't know where to look.

7. **Launch Dreamweaver and find the new menu option, button, or other interface feature that controls your new extension.**

   In many cases, all you have to do is open an existing page or create a new page in Dreamweaver and then open the newly added dialog box or select the new option from a menu.

Adobe is constantly updating the Exchange site available by clicking the Dreamweaver link at www.adobe.com/exchange. Visit it regularly to find new extensions you can download and install to enhance Dreamweaver's feature set.

Chapter 10

Showing Off with Multimedia

*G*et your Web pages singing and dancing with multimedia. Audio, video, and animation are exploding on the Web and transforming static pages into rich multimedia experiences. You can use Dreamweaver to link to multimedia files, or you can insert audio, video, and other files so that they play within your pages. You can even control when and how they play for your users.

Not all Web sites warrant multimedia; if your goal is to provide information in the fastest way possible to the broadest audience, text is still generally the best option. If you want to provide a richer experience for your users, to *show* rather than just *tell,* or to entertain as well as inform, adding audio, video, and animation can help you share more information more vividly and even make you look more professional.

The most complicated aspect of multimedia on the Web is choosing the best format for your audience, which is why you'll find a primer on audio and video formats in this chapter. You can't create or edit multimedia files in Dreamweaver. (You'll need a video or audio editing software program for that.) But after your files are ready, Dreamweaver makes adding them to your Web pages relatively easy.

As you discover in this chapter, inserting video, audio, and Flash files is similar to adding image files to Web pages, but with many more options, such as settings that control whether a video starts automatically or whether a user has to click the play button before it begins.

Many people surf the Web in their offices, in libraries, and in other locations where unexpected sound can be jarring, disruptive, or worse. Always give people a warning before you play video or audio and always give users a way to turn audio off quickly when necessary.

In this chapter, you also find instructions for using third-party services, such as YouTube or Vimeo, to host videos. With this approach, you upload your video to YouTube, Vimeo, or another service and then use Dreamweaver to add a snippet of code into your site so that the video plays on your page (even though it's hosted elsewhere). An advantage of this approach is that YouTube and other video sites are better at delivering video on the Web than most of the commercial Web servers that you're likely to use to host your site.

Understanding Multimedia Players

When you add sound, video, or any other kind of multimedia to a Web site, your visitors may need a special player (sometimes with an associated plug-in) to play or view your files.

Players are small programs that work alone or with a Web browser to add support for functions, such as playing sound, video, and animation files. Some of the best-known multimedia players are the Flash Player, Windows Media Player, and Apple QuickTime.

The challenge is that not everyone on the Web uses the same player, and viewers must have the correct player to view your multimedia files. As a result, you need a strategy that helps visitors play your multimedia easily, such as the following ones:

✔ Many Web developers offer audio and video in two or three formats so users can choose the one that best fits the players they already have.

✔ Some developers also include the same multimedia files in different file sizes so that visitors with slower connection speeds don't have to wait as long. Optimizing multimedia for the Web works much as it does with images: The smaller the file size, the lower the quality but the faster the file downloads.

✔ Many Web developers also include information about how visitors can download and install the best player if they need it to view the files.

✔ Increasingly, Web developers are using third-party services, such as YouTube or Vimeo, to host videos. You find instructions for using these services toward the end of this chapter.

You can use Dreamweaver to insert or link to any type of multimedia file, but only you can choose the format that's best for your audience. Although dozens of plug-ins are available for Web pages, the most common plug-ins on the Web today are Flash, Windows Media, and QuickTime.

In general, I recommend that you avoid the more obscure players unless you're offering specialized content that users have a good reason to download, such as a three-dimensional game that requires a special program to run.

Working with Adobe Flash

Adobe Flash is a favorite among Web designers because it's well supported on the Web (more than 90% of Internet users already have the Flash plug-in), and because you can use it to create audio files, videos, and animations.

Dreamweaver supports both of the popular Flash file types:

- **Flash files:** (extension `.swf`) The most versatile Flash format is the SWF file (pronounced SWIFF). Often referred to simply as *Flash files,* this format is sometimes called a Flash movie, even when it doesn't include video. Flash files with a `.swf` extension can include illustrations, photos, animation sequences, and video. In Dreamweaver, choose Insert⇨Media⇨SWF for this format. You find detailed instructions for working with this type of Flash file in the following section.

- **Flash video:** (extension `.flv`) As the name implies, Flash video is a video format, although it can also be used for audio files. To convert video into the Flash video format, you need the Flash Video Encoder. In Dreamweaver, use the Insert⇨Media⇨FLV option for this format. You find detailed instructions for working with `.flv` Flash files in the "Adding Flash audio and video files" section later in this chapter.

One thing that makes Flash files (with the `.swf` extension) so flexible and so fast on the Internet is that Flash uses *vector graphics* instead of *bitmaps.* Therefore, the graphics in Flash are based on mathematical descriptions *(vectors)* instead of dots *(bitmaps),* and those vector equations take up far less space than bitmapped images. Vector graphics can also be scaled up or down in size without affecting the image quality or the size of the downloaded file. This ability to scale makes Flash ideally suited for the many different monitor sizes that Web viewers use as well as for the tiny displays on cell phones and other handheld devices. You can even project Flash graphics on a wall or movie screen without losing quality, although any photographs or video files integrated into a Flash file may lose quality or look distorted at higher or lower resolutions.

To create a Flash file, you need Adobe Flash or a similar program that supports the Flash format. Because Flash is an open standard, you can create Flash files with a variety of programs, including Adobe Illustrator, which has an Export to SWF option. If want to know how to create full-featured Flash files, check out *Adobe Flash CS5 For Dummies,* by Ellen Finkelstein and Gurdy Leete.

Flash is great overall, but be aware of these important drawbacks:

- ✔ Flash is not supported by most mobile phone browsers, including the iPhone. As a result, if you try to view a site created with Flash on a mobile phone, you see only blank screen. To get around this problem, more and more Web designers are creating a second version of their Flash sites designed for mobile phones and linking it to their main site.

- ✔ If you need printouts for some reason, Flash may not print as well as you would hope.

- ✔ Flash may cause accessibility problems. Screen readers and other specialized viewers can't read the text in a Flash file any better than they can read text in an image file. To make Flash files more accessible, include detailed alternative text.

- ✔ Flash sites are generally more complicated to edit or update than sites created using HTML and CSS.

- ✔ Search engines may not read text in Flash files, which can hurt your page ranking in search results (although including alternative text can help with this limitation and Google is improving its ability to index flash pages).

- ✔ Sites created entirely in Flash are harder to link to, especially if you want to link to a particular page within a site and not just to the front page of the site. Similarly, it's harder (or impossible) to bookmark specific pages within a site designed with Flash.

Inserting Flash SWF files

Flash files, often called Flash *movies,* use the .swf extension and can include animations, graphics, photos, and even video. Thanks to Dreamweaver, these files are relatively easy to insert into a Web page. In this section, I assume you have a completed Flash file (an animation or other Flash movie), and you want to add it to your Web page.

You insert a Flash file much as you insert an image file. But because Flash can do so much more than a still image, you have a variety of settings and options for controlling how your Flash file plays.

Before you start, make sure to save the Flash file you want to insert in the main folder for your Web site (that is, the local site folder you set up, as I explain in Chapter 2). I recommend creating a multimedia subfolder in your main Web site folder for audio and other multimedia files, just as most designers create an image folder for image files.

To add a Flash file to a Web site, open an existing page or create a new document and save the file. Then follow these steps:

1. **Click where you want the Flash file to appear on your Web page.**

2. **If it's not already open, choose Window⟳Insert and then use the drop-down list to select the Common Insert panel.**

3. **From the Media drop-down list on the Common Insert panel, choose the SWF Flash option (see Figure 10-1).**

   You can also choose Insert⟳Media⟳SWF. The Select File dialog box appears.

4. **Browse to locate the Flash file that you want to insert in your page and click to select the file.**

5. **If you have accessibility options turned on, you're prompted to add alternative text to describe the Flash file. Enter a description of the file and click OK.**

   The dialog box closes, and the Flash file is inserted into your document.

Dreamweaver displays Flash as a gray box with the dimensions of the Flash file. To display the Flash file as it will appear in a Web browser with the Flash player, click to select it and then click the green Play button on the right side of the Property inspector. (In Figure 10-2, you see the Stop button because I've already clicked the Play button, which changed to the Stop button when the file began playing.) If you have the Flash player installed on your computer, the Flash file will also play when you preview the page in a browser.

Setting Flash properties

Like most HTML tags, the tags that link Flash and other multimedia files to Web pages have *attributes* (also called properties) that define how a file is displayed within a browser, controlling such actions as whether an animation plays automatically when a page is loaded or whether a visitor must click a link for the animation to begin. Dreamweaver automatically sets some of these options, such as the height and width of the Flash file, but you may want to specify others.

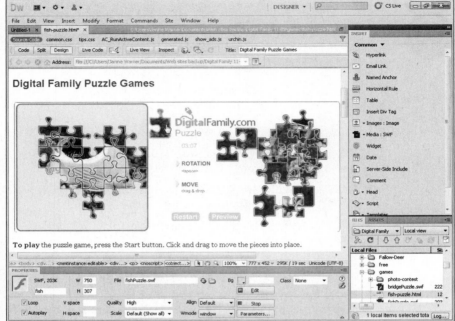

Figure 10-1:
To insert a Flash file, choose the SWF option from the Media drop-down list on the Common Insert panel.

To display Flash attributes in the Property inspector, click to select the gray box that represents a Flash file after it's inserted into a Web page. The following describes the Flash options included in the Property inspector, as shown in Figure 10-2.

If you don't see all the options in the Property inspector, click the expander arrow in the lower-right corner to display the more advanced options.

- **ID field:** Use the text field in the upper-left corner of the Property inspector, just to the right of the Flash icon, to assign a name to the file (in Figures 10-1 and 10-2, I've named the Flash file `fish`). You can enter any name; just don't use any spaces or special characters other than the dash or underscore. The name is important if you want to refer to the file in JavaScript or other programming, but you can leave this field blank if you are not using a script with your Flash file.

- **W (width):** Use this option to specify the width of the file. The file is measured in pixels.

- **H (height):** Use this option to specify the height of the file. The file is measured in pixels.

- **Reset Size:** (This icon is only visible if you have changed the size of a Flash file.) You can change the display size of a Flash file by clicking a corner and dragging it or by entering a number in the height or width fields. When the size of a Flash file has been altered, a small, circular icon appears just to the right of the height and width fields. Clicking this circular icon reverts the Flash file to its original size. You can resize Flash files, unlike images, video, and many other file types, without affecting image quality because they're vector-based. To keep the file proportionate, hold down the Shift key while you drag to resize the file.

Figure 10-2:
Select any
Flash file
to view or
change its
settings in
the Property
inspector.

 ✔ **File:** Dreamweaver automatically fills in this field when you insert a Flash file with the filename and path. You risk breaking the link to your flash file if you alter this field.

 ✔ **BG:** Click the color swatch to change the Background Color that appears behind the Flash file, or enter any hexadecimal color code, starting with the pound (#) sign.

 ✔ **Edit:** Click this button to open a Flash source file with the Adobe Flash program where you can edit it. Note that you can edit only the source Flash file. After saving the Flash file for Web use with the .swf extension, return to the original Flash file to edit it again.

 ✔ **Class:** Use this drop-down list to apply any class styles defined for the document.

 ✔ **Loop:** Selecting this box causes the Flash file to repeat (or *loop*). If you don't select this box, the Flash movie stops after it reaches the last frame.

 ✔ **Autoplay:** Selecting this box causes the Flash movie to play as soon as it downloads to the viewer's computer. If you don't select this box, whatever option you've set within the Flash file itself (such as onMouseOver or onMouseDown) is required to start the movie.

 ✔ **V Space (vertical space):** If you want blank space above or below the file, enter the number of pixels.

 ✔ **H Space (horizontal space):** If you want blank space on either side of the file, enter the number of pixels.

 ✔ **Quality:** This option enables you to prioritize the anti-aliasing options of your images versus the speed of playback. *Anti-aliasing,* which makes your files appear smoother, can slow down the rendering of each frame because the computer must first smooth the edges. The Quality parameter enables you to regulate how much the process is slowed by letting you set priorities based on the importance of appearance versus playback speed. You can choose from these Quality options:

- **Low:** Anti-aliasing is never used. Playback speed has priority over appearance.

- **High:** Anti-aliasing is always used. Appearance has priority over playback speed.

- **Auto High:** With this option, playback is set to begin with anti-aliasing turned on. However, if the frame rate supported by the user's computer drops too low, anti-aliasing automatically turns off to improve playback speed. This option emphasizes playback speed and appearance equally at first but sacrifices appearance for the sake of playback speed, if necessary.

- **Auto Low:** Playback begins with anti-aliasing turned off. If the Flash player detects that the processor can handle it, anti-aliasing is turned on. Use this option to emphasize speed at first but improve appearance whenever possible.

✔ **Scale:** Specify this option only if you change the file's original height and width size settings. The Scale parameter enables you to define how the Flash movie appears within those settings. The following options in the Scale drop-down list enable you to set preferences for how a scaled Flash movie appears within the window:

- **Default (show all):** This option enables the entire movie to appear in the specified area. The width and height proportions of the original movie are maintained and no distortion occurs, but borders may appear on two sides of the movie to fill the space.

- **No Border:** This option enables you to scale a Flash movie to fill a specified area. No borders appear and the original aspect ratio is maintained, but some cropping may occur.

- **Exact Fit:** The Flash movie is the exact width and height that are set. However, the original aspect ratio may not be maintained, and the movie may look squished.

✔ **Align:** This option controls the alignment of the file on the page. This setting works the same for plug-in files as for images.

✔ **Wmode:** Choose the Window option to display the Flash file in a rectangular window on a Web page. Choose Opaque to hide everything behind a Flash file when you move or resize it using JavaScript. Choose Transparent to show the background of the HTML page though any transparent portions of the Flash file.

✔ **Play button:** Click the green Play button to play a Flash file in Dreamweaver. Note that when the Play button is activated, the button changes to Stop (refer to Figure 10-2).

> ✔ **Parameters:** This button provides access to a dialog box where you can enter parameters specific to your Flash files.

Using scripts to make Flash function better

When you insert Flash or other multimedia files with Dreamweaver, the program creates a collection of JavaScript files that help the Flash file play properly. The files are named things like, AC_RunActiveContent.js, and are stored in a Scripts folder, which Dreamweaver automatically creates inside your local site folder. The first time Dreamweaver creates this file, a dialog box alerts you that you need to upload the script for your multimedia file to work properly. Make sure you include this script when you publish your site on your Web server.

If you don't include the script, your multimedia file may not play properly, or your visitors may be required to click the play button twice before the file begins to play.

With each new version of Dreamweaver, Adobe has changed the scripts included with Flash and other multimedia files. If you're editing a site that was created with an earlier version of Dreamweaver, it's a good idea to update these scripts by deleting and then reinserting the multimedia file to generate new scripts. Then, make sure you upload the page with the Flash or other multimedia file, as well as the Scripts folder.

Finding Flash resources online

One of the best places to read more about creating Flash files is on the Internet, where a wide range of Web sites offers everything from pre-designed Flash files you can easily customize to great ideas for getting the most from this award-winning technology. You may find these Web sites useful if you want to find out more about Flash:

✔ **Adobe** (www.adobe.com): You find loads of tips and tricks for creating and using Flash files (as well as many inspiring examples of Flash in action).

✔ **Swish** (www.swishzone.com): If you're looking for an alternative to Adobe Flash, Swish is a great little program that's more reasonably priced.

✔ **Flash Kit** (www.flashkit.com): You find a wide range of resources for Flash developers.

✔ **Go to and learn** (www.GoToAndLearn.com): Go here when you want free Flash tutorials as well as videos about developing Flash animations and working with ActionScript, the programming language used in Flash.

✔ **Flash Arcade** (www.flasharcade.com): This site has a collection of interactive games created in Flash.

Working with Video and Audio on the Web

As bandwidth has grown on the Web, the use of video files has grown more dramatically than almost any other multimedia file type. From YouTube to small personal Web sites, millions of video files are added to the Web every day. Adding a video file to a Web page with Dreamweaver is relatively easy, especially if you use the Flash video format described in the "Adding Flash audio and video files" section later in this chapter.

If you use another video format, such as Windows Media Video or QuickTime, you find instructions for adding files in those formats in the section, "Inserting audio and video files" also later in this chapter. You can specify video and audio settings, such as Autoplay, by changing setting parameters, an option that is a little more complicated if you use any format other than Flash video. You find instructions for managing these settings in Dreamweaver in the "Setting options for audio and video files," later in this chapter.

 Instead of hosting your video on your own Web server, an alternative is to upload video files to YouTube, Vimeo, or another video site and then include special code from that site in the HTML code of your Web pages so that the video plays within your pages, even though it's hosted on YouTube. You find instructions for using these kinds of services in the section "Using YouTube and Other Services to Host Videos," later in this chapter.

The first challenge to working with multimedia is choosing the right format and optimizing your video so it downloads quickly and still looks good. Unfortunately, no single video format works perfectly for everyone on the Web, but most new computers come with preinstalled video and audio players that play the most common file formats. If you use a Windows computer, you probably have Windows Media Player. If you use a Mac, you have QuickTime. Both video players can handle multiple video formats, so anyone with a relatively new computer can likely view video in common formats.

Streaming media plays faster

To *stream* multimedia means to play a file while it's downloading from the server. This is a valuable trick on the Web because video and audio files can take a long time to download. Here's how streaming works. When you click a link to a video file, your computer begins to download it from the server. If the video is hosted on a Web server that supports streaming, the video or audio file begins to play as soon as enough of the file downloads successfully to ensure an uninterrupted experience.

If you don't use streaming, the entire file may have to download before the media can play. Although the download time for streaming or nonstreaming files may be the same, streaming can greatly reduce the time your visitors wait before they can start viewing a video online.

Because Web servers that stream video are very expensive (part of why more and more people are hosting their videos on sites like YouTube or Vimeo, covered later in this chapter), Flash offers an option called *Progressive Download*. This option offers many of the same advantages of streaming because a video embedded with the Progressive setting will start playing before the entire file is downloaded, but there are some limitations. For example, you can't fast forward or back up as well with a video that is downloading using Progressive settings as you can with a video that is hosted on a Web server that supports streaming.

Comparing popular video formats

You can convert video from one file format to another relatively easily with most video-editing programs. You can open a video in AVI (Audio Video Interleave) format in a program, such as Adobe Premier Elements (a good video editor for beginners), and then choose File⇨Export to convert it to any of a dozen formatting and compression options. For example, you could convert an AVI file to the Windows Media format with the compression setting for a 56K modem or into the QuickTime format with the compression setting for a cable modem.

Editing video can get complicated, and optimizing video for the best quality with the fastest download time is both an art and a science, but the most basic process of converting a video file isn't difficult after you understand the conversion options. Because Flash video is increasingly popular and because the Flash video encoder is included most of the CS Adobe program suites, I've included basic instructions for using the encoder in the section, "Converting video files into Flash format with the Flash video encoder," later in this chapter.

The following sections provide a brief description of the most common digital video formats, their file extensions, and a Web address where you can find out more about each option.

Flash video

You can create Flash videos with Adobe Flash. Because the Flash player is so popular on the Web, many developers consider Flash one of the best options available today.

> **File extension:** .flv
>
> **Web site:** www.adobe.com

MP4

Part of MPEG-4, the MP4 format can be used for audio or video. This format is becoming increasingly popular, in part, because most mobile phones, including the iPhone, support it, making it a good alternative to .flv.

> **File extension:** .mp4
>
> **Web site:** No official site for this technology

Windows Media Video

Defined by Microsoft and popular on the PC, this video format supports streaming and plays with Windows Media Player as well as many other popular players.

> **File extension:** .wmv
>
> **Web site:** www.microsoft.com/windows/windowsmedia

QuickTime

The QuickTime player is built into the Macintosh operating system and is used by most Mac programs that include video or animation. QuickTime is a great format for video on the Web and supports streaming, but it's used primarily by those who favor Macs (although QuickTime files can be viewed on Windows computers as well).

> **File extension:** .qt, .mov
>
> **Web site:** www.quicktime.com

AVI

Created by Microsoft, AVI (Audio Video Interleave) is one the most common video formats on Windows computers and can play on most common video players. AVI is fine if you're viewing video on a CD or on your hard drive, where the file doesn't have to download, but you can't optimize AVI files well for use on the Internet. If your files are in AVI, convert them to one of the other formats before adding them to your Web site. Otherwise, you force your visitors to download unnecessarily large video files.

> **File extension:** .avi
>
> **Web site:** No one site about AVI exists, but you can find information if you search for *AVI* at www.microsoft.com.

Comparing popular audio formats

Audio works much like video on the Web. You can link to a sound file or embed the file into your page; either way, your visitors need to have the right player to listen to the file. You find instructions for adding both audio and video files to your pages in the following section, "Adding Audio and Video Files to Web Pages."

The following sections provide a brief description of the most common digital audio formats, their file extensions, and a Web address where you can find out more about each option.

MP3

One of the most successful audio compression formats, MP3 supports streaming audio. Most music you can download from the Internet is in MP3 format, and it's clearly the first choice of many Web developers. Most popular multimedia players on the Web can play MP3 files.

> **File extension:** .mp3
>
> **Web site:** No official site for this technology

Windows Audio

Microsoft's Windows Audio format supports streaming and can be played with Windows Media Player as well as many other popular players. It also offers digital rights management functionality.

> **File extension:** .wma
>
> **Web site:** www.microsoft.com/windows/windowsmedia

WAV

The WAV file format is popular in digital media because it offers the highest sound quality possible. Audio files in this format are often too big for use on the Web, averaging 10MB for a minute of audio. (In comparison, an MP3 file that is five times longer can be less than one-third the size.) Although WAV files are commonly used on the Internet because of their nearly universal compatibility, I recommend that you convert WAV files (especially for long audio clips) to one of the other audio formats.

> **File extension:** .wav
>
> **Web site:** No official Web site exists for WAV files, but you can find some documentation at www.microsoft.com when you search for *WAV*.

Adding Audio and Video Files to Web Pages

Like other multimedia files, you can link to an audio or a video file or you can insert multimedia files into a page. Linking to a multimedia file is as easy as linking to any other file, as you see in the instructions that follow. Inserting an audio or a video file is a little more complicated, but it lets a visitor play the file without leaving the Web page. Inserting audio and video files is covered in this section. If you're using Flash video or audio, see the "Adding Flash audio and video files" section, later in this chapter.

Linking to audio and video files

To use Dreamweaver to link to a video file, an audio file, or another multimedia file, follow these steps:

1. **Click to select the text, image, or other element you want to use to create a link.**

   If you're linking to a video file, a good trick is to take a single still image from the video and insert that into your Web page. Then create a link from that image to the video file.

2. **Choose Insert⇨Hyperlink or click the Hyperlink icon in the Common Insert panel.**

   The Hyperlink dialog box opens, as shown in Figure 10-3.

   Alternatively, you can click the Browse button just to the right of the Link field in the Property inspector. (The Browse button looks like a small file folder.)

Figure 10-3:
Link to an audio or a video file just as you'd create a link to another Web page.

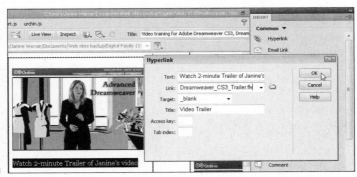

3. **Enter the text you want to serve as a link in the Text field.**

   If you selected a section of text on the page before opening the Hyperlink dialog box, that text automatically appears in the Text field.

4. **Enter the URL where the audio or video file is located.**

   Alternatively, click the Browse button (the small file folder icon) to the right of the Link field and browse your hard drive to find the video or audio file you want to link to.

   As with any other file you link to, make sure you've saved your audio or video files into your local site folder (which I explain how to set up in Chapter 2).

   Note that you can link to an audio or video file on another Web site, as I've done in the example shown in Figure 10-3, but you need to have the exact URL of the file's location.

5. **Click to select the file you want to link to and then click OK.**

   The dialog box closes, and the link is created automatically.

6. **(Optional) Choose blank from the Target drop-down list if you want the video file to open in a new browser window or tab.**

7. **To specify Accessibility settings, enter a Title, Access Key, and Tab Index.**

8. **Click OK to add the hyperlink and to close the Hyperlink dialog box.**

9. **Click the Preview button (at the top of the work area) to open the page in a browser, where you can test the link to your multimedia file.**

   Dreamweaver launches your specified Web browser and displays the page. If you have the necessary player, the file downloads, your player launches, and your file automatically plays.

Many people like to have multimedia files, such as video, pop up in a new browser window. To do this, create an HTML file and embed your multimedia file in it. Then use the Open Browser Window behavior in Dreamweaver to create a pop-up window that displays your multimedia page. For more on how to work with Dreamweaver behaviors, see Chapter 9.

Inserting audio and video files

When you insert an audio or a video file into a Web page, you can set the file to play automatically when the page loads (as long as your visitor has the necessary player), or you can require that your visitors click the Play button first. I recommend the second option. I like to give users control over when and how a video plays because I never want to get anyone in trouble if they're surfing the Web in an office or library where unexpected audio can be a problem.

Whether or not you set the file to play automatically, the advantage of embedding it into the page is that file will play within your Web page instead of opening in a separate window or player.

To use Dreamweaver to embed an audio or a video file into a Web page, follow these steps:

1. **Click where you want the file to appear on your Web page.**

2. **Select Common from the Insert panel, and in the Media drop-down list, choose Plugin (see Figure 10-4).**

   You can also choose Insert⇨Media⇨Plugin. The Select File dialog box appears.

   Use the Plugin option for all audio and video file types — except Flash video (`.flv`) files, covered in the next section.

Figure 10-4:
Use the Plugin option to insert any audio or video file that isn't saved in the Flash format.

3. **Browse your hard drive to locate the sound or video file you want inserted in your page and then click to select it.**

4. **Click OK.**

The dialog box closes, and the file is inserted automatically into the page. A small plug-in icon (resembling a puzzle piece) represents the file.

When you add audio or video, Dreamweaver doesn't automatically determine the height and width of the file, so you need to add the dimensions in the Property inspector after you insert the file. You can generally find the dimensions of a video file by opening it in a video-editing program and looking for the height and width, but it's often not necessary. You can set the height and width in Dreamweaver to whatever you want, irrespective of the video's actual dimensions, but the video may be distorted or lack quality if you make it much bigger than its actual size or fail to maintain its proportions. After you set the height and width in the Property inspector, the plug-in icon changes to reflect the specified size.

5. **Click the plug-in icon that represents the file in the Web page to display the file options in the Property inspector and specify your desired settings.**

You find a description of each option in the next section, "Setting options for audio and video files."

6. **Click the Preview button (at the top of the work area) to open the page in a browser.**

Dreamweaver doesn't include a Play button for audio and video files (unless they're in the Flash format). If you have the necessary player on your computer and set the file to Autoplay (the default setting), your file plays automatically when the page loads into the browser. To change video and audio settings that aren't included in the Property inspector, such as Autoplay, see the "Setting multimedia parameters" section later in this chapter.

Setting options for audio and video files

When you select an inserted multimedia file, such as a sound or a video file, the Property inspector displays the options for the file, as shown in Figure 10-5. Among these settings, the height and width are the most important. Unlike image files or Flash files, Dreamweaver can't automatically detect the height and width of other audio or video formats, so it's important to set these options in the Property inspector. To determine the height and width of a video file, you may need to open the file in a video-editing program. For audio files, set the height and width based on the size required for the player you're using.

The following describes the multimedia options available from the Property inspector:

- ✔ **ID field:** Use the text field in the upper-left corner of the Property inspector, just to the right of the plug-in icon, if you want to assign a name to the file. If you leave this field blank, Dreamweaver doesn't enter a name automatically unless you are using a file in a Flash format. The name is important only if you want to refer to the file in JavaScript.

- ✔ **W (width) and H (height):** Specify the measurement of the file in pixels.

- ✔ **Src (source):** This option specifies the name and path to the file. You can type a filename or click the Browse button (which looks like a small yellow folder) to browse for the file. This field is filled in automatically when you embed the file.

- ✔ **Plg URL:** This option enables you to provide a URL where viewers can download the plug-in if they don't already have it.

- ✔ **Align:** This option enables you to specify how the element aligns on the page. Alignment works just as it does for images.

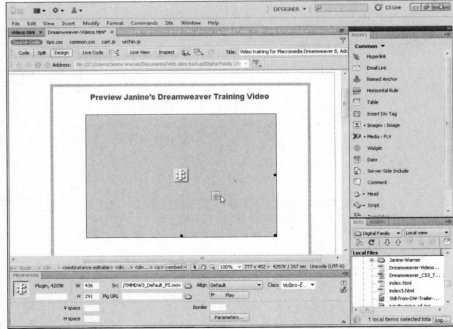

Figure 10-5:
Select an audio or a video file in Dreamweaver, such as the Windows Media video shown here, to display the properties for the file in the Property inspector.

✔ **Play button:** Click the green Play button to preview the media file. The media plug-in must be installed in Dreamweaver (in the Configuration/ Plugins folder) for it to be previewed in Dreamweaver.

✔ **Class:** Use this drop-down list to apply any style sheets defined for the document.

✔ **V Space (vertical space):** If you want blank space above and below the plug-in, enter the number of pixels here.

✔ **H Space (horizontal space):** If you want blank space on either side of the plug-in, enter the number of pixels or use a percentage to specify a portion of the browser window's width.

✔ **Border:** This option specifies the width of the border around the file when it's displayed.

✔ **Parameters:** Click this button to access a dialog box where you can enter additional parameters specific to the type of multimedia file you inserted. For more information, see the following section.

Setting multimedia parameters

You can use parameters to control a wide range of multimedia options, such as whether a video file or an audio file starts playing as soon as a page is loaded. Setting parameters isn't intuitive, and Dreamweaver doesn't do the best job of helping with these settings. However, with some research on the options for the file type you're using and a little care in using the Parameters dialog box in Dreamweaver, you can have a lot more control over your multimedia files.

In fairness to the programmers who created Dreamweaver, it'd be hard to include all the parameters for all the possible multimedia file types in use on the Web today, but they could've included the common ones. Because they don't, I offer you this brief primer on using the parameters setting and a few common options for a few common file types. You also find Web addresses where you can find more complete lists of parameters for a few of the most popular audio and video formats.

In Figure 10-6, you see the Parameters dialog box with settings for a Windows Media Video file. The following steps outline how the process works:

1. **To access the Parameters dialog box, click to select the multimedia file in the Web page and then click the Parameters button in the Property inspector.**

   The Parameters dialog box opens. The dialog box is blank unless you have already entered parameters for the selected file.

2. **Use the plus sign (+) at the top of the dialog box to add a parameter; use the minus sign (–) to delete a selected parameter.**

3. **On the left side of the dialog box, enter the name of the parameter, such as** autoplay; **on the right side, enter the value you want, such as** false, **which I've entered in this example to prevent the Windows Media Video file from playing automatically.**

You can move from the name side of the Parameters dialog box to the value side by pressing the Tab key or by clicking to insert your cursor.

Figure 10-6: Add parameters for additional audio and video settings.

To help you get started with parameters, here are some of the most common and valuable parameters:

✔ **Autoplay (or Autostart, depending on the file type):** By default, when you add video or audio to an HTML file, most browsers play the file as soon as the page loads (except Firefox, which gives users more control). If you want to prevent your multimedia files from playing automatically in Internet Explorer and other browsers, set the Autoplay or Autostart parameter to false. Think of true and false as on and off when it comes to parameters.

✔ **Loop:** This parameter enables you to control whether a video file or an audio file loops or continues to play over and over.

✔ **showControls:** This option makes it possible to hide the video or audio controls for a file.

Be careful about combining options like these. For example, if you set Autoplay to false and showControls to false, your visitor can never play your file. By default, the controls for most multimedia files are visible unless you set the showControls parameter to false.

Find more attributes for the Windows Media format at www.microsoft.com when you search for *Windows Media Player properties*, or go directly to http://msdn.microsoft.com/en-us/library/ms930698.aspx. For QuickTime attributes, visit www.apple.com and search for QuickTime Embed tag attributes or go directly to www.apple.com/quicktime/tutorials/embed2.html.

Adding Flash audio and video files

Flash video is the video format of choice among many designers because so many people have the Flash Player and the player's such a small and easy download for those who don't have it. Because Adobe owns both Flash and Dreamweaver, you find much better support for Flash files in Dreamweaver. An Insert dialog box makes it easy to set parameters for Flash. The Insert FLV dialog box is displayed in Figure 10-7. Dreamweaver can even automatically detect the size of Flash video files. You can also use Flash to create and insert audio files, displaying only the player (called a *skin* in Flash).

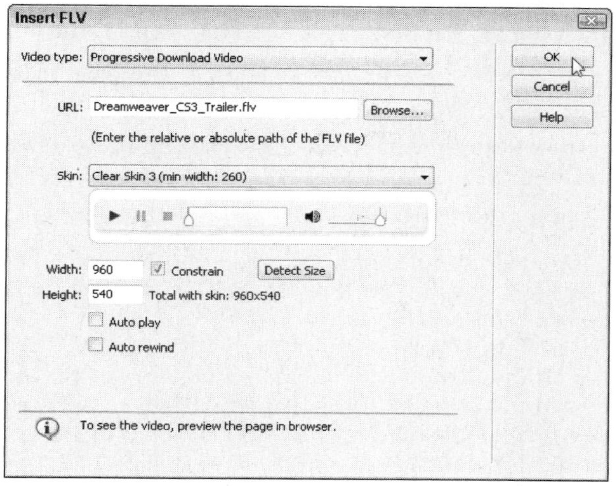

Figure 10-7: You can specify how a Flash video will be displayed in a Web page in the Insert FLV dialog box.

Follow these steps to insert a Flash video file into a Web page:

1. **Click where you want the file to appear on your Web page.**

2. **Choose Insert⇨Media⇨FLV.**

   The Insert FLV dialog box appears, as shown in Figure 10-7.

   Alternatively, you can choose FLV from the Media drop-down list in the Common Insert panel select (refer to Figure 10-1 at the beginning of this chapter).

3. **At the top of the dialog box, specify Streaming or Progressive.**

   You must have special server software to handle streaming video. Check with your Internet hosting service or system administrator to find out whether your Web server supports streaming Flash files. If not, choose Progressive, which offers some of the advantages of streaming and works on any Web server. For more this topic, read the sidebar "Streaming media plays faster," earlier in this chapter.

4. **Click the Browse button to the right of the URL field and browse to find the Flash FLV file you want to add to the page. Select the file and click OK.**

   Dreamweaver automatically adds the filename and path to your Flash file in the URL field.

5. **Choose a skin from the Skin drop-down list.**

   Dreamweaver calls the controls for a Flash file a *skin*. As you can see in Figure 10-7, a preview of the selected skin appears in the dialog box so you can better decide which one is best for your Flash file and your design. You can also create custom skins in Adobe Flash.

6. **Click the Detect Size button to insert the height and width of the inserted Flash file (if Dreamweaver hasn't already done so).**

7. **If you want the Flash video to play as soon as the page is loaded, select the Auto Play check box.**

8. **If you want the video to rewind after play is complete, select the Auto Rewind check box.**

9. **Click OK to insert the Flash file and close the dialog box.**

   The Flash file appears on the page, represented by a gray box that's the height and width of the file. To view the Flash video, preview the page in a Web browser.

When you insert a Flash video file and include a skin for the player, Dreamweaver creates a Flash file for the player with the .swf extension and saves the file in your local site folder. This Flash file contains the player controls and *must* be uploaded to your Web site when you publish the page with the Flash file for the player controls to work.

You can change the skin by clicking to select the inserted Flash file and using the Skin drop-down list in the Property inspector to select another option, as shown in Figure 10-8. Each time you choose a skin, Dreamweaver creates a new .swf file. You can delete any skins that aren't being used.

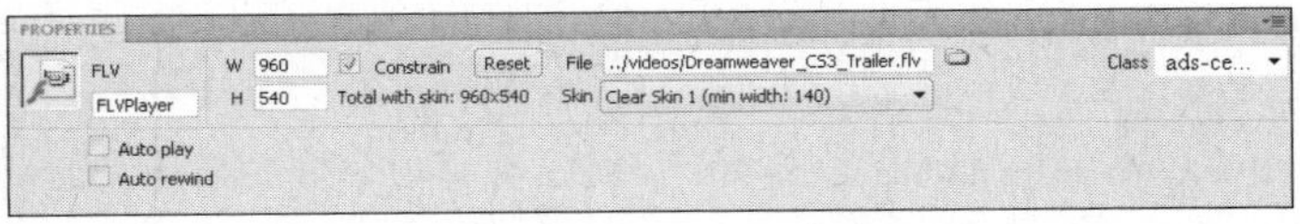

Figure 10-8:
Use the Property inspector to alter the settings for a Flash video.

PROPERTIES					
FLV	W 960	☑ Constrain Reset	File ../videos/Dreamweaver_CS3_Trailer.flv		Class ads-ce... ▾
FLVPlayer	H 540	Total with skin: 960x540	Skin Clear Skin 1 (min width: 140) ▾		
☐ Auto play					
☐ Auto rewind					

If you want to find out about other Flash options, visit www.adobe.com and search for *Flash Object and Embed tag attributes*. Or go directly to http://kb2.adobe.com/cps/127/tn_12701.html.

Converting video files into Flash format with the Flash video encoder

If you want to convert video from nearly any video format into the Flash video format, you can use the Flash video encoder, which is included in all the Adobe Create Suite packages that include Flash. The following exercise walks you through the process of converting a video file into Flash video with the Flash video encoder.

1. **Launch the Flash video encoder, as shown in Figure 10-9.**

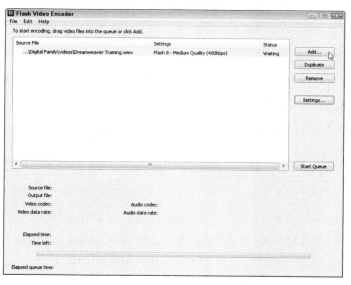

Figure 10-9:
The Flash video encoder is designed to convert video in nearly any format into the Flash video format.

2. **Click the Add button to load a video into the encoder that you want to convert into a Flash video file.**

   In this example, I added a short video clip that was saved in the Windows Media Video (WMV) format, but you can add video in a variety of formats, including AVI and QuickTime. For best results, start with a video that hasn't already been compressed.

3. **Click the Settings button.**

   The Flash Video Encoding Settings dialog box opens, as shown in Figure 10-10.

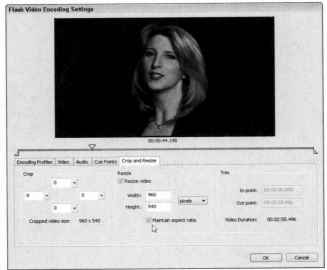

Figure 10-10:
The Flash
Video
Encoder
Settings
dialog box
includes
five different
tabs with
video set-
ting options.

4. **Click the Encoding Profiles tab and choose a Flash encoding profile.**

   The later the version of Flash, the better the encoding looks and the faster it plays, but here's the trade off: Not everyone has downloaded the latest version, so an earlier version may mean fewer visitors have to download the player to view your video. Because Flash is such a fast and easy program to download, the latest version is generally the best choice though.

5. **Click the Video tab and specify additional video settings.**

   a. **Make sure Encode Video is checked.** The video *codec* (which controls the compression of the video) is set automatically based on the Flash version you selected on the Encoding Profiles tab. Select Deinterlace only if you're encoding video that's interlaced, such as video captured from a television or VCR. Video that's already been encoded in a format like Windows Media doesn't need to be deinterlaced.

   b. **Set Framerate to the lowest setting that will look good to achieve the fastest download time.** If you're encoding a video that has lots of action, you need a higher frame rate, ideally 24 or better, or your video will lose details and look fuzzy in places. If you're converting a video, such as a Windows Media file that's already been encoded, your best option is to choose Same as Source to leave the frame-rate unchanged.

   c. Set the Quality to the lowest level that still looks good to get the fastest download times. Use the slider under the preview window to move through the frames of the video to see the effects of your settings.

6. **Click the Audio tab to adjust audio settings.**

   Under the Audio tab, adjust the Data rate. Again, the lower the number, the lower the quality but the faster the download. If your audio has only a single voice, you can set this quite low, and it'll still sound good. If your audio file has music, special sound effects, or other multifaceted audio, set the Data rate to at least 96 Kbps (kilobits per second).

7. **Use the Cue Points tab and insert cues in the file that make it easier for someone using the file to jump to a particular section.**

8. **Use the Crop and Resize tab to make the file physically smaller or larger.**

   Note that trying to increase the file size of a video can result in a severe loss of quality.

9. **After the settings are complete, click OK.**

   The Flash Video Encoder Settings dialog box closes, returning you to the Flash video encoder.

10. **Click Start Queue to begin the encoding process.**

   This process can take several minutes, even for a very short file. A small preview window in the bottom-right corner of the Flash video encoder enables you to watch the encoding process in action.

   When the encoding process is complete, the Flash video encoder has created a copy of the video file in the FLV Flash video format.

Using YouTube and Other Services to Host Videos

Instead of hosting your video on your own Web server, an increasingly popular alternative is to upload video files to YouTube, Vimeo, or another video hosting site and then include special code from that site in the HTML code of your Web pages. The video plays within your pages, even though it's not hosted on your Web server.

Adding video from a site like YouTube to your pages is easier and often works better than inserting video directly into your site. The many video hosting sites today range from expensive high-end services, such as BrightCove and Akamai, which handle big video clients like *The New York Times* and Showtime to free services, like YouTube.

YouTube is a great option if you want your video to reach the widest audience (for free) but when you upload a video to YouTube, you give up some of your rights to your video in exchange for having it hosted on the site. Similarly, when you add a video to your site from YouTube, you're stuck with the YouTube player, which includes the YouTube logo, as well as links to other videos on YouTube. Make sure to read through the terms and conditions on any video site you use so that you fully understand the rights (to your own video) you may be giving away and how the site may use your video in the future.

Vimeo is becoming increasingly popular because it offers a reasonably priced professional level of service that makes it easier to control the rights to your own videos and offers the option of adding videos to your pages without the Vimeo logo or links to other videos on the site

Today YouTube and Vimeo seem to offer the best options for most small- to medium-sized Web sites, but new competitors are emerging. The services that these video companies offer keep changing, so you may want to research the best services for your videos needs before you decide where to host your videos.

The advantages of hosting video on a site like YouTube or Vimeo include the following:

✔ **Better Video Compression:** Both YouTube and Vimeo optimize video for you when you upload it to their servers, and they often to a better job than you could yourself.

✔ **Deliver the right version to each visitor:** YouTube detects the connection speed and device of your visitors and delivers video accordingly. If you visit YouTube with an iPhone, you see the video in MP4 format. View the same video with a computer, and you see the Flash version. Similarly, if you have a fast 3G connection, you see a higher-resolution version. View the video with a slower connection, and you see a lower-quality version that loads faster.

✔ **Manage bandwidth costs:** These services can also help you save money. If your videos become popular and you host your own video, you may exceed the bandwidth limits of your Web host and incur additional fees. Because video uses more bandwidth than other types of content, overages can get costly. Hosting your video on YouTube or Vimeo means you'll never be surprised by extra bandwidth fees for video.

Hosting video on YouTube or Vimeo is easy. Here's how it works:

1. **Create an account on the site by filling out a form (or log into your account if you already have one).**

   If you want to use the professional-level services on Vimeo, you also must pay a fee.

2. **Upload your files to the site through your Web browser.**

   In this process, the video is uploaded and encoded, which can take a few minutes depending on the site and how busy it is.

3. **Follow the site's instructions for copying the code you need to embed your video on your Web site.**

4. **Open your Web page in Dreamweaver, and paste the code snippet into the HTML code on your page, in the place you want the video to appear.**

   Use Dreamweaver's split view to make it easy to find the right place to paste in the code.

Working with Java

Java is a programming language, similar to Basic, C, or C++, that you can use to create programs that run on a computer. What makes Java special is that it can run on any computer system and can display within a browser.

If you create a program in another programming language, you usually have to create one version for the Macintosh, another for the PC, and a third for Unix. But Java, created by Sun Microsystems, is platform-independent. Thus, developers can use it to create almost any kind of program — even complex programs, such as a sophisticated game or even a word processing program — that works on any type of computer without the user having to customize the code for each platform.

Another advantage of Java is that the program (dubbed an *applet*) can run within a Web browser, allowing the program to interact with different elements of the page or with other pages on the Web. Applets enable designers to add sophisticated capabilities to Web pages — irrespective of the visitor's operating system — making Java popular on the Internet. You can embed Java applets in Web pages, you can use Java to generate entire Web pages, or you can run Java applications separately after they download. Similar to Flash, Java requires a plug-in on the user's computer.

Inserting Java applets

To insert a Java applet in your Web page, follow these steps:

1. **Click where you want the applet to appear on your Web page.**

2. **Choose Insert⇨Media⇨Applet**

   The Select File dialog box appears.

   Alternatively, you can choose Applet from the Media drop-down list in the Common Insert panel (refer to Figure 10-1).

3. **Use the Browse button to locate the Java applet file you want to insert on the page.**

4. **Click to highlight the filename and then click OK to close the dialog box.**

   Dreamweaver doesn't display applets in the Dreamweaver work area. Instead, you see an icon that represents the applet. To view the applet on your Web page (the only way to see the applet in action), preview the page in a browser that supports applets, such as Firefox.

5. **Click the Applet icon to open the Property inspector.**

   You can set many options in the Property inspector. If you want to know more about these options, read on.

JavaScript is not Java

JavaScript is a scripting language; Java is a programming language. Despite the similarity in their names, the two have little in common. Although JavaScript is much more complex than HTML, it's much simpler than Java and has far fewer capabilities. Unlike Java, JavaScript can be written directly into HTML code to create interactive features, such as rollover effects. Dreamweaver uses JavaScript to create most of the features included in the Behaviors panel (covered in Chapter 9).

You can use Java to create more complex programming than you can create with JavaScript.

Java programs, or *applets,* are usually small, self-contained programs that can run on any operating system. If you search the Web for Java applets, you're likely to find cool little clocks, converters, and other programs that you can download and add to your Web pages. You can use Java to create programs that work on both the Mac and PC, an advantage over other programming languages that makes Java especially well-suited to the multiplatform world of Web design.

Setting Java parameters and other options

Like other file formats that require plug-ins or advanced browser support, the display of Java applets can be controlled by specifying a number of options. If you select a Java applet in Dreamweaver, the Property inspector displays the following options:

- **Applet name:** Use this field in the upper-left corner if you want to type a name for your applet. Dreamweaver doesn't apply a name if you leave this field blank. This name identifies the applet for scripting.

- **W (width):** This option specifies the width of the applet. You can set the measurement in pixels or as a percentage of the browser window's width.

- **H (height):** This option specifies the height of the applet. You can set the measurement in pixels or as a percentage of the browser window's height.

- **Code:** Dreamweaver automatically enters the code when you insert the file. Code specifies the content file of the applet. You can type your own filename or click the folder icon to choose a file.

- **Base:** Automatically entered when you insert the file, Base identifies the folder that contains the applet.

- **Align:** This option determines how the object aligns on the page. Alignment works just as it does for images.

- **Alt:** This option enables you to specify an alternative file, such as an image, that appears if the viewer's browser doesn't support Java. That way, the user doesn't see a broken file icon. If you type text in this field, the viewer sees this text; Dreamweaver writes it into the code by using the Alt attribute of the `<applet>` tag. If you use the folder icon to select an image, the viewer sees an image; Dreamweaver automatically inserts an `<img>` tag within the `<applet>` and `</applet>` tags of the applet.

- **V Space (vertical space):** If you want blank space above or below the applet, enter the number of pixels here.

- **H Space (horizontal space):** If you want blank space on either side of the applet, enter the number of pixels here.

- **Parameters:** Click this button to access a dialog box in which you can enter additional parameters for the applet.

- **Class:** Use this drop-down list to access style sheets created with CSS (Cascading Style Sheets).

You can find lots more information in *Java For Dummies,* 4th Edition, by Barry Burd.

Linking to PDFs

Adobe's Portable Document Format (PDF) has become increasingly popular on the Internet, and with good reason. Now that Acrobat Reader is widely distributed and even built into more recent browser versions, you can assume that most of your audience can read files in PDF.

PDF is a great option for files that you want to make easy to download in their entirety to be saved on a hard drive, as well as documents that you want printed exactly as they're designed. Because the PDF viewer is free, your users don't need expensive software, such as Microsoft Word or Lotus Notes, to view your documents.

In the early days, PDFs were limited to text and images, but the most recent versions support audio, video, and even Flash files meaning you can now create complex multimedia presentations in PDF format.

To add a PDF file to your Web site, simply copy the file into your local site folder and link to it as you'd link to any other Web page on your site. When you upload the page with the link to your PDF file, make sure to upload the PDF as well.

Chapter 11

Forms Follow Function

. . . .

. . . .

*F*orms follow function, to paraphrase the old saying. On the Web, many of the most advanced and interactive features you can add to a Web page require *forms* — structures for collecting information from users — information that can then be used in a variety of ways. Forms are commonly used to create guest books, contact forms, search-engine entry fields, chat rooms, and discussion areas.

When you design a form, Dreamweaver makes it relatively easy to create such controls as check boxes, radio buttons, and text boxes — (which show up on-screen as *fields* that the user fills in. Other common form elements include drop-down lists (which make it possible to add a long list of options to a page without taking up too much space) and Submit buttons (which a user must click when they finish filling out a form). You'll also find options in Dreamweaver for specifying text box sizes, character limits, and other features. After you build your form, you may want to consider formatting options, such as CSS (Cascading Style Sheets), to make it look good.

But if you want your form to actually do something, you have to pair it with a program on your Web server. One of the most confusing aspects of working with HTML forms is that they don't do much until you've connected them to a *script* (essentially a short program that executes a limited set of commands). Most forms are processed by Common Gateway Interface (CGI) scripts or some other program. These scripts can be written in different programming languages — including PHP, ASP.NET, C, C#, Java, and Perl. CGI scripts are far more complex than simple HTML files. Even experienced Web designers often purchase scripts created by a third party or hire experienced programmers to develop CGI scripts for them — especially for complex features, such as discussion boards or shopping carts.

Fortunately for those who don't have a computer science degree or a huge budget for programmers, many free and low-priced scripts are available on the Web. Search the Internet for *CGI scripts* and you'll find an impressive collection of ready-to-use programs, many of them free. Be aware, however, that when you download a program, you could be creating a security risk for your server (so look for trustworthy scripts with good reviews and support).

You also have to know how to configure and install any script you download on your Web server, which may require special access. How you install a script on your server depends on how your server is set up. Unfortunately, this book can't show you everything there is to know about working with all the different kinds of scripts available on the Web on all the different kinds of servers. (That would require a shelf full of books.) But I do try to give you an idea of what's involved in working with CGI scripts — and what to do in Dreamweaver to make sure your HTML form will work with a script.

The first part of this chapter includes instructions for creating the common elements in an HTML form, from radio buttons to text boxes. In the last part of the chapter, I include instructions for configuring a form to work with a common CGI script that you can use to send the contents of a form to any specified e-mail address. The steps and features covered in the final exercise also help you with other kinds of CGI scripts, but you should note that how you work with forms will depend on your Web hosting service and the specific configuration and requirements of your server.

You also need to create forms when you build dynamic Web sites using Dreamweaver's ColdFusion, ASP.NET, or PHP features. If you're creating a dynamic or database-driven site, use the features specific to those technologies, which are covered in Chapter 13. In this chapter, you find out how to create HTML forms in Dreamweaver.

Creating HTML Forms

No matter what kinds of fields you put in your form — radio buttons, check boxes, and text areas, for example — you start by inserting the `<form>` tag itself. Think of a `<form>` tag as the logical container for the instructions that create all the buttons, boxes, and so on that you place in your form.

Make sure you start with this first step — creating an HTML form — before you move on to the other exercises in this chapter.

The following exercise walks you through creating an HTML form. Start with an open page — either a new page or an existing page to which you want to add a form:

1. **Choose Insert⇨Form⇨Form or click the Form icon on the Forms Insert bar.**

   An empty `<form>` tag is inserted in your document and is displayed as a rectangle outlined by a red dotted line like the one shown in the Document area in Figure 11-1. This dotted line defines the boundaries of a form in the HTML code.

   You can control the display of invisible elements, such as `<form>` tags. Choose Edit⇨Preferences (Windows) or Dreamweaver⇨Preferences (Mac). Then, in the Invisible Elements category, select or deselect the Form Delimiter box. When the box is selected the form outline is visible in the Dreamweaver workspace, as you see in Figure 11-1.

2. **Click the red outline to select the `<form>` tag and display the `<form>` tag options in the Property inspector (as shown in the bottom of Figure 11-1).**

Figure 11-1: The Forms Insert bar provides easy access to all common form elements.

3. **In the Form ID text box, type a name.**

In this example, I entered the name **form1**. You can choose any name for this field as long as you don't use spaces, special characters, or punctuation. With your basic HTML form set up, you're ready to add elements to it, as explained in the following sections.

Before you begin filling your form with options, keep the following tips in mind:

- ✔ **The best way to get your form fields to line up nicely is to use CSS.** By creating styles that control the spacing and padding of form elements, you can make all your fields, buttons, and other elements line up neatly. (Chapters 5 and 6 cover CSS.)

- ✔ **After you design your form, your work isn't quite done; your form won't do anything unless you configure it to work with a script.** Although Dreamweaver doesn't provide any scripts, it does make linking your HTML forms to a script — or to a database — relatively easy. The section "Understanding How CGI Scripts Work" (later in this chapter) offers more details on making your form work with a script.

Match the script. Most fields displayed in the Property inspector when the `<form>` tag options are on-screen should be set to match those in the CGI script or other program that's used to collect and process the data from the form. You find instructions for filling in these fields in the "Configuring your form to work with a script" section, at the end of this chapter.

Use Accessibility Settings. The accompanying sidebar, "Making forms accessible," offers some practical examples of how the Accessibility settings in Dreamweaver can help you tweak your forms' characteristics to make them easier to use for all of the visitors to your site.

Making forms accessible

You can make your forms much easier to use and more accessible to all your visitors by using the `<label>` tag and other accessibility attributes with form items. Dreamweaver makes this easy by including an Input Tag Accessibility Attributes dialog box, as shown in the figure. For this dialog box to appear when you insert a form item such as a radio button or a check box, you must have accessibility features turned on in Dreamweaver's Preference settings. To turn on these features, choose Edit➪Preferences (Dreamweaver➪Preferences on a Mac); in the Preferences dialog box, click the Accessibility category, and select the Form Objects option.

With the accessibility options turned on, the Input Tag Accessibility Attributes dialog box opens automatically when you insert a form item (such as a radio button or a text box). Use this dialog box to specify the following options:

- ✔ **ID:** Use the ID field to assign a name to a form element. The name is important because it can be used to refer to the field in a script. The ID is also used if you choose Attach Label Tag Using 'For' Attribute option under the Style options. If you're not using the form with a script or a Label, you can leave this field blank, and Dreamweaver won't enter a name automatically.

✔ **Label:** Enter a name that describes the form element (radio button, check box, text field, whatever) — for example Email Address for a text field where you want the user to enter their e-mail address. The text you enter in the label field will appear next to a form field in the Web page, but if you enter it as a label and not just as text; it will have more meaning when it's read by a *screen reader* (a program that provides audible descriptions of screen elements to visually impaired users).

✔ **Style:** Check one of these three options to specify how the label should be included with the form field in the HTML code. The option Attach Label Tag Using 'For' Attribute is recommended as the best option for accessibility because it wraps the label tag around the entire form field, ensuring that the label and the form field will always be associated with each other. This option makes it easier to select a form field, such as a check box or radio button, because they can select the field by clicking anywhere in the text associated with it, instead of having to click precisely inside the check box or radio button.

✔ **Position:** Check the corresponding box to specify whether the label text should appear before or after each form item.

✔ **Access Key:** This attribute enables you to create a keyboard shortcut for each of your form items. You can enter any letter in this field, and your users can select the form item by holding down the Alt key (Windows) or the Control key (Macintosh) and typing the letter you specify. For example, if you enter **Q** as the Access Key, a visitor to your site who uses a Windows computer could press Alt+Q to select the form item.

✔ **Tab Index:** By default, a visitor to your site can use the Tab key to move from one form field to another in the order the form items appear on the page. With the Tab Index, you can specify the order in which the Tab key progresses from one form item to another. This is especially helpful if you have links and other form items on a page, and you want the user to be able to tab through them in a specific order. To control the order, assign a number to each form. Be sure to number your form items in ascending numerical order (as with 1, 2, 3) — and don't skip any numbers or the tab order will revert to the visual layout order.

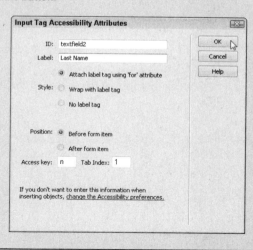

Input Tag Accessibility Attributes

ID: textfield2

Label: Last Name

Style: ⦿ Attach label tag using 'for' attribute
○ Wrap with label tag
○ No label tag

Position: ⦿ Before form item
○ After form item

Access key: n   Tab Index: 1

OK
Cancel
Help

If you don't want to enter this information when inserting objects, change the Accessibility preferences.

Creating radio buttons and check boxes

Radio buttons and check boxes make filling in a form easy for viewers of your site. Instead of making users type a word (such as **yes** or **no**), you can provide radio buttons and check boxes so users can simply click boxes or buttons to make a specific and consistent choice. Using buttons, check boxes, and multiple-choice lists, covered later in this chapter, can also help ensure that the data collected in a form is consistent.

What's the difference between radio buttons and check boxes? *Radio buttons* (like the pushbuttons on old car radios) enable users to select only one option from a group. Thus radio buttons are good for either/or options — or situations in which you want users to make only one selection. *Check boxes,* on the other hand, enable users to make multiple choices, so they're good for choose-all-that-apply situations or for situations that require approval, such as "Check this box if. . ."

Creating radio buttons

To create radio buttons on a form, follow these steps:

1. **Click to place your cursor inside the boundary of the** `<form>` **tag where you want to add a radio button.**

   If you haven't yet inserted the `<form>` tag, follow the steps in the section "Creating HTML Forms," earlier in this chapter.

2. **Click the Radio Button icon on the Forms Insert bar.**

   You can also choose Insert⇨Form⇨Radio Button. Either way, a radio button appears inside the form's red boundary line.

   If you have accessibility options turned on in Preferences, the Input Tag Accessibility Attributes dialog box opens. (See the sidebar "Making forms accessible" to find out more about these options.)

3. **Repeat Step 2 until you have the number of radio buttons you want.**

4. **Select one of the radio buttons on the form to reveal the radio button's properties in the Property inspector, as shown in Figure 11-2.**

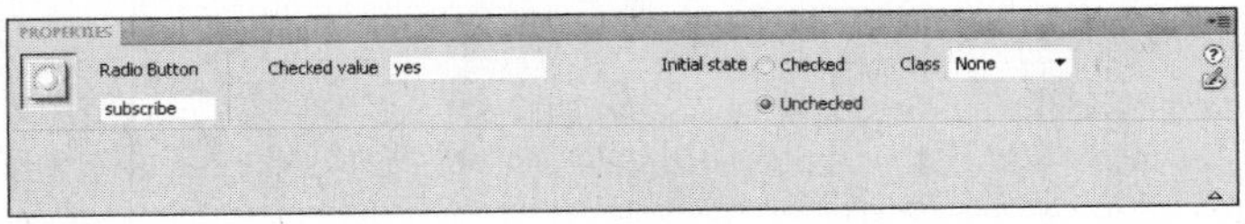

Figure 11-2:
Properties
of radio
buttons.

PROPERTIES						
Radio Button	Checked value	yes	Initial state	Checked	Class	None
subscribe				⊙ Unchecked		

5. **In the Radio Button text box on the far left of the Property inspector, type a name.**

   All radio buttons in a group should have the same name so that the browser associates them with one another and prevents users from selecting more than one. If you want users to be able to choose more than one item from a list, use check boxes instead, as described in the following section.

6. **In the Checked Value text box, type a name.**

   Each radio button in a group should have a different Checked Value name so it can be distinguished from the others. Naming radio buttons for the thing they represent is often a good practice; for example, _yes_ when the choice is yes and _no_ when it's no. If you're asking users about their favorite ice cream flavors, you might use as values the flavor each button represents.

   The Checked Value name is usually included in the data you get back when the form is processed and returned to you (the data collected by a form can be returned in an e-mail message or sent directly to a database or other data-storage option). How the data is returned depends on the CGI script or other programming used to process the form. If you're looking at the data later, interpreting it is easier if the name is something that makes sense to you.

7. **For the Initial State option, select Checked or Unchecked.**

   These two options determine whether the radio button on your form appears already selected when the Web page loads. Select Checked if you want to preselect a choice. You should set only one radio button option to be preselected; remember that the user can always override this setting by selecting another radio button.

8. **Select the other radio buttons one by one in the main design area and repeat Steps 5–7 to specify the properties in the Property inspector for each one.**

If you want to create a series of radio buttons, you'll find some advantages to using the Radio Group button in the Insert Form panel. Dreamweaver creates IDs for each radio button automatically. If you want to change these IDs, you may find it easier to change them in code view. You can split the screen between code and design views by clicking the Split view button at the top of the workspace.

If you want to format your form with CSS styles, you can create tag styles for the form, radio button, and other tags, or you can create class styles and apply them to any or all of your tags using the Class drop-down list in the

Property inspector. (You find more information about creating and applying styles in Chapters 5 and 6.)

If your form is complete, jump ahead to the "Finishing your form with Submit and Reset buttons" section, later in this chapter.

Creating check boxes

To create check boxes, follow these steps:

1. **Click to place your cursor inside the boundary of the** `<form>` **tag where you want to add a checkbox.**

   If you haven't yet inserted a `<form>` tag, follow the steps in the "Creating HTML Forms" section, earlier in this chapter.

2. **Click the Checkbox icon on the Forms Insert bar.**

   You can also choose Insert⇨Form⇨Check Box.

   If you have accessibility options turned on in Preferences, the Input Tag Accessibility Attributes dialog box opens. (See the sidebar "Making forms accessible," to find out more about these options.)

3. **Repeat Step 2 to place as many check boxes as you want.**

4. **Select one of the check boxes on your form to reveal the check-box properties in the Property inspector, as shown in Figure 11-3.**

Figure 11-3:
Properties
of check
boxes.

5. **In the Checkbox Name text box, type a name.**

   Use a distinct name for each check box. Users can select more than one check box, and you want to ensure that the information submitted is properly associated with each individual check box.

6. **In the Checked Value text box, type a name.**

   Every check box in a group should have a different Checked Value name so the CGI script can tell the boxes apart. Naming them for the things they represent is a good practice. As with radio buttons, the checked value is usually included in the data you get back when the form is processed and returned to you. If you're looking at the data later, it's easier to interpret if the name is something that makes sense to you.

If you're looking at the data later — say, reading an e-mail message that lists the text in the Checked Value box name and whatever the user entered into the field — is the data is easier to understand if the name is something that makes sense to you. For example, entering the word Chocolate instead of Option2 will result in data that looks like this: Chocolate=yes instead of Option2=yes.

7. For the Initial State option, select Checked or Unchecked.

This option determines whether the check box appears already selected when the Web page loads. Select Checked if you want to preselect a choice. A user can always override this preselection by clicking the text box again to deselect it.

8. Select the other check boxes one by one and repeat Steps 5–7 to set the properties in the Property inspector for each one.

If you want to create a series of check boxes, you'll find some advantages to using the Checkbox Group button in the Insert Form panel.

If your form is complete, jump ahead to the "Finishing your form with Submit and Reset buttons" section, later in this chapter.

Adding text fields and text areas

When you want users to enter text, such as a name, an e-mail address, or a comment, use a text field. To insert text fields, follow these steps:

1. Click to place your cursor inside the `<form>` tag where you want to add a text field.

If you haven't yet inserted a `<form>` tag, follow the steps in the "Creating HTML Forms" section, earlier in this chapter.

2. Click the Text Field icon on the Forms Insert bar.

You can also choose Insert⇨Form⇨Text Field. A text field box appears.

If you have accessibility options turned on in Preferences, the Input Tag Accessibility Attributes dialog box opens. (Refer to the "Making forms accessible" sidebar to find out more about these options.)

3. On the form, click to place your cursor next to the first text field and type a question or other text prompt.

For example, you may want to type **E-mail Address:** next to a text box where you want a user to enter an e-mail address.

4. Select the text field on your form to reveal the Text Field properties in the Property inspector, as shown in Figure 11-4.

Figure 11-4:
The
TextField
option
enables
users to
enter text.

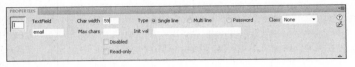

5. **In the TextField text box, type a name.**

   Each text area on a form should have a different text field name so the CGI script can distinguish it from the others. Naming text areas for the things they represent is usually best, but don't use any spaces or special characters (other than the hyphen or underscore). In Figure 11-4, you can see that I named the text field *email.* Many scripts return this name next to the contents of the text field a visitor enters at your Web site. If you're looking at the data later, you can interpret it more easily if the name corresponds to the choice.

6. **In the Char Width box, type the number of characters you want visible in the field.**

   This setting determines the width of the text field that appears on the page. In the example shown here, I've set the character width to 50 to create a text box that's more than wide enough for most e-mail addresses. How wide you make your text boxes depends on the amount of information you expect users to enter — and on the constraints of your design.

7. **In the Max Chars box, type the maximum number of characters you want to allow.**

   If you leave this field blank, users can type as many characters as they choose, even if their entries exceed the physical length of the text box specified in the Char Width field.

   I usually limit the number of characters only if I want to maintain consistency in the data (for example, I like to limit the State field to a two-character abbreviation). Creating drop-down lists, which require users to make a selection rather than risking that they might make a typo, is an even better way to ensure consistent data. You find instructions for creating drop-downs in the exercise that follows.

   You can set the Char Width field to be longer or shorter than the Max Chars field. If users type more characters than can appear in the text field, the text scrolls so that users can still see all the text they enter, even if it can't be displayed in the text field all at once.

8. **Next to Type, select one of the following options:**

   - **Single Line** creates a one-line text box, such as the kind I created for the hat size field shown in Figure 11-4.

   - **Multi Line** gives users space to enter text. (Note that if you select Multi Line, you also need to specify the number of lines you want the text area to cover by typing a number in the Num Lines field, which appears as an option when you choose Multi Line.)

   - **Password** is used if you're asking users to enter data that they might not want to display on-screen. This type of field causes entered data to appear as asterisks — and disables copying from the field (essential if you're going to keep the password secure).

9. **Use the Class drop-down list to apply any class CSS styles that may be defined in the site.**

   You can create class styles for many purposes, including formatting form elements. (For more about creating and applying class styles, see Chapters 5 and 6.)

10. **In the Init Val text box, type any text you want displayed when the form loads.**

    For example, you can include `Add e-mail address here` on the form in the text field under Comments. Users can delete the Init Val text or leave it and add more text in the same text field.

11. **If you're creating a multiline text area, specify the Wrap options.**

    The Wrap field controls how the users' data is displayed if it exceeds the length of the text field. Selecting Off or Default prevents the users' text from wrapping to the next line. (Note that this option is available only for multiline text boxes.)

12. **Select the other text areas one by one and repeat Steps 5–9 to set the properties in the Property inspector for each one.**

If your form is complete, jump ahead to the "Finishing your form with Submit and Reset buttons" section, later in this chapter.

Creating drop-down lists

When you want to give users a multiple-choice option but don't want to take up lots of space on the page, drop-down lists, such as the one shown in Figure 11-5, are an ideal solution. Drop-down lists are also a good option if you want to make sure that data collected in the form is consistent. For example, if you give users a list of state names instead of a text field, you don't have to worry about the fact that some people may enter the full state name, others may enter two letters, and still others may misspell the name. If the data collected in your form is simply e-mailed to you, consistency may be no big deal. But if the data goes into a database where it needs to match other related data, misspellings and other variations can cause big problems.

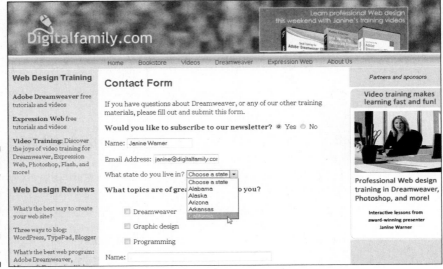

Figure 11-5:
The List/
Menu option
enables you
to create a
drop-down
list.

To create a drop-down list with Dreamweaver, follow these steps:

1. **Click to place your cursor inside the** `<form>` **tag where you want to add a drop-down list.**

   If you haven't yet created a `<form>` tag, follow the steps in the "Creating HTML Forms" section, earlier in this chapter.

2. **Click the List/Menu icon on the Forms Insert bar.**

   You can also choose Insert➪Form➪List/Menu. A drop-down list appears.

   If you have accessibility options turned on in Preferences, the Input Tag Accessibility Attributes dialog box opens. (Refer to the "Making forms accessible" sidebar, earlier in the chapter, for more about these options.)

3. **Click to place your cursor next to the List field and enter a question or other text prompt.**

   I typed **What state do you live in?**

4. Select the field that represents the list on your page to reveal the List/Menu properties in the Property inspector.

5. In the List/Menu text box, type a name.

Each list or menu on a form should have a different name so you can differentiate the lists when the form data is returned.

6. Next to Type, select the Menu or List option.

This step determines whether the form element is a drop-down list or a scrollable list. If you select List, you can specify the height and control of how many items are shown at a time. You can also specify whether a user can select more than one item. If you select Menu, these options aren't available.

7. Click the List Values button, at the upper-right of the Property inspector.

The List Values dialog box appears, as shown in Figure 11-6.

Item Label	Value
Choose a state	
Alabama	AL
Alaska	AK
Arizona	AZ
Arkansas	AR

OK · Cancel · Help

8. Enter the choices you want to make available.

Click the plus sign (+) to add an item label and then type the label text you want in the text box that appears in the dialog box. Item labels appear on the menu or list on the Web page in the order in which you enter them. Use the minus sign (–) to delete a selected option.

Press the Tab key to move the cursor to the Value side of the dialog box, where you can enter a value. Values are optional, but if they're present, they're sent to the server instead of the label text. This feature provides a way of including information that you don't want to display directly on the drop-down list. For example, if you enter **Alabama** as a label on the left, you can enter the abbreviation **AL** as a value on the right. If you enter **Alaska** as a label, you can enter **AK** as a value, and so on. That way, you visitors can select from a list that displays the full name of each state, but your script can collect only the two-letter abbreviations. If you don't enter a value, the label is used as the submitted data when the form is processed.

The first label entered in the List Values dialog box is the only one that's displayed on the page until a user clicks the drop-down arrow. Thus, it's good practice to include an instruction in this space, such as Choose a State, as shown in the example in Figures 11-5 and 11-6.

9. **Click OK to close the dialog box.**

Using jump menus

Many designers use *jump menus* (which take the user immediately to a different online location) as navigational elements because they can provide a list of links in a drop-down list without taking up lots of room on a Web page. You can also use a jump menu to launch an application or start an animation sequence. Jump menus are generally used as standalone features on a Web page, but they can be integrated into a form with other form items.

To create a jump menu, follow these steps:

1. **Click to place your cursor inside the** <form> **tag where you want to add a jump menu.**

   Alternatively, you can create a jump menu anywhere on a page. If there is no form tag in place, Dreamweaver adds one automatically around the jump menu's tag.

2. **Click the Jump Menu icon on the Forms Insert bar.**

   You can also choose Insert➪Form➪Jump Menu. The Insert Jump Menu dialog box opens.

3. **In the Text field, under Menu Items, type the name you want to display in the drop-down list.**

   Click the plus sign (+) to add more items. As you type items in the Text field, they appear in the Menu Items list, as shown in Figure 11-7.

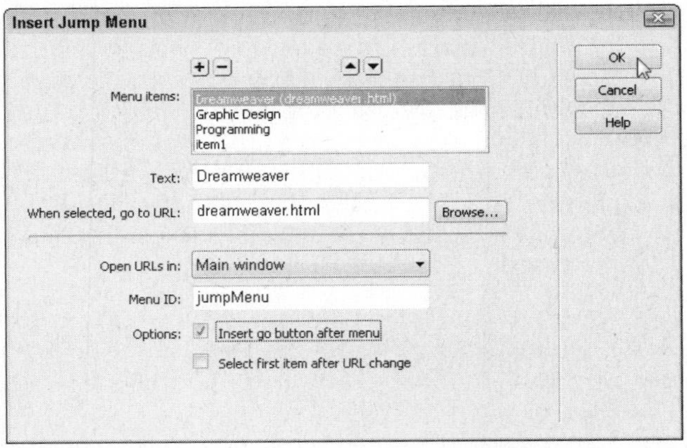

Figure 11-7:
When you create a jump menu, items you type in the Text field appear in the Menu Items list.

Insert Jump Menu

Menu items: Dreamweaver (dreamweaver.html)
Graphic Design
Programming
item1

Text: Dreamweaver

When selected, go to URL: dreamweaver.html   Browse...

Open URLs in: Main window

Menu ID: jumpMenu

Options: ☑ Insert go button after menu
☐ Select first item after URL change

OK
Cancel
Help

4. **Click the Browse button to locate the page you want to link to or type the URL for the page in the When Selected, Go to URL field.**

   You can link to a local file or enter any URL to link to a page on another Web site, and you can use the Browse button to specify the URL you want to link to.

5. **If you're using frames, use the Open URLs In field to specify a target.**

   If you're not using frames, the default is Main Window. When the user selects an option, the new page replaces the page he or she is viewing. (I explain how to target links in frames in Chapter 8.)

6. **If you want to enter a unique identifier for this menu, use the Menu ID field.**

   This option can be useful if you have multiple jump menus on a page. You can use any name you want, but you can't use spaces, special characters, or punctuation.

7. **If you want to force users to click a button to activate the selection, select the Insert Go Button after Menu option.**

   If you don't add a Go button, the linked page loads as soon as the user makes a selection. The Go button works like a Submit button for the jump-menu options.

Finishing your form with Submit and Reset buttons

For your users to be able to send their completed forms to you, create a Submit button, which, when clicked, tells the user's browser to send the form to the CGI script or other program that processes the form. You may also want to add a Reset button, which enables users to erase any information they've entered if they want to start over.

Many developers don't use the Reset button because they find it can be confusing to visitors (and annoying if it means they accidentally erase all the information they just entered). Because visitors can always leave a page before clicking the Submit button if they choose not to complete a form, the simplest way to avoid this problem is to avoid using a Reset button.

To create a Submit, Reset, or other button in Dreamweaver, follow these steps:

1. **Click to place your cursor inside the** `<form>` **tag where you want to add a button.**

   If you haven't yet inserted the `<form>` tag (which appears as a red dotted line around your form), follow the steps in the earlier section "Creating HTML Forms" before continuing with these steps. You might also want to enter at least one text field or other field option. There's not much point in having a Submit button if you don't provide any fields where a user can enter data to be submitted.

2. **Click the Button icon on the Forms Insert bar.**

   You can also choose Insert⇨Form⇨Button.

   If you have accessibility options turned on in Preferences, the Button Accessibility Attributes dialog box opens. (The "Making forms accessible" sidebar, earlier in the chapter, details these options.)

   A Submit button appears.

3. **Click to select the button.**

   The Property inspector changes to reveal the form button properties, as shown in Figure 11-8. You can change the button to a Reset button or other kind of button by altering the attributes in the Property inspector, as shown in the remaining steps.

Figure 11-8:
The form button properties.

4. **Next to Action, click the Submit Form or Reset Form option.**

   The Submit Form option invokes an action, such as sending user information to an e-mail address. The Reset Form option returns the page to the way it was when the page loaded. You can also select the None option, which creates a button that can be used for many purposes by combining it with a script.

5. **In the Value text box, type the text you want to display on the button.**

   You can type any text you want for the label, such as Search, Go, Clear, or Delete.

Having the user click a Submit button in a form doesn't do much unless you've configured the form to work with a CGI script or other program that collects or processes user-entered data.

Understanding How CGI Scripts Work

Common Gateway Interface (CGI) scripts are (as mentioned earlier), programs written in a programming language (such as Perl, Java, C++, ASP, or PHP) that work in tandem with your Web server to process data submitted by a user.

Think of CGI scripts as the engine behind an HTML form and many other automated features on a Web site. These scripts are much more complex to create than HTML pages — and these languages take much longer to figure out than HTML. CGI scripts reside and run on the server and are usually triggered by an action a user takes, such as clicking the Submit button on an HTML form.

A common scenario with a script may go like this:

1. A user loads a page, such as a guest book, fills out the HTML form, and clicks the Submit button.

2. The browser gathers all the data from the form and sends it to the Web server in a standard format.

3. The Web server takes the incoming data and hands it off to the CGI script that unpacks the data and does something with it — such as placing it in an e-mail message and sending the message to a specified e-mail address, or adding the data to a Web page where guest-book comments are posted.

4. The CGI script then sends instructions or a block of HTML back to the browser through the Web server to report on the outcome of the script and to complete any final actions, such as displaying a Thank You page.

Configuring your form to work with a script

After you create a form using the features covered in the previous sections of this chapter, configure the form to work with a CGI script or a program. To help you understand how this process works, I use the common `formmail.pl` script in the following exercise. This clever little script is designed to collect data entered into an HTML form and send it to a specified e-mail address. You can find out more about `formmail.pl` at `www.scriptarchive.com` (a great place to find lots of free CGI scripts).

Every script is different. The details of how you install and configure a script depend on the individual program — and on how your server is set up.

If your service provider doesn't offer a mail script to use in your form, you can download and configure the script if you have the right access on your server (*and* knowledge of how your server is configured). Ask your service provider for more information. If your service provider doesn't provide the interactive scripts you want, you may want to consider moving your site to a hosting service that does provide CGI scripts you can use.

The following exercise shows you how to use Dreamweaver with the `formmail.pl` script. This gives you a good introduction to how you'd set up any form to work with any script — but be aware that you may have to alter some of the steps to work with the program you're using:

1. **Select the `<form>` tag that surrounds your form by clicking anywhere on the red dotted line that represents the boundary of the `<form>` tag (or by clicking the `<form>` tag in the tag selector at the bottom of the work area), as shown in Figure 11-9.**

   With the `<form>` tag selected, the Property inspector changes to feature the `<form>` tag options. *Note:* All HTML forms must be enclosed by the `<form>` tag. If your script doesn't have a `<form>` tag, add one around the entire contents of your form by following the steps in the "Creating HTML Forms" section found earlier in this chapter.

   To select the `<form>` tag in Dreamweaver, place your cursor anywhere in the body of your form and then use the tag selector at the bottom of the work area to select the `<form>` tag. Make sure you've selected the `<form>` tag and not just one of the form elements, such as the text box I created in this form for comments.

Figure 11-9: You can use the tag selector to select the `<form>` tag and display form properties in the Property inspector.

2. In the Property inspector, give your form a name.

Dreamweaver automatically gives each form you create a distinct name (form1, form2, and so on) — but I prefer to change the name to something that has more meaning, such as *contact* for this contact form. You can name your form whatever you like; just don't use spaces or special characters.

3. Specify the action for the form.

For the `formmail.pl` script used in this example (as well as many other scripts you might use), the action is simply the path to the script's location on your server. In Figure 11-10, you can see that I've entered the address `/cgi-bin/formmail.pl`. The address you enter depends on your service provider; a common convention is to call the folder where CGI scripts are stored `cgi-bin`. The last part of the address (`formmail.pl`) is the name of the script. (In this case, it's a Perl script, indicated by the `.pl` extension.)

You can only use the Browse button (the yellow folder icon in the Property inspector) to enter an address automatically in the Action field if you're working on a live server — and Dreamweaver has identified the location of your script — or if you have the script on your local system in the same directory structure that exists on your server. In most cases, it's simplest just to ask your service provider or programmer for the address and type it in the Action field.

Figure 11-10:
In the Action field, enter the path to the script.

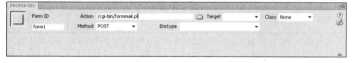

4. In the Method field, use the drop-down arrow to choose Get, Post, or Default.

Again, what you choose depends on your script, but Dreamweaver's default is Post. If you're using a script, such as `formmail`, which is featured in the final sections of this chapter, the best option is Post.

The Get option is generally used for nondestructive, safe form transactions that may be repeated, such as those done with a search engine. Transactions with the Get option are generally stored in the log files on a server and in a browser's history files, so this option isn't recommended for sensitive data, such as financial information. The Post option is generally used for transactions that occur only once — such as sending an e-mail with the data from a form, registering for a service, or unsubscribing to a newsletter. The Post option can also handle larger chunks of data than Get.

5. **Click the Target option to specify what the browser does when the submit action is completed.**

If you choose _blank, the results page opens in a new browser window. If you leave this field blank, the browser window is simply replaced with the results page. A results page is usually a simple HTML page with a message (such as *Thanks for playing*) delivered when the Submit button is clicked.

6. **Use the Enctype field to specify how the data is formatted when it's returned (see Figure 11-11).**

For example, if you're using a form mail script, the `Enctype` field determines how the text appears in your e-mail when the contents of the form are sent to you. By default, this field is blank.

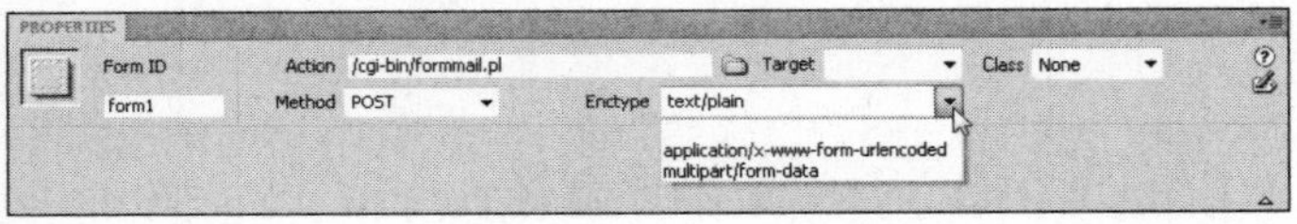

Figure 11-11:
Enter a type in the Enctype field.

7. **Use the Class field at the far right of the Property inspector to apply a CSS style to the form.**

In this example, I applied CSS to some elements in the form, such as the text, but not to the entire form.

That takes care of all the options in the Property inspector. You still have one more task, however: inserting a hidden form field into this form to make it work with the `formmail.pl` script, as shown in the next exercise.

Using hidden fields

Many scripts, including the `formmail.pl` script, require the use of *hidden fields* — fields that hold data you want associated with a form but not shown to visitors to a site (such as the e-mail address to which a form is sent when a visitor clicks the Submit button). To insert and use a hidden field, follow these steps:

1. **Click to place your cursor inside the** `<form>` **tag.**

   If you haven't yet inserted the `<form>` tag (which appears as a red dotted line around your form), follow the steps in the first exercise in the "Creating HTML Forms" section before continuing with this exercise.

   Even though the hidden field doesn't appear in the form area, make sure that it's inside the `<form>` tag before you add a hidden field. Placing your cursor at the top or bottom of the form area before inserting a hidden field is a good option because it makes the hidden field easier to find in the HTML code.

   After the hidden field is inserted into the `<form>` tag, the Property inspector changes to feature the Hidden Field options (shown in Figure 11-12).

2. **In the Property inspector, enter a name.**

   If you're using `formmail.pl`, you'd enter **recipient** as the name and the e-mail address where you want the form data sent as the value. You can even enter more than one e-mail address, separated by commas. So, for example, I could enter **janine@jcwarner.com, janine@digitalfamily.com** in the Value field, and the data from the form would be e-mailed to both these e-mail addresses when a user clicks the Submit button (as shown in Figure 11-12.)

Figure 11-12:
The Hidden Field properties.

3. **Click to place your cursor inside the** `<form>` **tag and then click the Hidden Field icon in the Forms Insert Bar to add another hidden field to create a subject line.**

4. **In the Property inspector, enter the name** subject**; in the Value field, include a subject line you want inserted into the e-mail message automatically when a user submits the form.**

   In this example, I entered **Contact Information from DigitalFamily.com** as the value.

   You can add many other hidden fields to a form, depending on the script you're using and on how much you want to customize the results.

That's it. Assuming all fields are filled in correctly and `formmail.pl` (or a similar script) is properly installed and configured on your server, you should receive via e-mail any data a user enters into your form and submits.

Using form validation to check data

When you create a form, it's good practice to include features that validate the form as a user submits it. For example, you can use form validation to ensure that a user has entered an e-mail address in a text field. If they have not, you can return the form with a message stating that the e-mail address field is required.

You can set up validation for forms in many ways, but the simplest way in Dreamweaver is to use the Spry form fields, which I cover in more detail on my Web site at DigitalFamily. com.

There are many reasons to create forms on the Web, but e-mailing the contents of a contact form is one of the most common. I hope this little exercise has helped give you an idea of what to do to make your HTML forms interact with a CGI script on your server.

Most service providers offer a collection of scripts you can use to create forms for common features of Web sites, such as guest books and contact forms. All you have to do is create the HTML part of the form and then specify the form fields to interact with the script on your server. Check the Web site of your Web-hosting service for instructions specific to the scripts available on your server.

Chapter 12

Creating AJAX Features with Spry

* *

In This Chapter

▶ Creating drop-down menus

▶ Creating collapsible and tabbed panels

▶ Working with Spry validation widgets

* *

*1*f you still think AJAX (Asynchronous JavaScript and XML) is just something you can use to clean the house, you're missing out on one of the greatest innovations in Web design. On the Internet, AJAX combines JavaScript and XML to create highly interactive features, such as drop-down menus and panels that can be opened and closed without reloading a Web page.

To make it easier to create these advanced features, Dreamweaver includes a collection of widgets known as the Spry Framework. Even if you don't know how to write JavaScript, XML, or CSS, you can use to Spry add AJAX features to your Web pages, such as drop-down menus (like the one shown in Figure 12-1), collapsible and tabbed panels, and form validation features, which I cover in this chapter.

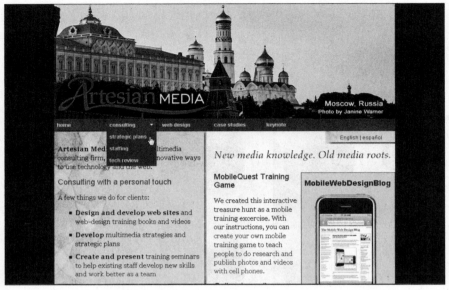

Figure 12-1:
You can create drop-down menus like these with the Spry menu in Dreamweaver.

Making Magic with AJAX

Web designers are all a buzz about AJAX because it enables you to create more interactive pages that load faster than similar pages created with previous Web technologies. AJAX also enables designers to add features that a Web page visitor can change without having to reload the entire page.

For example, at the highly popular iGoogle page of the Google search engine (available at www.igoogle.com), AJAX enables you to open and close the weather box, calendar, and other features on the site, as well as move boxes around the page without reloading the page. Although iGoogle is a very advanced example of AJAX, it's a great example of what's possible.

Dreamweaver's Spry features are designed to make it easy to create some of these kinds of features, such as panels that open and close, the way the weather content box on iGoogle opens or closes.

To save you from having to write the code for these kinds of features yourself, Dreamweaver includes a collection of widgets that instantly adds things like collapsible panels and drop-down menus to your pages, and includes editing tools for customizing these features without knowing JavaScript. To view the list of AJAX widgets available in Dreamweaver, open the Spry Insert panel by choosing Spry from the Insert panel drop-down menu shown in Figure 12-2.

Creating Drop-Down Menus with AJAX

An increasingly popular option for navigation bars, drop-down menus can provide a menu (or list) of links to the main sections of a Web site, with a secondary menu of links to the subcategories within those sections. You can even create a third layer with the Spry Menu Bar widget.

With the Dreamweaver Spry Menu Bar, you can create menus that span horizontally or vertically. As you see in the following steps, you simply choose which way you want the menu to span when you insert it from the Spry menu.

To create a drop-down menu with the Spry Menu Bar widget, follow these steps:

1. **Place your cursor on a page where you want the menu to appear.**

   If you haven't already saved your page, make sure you save it before adding Spry features, or Dreamweaver will prompt you with a warning message that you need to do so.

2. **Choose Insert➪Spry➪Spry Menu Bar.**

   Alternatively, you can click the Spry Menu Bar option in the Spry Insert panel, visible in Figure 12-3.

   The Spry Menu Bar dialog box appears.

3. **In the Spry Menu Bar dialog box, choose Horizontal or Vertical.**

   Horizontal creates a menu that drops down into a page; Vertical creates a menu that opens out to the right.

4. **Click OK.**

   A menu with four items and several subitems is created and inserted into the page.

5. **Enter your own text for the menu items.**

   You can edit the text for the top-level items in the main workspace by simply clicking and dragging to select the generic text, such as Item1, and then typing to replace it.

   In general, making changes to menu bar items in the Property inspector is best. I explain how in the remaining steps. To change formatting options, such as color, font face, and size, make changes to the style sheet rules, described in Step 14.

6. **Click the blue Menu Bar tab on the top of the menu bar you inserted in the design area to display the settings in the Property inspector, as shown in Figure 12-3.**

   You find settings to add, remove, edit, and change the order of items and subitems in the Property inspector.

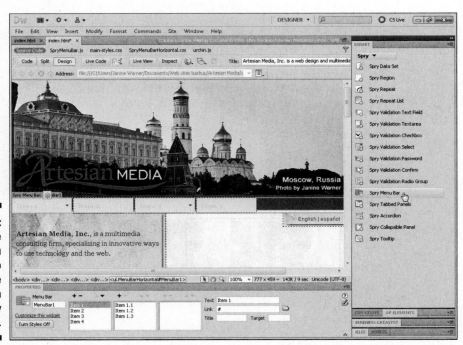

Figure 12-3: Click the blue Menu Bar tab to display the options in the Property inspector.

7. **To change the name of an item or subitem, click to select the item in the Property inspector and then type a new name in the Text field on the far-right side of the Property inspector, as shown in Figures 12-3 and 12-4.**

8. **To link a menu item, select the item name and enter a URL in the Link field or click the Browse button (which looks like a file folder), and select the page you want to link to (see Figure 12-4).**

9. **To remove an item, select it and then click the minus (–) sign at the top of the field in the Property inspector.**

   A deleted item is removed from the menu in the Property inspector as well as the main work area.

10. **To add an item, select the plus (+) sign at the top of the item field in the Property inspector.**

    When you add an item, it appears in the Property inspector menu as well as in the menu bar in the main work area.

11. **To add a subitem, select the item you want the subitem to appear under and then click the plus (+) sign in the item box to the right of the selected item (refer to Figure 12-3).**

12. **To change the order of items, click to select an item name and then use the arrows at the top of each item box.**

    Items move up and down the menu when you click the up or down arrows. Items appear in the Web page in the order they appear in the Property inspector.

Figure 12-4:
Edit any item selected in the Property inspector with the Text, Link, Title, and Target fields.

13. **Choose File⇨Save to save the page, and when the Copy Dependent Files dialog box appears, click OK to automatically generate all the related files.**

    You must upload these files to your Web server when you upload the Web page for the Spry features to work.

14. To change the appearance of a drop-down menu, edit the corresponding CSS style rules.

CSS (Cascading Style Sheets) style rules determine the text size, font, background color, and other formatting features. When you create a menu bar, a collection of CSS styles are generated automatically and saved in an external CSS file dubbed `SpryMenuBarHorizontal.CSS` (for horizontal menus) or `SpryMenuBarVertical.CSS` (for vertical menus). You can access these styles through the CSS Styles panel, shown in Figure 12-5.

Here are a few examples of how Spry menu bar styles can be edited:

a. **To change the font size or face, double-click the style name** `ul.MenuBarHorizontal` **and alter the corresponding Type category settings.** In the example, shown here, I've changed the font size to 90 percent, which will make the text in the menu display at 90 percent of the size of the default text setting for the page.

b. **You can remove or edit the border of a menu bar by editing the border settings in the style** `ul.MenuBarHorizontal ul.` (In the example shown here, I removed the border by simply deleting all the settings for the border.)

c. **You can change the text and background colors for the active links (effectively changing the colors of the menu bar when the page first loads) by changing the colors for the rule** `ul.MenuBarHorizontal a.`

To find other settings you may want to change, click to select each of the style names in the Spry Menu Bar style sheet and use the CSS Properties pane, in the lower half of the CSS Styles panel, to view the rules that have been defined for each style. By simply clicking through the collection of styles, you can identify each of the settings in a drop-down menu (or any other Spry feature) and determine where you'll need to edit them to change the appearance of each element. You find more detailed instructions for creating and editing style rules in Chapters 5 and 6.

15. Click the globe icon at the top of the workspace to preview your work in a browser.

Here you can see how the styles appear in the menu and test the drop-down effects and links.

The example in Figure 12-6 is in the Firefox browser.

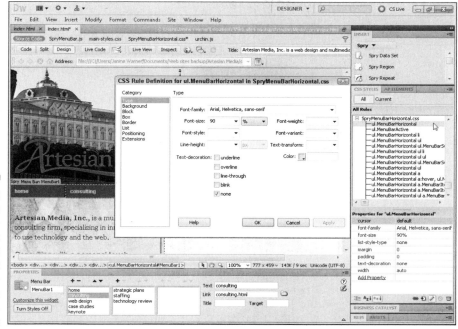

Figure 12-5:
To change the appearance of a drop-down menu, edit the corresponding CSS styles.

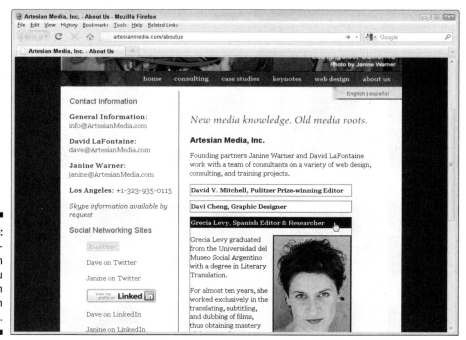

Figure 12-6:
The collapsible panel in this menu is shown in the open position.

Creating Collapsible Panels

The Spry Collapsible Panel option makes it easy to add panels that can be opened or closed on a Web page. This AJAX feature enables you to make better use of the space on a page by making it easy to display more information in less space within a browser window.

In Figures 12-6, you can see how I used collapsible panels to contain the biography of each partner and consultant in a consulting firm. The result is that you can easily see the names of all the consultants on one page. To view a consultant's bio, a user need only click the tab at the top of the panel (where the consultant's name appears), and the panel opens instantly. In Figure 12-6 you can see that the bio for Designer Davi Cheng is open while the others on the page are all closed. The beauty of AJAX is that the page doesn't have to be reloaded for the panels to open or close. Click once on a tab and a panel opens instantly. If a user clicks the tab again, the panel closes. Collapsible panels can be used to display text and images. You can also include multimedia files in panels, such as audio, video, and Flash files.

When you create collapsible panels with the Spry menu in Dreamweaver, you can set the panels so that they're closed or opened when a page is first loaded. Because each panel is created separately, you can create a page that displays all panels open, all panels closed, or a mix of the two options.

Follow these steps to create a collapsible panel:

1. **Place your cursor on a page where you want the collapsible panel to appear.**

2. **Choose Insert⇨Spry⇨Spry Collapsible Panel.**

   Alternatively, you can click the Spry Collapsible Panel icon in the Spry Insert panel, as shown in Figure 12-7.

   A Spry collapsible panel appears in the page, as shown in Figure 12-7.

3. **Click and drag to select the word Tab and replace it with the text you want to appear in the panel's Tab area.**

   By default, the text in the Tab area is bold, but you can change that by altering the corresponding CSS rule.

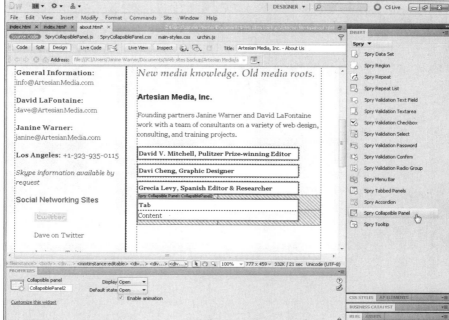

Figure 12-7:
The Spry
Collapsible
Panel option
adds one
panel to a
Web page,
but you can
use it mul-
tiple times
to create
a series of
panels.

4. **Click to select the word Content in the main area of the panel and enter any text or images you want to display.**

   You can copy text into a panel by pasting it just as you'd paste text anywhere else on the page. Similarly, you insert images into panels just as you would anywhere else on a page by choosing Insert⇨Image and selecting the GIF, JPEG, or PNG file you want to display. (Chapter 3 covers images on the Web if you need help preparing or converting images into these formats.)

   When you paste text into a panel, choose Edit⇨Paste Special to choose the amount of formatting you want to preserve in the text you paste in Dreamweaver. Limiting the amount of formatting preserved can cut down on potential style conflicts.

5. **Click the blue Spry Collapsible Panel tab at the top of the panel in the design area.**

   When you correctly click the blue tab, the panel settings immediately appear in the Property inspector, as shown in Figure 12-7. Click anywhere else on the page, and the inspector returns to its default settings.

6. **From the Display drop-down menu in the Property inspector, choose Closed.**

   The Closed option immediately closes the panel in the main workspace in Dreamweaver. This setting only affects the way the panel displays in the Dreamweaver workspace.

7. **From the Default State drop-down menu in the Property inspector, choose Closed.**

   This setting controls how the panel displays in a Web browser. Choosing Closed means the panel is closed when the page loads. If you choose Open, the panel appears open when the page is loaded.

8. **Make sure the Enable Animation check box is selected if you want the panel to open and close when a user clicks the tab.**

9. **To change the appearance of the panel, such as the font face or color, edit the corresponding CSS rule.**

   For example, to edit the background color of the tab, or the font face, style, or color, select the `.CollapsiblePanelTab` style and alter the settings in the Properties panel in the lower half of the CSS Styles panel, as shown in Figure 12-8. Alternatively, you can double-click any style name to launch the CSS Rule Definition dialog box to make your changes there. You find more detailed instructions for creating and editing styles in Chapters 5 and 6.

10. **Choose File➪Save to save the page, and when the Copy Dependent Files dialog box appears, click OK to automatically generate all the related files.**

    You must upload these files to your Web server when you upload the Web page for the Spry features to work.

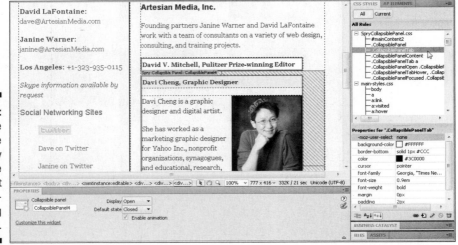

Figure 12-8: To alter the appearance of a Spry collapsible panel, edit the corresponding CSS rule.

11. **Click the globe icon at the top of the workspace to preview your work in a browser.**

Creating Tabbed Panels

The Spry Tabbed Panel option makes it easy to add a series of panels that display or hide content corresponding to a series of tabs, as shown in Figure 12-9. Similar to the collapsible panels, this AJAX feature lets you display more information in less space within a browser window.

Similar to the collapsible panels, tabbed panels can be used to display text, images, and multimedia.

When you create tabbed panels with the Spry menu in Dreamweaver, you can control the order of the tabs, effectively controlling what content appears when the page is first loaded.

Figure 12-9:
Tabbed panels enable you to change the content displayed on a Web page when a visitor clicks a tab.

Follow these steps to create a tabbed panel:

1. **Place your cursor on a page where you want the tabbed panel to appear.**

2. **Choose Insert⇨Spry⇨Spry Tabbed Panels.**

   Alternatively, you can click the Spry Tabbed Panels icon in the Spry Insert panel, as shown in Figure 12-10.

   A Spry tabbed panel appears on the page, as shown in Figure 12-10.

3. **Click and drag to select the word Tab in the main workspace and replace it with the text you want to appear in the panel's Tab area.**

   You can edit the contents of the tabs only in the workspace, not in the Property inspector.

   By default, the text in the Tab area is bold and black, but you can change that by altering the corresponding CSS rule.

4. **Click the blue Spry Tabbed Panels tab at the top of the panel set in the design area.**

   When you correctly click the blue tab, the settings immediately appear in the Property inspector, as shown in Figure 12-10. Click outside the blue boxed area, and the Property inspector returns to its default settings.

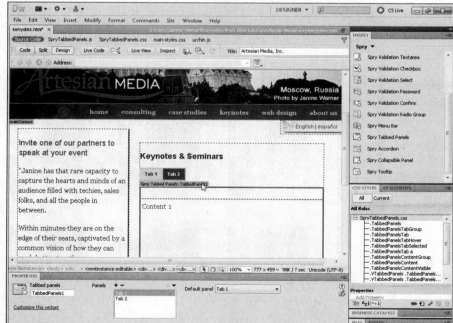

Figure 12-10: The Spry Tabbed Panel option adds a tabbed panel to a Web page.

5. **To add tabs, click the plus (+) icon in the Property inspector, as shown in Figure 12-10.**

   New tabs appear in the workspace.

6. **To change the order of tabs, click to select the tab name in the Property inspector and then use the arrows in the Panels field to move the panel.**

   Panel names move up and down the menu as the order is changed. Panels and their corresponding tabs appear in the Web page in the order they appear in the Property inspector.

7. **Use the Default Panel drop-down menu to choose the tab you want to display when the page is first loaded into a Web browser.**

   The drop-down menu corresponds to the names you give each tab in the workspace.

8. **To add content, select the word Content in the main area of any selected tab panel and enter text, images, or multimedia.**

   You can copy text into a panel by pasting it just as you'd paste text anywhere else on the page. Similarly, insert images into panels just as you would anywhere else on a page by choosing Insert⇨Image and then selecting the GIF, JPEG, or PNG file you want to display. You can also add multimedia, such as Flash video files. (Find instructions for adding multimedia to Web pages in Chapter 10.)

9. **To change the appearance of a tab or a panel, such as the font face or color, edit the corresponding CSS rule.**

   For example, to edit the background color of the tabs, click to select the `.TabbedPanelsTab` style and alter the settings in the Properties panel in the lower half of the CSS Styles panel. Alternatively, you can double-click any style name to launch the CSS Rule Definition dialog box to make your changes there. You find more detailed instructions for creating and editing styles in Chapters 5 and 6.

   In tabbed panels styles, the tab background colors are controlled by two different styles — the `.TabbedPanelsTab` and the `.TabbedPanelsTabSelected` styles. As a result, you can specify a different background color and other formatting settings to distinguish the tab that's selected from the tabs that aren't selected.

10. **Choose File⇨Save to save the page, and when the Copy Dependent Files dialog box appears, click OK to automatically generate all the related files.**

    You must upload these files to your Web server when you upload the Web page for the Spry features to work.

11. **Click the globe icon at the top of the workspace to preview your work in a browser.**

Using Spry Validation Widgets

The Spry menu also includes a collection of validation widgets you can use to create form elements with built-in validation features. For example, you can use the Text Field Validation widget to verify whether a visitor has filled in a specified minimum number of characters — a handy way to ensure that someone has filled in all the digits in a phone number or Social Security number. You can also add hints to a text field to provide additional instructions.

Similarly, you can use the Validation Checkbox widget to verify that a check box has been selected. This is common, for example, when you have a legal disclaimer or contract and want to ensure that a visitor selects the Accept box before progressing into another area of your site, as shown in Figure 12-11.

To use these widgets, click to select the Spry validation option you want to use, such as the Spry Validation Text Area or the Spry Validation Checkbox (see Figure 12-11). If you have not already inserted the HTML form tag, Dreamweaver offers to do it for you. (You find more instructions for creating form elements in Chapter 11).

To use the Spry Validation Checkbox Wizard to require that users select one or more check boxes on a Web page, follow these steps:

1. **Click to place your cursor in the page where you want the checkbox to appear.**

2. **Choose Insert⇨Spry⇨Spry Validation Checkbox.**

   Alternatively, you can click the Spry Validation Checkbox icon in the Spry Insert panel.

3. **If you are not adding the check box to an area that already includes a form tag, the Add Form Tag dialog box opens. To create the form tag as you create the text box, click Yes.**

4. **Specify validation requirements in the Property inspector.**

   When you add a validation widget to a form element, such as the check box shown in this example, the Property inspector automatically displays the properties for that validation option. If those properties aren't visible, click the blue Spry tab just above the form element to display them.

5. **To require that users select a check box, choose Required from the Preview States drop-down menu in the Property inspector.**

   Dreamweaver automatically adds Please Make a Selection, just to the right of the check box in the workspace. You can edit this text by selecting it in the workspace and typing any message you want, such as, **You must accept our policy to continue.**

The validation message displays only if a visitor fails to select the check box before clicking the Submit button.

6. **Choose File⇨Save to save the page, and when the Copy Dependent Files dialog box appears, click OK to automatically generate all the related files.**

For the Spry features work, you must upload these files to your Web server when you upload the Web page.

7. **Click the globe icon at the top of the workspace to preview your work in a browser where you can test the validation features.**

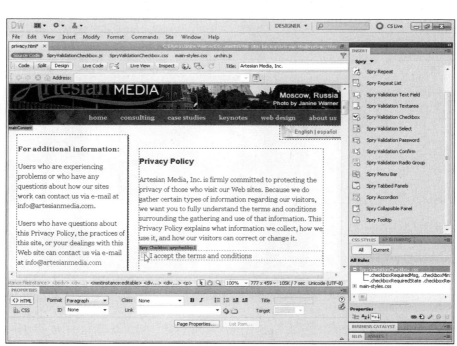

Figure 12-11:
You can use the Checkbox Validation widget to require that visitors select a check box before continuing to another page in your site.

Chapter 13

Creating Dynamic Web Sites

*B*efore you start down the path of working on a dynamic Web site, let me warn you of two things. First, creating a dynamic Web site is far more complex than creating the static-page Web sites described in the rest of this book. Second, there is no way I can possibly cover everything you'd need to know to create a dynamic site as complex as Amazon.com or CNN.com in one book.

But don't despair! Thousands of programmers have done the heavy lifting to build open-source (that is, free) code for dynamic sites, and Dreamweaver is the perfect tool to take an "off-the-shelf" dynamic site and customize it to make it really your own.

This chapter shows you how dynamic sites work, why they're important, and how Dreamweaver can be used to create and edit them. You also find a review of the most common technologies used to create dynamic sites — PHP, ASP.Net, ColdFusion, and JSP — and an explanation of how these technologies are used to create everything from Disney.com to blogging programs like WordPress. At the end of this chapter, you find an introduction to Dreamweaver's most advanced features, which are designed for developing and editing dynamic Web sites.

Although most of this book focuses on creating static page sites, the skills you try out throughout this book — such as how to optimize images for the Web and how to create Cascading Styles Sheets — apply equally well to both static and dynamic Web sites. (In Chapter 1, you find a comparison of static and dynamic sites and the templates used in each of these site types.)

If you want to get further into using the most advanced Dreamweaver features introduced in this chapter, you can find more information in *Dreamweaver CS5 All-in-One Desk Reference For Dummies,* by Sue Jenkins, Michele E. Davis, and Jon A. Phillips; or *Dreamweaver CS5 Bible,* by Joseph Lowery (Wiley).

Understanding Dynamic Web Sites

Dynamic Web sites are so powerful because you can draw information out of a *data source* (such as a database), as a visitor arrives at your Web site and use it to create a new Web page in real time, that responds to the visitor — that is, a *dynamic* page. The ability to create Web pages on the fly is what enables a site to show a page featuring books on dog costumes to one visitor and show a page with books about dancing cats to another visitor.

In addition to databases, you can use other data sources (such as XML files or RSS feeds) to display data dynamically. You can also combine multiple sources to create one very complex page. For example, the pages you see on many news sites (such as CNN) combine information from articles that come from one data source with advertising that comes from another. Connecting different data sources to the same Web page enables CNN to produce up-to-date news pages with breaking news and the latest weather report, as well as ever-changing advertising, because they create each page on-the-fly as visitors arrive at the site.

A simple example of a dynamic Web site feature is a search engine, which works (generally) like this:

1. You type what you want to find into a search field.

2. When you submit your request, that information is passed from your Web browser to a database (using a script or Web technology), written in a programming language such as PHP.

3. That same script, or one that works cooperatively with it, then compares what you entered into the search field with the contents of the database and returns a list of results that are displayed in a single page. Thus, the information that a visitor enters results in a unique, dynamically generated Web page with a list of results that are relevant (ideally, anyway!) to the search request.

If you're starting to think you'll never be able to add dynamic features to your Web site, take heart in the fact that more and more services save you the complex programming needed to add these kinds of high-end features. For example, the easiest way to add search to a Web site (even a static-page site) is Google's free search engine. You can download a snippet of code from the Google Web site and add it to your own site for free, effectively adding a complex search engine on your site, even if you're not a programmer. Visit www.google.com/cse for details.

Appreciating dynamic sites' advantages

A dynamic Web site has many advantages beyond the capability to search another Web site. Suppose you have a Web site where you sell 657 kinds of candy. Here's how a static site stacks up against a dynamic site:

✔ **With a *dynamic* Web site,** you create just *one* page template with the design for your candy products pages — and then you add special code that dynamically pulls product name, image, description, and any other pertinent information from a database and displays it in that one page template each time a visitor requests one of the 657 kinds of candy. That means you don't actually have 657 pages, you have one template and a database full of content. That allows you to update, sort, mix and match your candy data — whenever and however you want — to create a virtually infinite number of pages that exist only as long as visitors to your site are viewing them.

✔ **On a *static* Web site,** you'd have to create 657 pages, one for each candy product. If you ever wanted to change the way those pages look, you'd have to change all 657 pages. Although using Dreamweaver templates (covered in Chapter 7) will get you some of the same advantages you'd get from a dynamic site — such as doing some global updates to common parts of a page — you still have to go through each and every one of those 657 distinct pages, and then upload all of them to your Web server.

When you compare the two types of site, dynamic Web sites clearly offer advantages to site owners who have a lot of data, such as items for sale, to display in a consistent format:

✔ **A dynamic site saves time** because you don't have to create individual pages for every product or for every different type of product listing. With a dynamic site, you invest more time upfront, but if you're working on a site that's more than 100 pages or so, the dynamic approach is probably more efficient in the long run.

✔ **Dynamic sites enable you to display the same product information in different combinations.** So, for example, you could create one template that displayed only the name and photo of each kind of candy in a long list, and then another template that displayed all the product information for each type of candy, including a detailed description, pricing information, additional photos, and so on. (If you've ever shopped on Amazon.com or Godiva.com, you're familiar with the concept.) You could also create one page that listed only chocolate candy and another that listed jelly beans. One big advantage is that if you change the name of a candy bar, you simply change the name once in the database, and it's automatically changed on all the pages created from that entry in the database.

Comparing server-side versus client-side scripts

Two types of dynamic Web technology exist: Web pages created with server-side scripting and those created with client-side scripting.

Client-side scripting can be executed on the client — which (for our purposes) means it's done in the Web browser on your computer. For example, the rollover behaviors covered in Chapter 9 and the drop-down menus covered in Chapter 12 both make substantial use of JavaScript to make images and links change *dynamically* on a Web page. Those changes are handled on your computer by function calls to your processor, memory, and video card. Client-side scripts enable you to create some very cool features, but their uses are more limited than those of server-side scripts.

Server-side scripting is installed and executed on a Web server. This chapter focuses on the kinds of dynamic sites you can create with server-side scripting — which enables a dynamic site to function with far more complexity — for example, pulling data from more than one data source to give potential customers on an e-commerce site custom-tailored recommendations based on the search terms they enter, as well as on the company's current inventory. An example is a message that says something like, "You looked for jelly beans, and we think you might also like the jelly bean bouquets we have on sale this week."

✔ **Dynamic sites enable you to create links between pages with related information — automatically — so visitors can drill down to find the details they want.** For example, you can set up one template that is designed to display the kinds of candy you sell, but specify that only ten items should appear on each page. Your dynamic site will then respond automatically — generating as many pages as needed to display all your products (at ten per page), and linking each page to the next. If you add more products to the database, the system generates more pages as needed, also automatically.

Considering the disadvantages of a dynamic Web site

Before you get too excited about all the advantages of a dynamic Web site, keep in mind the few disadvantages as well. Dynamic sites are harder to develop and require much more advanced skills to create and maintain. They can also be more expensive to host on a commercial service provider because they require more resources, and software, on your Web server.

Then consider that all the advantages of being able to replicate pages quickly come with the disadvantage that you can't vary the designs as much from page to page. That's one of the reasons that so many blogs have such a similar look. Although you can change the design in a dynamic site on every page, it's much harder to develop the page designs, and the more variations on the design, the less efficient it is. Thus, when you create a dynamic Web site, what you save in automation, you give up in design control. If you want to create a site with really great, interesting, and varied designs, you may be best served by a static page design. As a general rule, any site with less than 10 or 20 pages is almost certainly better (and more easily) created as a static site. And although I generally recommend that you graduate to a dynamic site after your site grows to more than 100 pages, I have managed static sites as big as 3,000 pages using Dreamweaver's templates.

Blogs are dynamic sites, too

Many people are confused by the difference between a Web site and blog. Essentially a blog is just a special kind of dynamic Web site, often called a *content management system* (CMS) because it's used to manage content (all those blog posts, pictures, and comments). Many content management systems are in use on the Web today. The open source programs Joomla! and Drupal are among some of the most popular, but blogs are designed to be so easy, even actors and politicians can use them.

The advantage of a blog is that you can start your blog site with all the dynamic functionality prebuilt for you. Seemingly all you have to do with most blog programs (including Blogger, WordPress, and TypePad) is set up an account and then add your own words and pictures. Most people find blogging as easy as using a word processor. (And it *can* be, except that a lot is happening behind the scenes.)

From a technical standpoint, blogs combine upfront functionality with back-stage administrative tools — both of which work dynamically. On the front end, the dynamic technology pulls content from a database to display to visitors to the blog. On the back end, dynamic technology enables bloggers to use *any* Web browser to enter headlines, images, and text into the database. (See my example of how a blog works in the next section.)

Blogging enables people who aren't programmers to create sites easily, using some of the most advanced technology on the Web. The result is a paradox: It's easier to create a blog than a static site (and super easy to post articles and photos), but much harder to edit the design of a blog than a static site.

This seeming contradiction makes a little more sense if you can compare setting up a blog to building a house. Using a blogging program that sets up the underlying dynamic functionality for you is a little like buying a prefabricated house. With a prefab, you let someone else work out all the design and engineering challenges and put together the pieces. Then all you have to do is move in your furniture and paint your name on the mailbox.

You need advanced technical knowledge, however, if you're editing the underlying code of a blog (or building a blog from scratch). It's almost like building your own house by drawing your own plans and constructing it yourself.

Continuing with the prefab metaphor, when you're working on a blog, rearranging the furniture and even painting the walls isn't that hard. But what if you decide you want to add on a second story or take down the wall between the kitchen and the dining room? Well, now, *that* requires an engineer who has to first figure out the electrical wiring and plumbing that the original designer put in — and then ensure that the changes you have in mind don't conflict with a hidden quirk that could make a load-bearing wall collapse.

The blog equivalent is that you need a programmer for substantive changes such as adding new page designs or changing the functionality of how you add images — and you have to make sure that all that new programming is set up to work properly on your Web server (which is a bit like needing permits from the city to add a second story).

Here's a quick look at some popular ready-made blogging tools and content management systems:

- **The simplest blogging tool:** For pure ease of use and setup, Blogger.com is a popular choice, but you won't have as many options for customizing the design or adding additional features.

- **Most popular blogging tool:** WordPress is by far the most popular blogging program among serious bloggers. WordPress is relatively easy to set up and administer, but it offers many additional options for customizing the design and adding features, which can get increasingly complex. Also confusing to many people, there are two ways to use WordPress. Visit www.WordPress.org if you want to create a free blog using the simplest options. Visit www.WordPress.com to take advantage of the full power of the program.

- **For developing more complex sites:** Joomla! (www.joomla.org) and Drupal (www.drupal.org) offer similar advantages to blogging, but with more features and more flexibility. You still need the equivalent of an engineer (programmer) to move walls, but it gives you more of a head start if you want to build something more complex, like an office building (or online magazine).

- **For adding e-commerce to a dynamic site:** WordPress, Joomla!, and Drupal can also be paired with other programs, such as Zen Cart or OS Commerce, which add shopping-cart and e-commerce capabilities with the same replicable model.

Using Dreamweaver to edit a blog

So where does Dreamweaver fit into the creation of dynamic sites, especially blogs? Well, you *can* create a completely custom dynamic site with Dreamweaver, but these days most smart Web designers start with a program like WordPress — and *then* use Dreamweaver to create and edit the templates that control the design.

The templates used in WordPress, Joomla!, and other content management systems are all created with XHTML and CSS (combined with more advanced programming), using Web technology such as a hypertext preprocessor (PHP) that makes everything work dynamically. Thus, the same CSS and XHTML skills you covered in the rest of this book apply to editing the basic design of WordPress templates.

Editing a WordPress template is kind of like being your own handyman: You don't have to be able to rewire the entire house to replace a light fixture, but you need to know the basics of how wiring works or you risk electrocuting yourself.

Search the Web, and you'll find thousands of templates for WordPress. Downloading and installing templates is relatively easy, but editing them can get complicated quickly. Using what you learn in Chapters 5 and 6 of this book, you can edit the CSS style sheets that control the appearance of your template pages and can change design elements, such as colors and fonts without advanced skills. However, keep in mind that templates you download from the Web come from many different designers, and the CSS may not be written or organized the way you (or I) might prefer. The first task in editing the CSS in a WordPress template is often deciphering how the styles are defined.

If you want to create your own template or change the programming code that specifies how data is pulled from the database, you need to learn a programming language, such as PHP, used in most blogging programs. To help you keep things in perspective, most people can get the hang of XHTML and CSS in a couple of weeks, but many people study programming in a language like PHP for two or more years.

After you have the necessary programming skills, there's one other big challenge to making this all work: Because dynamic Web sites like WordPress use server-side scripts to generate pages, you need a lot more than Dreamweaver on your computer to make everything work. Installing WordPress on your hard drive is just the start — you also have to set up a Web server and other software on your computer before you can view dynamic Web pages. Setting your computer up to work as a Web server is not as hard as it sounds, but it's not as easy as installing most software programs (such as Dreamweaver). How you do it depends on what kind of computer you're using and what kind of programming was used to create the dynamic site. You find out more about the programming options (PHP, JSP, and so on) and about setting up a local Web server, later in this chapter.

If you just want to edit the CSS styles or make minor changes to a WordPress template without having to install WordPress and set up a server on your local computer, you can copy just the CSS file to your computer, edit it in Dreamweaver, and then upload it back to the server. You find tips for the simplest ways to use Dreamweaver to edit WordPress templates on my Web site at www.DigitalFamily.com/wordpress.

Studying a dynamic site in action

To help you better appreciate how a dynamic Web site works, this section takes a closer look at how a blog works. The following steps are designed to give you a tour of the front end, which visitors to a blog see, as well as the back end, which the blogger uses to add content to the database. This is a common way that many dynamic Web sites are built:

1. **Point your browser to** www.mobilewebdesignblog.com.

2. **On the home page, you see the first part of the most recent post in the database for this site, as shown in Figure 13-1.**

Figure 13-1:
My Mobile Web Design blog's front page displays the first couple of paragraphs for each post in the database. Each headline links to a complete post.

3. **Click the headline on the front page and the browser displays a new page, created dynamically, which displays the entire post.**

   You can also click the link at the bottom of the text that reads Click to Continue Reading, as you can see in Figure 13-1.

   When you view pages like this, keep in mind that there's really only one copy of the article stored in the database. When you click a linked headline, the PHP technology pulls the complete post from the database, inserts it into the same template, and displays it as a new page in the Web browser in place of the page that displayed the link you clicked. Another advantage of blogging programs is they can set these links for you automatically. Thus, you simply enter a story into the system and the program automatically turns the headline into a link and inserts the text Click here to continue reading with a link to the full version of the story.

Behind the scenes of this same blog is a set of administrative pages, also generated dynamically. (See Figure 13-2.) As the author of the blog, I use the administrative pages to enter headlines, articles, images, and even specify how much of the story I want to appear on the front page before the link to the full story. The administrative tools (or in WordPress terms, the Dashboard) is the interface I use to enter information into the database. That information is then displayed on the front-end page, according to the settings in the blog software.

Figure 13-2:
To add posts to my Mobile Web Design blog, I use back-end features to enter headlines, images, and text into the database.

Creating Dynamic Sites: Key Concepts

When you create dynamic Web sites, you need one program to create the data source (which is usually a database or an XML file) and another program or Web technology to connect the data source to your Web pages. In the sections that follow, you find a description of the five technologies that Dreamweaver supports for creating dynamic sites: PHP, JSP, ASP, ASP.NET, and ColdFusion.

There are many types of data sources. The most powerful option is a high-end database, such as MySQL, but you can also use simpler database programs, including Microsoft Access. XML files, which are specially designed text files, can also be used a data sources. WordPress, like many blogs, combines a MySQL database with PHP.

Comparing options for dynamic Web site development

One of the most complicated aspects of how dynamic sites work is how you set up the connection between the Web site that your visitor's see and the data source that contains all your articles, images, and other content. Essentially, this puzzle has three pieces: the data source, the Web server, and the Web technology that makes the two work together.

There are many ways to set up this connection. You can create a very simple script using a programming language like Java, or you can create a highly complex combination of programs that work in tandem to complete many tasks simultaneously. For example, displaying XML data on a Web page requires a relatively simple program. A far more complex setup collects information about a user's shopping habits and then compares that with data from multiple sources before generating a Web page specific to the visitor. Depending on the complexity of the dynamic site and the data source, you may also need an application server, as well as a Web server and a database.

Dreamweaver supports five popular technologies that can be used to connect a data source to a Web site (described in detail in the following sections):

- Active Server Pages (ASP)
- ASP.NET
- JavaServer Pages (JSP)
- Adobe ColdFusion
- PHP (which stands for *PHP Hypertext Preprocessor* — a recursive acronym, for you wordsmiths)

Although all five vary in technical specifications and requirements, they offer similar functionality:

- All provide the capability to generate Web pages dynamically.
- All can be used to connect your Web site to a database or other data source.
- Using server-side code, all can display information from a database and create XHTML based on certain criteria — such as the actions or data entered by a visitor to your site.

Although I don't recommend any one of these options over another, one consideration is important: Make sure that your choice works on your Web server. Not all Web servers are set up to handle each and every one of these technologies. The following descriptions are designed to help you make a more informed decision about which option best serves your needs.

ASP

Extension: .asp

Although Microsoft recommends that you replace ASP (Active Server Pages, the first Microsoft server-side script engine for dynamically generated Web pages) with ASP.NET, many active sites on the Web still use ASP. ASP was built into the Windows 2003 Server, Windows 2000, Windows XP Professional, and Windows Vista at no additional cost. ASP can also be used with other Microsoft development tools such as IIS (Internet Information Services) or Personal Web Server (which is useful for building and testing your Web site on your local hard drive). ASP isn't a standalone programming language; much of the code you write for ASP pages is in VBScript or *JScript* (Microsoft's version of JavaScript). You can check out www.4guysfromrolla.com to find out more about ASP in what more closely resembles plain English.

ASP.NET

Extension: .aspx

ASP.NET is Microsoft's replacement for ASP. According to Microsoft, ASP. NET "is a unified Web development model that includes the services necessary for you to build enterprise-class Web applications with a minimum of coding. ASP.NET is part of the .NET Framework, and when coding ASP.NET applications you have access to classes in the .NET Framework."

ASP.NET isn't a programming language itself, but a framework within which you can code applications in any language that's compatible with the common language runtime (CLR). These languages include Microsoft Visual Basic, C#, JScript .NET, and J#. ASP.NET isn't just an upgrade of ASP, either; it's a complete redesign of the framework. You can find more information at msdn.microsoft.com/asp.net and www.asp.net.

Adobe ColdFusion

Extension: .cfm

According to Adobe, ColdFusion software enables developers to build, deploy, and maintain Internet applications. You can use ColdFusion to create a variety of highly complex dynamic Web sites. Because Adobe owns ColdFusion, it is integrated into Dreamweaver better than the other options, and ColdFusion is probably the easiest to learn because it includes custom tags designed to simplify setting up common features of a dynamic site. ColdFusion is similar to JSP (like JSP, it's ultimately based on Java). ColdFusion also includes built-in XML processing. The biggest limitation: You need special server software for ColdFusion, which is expensive to run yourself and not offered by all Web hosting companies. You can read more about ColdFusion at www.adobe.com/products/coldfusion.

JavaServer Pages (JSP)

Extension: `.jsp`

According to Oracle, JavaServer Pages (JSP) technology provides a simplified, fast way to create dynamic Web content. JSP technology enables rapid development of Web-based applications that are server- and platform-independent. With JSP, you can create and keep the dynamic code separate from the HTML pages — or you can embed the JSP code into the page. Unless you're a hardcore programmer, however, this language isn't for you. JSP is horribly complex. You can find out more about JSP at `http://java.sun.com/products/jsp`.

PHP

Extension: `.php`

PHP is a popular scripting language that is especially suited for Web development and can be embedded into HTML. Many open-source programs, such as WordPress and Joomla!, are built using PHP. Because it works on most Web servers and because so much free support is available, PHP is a favorite among Web programmers. PHP is most often used with databases created with MySQL (a popular open-source database program). PHP is right at home on UNIX-based servers. However, you can download Windows binaries from `www.php.net` to run *Apache* (server software typically used with PHP) from any version of Windows. The PHP scripting language is based on C, Perl, and Java. Check out *PHP and MySQL For Dummies,* 4th Edition, by Janet Valade to learn more or visit `www.php.net`.

Setting up your computer to work with dynamic Web pages

Another challenge when it comes to creating dynamic sites is that you can't just preview dynamic Web pages the way you can preview the static pages using nothing but a Web browser on your hard drive. When your Web site is dynamic, previewing your pages isn't that simple, because you need a Web server to *serve* the page to a browser. You may also need database software, application software, and other programs (such as WordPress, if your dynamic site is a blog).

Here's a closer look at these components:

- ✔ **Web server:** This term commonly refers to two things: (a) a piece of computer hardware on which a Web site is stored (usually a high-powered computer) and (b) the software on that computer that enables it to work as a server. A Web server responds to requests from a Web browser by serving up Web pages based on those requests.

If you can run Dreamweaver CS5, you're a step ahead: Your personal computer should be more than powerful enough to act as a Web server. The main reason most of us don't use our own computers as Web servers is that we lack the high-end Internet connection you find at most commercial service providers.

✔ **Data source:** The best dynamic sites are created by connecting a database to a Web site. Thus, in addition to a Web server, you may need to install a database program, such as MySQL or Microsoft Access.

✔ **Application server:** You may also need to set up an *application server,* which helps the Web server process specially marked Web pages. When the browser requests one of these pages, the Web server hands off the page to the application server, which processes the page before sending it to the browser.

Fortunately, you're not the only one who has ever had to set up a computer to serve dynamic Web pages; some smart programmers have put together packages with all the software you need to mimic the functions of the kind of Web server that will host your site when it's published online. (You find a list of software and server options in the next section.)

Installing Web servers and related software

Many different server programs are in use on the Web today. Big commercial service providers use sophisticated server programs to host Web sites for many clients on one computer — but a number of simple options work well on desktop computers.

Until you set up a local Web server and set the proper permissions on your local computer, you won't be able to create and test a dynamic site, regardless of whether you write the programming code yourself or use a CMS, such as WordPress or Joomla!.

Here's a list of a few popular Web server packages you can install on Mac or Windows computers:

✔ **MAMP** stands for Macintosh, Apache, MySQL, and PHP. Essentially MAMP collects all the programs you need in one specially designed package. The idea is to simplify the setup of a local Web server and the related software you need for developing and testing a dynamic Web site with Dreamweaver on any computer running Mac OS X. (You can find MAMP at www.mamp.info.)

✔ **MoWeS** enables you to set up a WAMP (Windows, Apache, MySQL, and PHP) system on any Windows system. As with MAMP, this package makes it easier to set up and install all the software you need to develop a dynamic site — in this case, on a Windows computer. (To learn more, visit `www.mowes.chsoftware.net`.)

✔ **Easy PHP** gives you everything you need in one nifty package. This pre-configured collection of tools includes an Apache Web server, MySQL database, and PHP. (Download it for free from `www.easyphp.org`.)

✔ **Microsoft Internet Information Services (IIS)**, formerly called Internet Information Server, is a set of software tools that also works well for testing dynamic Web pages on a Windows computer and serves as both a Web server and an application server. If you're running an edition of Windows 7, Vista, or Windows XP that supports IIS, all you have to do is make sure you've enabled IIS — and that you've set up the necessary permissions to use it on your computer. (Learn more at `www.microsoft.com/iis`.)

If you're creating a custom dynamic site, after you set up the server software and related software listed in this section, you're ready to go. However, if you're using a blogging tool or other CMS (such as WordPress or Joomla!), you must also install those programs and set up the blog on your local computer in exactly the way you intend to set it up on your Web server.

Exploring Database and Related Panels

In Dreamweaver, the most fundamental elements of creating a dynamic Web site are in the Application panel, which includes the Databases, Bindings, Components, and Server Behaviors panels. In this section, I introduce you to these panels and how they work together to help you create a dynamic site.

The Databases panel

The Databases panel lets you look at the databases on your application server. In the Databases panel, you can view your entire database structure within Dreamweaver — tables, fields, views, and stored procedures — without needing to use separate database software.

You can find the Databases panel by choosing Window➪Databases.

In Figure 13-3, you see a connection established to the Contacts database. You can view all the fields in that database by clicking the plus (+) sign next to Contacts.

Figure 13-3:
Dream-
weaver
includes
Databases,
Bindings,
and Server
Behaviors
panels.

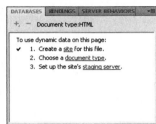

The Bindings panel

The Bindings panel enables you to add and remove dynamic-content data sources from your document. The number and kinds of available data sources can vary, depending on whether you use ASP.NET, PHP, JSP, or some other server technology. A *data source* — essentially wherever you get the information to use on your dynamic Web page — can be a *recordset* from a database — that is, a file used to hold a collection of data. After you create a recordset, the data can be displayed on a Web page.

If you don't see the Bindings panel, you can open it by choosing Window➪ Bindings.

With the Bindings panel, you can access data sources in several ways. You can find out what data-source objects you have available by clicking the plus sign (+) in the Bindings panel to display the Add Bindings pop-up menu.

The Server Behaviors panel

Server behaviors are server-side scripts that perform some type of action. Through the Server Behaviors panel, you can add server-side scripts (such as those for user authentication and record navigation) to your pages. Server behaviors available to you vary depending on the server technology you use.

You can get to the Server Behaviors panel by choosing Window➪Server Behaviors.

You can view the available server behaviors by clicking the plus sign (+) in the Server Behaviors panel to get the Server Behaviors pop-up menu.

The Components panel

Components are reusable bits of code that you can create and insert directly into your pages. To open the Components panel, choose Window⇨ Components. In Dreamweaver, you can create components for JSP, ColdFusion, and ASP.NET pages to use (in Web-server-speak, *consume*) Web services, display information, or accommodate just about any other use you can imagine.

Chapter 14

Managing Web Sites with Adobe InContext and Business Catalyst

*I*f you design Web sites for clients — or you're creating a site that you want others to be able to update (without their having to learn Dreamweaver) — you're sure to love the features covered in this chapter. Adobe now offers two online services — InContext Editing and Business Catalyst — that can greatly improve your ability to serve clients and other contributors to a Web site by enabling others to update a Web site created in Dreamweaver more easily than ever before.

✔ **InContext Editing** is a Web-based tool that enables anyone with password access to your server to make updates to a Dreamweaver Web site through a Web browser. That means the people making the updates (your clients, colleagues, club members, and so on) don't have to buy or install any new software (not even Dreamweaver). They can simply use any one of the most popular Web browsers: Firefox, Internet Explorer, or Safari.

✔ **Business Catalyst** is the newest of Dreamweaver's online tools, and is available for the first time as an integrated feature in Dreamweaver CS5. Adobe acquired Business Catalyst and is using it to add an extensive array of online services — including an e-commerce shopping cart, bulk-mail features, analytics, and more.

Most of this chapter covers how to design sites for InContext Editing (abbreviated as ICE). First you discover how to set up a site to work with InContext Editing. Then I show how incredibly easy it is for your clients, coworkers, friends, your Aunt Maude, or anyone else you know to edit a site after you set it up with ICE.

At the end of this chapter, you find an introduction to the features in Business Catalyst. Although Business Catalyst greatly extends the functionality of Dreamweaver, it is a completely new set of tools. As with InContext Editing, Business Catalyst uses a Web interface that enables you to administer its features through a Web browser. Unlike ICE, however, Business Catalyst includes so many new features of its own that it's way beyond the scope of this Dreamweaver book. (You'll find great help files and tutorials on the Business Catalyst site.) To help you appreciate how you can use Business Catalyst and what it's capable of, I include an overview of the features of this new tool set at the end of this chapter.

Understanding InContext Editing

The beauty of Adobe's InContext Editing is that you (or someone else) can easily update any site created with Dreamweaver as easily as you might update a site created with a blog program (such as WordPress).

To use InContext Editing, you create and design a page in Dreamweaver just as you would design any other page — and then you add a little special code to indicate which areas of the page may be edited using the online InContext tools. The process is quite similar to the process of creating Dreamweaver templates (covered in Chapter 7). You can even use InContext in combination with Dreamweaver's templates, but you have to add more code for the InContext features, covered in the sections that follow.

You cannot use InContext Editing with sites that use advanced programming options such as ASP.NET, PHP, or ColdFusion. Indeed, the advantage of InContext is that you *don't* have to use advanced programming languages such as PHP. Although those advanced capabilities make WordPress easy if you want to create a blog post, they also make it really hard to use if you want to edit the design of the blog. Similarly, many Web developers have spent enormous amounts of time using very complex programming, such as PHP or ASP. NET, to create administrative tools in Dreamweaver that their clients can use to update a site easily. (You learn more about how blogs work and the features in Dreamweaver you can use with programming languages, such as PHP, in Chapter 13.)

There are two ways to create pages in Dreamweaver that work with InConext Editing:

> ✔ **A single page with ICE features:** In the first exercise that follows, you start by creating a single HTML page using any one of the CSS layouts included in Dreamweaver, and then select the InContext option as you create the page. With this option, the InContext editing region is added to the page automatically, but the page will *not* work as a Dreamweaver template.

✔ **A Dreamweaver template with ICE features:** The second exercise that follows includes instructions for creating a Dreamweaver template and then adding ICE code. These same instructions work well if you want to alter any site that already uses Dreamweaver templates to support the InContext Editing features, including sites created with Dreamweaver CS3 or CS4.

You can learn more about InContext Editing at `www.adobe.com/products/incontextediting`, shown in Figure 14-1. To update a Web site created using Dreamweaver's ICE features, you can log in at `http://incontextediting.adobe.com`.

Figure 14-1: InContext Editing in an online tool that works with Dreamweaver to enable anyone to update a Web site with a Web browser.

Creating new ICE pages using Dreamweaver's CSS layouts

To create a new page using one of Dreamweaver's CSS layouts, make sure you've completed the site setup process (covered at the beginning of Chapter 2), and then follow these instructions:

1. **Choose File⇨New.**

   The New Document dialog box appears (see Figure 14-2).

2. **Choose Blank Page from the left column and HTML from the Page Type column in the middle.**

   You must choose Blank Page (not Blank Template) from the left column to use the automated InContext features in version CS5.

You cannot use InContext Editing with sites that use advanced programming options, such as ASP.NET, PHP, or ColdFusion.

3. Select any of the CSS layouts listed in the Layout section.

For this example, I chose 1 Column Fixed, Centered, Header and Footer.

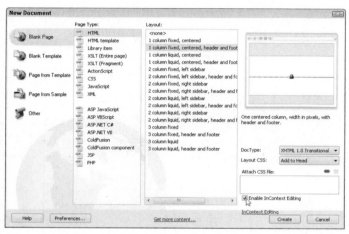

Figure 14-2:
When you select the name of a CSS layout in the New Document dialog box, a preview is displayed in the top-right corner.

4. From the Layout CSS drop-down list at the bottom right of the New Document window, choose the type of style sheet you want to create as you create the page.

- **Add to Head** creates an internal style sheet and includes all the styles for the layout in the Head area of the new document.

- **Create New File** creates a new external style sheet with all the page styles as you create the new document with the design.

- **Link to Existing File** adds the style sheet information for the new document to an existing external style sheet.

You can always change how the style sheet is set up later on, by moving styles from an internal style sheet to an external one or from one external style sheet to another. (See Chapter 5 for details.)

5. Click to select the Enable InContext Editing check box at the bottom right of the New Document window.

The feature activates Adobe's automated InContext Editing features, which inserts a line of code at the top of the page and makes the main area of the selected CSS Layout an editable region with the additional code needed for InContext Editing.

6. Click Create.

The new page is created and opened in the main workspace.

If you chose Create New File from the Layout CSS drop-down list, a dialog box prompts you to save the style sheet separately. If the styles are contained in an internal style sheet or you chose to add them to an existing style sheet, they're created automatically as the page is created.

7. Choose File⇨Save to save the page and styles.

The Save As dialog box opens.

It's good practice to save any Web page when you first create it, but this is especially true when creating InContext pages.

8. Enter a name for the page and click Save.

The page is saved and the Copy Dependent Files dialog box opens, as shown in Figure 14-3.

Be sure to save all the pages of a Web site, including external style sheets and any dependent files, in your local site folder. You find more about defining a Web site and specifying a local site folder in Dreamweaver in Chapter 2.

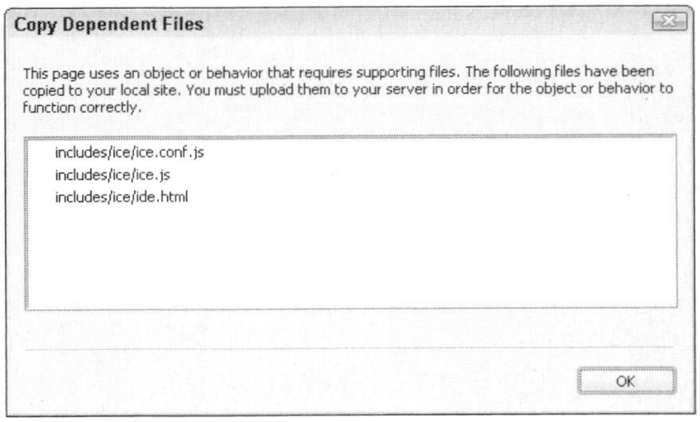

Figure 14-3:
When you save an InContext template, Dream-weaver creates a collection of includes files auto-matically. These files must be uploaded to your Web server.

Copy Dependent Files

This page uses an object or behavior that requires supporting files. The following files have been copied to your local site. You must upload them to your server in order for the object or behavior to function correctly.

```
includes/ice/ice.conf.js
includes/ice/ice.js
includes/ice/ide.html
```

OK

9. In the Copy Dependent Files dialog box (see Figure 14-3), click OK to save the ICE files.

Dreamweaver creates a folder called `includes` with a subfolder called `ice`, — and saves these files into the subfolder in your local site folder automatically. For the ICE features to work, you must upload the `includes` folder, as well as the `ice` subfolder and files, to your Web server when you publish your site.

10. **Click to select the blue Editable Region tab at the top of the main content area, and in the Property inspector, specify the options you want, as shown in the bottom of Figure 14-4.**

    Use the InContext Editing options available in the Property inspector to limit what someone can change in the page using the online tools. You can check or uncheck each of the options to control whether each feature is available when someone edits the page using a Web browser. For example, you could enable someone editing the page using the online InContext Editing tools to change whether text is bold or italic, but not enable changes to the font color. Or you could enable someone to change the text on the page, but not the formatting by clicking the Uncheck All button, as shown in Figure 14-4.

    See Table 14-1 for an explanation of each option for InContext Editable regions.

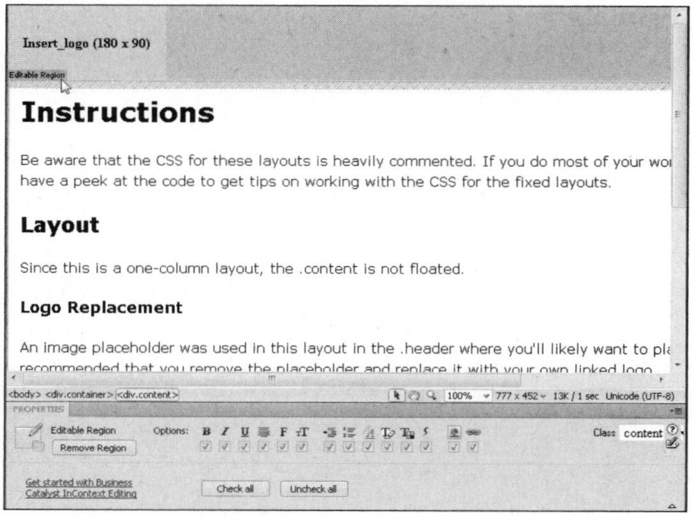

Figure 14-4:
You can specify which formatting options, such as font face or font size, can be changed within an InContext editable region.

Insert_logo (180 x 90)

Editable Region

Instructions

Be aware that the CSS for these layouts is heavily commented. If you do most of your wor have a peek at the code to get tips on working with the CSS for the fixed layouts.

Layout

Since this is a one-column layout, the .content is not floated.

Logo Replacement

An image placeholder was used in this layout in the .header where you'll likely want to pla recommended that you remove the placeholder and replace it with your own linked logo

11. **Design the page as you would design any other Web page using Dreamweaver's many features to add images, format text, define styles, and so on.**

12. **To add more editable regions, click to select any tag, such as an image, unordered list, or `<div>` tag and choose Insert➪InContext Editing➪Editable Region.**

    - If you select any element within an existing ICE editable region, Dreamweaver gives you a warning message that you cannot create editable regions within other editable regions.

    - If you selected a `<div>` tag that was not already contained within an editable region, it's turned into an editable region automatically — and no dialog box opens.

- If you selected an tag, such as an `<h1>` tag or unordered list (`<ul>`) tag, the Create Editable Region dialog box opens (see Figure 14-5). You have two choices: add a `<div>` tag around the selected element, or transform the parent (meaning the `<div>` tag that surrounds the selected element).

When you choose Transform the Parent Tag into an Editable Region, Dreamweaver selects the most immediate `<div>` tag that surrounds the selected element and makes everything in that `<div>` tag editable by adding the necessary code to make it an ICE editable region.

When you choose Wrap Current Selection with a DIV Tag and Then Transform It, only the item you selected becomes editable. In the example shown in Figure 14-5, I'm making only the heading in the `<h1>` tag that I selected an editable region by choosing to wrap it.

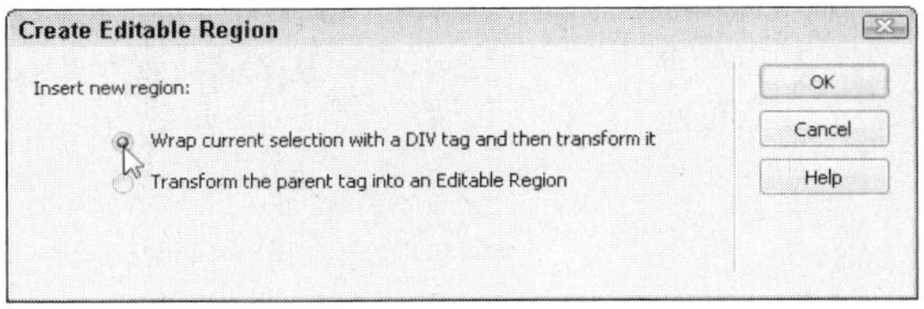

Figure 14-5:
The Create Editable Region dialog box.

13. **When the page is complete, use Dreamweaver built-in publishing features to upload the page to your Web server. (You find detailed instructions in Chapter 4.)**

Before you can use the InContext Editing features, you must upload the page to a Web server and set up the site at

```
http://incontextediting.adobe.com/
```

You find detailed instructions in the sections "Setting up an InContext site online" and "Editing an InContext page with a Web browser," later in this chapter.

Table 14-1   InContext Editing Options in the Property Inspector

Icon	Option	Controls the Use of InContext Editing To
 **B**	Bold	Make text bold or not bold.
 *I*	Italic	Make text italic or not italic.

(continued)

Table 14-1 *(continued)*

Icon	Option	Controls the Use of InContext Editing To
U	Underline	Make text underlined or not underlined (as a general rule, it's best to deselect this option to prevent the use of underlines for anything other than links).
≡	Right, left, and center alignment	Align text, images, and other elements to the left or right of the page. (Note: It's far better to create class styles to align images and other elements and then make those styles accessible in ICE. You find instructions for this in the exercise using CSS with InContext Editing.)
F	Font Face	Change the font of selected text.
ᴛT	Font Size	Change the size of selected text.
⁺≡	Indent or Outdent	Cause selected text to become indented or outdented respectively.
¹≡ ²≡	Numbered and Bulleted lists	Change a selected text to a bulleted or numbered list.
A	Paragraph styles	Format selected text using the paragraph and heading tags, H1, H2, H3, and so on.
T✎	Background Color	Change the background color of the page or any selected element (such as a `<div>` tag) that is editable.
T▣	Font Color	Change the color of selected text.
ſ	CSS Styles	Apply styles from an attached style sheet.
▦	Image/Media	Insert an image or other type of media.
✎	Hyperlink	Create a link.

Creating repeating regions with ICE

The advantage of a repeating region is that you can enable people who are editing the site online through the InContext Web site to create multiple collections of elements all at once. For example, you could create an editable region with formatted areas for the name and biography of an employee. If you want to list only one employee on the page, creating a single editable region (as you did in the previous exercise) is fine. If, however, you want to be able to add more employee names and bios to the page, creating a repeating region would enable a user to copy the entire section each additional employee.

Follow these steps to add a repeating editable region to a page that uses InContext Editing:

1. **Create a new page or open an existing page. Then click to insert your cursor anywhere you want to add an InContext repeating editable region.**

2. **On the page, click to select any HTML block tag (such as a heading tag, unordered list, or `<div>` tag) that you want to turn into an InContext editable region.**

   Although `<div>` tags themselves are ideal as InContext editable regions, Dreamweaver will add a `<div>` tag around whatever you select.

   In Figure 14-6, you see the tag selector at the bottom of the workspace, an ideal way to select a tag before using the InContext Insert panel to turn it into an editable region.

3. **Choose InContext Editing from the Insert panel drop-down menu to open the options for editable regions (see Figure 14-6).**

   Alternatively you can choose Insert⇨InContext Editing and then select Repeating Editable Region from the fly-out menu.

4. **Click Create Repeating Region, as shown in Figure 14-6.**

   The options available to you when you create a repeating region are the same as those available when you add an editable region. (See Step 12 in the preceding section for details.)

5. **Choose File⇨Save to save the page.**

   If you haven't already added InContext features to the site, Dreamweaver opens the Copy Dependent Files dialog box (shown in Figure 14-3 earlier in the chapter). Click OK and Dreamweaver automatically creates a folder called `includes` with a subfolder called `ice` — and saves these files into the subfolder in your local site folder. For the ICE features to work, you must upload the `includes` folder, as well as the `ice` subfolder and files, to your Web server when you publish your site.

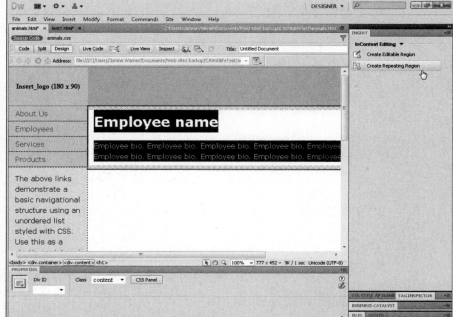

Figure 14-6:
Using the
tag selector
to select a
<div> tag
or other
element
and the
InContext
insert panel
to add the
selection as
a repeating
editable
region.

6. **When the page is complete, use the Dreamweaver built-in publishing features to upload the page to your Web server. (You find detailed instructions in Chapter 4.)**

   Before you can use the InContext Editing features, you must upload the page to a Web server and set up the site at `http://incontextediting.adobe.com/`. You find detailed instructions in the sections "Setting up an InContext site online" and "Editing an InContext page with a Web browser," later in this chapter.

Using CSS with ICE

You can combine the power of CSS with InContext Editing, but you can make only class and tag styles available to anyone who has access through ICE.

To make styles work with ICE, follow these steps:

1. **Define the styles as class styles, as you do in the section that follows.**

2. **Make the style sheet available by choosing Insert⇨InContext Editing⇨ Manage Available CSS Classes.**

3. **In the Manage Available CSS Classes dialog box that appears, click the check box next to any external style sheets that you want to make available when someone edits the page using InContext Editor.**

Combining Dreamweaver templates with ICE features

For the best of both worlds, combine InContext Editing and Dreamweaver's templates. ICE is great because it enables anyone with password access to edit a site online with a Web browser — but Dreamweaver's templates also offer valuable features. One such capability is creating new pages within Dreamweaver based on the template, and the option to update many pages at once by editing the locked regions of a template — a big timesaver.

In Chapter 7, you find detailed instructions for creating and working with Dreamweaver templates. In this section, you find instructions for combining InContext Editing with Dreamweaver's templates.

You can convert a page you created using the automated InContext Editing features (covered in the previous exercise) into a Dreamweaver template. However, I strongly recommend that you do it the other way around: Adding InContext Editing regions to a Dreamweaver template is easy; if you start by creating a simple HTML page with InContext Editing, turning it into a fully functional Dreamweaver template requires adding code manually to the head region of page (which gets complicated quickly).

To create a Dreamweaver template with editable regions and make the site editable with InContext Editing, follow these steps:

1. **Choose File⇨New.**

   The New Document window opens.

2. **In the list on the left, click the Blank Template option.**

3. **In the Template Type list, choose HTML Template.**

   You can only use InContext Editing with HTML Templates. InContext Editing does not work on pages that use advanced programming options, such as ASP.NET, PHP, or ColdFusion.

4. **In the Layout area, choose <none> to create a blank page or select any of the predesigned CSS layouts.**

   Unlike the previous exercise (where you used one of Dreamweaver's CSS layouts), if you create a Dreamweaver template and then add ICE features, using a CSS layout is optional. (You find instructions for customizing Dreamweaver's CSS layouts, as well as for creating a new layout in a blank page, in Chapter 6.)

5. **Click the Create button.**

   A new blank template is created and opens in the main work area; the New Document dialog box closes.

6. **Choose File➪Save.**

   If you haven't disabled the dialog box, a warning appears, stating that the template doesn't have any editable regions and asking whether you really want to save it. Click Yes to continue. (You find instructions for creating editable regions in the template in Step 10.)

7. **Click OK to save the page.**

   The Save window appears with the Templates folder open. You must save all your Dreamweaver templates in the Templates folder. (If you don't already have a folder named Templates in your local site folder, Dreamweaver creates one for you when you create your first template.)

8. **Give the template a name and click Save.**

   The template is saved automatically with a .dwt extension, which designates the file as a Dreamweaver template.

9. **Add images, text, and other elements as you would in any other Dreamweaver file.**

   You find instructions for designing Web pages throughout this book.

   You create a Dreamweaver page design in a template, just as you would in any other Web page.

10. **To create an editable region in a Dreamweaver template:**

    a. **Select an image or content area defined by a** <div> **tag.**

       A handy way to select a section surrounded by a <div> tag is to place your cursor anywhere in that area of the page, and then use the tag selector at the bottom of the workspace to select the <div>, as shown at the bottom of Figure 14-6 earlier in this chapter.

    b. **Choose Insert➪New Template Object➪New Editable Region.**

       The New Editable Region dialog box opens.

    c. **Give the new editable region a name.**

       I recommend something that identifies the type of content it is, such as **mainContent**.

       The region you define as editable becomes an area that can be changed in any page created from the template. You can have multiple editable regions in one template, and you have the option to make any or all of those regions editable with InContext.

d. Click OK.

The editable region is enclosed in a light blue box with a light blue tab at the top left of the box, identified by the name you entered into the New Editable Region dialog box.

To create additional editable regions, repeat Steps a–d.

11. When you finish designing the page and add all the editable regions you want, choose File⇨Save to save your template.

When you save a new template page (or you save an existing page as a template), Dreamweaver adds the .dwt extension automatically and saves the file into a Templates folder.

12. To add the capability to use InContext Editing on any of the editable regions in the template, first click to select the editable region.

The best way to make sure you've selected the editable region is to place your cursor anywhere on the page that's part of the region you want to make editable, and then click the <div> tag in the Quick Tag Selector, as shown in Figure 14-7.

When you create an editable region in a Dreamweaver template, Dreamweaver adds special code to identify it as an editable area of the template. When you use the InContext features to make a region editable, Dreamweaver adds additional code to the template. It's important to make sure that the ICE code is outside the Dreamweaver template code, which means the ICE code can be edited only in the template itself, not in any page created from the template. Doing so ensures that you don't accidentally delete the code in a page created from the template — and that if you *do* modify the ICE code later, those changes are updated in all pages created from the template. (For more on how to edit Dreamweaver templates, see Chapter 7.)

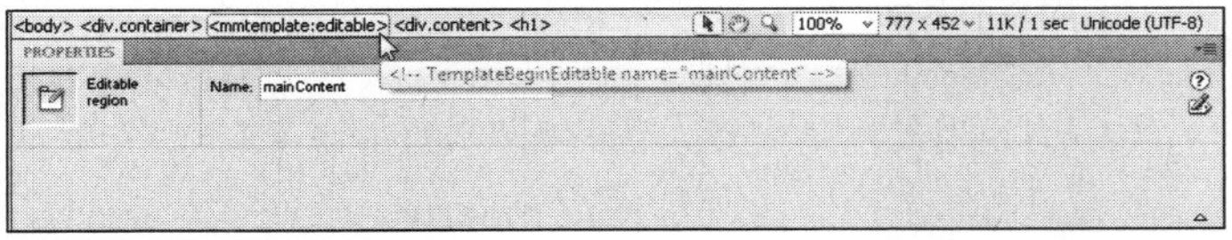

Figure 14-7:
Using the
Quick Tag
Selector to
select the
editable
region itself,
not a tag
inside it.

| <body> <div.container> <mmtemplate:editable> <div.content> <h1> | | 100% | 777 x 452 | 11K / 1 sec | Unicode (UTF-8) |

PROPERTIES

Editable region   Name: mainContent   <!-- TemplateBeginEditable name="mainContent" -->

13. To make the selected editable region editable using InContext Editing, choose Insert⇨InContext Editing⇨Create Editable Region.

The Create Editable Region dialog box opens.

14. In the Create Editable Region dialog box, click to select the radio button next to Wrap the Entire Template Editable Region with a DIV Tag and Then Transform It, and then click OK.

Dreamweaver inserts a <div> tag around the selected content — and the editable region tag — automatically, as shown in Figure 14-8.

Figure 14-8:
Split view shows tabs for both editable regions in Dreamweaver's workspace, as well as the code that creates the editable region for InContext Editing.

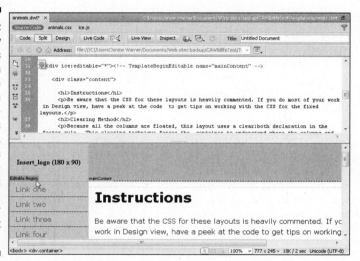

15. Choose File⇨Save to save the template.

If you haven't already added InContext features to the site, Dreamweaver opens the Copy Dependent Files dialog box (refer to Figure 14-3). Click OK and Dreamweaver automatically creates a folder called `includes` with a subfolder called `ice` — and saves these files into the subfolder in your local site folder. For the ICE features to work, you must upload the `includes` folder, as well as the `ice` subfolder and files, to your Web server when you publish your site.

16. After the template is complete, you can create new pages from the template in Dreamweaver, and use the template to make updates to all the pages from the template, just as you would with any other Dreamweaver template.

You find instructions for both tasks in Chapter 7.

17. **When the page is complete, use Dreamweaver built-in publishing features to upload the page to your Web server.**

    You find detailed instructions in Chapter 4.

    Before you can use the InContext Editing features, you must upload the page to a Web server and set up the site at `http://incontextediting.adobe.com/`. You find detailed instructions in the sections "Setting up an InContext site online" and "Editing an InContext page with a Web browser," later in this chapter.

Adding ICE to an existing template-based site

If you're like many Web designers, you may already have Web sites that use Dreamweaver templates and want to add InContext Editing to manage the sites and simplify contributors' access to pages on the site.

You can add InContext Editing features to an existing site by using much the same approach covered in the previous section — but when you're working on an existing site, keep in mind the following:

✔ When you add an InContext editable region to a page that already includes Dreamweaver template editable regions, make sure that the ICE code is outside the Dreamweaver template code. This prevents the ICE code from being edited or deleted in any page created from the template. (For more on how to edit Dreamweaver templates, see Chapter 7.)

✔ When you add an editable region using InContext Editing, Dreamweaver adds a `<div>` tag with the ICE code around whatever you've selected. *Don't give the InContext `<div>` tag any additional formatting or CSS styles.* (Note that this additional `<div>` tag won't change the layout of the page.)

Setting up an InContext site online

To set up a site so its pages can be edited using Adobe's InContext Editing online tools, you must first set up the site at `http://incontextediting.adobe.com/`, as shown in Figure 14-9. You need take this step only once per Web site to activate the online features; you can create as many user accounts as you like for each site so multiple people can edit the site after it's set up.

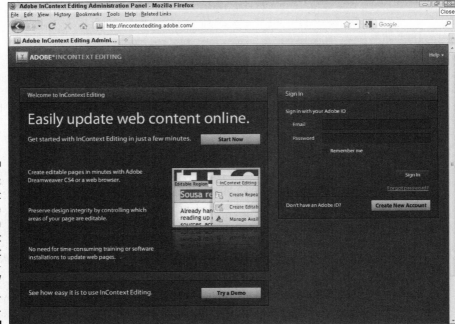

Figure 14-9:
To edit
a page
online with
InContext
Editing, start
by visit-
ing http://
InContext.
Adobe.com.

To set up a site and create a new user account for your InContext Editing site, follow these steps:

1. **Open the Web site** `http://incontextediting.adobe.com/` **(see in Figure 14-9), in a recent version of the Firefox, Internet Explorer, or Safari Web browser.**

2. **Fill out the form that opens.**

   Be sure to enter a name, a valid e-mail address (that has not already been used to create an InContext account), and a password that is at least six characters long.

   The account you create here becomes a master account login that can manage multiple sites and different users.

3. **Click the Create New Account button.**

4. **Verify the e-mail address you entered.**

   When you create a new account, Adobe sends a verification e-mail from `incontextediting-admin@adobe.com`. You must click the link in that e-mail to verify the address before you can use the new account to log in.

5. **Enter the e-mail address and password to sign into the InContext Account.**

The Adobe InContext Editing home page opens.

6. **Click the Manage Sites link at the top of the Adobe InContext Editing home page.**

   The Manage Sites page opens. If you already have sites set up with InContext, they're listed on this page; if you're new to InContext, the page is blank.

7. **Click the Add Site button at the top of the Manage Sites Page.**

   The Add Site window opens, as shown in Figure 14-10.

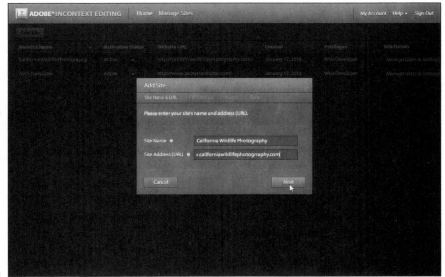

Figure 14-10:
You can manage multiple Web sites through one account at http:// InContext. Adobe.com.

8. **Enter the name and URL of the site and click Next.**

   The FTP Settings window opens.

9. **Enter the FTP access information you use to connect to your Web server and then click the Test button to confirm it works. After you've successfully established a connection, click Next.**

   The Assets window opens.

   If you use a secure server, choose SFTP from the drop-down menu at the top of the window. Your FTP Access information is specific to your Web server; you need to get this information from your service provider if you don't have it. *Note:* This is the same information you enter into the Server dialog box in Dreamweaver's site-publishing features (covered in Chapter 4).

10. Fill in the fields in the Assets window and click Save.

For most Web servers, the first two fields in the Assets window are optional, but InContext Editing works better if you type in the name of the main folder on your server (the one that corresponds to the local site folder on your hard drive). If you get an error message that InContext can't write to your server, you may have to enter the folder name on your server. You can leave the Media Folder field blank — or enter the location of your images folder (or any other media folder you want to specify). Whatever folder you enter here opens automatically if a user tries to add an image or other media file using the InContext Editing tools covered in the next section.

The third field in the Assets window lists all the common names for the main page of a Web site. You can delete all the names in this field except the one that represents name of the main page of your site. Many Web servers are set up for `index.html` as the main page, but if you use a Windows server, the page may be `default.htm`.

11. In the final setup window, labeled Done, click Invite User to add a new user who can edit the site, as shown in Figure 14-11.

The Invite User window opens.

If you don't want anyone else to edit the site, or you're eager to test it out before you set up any new users, click Edit. You can always add more users later by clicking the Invite User button one the Manage Sites page.

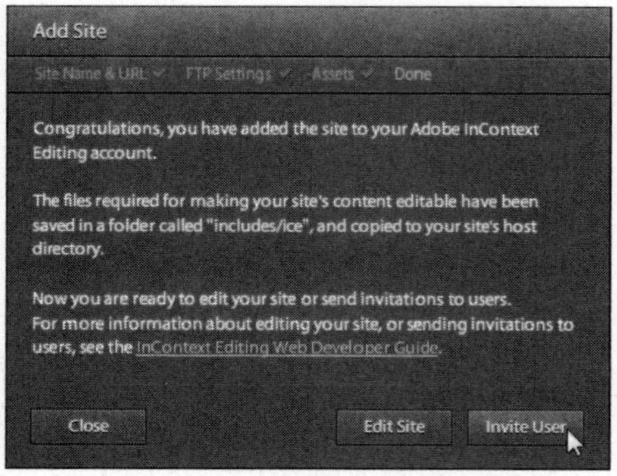

Figure 14-11: Completing site setup: You can go directly to the site by clicking Edit or add a login for a new user by clicking Invite User.

Add Site

Site Name & URL ✓ FTP Settings ✓ Assets ✓ Done

Congratulations, you have added the site to your Adobe InContext Editing account.

The files required for making your site's content editable have been saved in a folder called "includes/ice", and copied to your site's host directory.

Now you are ready to edit your site or send invitations to users. For more information about editing your site, or sending invitations to users, see the InContext Editing Web Developer Guide.

Close   Edit Site   Invite User

12. In the Invite User window, enter a name and e-mail address and then choose Editor or Publisher from the Privileges drop-down list. Click Invite.

An e-mail is sent to the new user and the Manage Users window opens.

Choose Editor if you want to limit how the user can edit the site by applying the restrictions you specified when you set up the ICE options in Dreamweaver.

Choose Publisher if you want the user to have additional editing options.

If you want to see the e-mail that is sent to you user, select the check box next to Send Me a Copy of the E-Mail.

Managing ICE sites

After you set up one or more sites with InContext Editing online, you may need to manage settings, invite more users, and so on. This section explains a few of the key ways you can manage your sites.

To access the Manage Users window, shown in Figure 14-12, log into your InContext Editing account, and click the name of the site you want to edit. In the window, you have several options:

✔ Click Invite User to add more users.

✔ Click the name of any user to edit their profile.

✔ Click the View/Edit Site button to open the site in a new browser window where you can edit the pages using the InContext Editor (see the following section for details).

✔ Click the Configure Site tab (just to the right of Manage Users) to edit the FTP access and other settings for the site. You have to re-enter your main account password to access this page.

✔ Click the Manage Sites link at the very top of the page to return to the main InContext Editing page (as shown in Figure 14-13), where you can access all the sites you've set up through your master account.

Figure 14-12:
The Manage Users window's links and buttons for adding new users, editing the site, and changing site configuration.

You open the Manage Sites window, shown in Figure 14-13, by clicking the Manage Sites link at the top of any screen after you log into InContext Editing.

Here you can manage all the sites you have set up in InContext Editing. One advantage of InContext Editing is that you can use it to manage many sites. Thus you can easily access multiple sites, while limiting the access of the users you set up to only the site you want them to edit.

From the Manage Sites page, you have several options:

✔ Use the drop-down list next to the site name to make the site Active or Inactive. When you make a site Inactive, you disable any user accounts you have created for that site.

✔ Click the URL of the site to open the site in the InContext Editor where you can make changes through your Web browser, as you discover in the following section.

✔ Click the Manage Users and Setting button next to each site name to open the corresponding Manage Users window (refer to Figure 14-12).

Figure 14-13: The Manage Sites window provides access to all the sites you've set up with InContext Editing.

Editing an InContext page with a Web browser

Setting up a site to use InContext Editing has a few complexities (as described in the previous sections in this chapter) — but using InContext Editing to make changes to a Web site is remarkably easy. That said, those of us who have worked with clients (or have had to teach complete novices how to do even simple things on a computer) know that *easy* is a relative term.

This final section is designed to help you help your clients — or anyone else you want to give access to a site using InContext Editing. If you've gotten this far in this book, using InContext Editing is probably easy enough that you could do without my help. So consider this section a way to get a quick overview of how InContext Editing works for your users — and a handy reference for yourself if you have to provide technical support by phone or e-mail to someone who is just getting started with Web design.

The first challenge — and potentially the biggest one — is that anyone you invite as a user must verify the invitation by clicking a link in an e-mail message sent for that purpose — and then entering an Adobe ID. If the person you invited does not already have an Adobe ID, he or she will have to create one in order to log in and start editing the site.

The following steps walk you through the process of editing an InContext site, starting with the e-mail invitation sent to a new user. It's a great exercise to send yourself an invitation and go through the process once so you know how it works. Here's the procedure:

1. **Open your e-mail program and look for a message with the subject line: Invitation to use Adobe InContext Editing.**

   This message contains several links.

2. **To visit the site and activate the account, click the link that appears just after the following text:**

   ```
   To view and accept the invitation, click the link
         below or copy and paste the following URL into
         your browser.
   ```

   The Web site in the invitation opens in the browser, and the Adobe InContext Editing Invitation pop-up window opens on top of it (as shown in Figure 14-14).

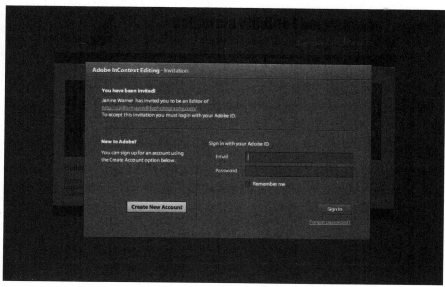

Figure 14-14: Every new user must verify an InContext Account by entering an Adobe ID. Users who have no Adobe ID must create one before accessing a site using InContext.

3. Enter your Adobe ID user name and password and click Sign In.

Many people don't even realize they already have an Adobe account. If you've ever downloaded software or anything else that required an account at Adobe.com, you can use the same Adobe ID you created at that time to activate your new InContext Editing account. If you think you have an account but don't remember your login information, you can retrieve your password: Click the Forgot password? link just under the Sign In button and follow the steps it provides. After you've reset the password, you can return to the login page and log in to InContext Editing.

Every Adobe ID account requires a unique e-mail address — so if you've created an Adobe ID in the past and try to do so again with the same e-mail address, you're informed that the e-mail address you typed in is already in use. You can create multiple Adobe IDs with different e-mail addresses, but Adobe prefers that you use the same ID.

4. After you log in, click the big green Edit Page button at the top-right of the browser window, as shown in Figure 14-15, to open the page in the InContext Editor.

Figure 14-15: Click the Edit Page button to open the InContext Editing tools.

5. Navigate around the site in the browser until you get to a page you want to edit.

You can click any link on any page, just as you would if you were simply viewing the site in a Web browser.

6. Click the Edit Page button to open the InContext Editing Tools.

7. **Click to place your cursor in an editable area of the page, and then use the editing options across the top of the browser window (as shown in Figure 14-16).**

   Across the top of the screen, you find common editing options — such as font face and font size — unless they've been turned off in Dreamweaver (as described in the earlier sections in this chapter.)

   Use the Advanced drop-down list at the far-right top of the page to access heading styles, font color, and highlight options.

   You can edit only those areas of a page that are set up as InContext editable regions (as described in earlier in this chapter). If you are working with a client or other contributor, you may have to explain which areas of the page can be edited and which cannot. For example, in the site shown in Figure 14-16, I've set up the three photos in the main area of the page, and the text below each one, in editable regions. However, the links and banner at the top of the page are not editable and can only be changed in Dreamweaver.

Figure 14-16:
Once you're logged in, you can make changes to any text, images, or other content on the page in an editable region.

8. **Click the Save Draft button in the bottom-right corner of the browser window to save your changes without changing the page on the public Web site.**

   The InContext Editing tool saves a copy of the page on the Adobe server where you are editing it.

   Saving your page regularly is good practice because otherwise, if your Internet connection is interrupted for any reason, you can lose your work.

9. **Click the Done button in the bottom-right corner of the browser window to save your changes and close the editing tools.**

   The editing features are closed, and you can use the navigation buttons or type in any URL to move to another page. Again, with this option, the InContext Editing tool saves a copy of the page on the Adobe server but does not publish it to the Web site.

10. **Click the Publish Draft button in the bottom-right corner of the browser window to apply the changes to the live Web site. Click Discard Draft to delete it.**

    Remember, when you click Publish Draft your changes are immediately applied to the live Web site.

If you make changes to a Web site in Dreamweaver while someone is viewing the site in InContext, and then upload the page to a server using Dreamweaver's FTP options, the changes aren't immediately visible in the InContext Editor, even if you use the Refesh/Reload button in the Web browser. Although Refresh/Reload works well when you're just testing a site in a browser, this feature doesn't work with InContext. Instead, you have to log out, clear the browser's cache, and log back in to see the changes. (Alternatively, you can switch to another Web browser and log in fresh to see the changes made in Dreamweaver in the InContext Editor right away.)

Returning to an InContext site

After you set up an active account, you don't have to use the link in the verification e-mail if you want to access the site and edit it using InContext. Instead, follow these steps:

1. **Open the site's URL in Firefox, Internet Explorer, or Safari.**

2. **Press Ctrl+E (Windows) or ⌘+E (on a Mac) to open a sign in window and display the InContext Editing tools.**

3. **After you're logged in, you can navigate around the site in the browser by clicking any link on any page, just as you would if you were simply viewing the site in a browser.**

4. **When you reach a page you want to edit, click the Edit Page button to open the InContext Editing Tools.**

5. **Choose Save Draft to save your work without publishing it, choose Done (to save a draft and close the tools), choose Publish Draft to save your changes and publish them to the Web site.**

Appreciating Business Catalyst

The newest of Dreamweaver's online tools, Business Catalyst, is available for the first time as an integrated feature in Dreamweaver CS5 and its features are being added to InContext Editing so that you can combine the power of both tools. Adobe acquired Business Catalyst and is using it to add an extensive array of online services to the set of options built into Dreamweaver.

Although Business Catalyst greatly extends the functionality of Dreamweaver and works in conjunction with InContext Editing, Business Catalyst is a completely new set of tools. As does ICE, Business Catalyst uses a Web interface that enables you to administer its features through a Web browser. Unlike ICE, however, Business Catalyst includes so many new features of its own that it's way beyond the scope of this book.

You can find great help files and tutorials on the Business Catalyst site (http://businesscatalyst.com/). To help you appreciate how you can use Business Catalyst and its capabilities, the following is an overview of the features included in this new toolset:

- **Content Management System:** With Business Catalyst, you can enable users to edit your Web site through a browser, using the SiteWalk Editing features.

- **E-commerce:** Business Catalyst includes a sophisticated e-commerce shopping cart that can be integrated with most popular payment gateways, including PayPal and Google Checkout. Keep in mind, however, that setting up a payment gateway requires advanced skills on a Web server. To use such a service securely, you need to purchase an SSL Certificate — and may have to pay additional fees to your hosting service for a static IP address and other technical requirements for a secure server.

- **Integrated database:** Use the integrated database to manage customer orders, bulk e-mail messages, and more.

- **Web apps and module manager:** Use the integrated Web Apps to make content searchable, create reusable content snippets, and add functionality.

- **Community management:** Enable any visitor to your site to comment on any content, including product listings.

- **Built-in SEO support:** Use the integrated features to help ensure that your site follows search-engine optimization guidelines and scores high in search-engine results.

- **RSS feeds:** Use the integrated RSS feed features to set up blog-like RSS feeds or create as many RSS channels as you want so your site can share content with other Web sites or bloggers.

- ✔ **Secure members-only area:** Create user logins, easily e-mail access information, and set up user accounts with expiration dates and varying levels of access.

- ✔ **Web-site reporting and analytics:** Similar to the features in the popular Google Analytics software, but these analytics don't require a separate login or set up with another company.

- ✔ **Community forums:** Create and moderate user forums, manage user access, and manage discussions using threads and posts.

- ✔ **Blog features:** Set up an integrated blog to go with your Web site.

- ✔ **Photo galleries:** Easily create and add photo galleries to your site.

- ✔ **Ad rotators:** Set up ad spaces on your site that rotate advertisers' messages, as well as manage impressions and reporting.

- ✔ **Metadata:** Built in metadata framework makes it easier to create a sophisticated search features on your site and fill in the metadata fields recommended for search engines.

Part IV
The Part of Tens

The 5th Wave

By Rich Tennant

"Just how accurately should my Web site reflect my place of business?"

In this part . . .

The Part of Tens features a collection of timesaving tips and great online resources. In Chapter 15, you find a collection of Web sites that can help you with some of the things you won't find in Dreamweaver, such as domain registration. You also discover how to add detailed traffic tracking and e-commerce features and how to design and manage e-mail newsletters and other bulk e-mail messages. In Chapter 16, you find ten timesaving tips to help you get the most out of Dreamweaver.

Chapter 15

Ten Resources You May Need

In This Chapter

▶ Finding domain registration services

▶ Protecting your e-mail address

▶ Highlighting your links with pop-ups

▶ Selling stuff on the Web and tracking your traffic

▶ Surveying your site visitors

▶ Creating templates and keeping up with Web standards

▶ Using Adobe.com and Favicon

*A*lthough Dreamweaver is a wonderful tool for creating Web sites, it can't handle everything you need to put a site online. For example, you can't register a domain name using Dreamweaver, or create a Favicon, a special kind of image that appears in the top of a Web browser. I added this chapter to offer you a handy list of online resources that can help you finish your site when you need to go beyond the features in Dreamweaver.

Some of the online services featured in this chapter are now available in Dreamweaver if you use the new Business Catalyst covered in Chapter 14. This suite of tools, new in Dreamweaver CS5, includes online traffic reporting features, a shopping cart for e-commerce, and features that make it possible to manage an online contact list and send bulk e-mail efficiently. The online services featured in this chapter are also offered in Business Catalyst, are included this book to help you appreciate your options. Most of the services highlighted in this chapter, such as domain registration, are not included in any of Dreamweaver's other features.

Registering a Domain Name

The address for your Web site is its *domain name*. The domain name is what visitors need to know to find your Web site. For example, you can visit my Digital Family Web site at www.DigitalFamily.com.

Even before you start building your Web site, I recommend that you register your own domain name. The process is simple, painless, and costs less than $10 per year, but it can take from a few hours to a few days for the domain registration process to be completed.

You can register any domain name that hasn't already been taken by someone else, and for free, you can check to see whether a domain name is already taken. Just visit any domain registrar, such as `www.godaddy.com` or `1and1.com`, and enter the domain name you want into the search field on the main page of the registrar's site. If the name you want is no longer available, most registration services will give you a list of recommended alternatives.

Most domain registration services also provide Web hosting services, but you don't have to host your site at the same place where you register the name. You can set up a Web server anywhere you want and then use the domain management settings at your domain registration service to point your name to the server where your Web site is hosted.

When you enter a domain name into a Web browser, everything before the extension (the `.com`, `.net`, or `.org` part) can be written in uppercase or lowercase, and it will work just fine. However, if you want to go to a specific page within a Web site, such as `www.DigitalFamily.com/videos`, the text that comes after the extension is often case sensitive. Because the part before the `.com` doesn't matter, I find it easier to recognize domain names when they're written with capital letters. So, for example, I use `www.DigitalFamily.com` on my business cards instead of `www.digitalfamily.com`.

Protecting Your E-Mail Address from Spammers

Spammers gather millions of e-mail addresses from Web sites every day by collecting e-mail addresses from links on Web pages. Web designers often include an e-mail link so visitors can easily contact them. Unfortunately, those simple e-mail links enable spammers to easily gather e-mail addresses automatically.

To help counter this problem, the programmers at AddressMunger.com have come up with a special way of "hiding" e-mail addresses from the automated bots that spammers use. When you add this special code to your Web pages and use AddressMunger to create the e-mail links on your Web pages, your visitors can still e-mail you easily, but spammer's can't read your e-mail address. It's an easy way to cut down on all that spam in your inbox.

Highlighting Links with Pop-Ups

An innovative online service creates a small pop-up preview of any page you link to on your site, as you see in Figure 15-1. You simply sign up (for free) at Snap.com and use its online tool to generate special code, which you copy and paste into the code in your Web pages.

Figure 15-1: You can create links with pop-up previews with Snap. com.

With Snap.com's unique pop-ups, your visitors see a preview of the page or site that you've linked when they roll their cursors over a link. Adding this feature is a great way to give visitors a little more information as they peruse your pages and to highlight the links on your site.

Selling Stuff on the Web

You can sell things online in many ways. As a general rule, I recommend that you start simple and add more complex and expensive options after you know that you'll make money with your site.

At the simple end of the spectrum, you can add a purchase button with the services offered at www.PayPal.com or checkout.google.com. Moving up in complexity and price, you can create a shopping system at smallbusiness.yahoo.com/ecommerce. If you want a more custom solution and the ability to create your own shopping cart, check out the powerful, highly customizable, Dreamweaver-compatible programs at www.WebAssist.com or www.cartweaver.com.

Keeping Track of Traffic

Most Web hosting services provide basic log reports and traffic information, but if you want to know for sure how people are finding your Web site and what they're doing after they arrive, consider using a service like Google Analytics (www.google.com/analytics), StatCounter.com, or WebSTAT.com.

To use any of these services, set up an account and copy a bit of code from the site into your Web pages. (The procedure is a simple copy-and-paste that you can do with code view in Dreamweaver.) Google Analytics, StatCounter and other services then use that bit of code to track your traffic.

Visit any of the services, such as Google Analytics, for a demo and a sample report that illustrates the kind of information you can collect, including what search terms someone used to find your site through a search engine. Studying how people use your Web site is one of the best ways to determine how to improve your site's content and design.

For instructions on how to copy and paste code from a site like Google Analytics into the pages of your site in Dreamweaver, read the tutorial on the very similar service, Google Adsense, on my Web site at www. DigitalFamily.com/dreamweaver.

Taking Your Site's Temperature with a Heat Map

Adding a heat map to your Web site is a great way to discover what people find most interesting on each page of your site. Analytics, covered in the previous section, measure overall traffic patterns on the different pages of your site; heat maps are designed to show you the popularity of the different elements on each page of your Web site.

When you add a heat map to your site, you get a visual snapshot showing the "hot areas" — the links, text, images, and other elements on a page that attract the most attention from your visitors. To learn more about how heat maps work, visit www.clickdensity.com or www.crazyegg.com.

Surveying Your Visitors

Want to know what your visitors really think? Ask them. You can create a free, online survey at SurveyMonkey.com and link to it from your Web site. With SurveyMonkey, you create the survey using a Web browser. The site then automatically tallies the results and presents them in a series of reports and pie charts. The survey results are a great way to impress your board of directors at the next annual meeting.

Keeping Up with Web Standards at W3.org

If you want to keep up with the latest developments in Web design and make sure you're following standards, there's no better place than W3.org, the official Web site of the organization that sets Web standards. You can find loads of information on this nonprofit site, including the full specification for HTML, CSS, and much more. You can also test your Web pages for compliance with W3C standards by entering a page's URL into the CSS validator at jigsaw.w3.org/css-validator, or the MarkUp validator at validator.w3.org.

Extending Dreamweaver at Adobe.com

Visit the Dreamweaver Exchange Site at www.adobe.com/cfusion/exchange/ to find a vast collection of extensions you can use to add behaviors and other features to Dreamweaver. To install them, use the Extensions Manager, which I cover in Chapter 10.

While you're at the site, check out the growing collection of Adobe tutorials, updates, and resources at www.adobe.com/devnet/dreamweaver. Among the resources, check out the new CSS section, where you'll find the latest in CSS tips, tricks, and workarounds.

Dressing Up the Address Bar with a Favicon

Have you ever wondered how to add a custom graphic to the address bar at the top of browsers like Internet Explorer or Firefox? Google adds a capital *G*, Adobe adds its logo, and you can add an image, too. But first you have to get the image in the right format.

To convert an image into a Favicon, visit Favicon.com, where you can upload a graphic and have it converted for free. Then just add that image to the root level of your main site folder (that is, your local site folder). The next time you preview your page in a browser, the image automatically displays in the address bar.

Chapter 16

Ten Ways to Promote Your Site

*W*hat if you build a Web site and nobody comes? Unfortunately, that's an all-too-common problem on the Internet. And, that's why I end this book by pointing you to a few places where you can promote your Web site. Driving significant traffic to the pages of a site requires a significant amount of time or money or an incredibly compelling message. If you can manage all three, you should do very well indeed. In this chapter, you find tips and online resources to help bring people to your Web site.

Scoring High in Search Engines

The buzzword here is *search engine optimization,* or *SEO,* a process designed to help you attract more attention from search engines like Google, Bing, and Yahoo! The goal is to get your site higher on the search results page than your competitors.

Scoring high in Web searches is complicated because millions of sites vie for the top spots and search engines use complex formulas to determine which Web site should match any given keyword search. Search engines also guard their formulas for prioritizing Web sites more carefully than Coca-Cola guards its recipe. And if that doesn't make it complicated enough, most search engines change their formulas regularly. (*How* regularly is also secret.)

Thousands of companies and services promise to "get you in the top 10 matches" on search engines for as little as $19.99. Be wary of these services. The truly good ones charge hundreds or even thousands of dollars per month (with good reason), and the bad ones can get you delisted from search engines for breaking the rules with old tricks like inserting the word *sex* into your code when you're site is really about car maintenance. Most SEO experts agree that the best way to score high in search engines is to provide useful information on your site and to use appropriate keywords effectively.

For the most part, search engines score sites based on the words and images on Web pages and on how well a site's content matches the keywords that are searched. For example, if you own a B&B in Point Reyes Station, California, you should include *at least* the name Point Reyes Station on your Web site because the term B&B has many competitors, and people searching for lodging in the area are likely to include the town's name in their search.

A great way to determine how best to make your own site search engine friendly is to search for keywords that you want to lead people to your site and then study the Web sites that match those words already. Often, the best way to move your Web site up the ranks in search results is to emulate the strategies of other sites that are already doing well.

Achieving the best placement, especially for popular keywords, is a full-time job, but here are a few tips that most SEO specialists agree are likely to help you score better in search engine searches.

- ✔ **Invite other sites to link to you.** Popular belief is that Google rewards people who attract the most links to their sites, especially if those sites already have good rankings themselves. It makes sense: If lots of other Web sites consider your site good enough to send their visitors to you, you probably have something of value to offer.

- ✔ **Fill your site with fresh, original content related to your business or industry.** Include tips, articles, tutorials, and other content that's valuable to your visitors, and don't stop there. Keeping your content updated by adding fresh information on a regular basis is another great way to keep search engines — and visitors — interested.

- ✔ **Develop a list of keywords and a good description for your site.** The trick to writing a good Web site description is making it concise (every word counts), packing it with your most important keywords, and phrasing it so that it reads like a sentence (not just a list of words). Include this description toward the top of your home page in the *meta description tag,* which is a special tag that can be used to add information just for search engines. (You find instructions for adding meta descriptions and keyword content in Chapter 2.)

Why all this search engine secrecy?

The people who run sites like Google and Bing want to deliver the best results when someone conducts a search — not just a list of the sites that reflect smart Web marketers' ability to figure out how to trick their way into top position. Because much money can be made at the top of search results lists, Web marketers spend countless hours testing how search engines work to come up with their best guesses about the criteria that search engines are using and how best to move their sites up the list.

The result is sort of a cat-and-mouse game, with search engines changing the rules to thwart the most calculated efforts of specialists in SEO, and people who specialize in SEO charging big bucks to figure out the secret formula that can put you on top.

✔ **Include your most important keywords in the title of your Web page and the name of the file.** The title doesn't appear in the body of a Web page; the title appears at the top of the browser window. You can add or edit the title of a page in Dreamweaver by changing the text in the Title field at the very top of the workspace. Similarly, including keywords in the filename of each page in your Web site can also boost rankings.

✔ **Include keywords in the headings on your Web page.** Most search engines place higher priority on keywords that appear in the headings on a page, but only if you use XHTML heading tags to style those headlines. Heading tags, which include `<h1>` (the biggest) through `<h6>` (the smallest), identify text as headings in a way that search engines easily recognize.

✔ **Don't expect instant (or permanent) results.** Even if you do everything right in the search engine optimization game, you might still have to wait for the results of your efforts. Some search engines can take weeks or months to reflect changes to Web pages on the Internet. Search engines, such as Google, generally update the most popular sites very quickly while lagging weeks or months behind in updating less-visited sites.

A great place to learn more about how search engines work and how to achieve the best ranking is www.searchenginewatch.com.

Buying Traffic (Yes, You Really Can!)

In addition to the "natural" results that search engines deliver when someone does a keyword search, buying keywords on search engines helps to ensure that your site is listed when someone searches for words that are relevant to your site, although the process is far more complex than most people realize. Search engine ads generally appear at the top and right side of most search-result pages.

Not all keywords sell for the same price. Using a complex bidding process, most search engines charge significantly more for the most popular keywords. Adding to the complexity, the results of those keywords for your site can vary dramatically based on a dizzying array of factors. For example, the expensive keyword *Hawaii* may bring the most amount of traffic to your site, but the lower-priced keyword *luau* may result in more reservations to your hotel. Because it's possible to measure not only the traffic from a keyword search but also the actions of the person who clicks that keyword, you can measure and compare the effectiveness of nearly every aspect of search engine advertising.

Again, this process can be highly complex. Just consider the following:

✔ **The real art of developing a list of keywords for search engine advertising requires more than just brainstorming a few words related to your business.** The best SEO companies come up with hundreds or thousands of keywords and phrases and then track the results to find the best return on each dollar spent for the keywords (for example, how many paying customers arrive via each keyword or phrase and how much do they buy). Thus, running a campaign with 10,000 words might not cost much more than running a campaign with 100 words and might prove much more effective over time.

✔ **The most sophisticated ad campaigns involve creating special Web pages to go with each keyword ad.** For example, you can create a special page (often called a *landing page*) on your Hawaiian hotel site for people who click on the search term **scuba diving** that is different from the page for those who click the search term **health spa**.

You can learn more about how to make the most of your keyword ads by carefully reading the instructions and tips on any site where you plan to advertise.

Google AdSense offers the largest online advertising program for keywords. Just visit www.google.com/adsense to find detailed instructions and a number of tips and tools to help you develop the best campaign and measure the results.

In addition to buying ads on Google, you can include Google Ads on your own Web site to earn advertising income. This program is called Google AdWords, and you can learn more about it at http://adwords.google.com.

Using Social Networking Sites for Promotion

Social networking, the art of meeting and building contacts on the Web, is an increasingly popular way to increase your personal and professional contacts, make new friends, develop professional relationships, and even find a new job. You can also use social networking sites to promote your personal or business Web site. *Netiquette* (Internet etiquette) calls for a subtle approach to promoting your site in these kinds of environments, but simply including your Web address in your online profile can help drive new people to your site.

Here's what you can expect to find among the most popular social networking sites:

- **Facebook:** (www.facebook.com) Facebook wins top place as the fastest-growing social networking site on the Web, and its broad appeal makes it an excellent place to promote your Web site. Facebook was originally considered a vanity site and a place for college students, but its professional power is growing with its ever-expanding audience.

- **LinkedIn:** (www.linkedin.com) This is *the* site for professional connections and online business networking. If you're online to develop business contacts with other professionals, especially if you're job hunting or trying to attract new business clients, this is a powerful place to promote yourself and your Web site. Unlike Facebook and MySpace, LinkedIn is all business.

- **MySpace:** (www.myspace.com) One of the all-time most popular social networking sites, MySpace, enables you to create a profile site, add music, write a blog, and post as many photos as you want to share with the world. Although the site has dominated the social networking landscape on the Internet, at the time of this writing, it was rapidly falling behind its biggest competitor, Facebook. Still, its huge online audience is a popular place for musicians, performers, and many others to promote themselves and their Web sites.

- **Ecademy:** (www.ecademy.com) Similar to LinkedIn, Ecademy is a site where professionals network, seek new clients, hunt for jobs, and recruit employees. What makes Ecademy different is that it's much more international, with an especially strong audience in Europe and Asia.

- **Ning:** (www.ning.com) You can create your own social networking site at Ning and invite your friends and colleagues to create profiles there in your own exclusive social network environment.

✔ **Twitter:** (www.twitter.com) Best described as "microblogging," Twitter makes it easy to connect with people online and share brief bursts of information, called tweets. Twitter limits you to no more than 140 characters per post, which may seem restrictive at first, but seems to be the secret to Twitter's success. Because you can post to Twitter from a computer, cell phone, or any other Internet-enabled device, and because the posts are so brief, people tend to update Twitter more frequently than other services, making it a great place to follow trends, news events, and other information in real time.

Ranking on Social Bookmarking Sites

Social bookmarking sites rank the popularity of Web pages by the number of votes they get. The result is that these sites are excellent resources for people who want to keep up with what's popular online. Most enable anyone to vote on a site.

Getting your site listed on social bookmarking sites is a highly effective way to increase traffic. Dozens of these sites and services exist, with more sure to come, and they feature catchy and unusual names, like Digg (http://digg.com), delicious (http://delicious.com), StumbleUpon (www.stumbleupon.com), and reddit (www.reddit.com).

Although you can submit your own pages on any of these sites, it's generally frowned upon, and if you do it too frequently, you can be banned. Besides, your one little vote won't make much difference anyway. A better method is to add a button to your site from each of these services so that visitors can easily vote for you. If you're a blogger, you can add a button each time you post. You can get the buttons (called *chicklets*) for free and add them to your pages by simply inserting a little code you generate on the social networking site.

Enticing Visitors to Return for Updates

One of the best ways to improve traffic to your site is through repeat visitors, and regular updates to your site can make all the difference. If you want your visitors to know when to look for updates, consider making regular changes to your Web site. Add a post to your blog every Thursday morning, for example, or post your newest photos to the site on Saturday mornings. Regular updates help get people in the habit of visiting your site.

Gathering Ideas from Other Web Sites

One of the best ways to create good habits in Web design is to visit other people's Web sites and study what works and what doesn't on their pages, with special attention to the following:

- ✔ Check out the title of the page, any descriptive text, or keywords that are used throughout the site.
- ✔ Ask yourself what you like about the site and why you like it.
- ✔ Determine whether you can easily find the information you're most interested in and how easily you can navigate around the site.

Sometimes the best way to discover the problems in your own Web site is to look for problems on someone else's site and then return to yours with a fresh perspective.

Marketing a Web Site to the Media

Attracting traditional media attention to your Web site is like attracting it to any other business. The trick is to tell a good story and get the attention of someone who can write about it in a publication that your target audience reads. If you're looking for press coverage, make sure to include a Press section on your Web site with contact information, story ideas, and any other press coverage you've received.

Don't wait for journalists to come to you! You should never pester a reporter with a barrage of e-mails, press releases, or phone calls, but a well-timed or well-pitched message can get the attention of a reporter *and* the desired result — your Web address in the press. One good way to find journalists who might be interested in your site is to visit related sites and study their Press sections to find out who has been writing about the site. Note not only the publication but also the writer. Then send a note directly to that person with a message that starts like this:

Dear *fabulous journalist* <insert *that person's name,* of course>:

I enjoyed reading the article you wrote on the XYZ company and thought that you might be interested in what we're doing.

Keep your message brief, and try to include a news hook and story idea that go beyond just promoting your business. For example, rather than tell a reporter that you have the best B&B site in northern California, pitch a story about the best hikes in the area. With any luck, the article on great hikes will include a quote from you and a mention of your B&B's Web site (especially if the reporter can send readers to your online list of hiking tips).

Unleashing the Power of Viral Marketing

Viral marketing is another of the marketing industry's buzzwords in the digital age. The idea is that a message (a video, an article, or a photo, for example) is so exciting, fun, and compelling that people want to share it with each other, passing it on to their friends, who then pass it on to their friends, until it spreads like a virus. Such messages are often sent via e-mail, blogs, or chat, which can make the ever-expanding impact happen at an almost instantaneous pace.

Tap in to the power of viral marketing, and you can become an overnight sensation. Humor seems to be the most effective strategy. Among the mainstays of the viral phenomena are those silly photos of cats with clever sayings. Known as the LOL cats, these photos have spawned several Web sites, like Icanhascheeseburger.com. Funny video clips — the kind you would expect to see featured on a show like *America's Funniest Home Videos* — are also highly viral because they're shared around the Web.

To use viral marketing to attract traffic to your Web site, include a section with funny photos, industry jokes, or a Top 10 list, and you might just get visitors to tell their friends about your site.

Blogging, Blogging, Blogging

By creating a blog for your Web site, you can easily add fresh content. Blogs are designed for frequent updates, and when you become a blogger, you also join the ranks of a prolific group of writers who regularly refer their readers to each other's Web sites.

Don't launch a blog without considering the commitment it requires. For your blog to attract traffic and serve as an effective marketing tool, you must

- ✔ Feature interesting, relevant information for your audience.
- ✔ Update the blog regularly.
- ✔ Take the time to participate in other people's blogs. Adding relevant tips and thoughtful comments to other people's blogs is an excellent way to get their visitors to come back to your Web site.

Check out *Blogging For Dummies*, 3rd Edition, by Susannah Gardner and Shane Birley, if you're interested in exploring blogging.

Using Twitter to Promote Your Site

One of the most popular new forms of social media can be found at www. twitter.com. Twitter makes it easy to register and start sharing your words of wisdom, but you have to keep it brief — a way of posting called *microblogging*. Twitter limits users to 140 characters (about a sentence) of text per post. At first, many users complained that Twitter was a trivial place where people shared too many boring details, such as, "I'm going to lunch at my favorite diner now."

But Twitter has evolved into an incredibly popular way for friends to stay in touch and for businesses, actors, and others to promote themselves. Just visit www.twitter.com, and register for a free account. Then you can start posting short messages about what you're doing, what you're thinking, or questions you're pondering. After you sign up, you can also subscribe to the Twitter feed of anyone else who uses Twitter and thus see others' comments, called *tweets,* in a real-time stream on your home page.

Telling Everyone You Know

Many people are either too shy or too busy to reach out to their friends, family, and personal contacts when they launch a Web site. Don't overlook your most obvious supporters. Launching a new Web site or redesigning an existing site is an excellent excuse to e-mail personal and professional contacts. To make the announcement even more fun, consider sending an e-card with a colorful character, animation, or music to dramatize your announcement.

Hallmark.com is one of my favorite e-card sites because it has lots of free cards with clever sayings, professional designs, and interactive animations. Most of its free e-cards even include sound. BlueMountain.com is another useful e-card site, but you have to pay for the pleasure of sending its professional greetings. When choosing an e-card to announce your Web site, look for blank cards or the Friendship and Any Occasion sections, where you can find messages that are easily personalized for nearly any kind of Web site.

Make sure you include your URL on all your marketing and other materials, too. Prominently display your Web address on your business cards, brochures, stationery, and anywhere else you promote your business (such as your e-mail signature).

Index

• *G* •

• *H* •

Business/Accounting & Bookkeeping

Bookkeeping For Dummies
978-0-7645-9848-7

eBay Business
All-in-One For Dummies,
2nd Edition
978-0-470-38536-4

Job Interviews
For Dummies,
3rd Edition
978-0-470-17748-8

Resumes For Dummies,
5th Edition
978-0-470-08037-5

Stock Investing
For Dummies,
3rd Edition
978-0-470-40114-9

Successful Time
Management
For Dummies
978-0-470-29034-7

Computer Hardware

BlackBerry For Dummies,
3rd Edition
978-0-470-45762-7

Computers For Seniors
For Dummies
978-0-470-24055-7

iPhone For Dummies,
2nd Edition
978-0-470-42342-4

Laptops For Dummies,
3rd Edition
978-0-470-27759-1

Macs For Dummies,
10th Edition
978-0-470-27817-8

Cooking & Entertaining

Cooking Basics
For Dummies,
3rd Edition
978-0-7645-7206-7

Wine For Dummies,
4th Edition
978-0-470-04579-4

Diet & Nutrition

Dieting For Dummies,
2nd Edition
978-0-7645-4149-0

Nutrition For Dummies,
4th Edition
978-0-471-79868-2

Weight Training
For Dummies,
3rd Edition
978-0-471-76845-6

Digital Photography

Digital Photography
For Dummies,
6th Edition
978-0-470-25074-7

Photoshop Elements 7
For Dummies
978-0-470-39700-8

Gardening

Gardening Basics
For Dummies
978-0-470-03749-2

Organic Gardening
For Dummies,
2nd Edition
978-0-470-43067-5

Green/Sustainable

Green Building
& Remodeling
For Dummies
978-0-470-17559-0

Green Cleaning
For Dummies
978-0-470-39106-8

Green IT For Dummies
978-0-470-38688-0

Health

Diabetes For Dummies,
3rd Edition
978-0-470-27086-8

Food Allergies
For Dummies
978-0-470-09584-3

Living Gluten-Free
For Dummies
978-0-471-77383-2

Hobbies/General

Chess For Dummies,
2nd Edition
978-0-7645-8404-6

Drawing For Dummies
978-0-7645-5476-6

Knitting For Dummies,
2nd Edition
978-0-470-28747-7

Organizing For Dummies
978-0-7645-5300-4

SuDoku For Dummies
978-0-470-01892-7

Home Improvement

Energy Efficient Homes
For Dummies
978-0-470-37602-7

Home Theater
For Dummies,
3rd Edition
978-0-470-41189-6

Living the Country Lifestyle
All-in-One For Dummies
978-0-470-43061-3

Solar Power Your Home
For Dummies
978-0-470-17569-9

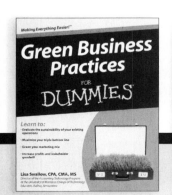

Internet

Blogging For Dummies,
2nd Edition
978-0-470-23017-6

eBay For Dummies,
6th Edition
978-0-470-49741-8

Facebook For Dummies
978-0-470-26273-3

Google Blogger
For Dummies
978-0-470-40742-4

Web Marketing
For Dummies,
2nd Edition
978-0-470-37181-7

WordPress For Dummies,
2nd Edition
978-0-470-40296-2

Language & Foreign Language

French For Dummies
978-0-7645-5193-2

Italian Phrases
For Dummies
978-0-7645-7203-6

Spanish For Dummies
978-0-7645-5194-9

Spanish For Dummies,
Audio Set
978-0-470-09585-0

Macintosh

Mac OS X Snow Leopard
For Dummies
978-0-470-43543-4

Math & Science

Algebra I For Dummies,
2nd Edition
978-0-470-55964-2

Biology For Dummies
978-0-7645-5326-4

Calculus For Dummies
978-0-7645-2498-1

Chemistry For Dummies
978-0-7645-5430-8

Microsoft Office

Excel 2007 For Dummies
978-0-470-03737-9

Office 2007 All-in-One
Desk Reference
For Dummies
978-0-471-78279-7

Music

Guitar For Dummies,
2nd Edition
978-0-7645-9904-0

iPod & iTunes
For Dummies,
6th Edition
978-0-470-39062-7

Piano Exercises
For Dummies
978-0-470-38765-8

Parenting & Education

Parenting For Dummies,
2nd Edition
978-0-7645-5418-6

Type 1 Diabetes
For Dummies
978-0-470-17811-9

Pets

Cats For Dummies,
2nd Edition
978-0-7645-5275-5

Dog Training For Dummies,
2nd Edition
978-0-7645-8418-3

Puppies For Dummies,
2nd Edition
978-0-470-03717-1

Religion & Inspiration

The Bible For Dummies
978-0-7645-5296-0

Catholicism For Dummies
978-0-7645-5391-2

Women in the Bible
For Dummies
978-0-7645-8475-6

Self-Help & Relationship

Anger Management
For Dummies
978-0-470-03715-7

Overcoming Anxiety
For Dummies
978-0-7645-5447-6

Sports

Baseball For Dummies,
3rd Edition
978-0-7645-7537-2

Basketball For Dummies,
2nd Edition
978-0-7645-5248-9

Golf For Dummies,
3rd Edition
978-0-471-76871-5

Web Development

Web Design All-in-One
For Dummies
978-0-470-41796-6

Windows Vista

Windows Vista
For Dummies
978-0-471-75421-3